# POLICY-MAKING IN BRITAIN

## CONTRIBUTORS

Samuel Brittan
*Financial Times*

D. N. Chester
*Nuffield College, Oxford*

Harry Eckstein
*Princeton University*

Ron Hall
*Sunday Times*

Jenifer Hart
*St Anne's College*

Keith Hindell
*British Broadcasting Corporation*

Clive Irving
*London Weekend Television*

George W. Jones
*London School of Economics*

Tom Lupton
*Manchester Business School*

W. J. M. Mackenzie
*Glasgow University*

Ernest Marples
*Conservative MP*

Laurence W. Martin
*King's College, London*

Harve Mossawir
*University of Alabama*

Richard Neustadt
*John F. Kennedy Institute, Harvard*

J. Roland Pennock
*Swarthmore College*

Political and Economic Planning
*London*

Jorgen Rasmussen
*Vanderbilt University*

John P. Roche
*Brandeis University*

Richard Rose
*Strathclyde University*

Stephen Sachs
*U.S. Attorney, District of Maryland*

Lord Strang
*Foreign Office (retired)*

*The Times*
Political Staff

Patrick Gordon Walker
*Labour MP*

Jeremy Wallington
*Granada TV*

Alan Watkins
*New Statesman*

Sir Kenneth Wheare
*Exeter College, Oxford*

F. M. G. Willson
*University of California, Santa Cruz*

C. Shirley Wilson, *lately of Manchester University*

# POLICY-MAKING IN BRITAIN

## A Reader in Government

EDITED BY

RICHARD ROSE

*University of Strathclyde*

MACMILLAN

London · Melbourne · Toronto

1969

*By the same author*

★

INFLUENCING VOTERS

STUDIES IN BRITISH POLITICS

POLITICS IN ENGLAND

MUST LABOUR LOSE? (*with Mark Abrams*)

THE BRITISH GENERAL ELECTION OF 1959 (*with D. E. Butler*)



*Published by*
MACMILLAN AND CO LTD
*Little Essex Street London* WC2
*and also at Bombay Calcutta and Madras*
*Macmillan South Africa (Publishers) Pty Ltd Johannesburg*
*The Macmillan Company of Australia Pty Ltd Melbourne*
*The Macmillan Company of Canada Ltd Toronto*

*Printed in Great Britain by*
WESTERN PRINTING SERVICES LTD
*Bristol*

# CONTENTS

# ACKNOWLEDGEMENTS

THE study of policy-making involves the gradual accumulation of information, concepts and hypotheses by many people over a lengthy period of time. The debt that any student in this field owes to others, whether personal friends or individuals known only through their writings, is large. An editor of a collection of articles is especially indebted to the efforts of others. It is a pleasure to acknowledge what the editor has learned from other authors by the practical device of securing wider circulation for work originally printed elsewhere. The source of publication is listed at the beginning of each article and this represents formal permission to reprint.

The original idea for this reader came from an after-dinner conversation with Professor Samuel J. Eldersveld of the University of Michigan. The *Political Behavior* reader that he co-edited was a pioneering book contributing much to the scientific education of the editor while a research student at Oxford; three years in residence there provided an excellent chance to observe the Cromwellian profiles of policy-makers and embryonic policy-makers. The immediate stimulus to edit this book came from writing *Politics in England*, which sets out the editor's interpretation of British politics; the articles presented here illustrate and complement the generalisations there.

While British government has been the subject of scholarly attention at least since the time of the Venerable Bede, much that has been written is of a historical or descriptive nature. The merits of such approaches are considerable, but they are different from those of modern social science. As social science ideas have come to be applied to the study of British politics, the politics of the masses first attracted attention. Hence the first reader — *Studies in British Politics* — concentrated upon political culture, socialisation, elections, communication, pressure groups and parties. This companion volume has appeared later because of the time required to accumulate a collection of articles that analyse British policy-making in ways relevant to contemporary social science thinking. A special effort, too, has been made to ensure that the articles collected, while written independently of each other, form an *ensemble*.

Many ideas underlying the point of view represented by this collection have been shaped by conversations with a wide range of persons in university environments, Westminster and Whitehall. Dr John Lees, now Lecturer in American Studies at Keele, assisted greatly in compiling the preliminary bibliography. The box made and decorated by Clare, Charles and Lincoln Rose for filing bibliography cards has served for this second reader. Mrs J. McGlone and Mrs R. Johnstone assisted in the considerable secretarial work involved. My wife, Rosemary, has listened patiently while the problems of an editor were recited to her.

The diagrams on pages 21–5 are reproduced by kind permission of the Manchester School of Economics and the Kraus-Thomson Organisation.

RICHARD ROSE

*University of Strathclyde*
*4 July 1968*

# INTRODUCTION

THE policies of government, for better or for ill, are important to everyone. Acts of government influence the necessities of health, education, employment, and sustenance in old age. Government also makes collective provision for amenities, and its action or inaction thus contributes much to the total environment of cities, towns and rural areas. While the influence of Britain in foreign policy has declined greatly in recent decades, the total impact of foreign-policy decisions upon the British people has vastly increased. Moreover, domestic policies have grown greatly in significance, from the time in the 1790s when government expenditure represented one-eighth of the gross national product, until the present, when it represents nearly two-fifths of the gross national product.[1] As the importance of public policy-making grows, government has become a far more complex set of institutions than those envisioned by our pre-industrial forebears.

Policy-making is, unfortunately, an ambiguous phrase. It can refer to the intentions of politicians as well as to the outcomes of their activities. Usually it refers to intentions rather than consequences. When a political party or a group of lobbyists is said to have a policy to handle a problem, this means that the group has put forward a prescriptive statement of intent. In the language of politics, any set of recommendations about what ought to be done or what will be done when power changes hands constitutes a policy. Whether the set of intentions is clear or vague, based on evidence or conjecture, or comprehensive or disconnected in its reasoning, is neither here nor there. It is a policy nonetheless. In some cases, these statements of intent become adopted as government policy. This means that a set of intentions has been endorsed in the form of an Act of Parliament, a statement in the House of Commons, or a directive to a group of Whitehall civil servants. While government policies often require legislation, increasingly in economic planning as in foreign affairs, ministers enunciate policy intentions which neither have, nor can hope to enjoy, the sanctions of binding legislation to carry them out.

The intentions of policy-makers are not automatically converted

[1] See the very useful article of Jindrich Veverka, 'The Growth of Government Expenditure in the United Kingdom Since 1790', *Scottish Journal of Political Economy*, x i (1963) 114.

into the outcomes they desire. The study of the outcomes of government policies is sadly neglected, even though the consequences of government bills and administrative directives are usually disputable, if not highly conjectural. Policies requiring no more than simple administrative actions to carry through may, in the event be frustrated by conflicts between the substantive goals of policy-makers and the procedural norms of administrators.[2] Policies that are backed by the sanctions of criminal law may enjoy prompt if grudging respect from all but a small minority of the population. As government involvement in the mixed-economy welfare state grows, the success of policies rests upon co-operation with businessmen and trade unionists outside control by legal sanctions. Such people must be convinced that co-operation with the Government is to their benefit, or, at least, helps achieve values and goals generally regarded as desirable throughout society. Foreign policy is the extreme example of governmental dependence upon the co-operation of those outside its jurisdiction, for the co-operation of a number of sovereign states is necessary if a policy intention of British government is to produce the desired outcome. Moreover, policies are frequently modified on a *de facto* basis by environmental changes greatly altering conditions crucial in the initial formulation of a policy.

Policy-making involves a long series of more-or-less related activities, rather than a single, discrete decision taken in Downing Street, Westminster, Whitehall or Washington. It thus covers far more than the term decision-making.[3] The study of decision-making usually involves analysing the intentions of policy-makers up to and including the point at which binding governmental action is taken. Much less attention is given to the consequences of these decisions in subsequent years. For example, a decision to clear slums from a city, however good the faith and intelligence of its makers, may retrospectively be seen as a decision that has simply transferred slum conditions from one part of a city to another. A more important limitation upon the decision-making approach is that it requires action to be taken by a relatively small number of people within a well-defined and bounded setting. It is, for example, much easier to study the small group decision to take Britain to war in Suez in 1956 than it is to study the multitude of separate decisions that led to the British economic crises of the 1960s. Outcomes may be affected less by conscious deci-

[2] See Harry Eckstein's article 'Planning', printed on pp. 221 ff.

[3] For a clear and able statement of the decision-making approach see Robert A. Dahl, 'A Critique of the Ruling Elite Model', *American Political Science Review*, LII ii (1958), and, for a comment on its limitations, see Peter Bachrach and Morton Baratz, 'Two Faces of Power', ibid. LVI iv (1962).

sions to act than by conscious or unconscious preferences for inaction. For example, in the years up to the passage of the first Act restricting coloured immigration in 1963, the refusal of the Government to alter existing regulations on Commonwealth immigration had very considerable consequences for race-relations policy.

The sense of continuous activity and adjustment involved in policy-making is best conveyed by describing it as a process, rather than as a single, once-for-all act. The policy-making process may be said to begin when uncertainties are consciously articulated in the form of political demands, or registered by observant civil servants noting that the instructions they have been given to carry out no longer have quite the consequences that their authors intended. In both cases, the uncertainty involves differences of opinion about what should be done. In other instances, the uncertainty may be more readily seen by an outside observer, aware of conflicts between what people think they are doing and what is happening in consequence of their actions. It is important to note that a point in time selected as ending the analysis of one policy may be conterminous with the point at which a new process starts. For instance, a study of policy-making concentrating upon the introduction of compulsory but differentiated secondary education in the 1944 Education Act would probably conclude at a point in the late 1950s when it had become apparent that the outcome was not the parity of opportunity and esteem which its proponents had hoped for. A new study, concentrating upon the development of the comprehensive secondary schools policy, could begin where a study of the 1944 Act concludes, or it could begin by returning to look again at the original intentions of the proponents of the 1944 Education Act.

The organisation of this book reflects the diverse influences that can bear upon policy-making, from the social origins of men who make decisions to the ability or inability of government officials to keep track of what is happening in their own society. The first chapter concerns the recruitment of policy-makers. Knowing how men are selected to participate in policy-making is a necessary, although hardly sufficient, condition of understanding how the process works. The second chapter considers how men behave once in office. The behaviour of individuals in office is not only a reflection of their previous backgrounds, but also of the institutional constraints which constantly affect politicians with widely diverse personalities. The case studies in the third chapter provide illustrations of policy-making, both in the textbook form of the drafting of an Act of Parliament and in accounts of more subtle ways in which government operates. The concluding chapter brings together studies of patterns of activity which are common to many different kinds of policies, such as the influence of the civil service. It also includes attempts to characterise the general structure of the policy process.

In selecting articles for this reader, the chief criteria have been quality, relevance, permanence and difficulty of access. The emphasis upon quality is self-justifying, but it is worth noting that merit may take different forms. Relevance refers to the significance of an article for the main themes of the volume; concern with producing an *ensemble* of articles embracing the whole range of policy-making has led to the omission of some articles of value which would have distracted attention from the main themes of this book. Concern with permanence has excluded studies primarily of topical interest. No selections are from books that have long been familiar to students of British politics, and deserve reading in their entirety. Bibliographical notes provide guidance to many of these books. At the margin, selections have been biased towards documents which are not conveniently accessible in public or university libraries.

The authors in this volume write from a variety of perspectives — political scientist, sociologist, journalist, civil servant and cabinet minister. Knowing a man's normal mode of employment is hardly the best way to assess the quality of what he has written. Variations in backgrounds do explain differences in styles of writing and in perspectives. On balance, these differences are worth while, if one assumes that no single approach to the study of politics provides all the most useful answers. Reading hundreds of articles about policy-making in Britain provided ample opportunity for the editor to document the simple but often neglected truism that the key distinction in political analysis is not between the party labels of academic disciplines, but rather between things that, of their kind, are excellent, good, indifferent or downright bad.

The scope of the book is large but not limitless. Extra-governmental influences — political culture, political socialisation, communications procedures, pressure groups and parties — are covered by a companion volume, *Studies in British Politics*.[4] The decision to concentrate upon the process of policy-making, rather than upon particular formal institutions of government, has produced a balance of selections that may strike some readers as unconventional. For example, the articles about relations between civil servants and ministers illustrate better than any theoretical polemic how the line between policy-making and administration is much less clear-cut than that which normally separates policy-makers (i.e., elected

[4] Edited by Richard Rose (London: Macmillan; New York: St Martin's Press, 1966).

officials) from administrators (i.e., civil servants) in textbooks of British government. The volume contains relatively little about the routine activities of MPs, for the simple reason that policy-making studies have had little need to give attention to many matters that receive close scrutiny from those who write about Parliament. If the parliamentary reformers have their way, then some day a revised edition of this book can register their success by giving increased attention to events inside the Palace of Westminster. In view of the considerable amount of research on local politics now in progress, one can more confidently state that a revised edition, appearing sometime in the 1970s, should contain more examples of policy-making studies in local politics, a field still dominated by a concern with institutions rather than outcomes. The reader concentrates upon post-war British politics for the simple reason that, while the historical sources of contemporary British politics are extremely important, their proper study requires a separate volume, one which the editor hopes to bring out in due course.

The articles are primarily analytic rather than prescriptive in tone. This is not meant to imply that the values of politicians and those who write about politics are irrelevant to the study of politics. In a number of selections, most notably the study concerned with the restriction of coloured immigrants, conflicts concerning political values are prominent and explicit. In many articles, value judgements refer to preferences concerning the structure of government, rather than to the ends of government. This emphasis can be justified by noting that there is no lack of literature prescribing policies for Britain today; much of it dates badly. One reason why primarily prescriptive policy manifestos fail to stand the test of time and common sense is that their authors usually omit to analyse carefully the existing structure of British government, including obstacles to its reform. Some of the selections that follow do contain, explicitly or implicitly, suggestions for altering the structure of British government in ways that could perhaps help policy-makers to achieve their goals. On the other hand, some contributions suggest that the problems diagnosed are not amenable to solution, in the short term or even in the long run. In a sense, then, this volume can help calculate the relationship between what is possible and what is desired, even though the result of this calculus may be far from felicific.

In sum that familiar and homely term 'British government' is a high-order abstraction that is difficult to connect with simple, empirical referents. If one hailed a taxi in central London and asked to be driven to the centre of British government, the driver might arguably deposit his fare in Downing Street, the middle of Whitehall, the Palace of Westminster or Buckingham Palace. During certain kinds of policy crises, he might head for the entrance to the Bank of England, or Heathrow Airport and a jet plane going to Zürich or Washington.[5] There is something to be said, empirically if not constitutionally, for each of these choices. In order to decide how important each of these institutions is in British government, we must descend from the heights of abstraction, represented by that mystical pinnacle 'sovereignty', and consider precise and empirically testable questions, such as: What are the chief problem areas which require policy decisions from government? Who are the actors involved in each area? What are the methods of deliberation? What strategies of influence are employed? and, How much influence does *any* sector of government have upon the eventual outcome? For a tentative discussion of a few answers, the interested reader is referred to chapter 9 of the editor's *Politics in England*. Briefly summarised, its argument is that policy-making in Britain is, in Bagehot's term, composite: 'the supreme power is divided between many bodies and functionaries'. The person who begins to study the processes of policy-making by asking the question — where does power lie? — begins with the fallacious assumption that power must be located in some simple, single place. Variations in the content of policies cause variations in modes of policy-making. Foreign policy, local government reform, penal policy and wage freezes each involve distinctive policy processes. To say this is not to argue that a new form of policy-making is required for every new issue that arises. In practice, the great bulk of new issues involve men who bring with them habits of action and expectations acquired from long participation in other policy decisions. It is therefore reasonable to seek accurate yet general answers to questions about the circumstances in which policy-making places primary emphasis upon the Prime Minister, upon pressure groups, MPs, civil servants, public opinion or some foreign power. Asking the right question is at least half the answer.

[5] On the influence of groups outside Britain, see the specific arguments of Morris Davis, 'Some Neglected Aspects of British Pressure Groups', *Midwest Journal of Political Science*, VII i (1963).

## Bibliographical Note

The approach to British politics outlined in this introduction is implicit in much of the pre-1914 literature about the government, but since that time most books have described government in narrowly legalistic terms. For exceptions, see e.g. Richard Rose, *Politics in England* (London: Faber, 1965), especially ch. 9, and Jean Blondel, *Voters, Parties and Leaders* (Harmondsworth: Penguin, 1963) especially chs 6–10. A blend of old and new approaches can be found in S. H. Beer, *Modern British Politics* (London: Faber, 1965 — published in New York as *British Politics in the Collectivist Age*), and A. H. Birch, *The British System of Government* (London: Allen & Unwin, 1967). As explained above, analyses of extra-governmental institutions are contained in *Studies in British Politics*, editor, Richard Rose (London: Macmillan, 1966).

General discussions of the policy-making process can be found, explicitly or implicitly, in many books on politics. Unfortunately, the literature on decision-making at times purchases conceptual elegance at the price of remoteness from observation of political life. Among recent books providing stimulating overviews of policy-making, one might note, *inter alia*, David Truman, *The Governmental Process* (New York: Knopf, 1951), Robert A. Dahl and Charles E. Lindblom, *Politics, Economics and Welfare* (New York: Harper, 1953), Harold Lasswell and Abraham Kaplan, *Power and Society* (New Haven: Yale University Press, 1950), and David Braybrooke and Charles E. Lindblom, *A Strategy of Decision: Policy Evaluation as a Social Process* (New York: Free Press, 1963).

CHAPTER I

# POLITICAL RECRUITMENT

POLICY-MAKING is a matter of men as well as measures. Without a number of specialist persons to carry out administrative and public duties, no government could long survive, least of all in a complex society such as Britain today. It does not, however, follow that because recruiting politicians is a necessary condition of government, it is of first importance in the policy-making activities of government. Some writers argue that the way in which politicians are recruited is of little significance, because the imperatives of environment and circumstance will drive all office-holders to make the same kinds of decisions. Others hold the same conclusion on the ground that whatever the views of men before they gain office, once there ambition will drive them to take the decisions most popular with the electorate. By contrast, the exponents of doctrines of individual leadership suggest that government works best when men of considerable insight and initiative are recruited for offices from which they can then initiate new and presumptively desirable policies. Belief in the continued loyalty of political leaders to their social origins also implies a strong link between the measures of government and recruitment procedures. In this model, too, a change in policy can be achieved by deposing political leaders from one class background and substituting leaders from another class.

In studying political recruitment, the first task is examining the jobs to be filled. Many writers on British Government attempt to distinguish 'political' from 'non-political' jobs. Political jobs are defined as offices acquired by popular election; all other appointments are said to be 'non-political'. The distinction cannot be justified. Whether a person undertakes political activity is determined by what he does in his job, not by the method of recruitment. For example, some MPs may pursue apolitical or commercial careers while technically remaining Members of Parliament, just as senior civil servants during an economic crisis may be asked to give advice or take initiatives regarding policies of considerable political significance. Extra-governmental friends of politicians may also play political roles, without inhibitions arising from their lack of a civil service or parliamentary status. The conventional language also errs in that it suggests people are either political, or non-political. The distinction is more aptly understood as a matter of degree; people in public offices are either more or less political, that is, they vary in the extent of their influence upon policy-making.

In terms of recruitment procedures, we can distinguish at least four different methods. The first and most familiar is recruitment by election. This is the way into the House of Commons or the local government council chamber, but it is not used elsewhere. The second route is through competitive examination. The majority of individuals employed in the civil service, especially at the higher salary levels, are recruited in this manner. The third method involves promotion or appointment by a formal patron. The term 'patron' emphasises that when a Prime Minister appoints a man to a ministerial position, or to a position of authority in a nationalised industry, he expects the recipient to show deference to him, whether or not his appointee remains formally responsible to him. Today, patronage has none of the overtones of financial corruption that once marked British government, but the exercise of patronage remains a means by which those enjoying powers of appointment can extend their influence. A complementary but less clearly defined process of recruitment involves informal co-option to a position of influence which may never be regularised by the award of a formal office. Examples in this category include the economists, journalists and academics known to have the ear of a cabinet minister, or those in the entourage of the Prime Minister in Downing Street, people whose informal relationship may be much different from that suggested by the title of press adviser or personal assistant.

In the policy-making process, one might hypothesise that differences in modes of recruitment would be associated with different conceptions of how to act in the policy process. In theory, elected politicians are expected to be specially responsive to popular preferences, holders of office by competitive examination are expected to be capable of applying technocratic criteria in evaluating policies, and recipients of patronage or co-option to be sensitive to those who have selected them for their current post or those who control appointments to the next job that stimulates their ambition. The difficulty in applying such theories is twofold. Many people prominent in policy-making in Britain have been subject to more than one means of recruitment. For example, a cabinet minister is first of all elected from a constituency, and then a recipient of the Prime Minister's patronage. A civil servant enters office by competitive examination, but rises to the top through promotion by formal civil service patrons and by co-option. Moreover, any deductions about motivation and behaviour drawn from analysis of general patterns of recruitment will not apply to those individuals who lack the desire to continue rising in their careers, or those who perceive the most certain path to promotion as different from those outlined above.

The complexities of government, not to mention the complexities of human nature, greatly limit the value of any attempt to deduce the policy preferences of politicians from a simple analysis of social origins. Such a deduction assumes that, say, parental occupation or secondary education is an influence which overrides later individual experiences, and operates equally upon nearly all individuals who share this attribute. Such assumptions would best be treated with scepticism in the absence of stronger empirical evidence than currently exists. The value of analysing the social origins of politicians lies in a different direction. Given that high political office is honoured, then studying the common characteristics of men in high office tells us much about the things that a society values. In Britain, one can trace the gradual shift from emphasis upon the virtues of ancestry, of inherited wealth and genteel upbringing, to those of formal educational achievement. Incidentally, all of these characteristics are acquired *before* an individual reaches voting age. Wealth, trade union office and, in a few cases, technical expertise, are the chief characteristics that an *adult* may acquire to increase his suitability for elective office. Analysing the social origins of politicians may be of greater use as a measure of the prevailing values of the culture than it is as a means of predicting or explaining policy-making in government.

## Bibliographical Note

The literature on the recruitment of British politicians is substantial, concentrating attention upon the social origins of its subjects. The best general survey of the literature is W. L. Guttsman, *The British Political Elite* (London: MacGibbon & Kee, 1963). It is particularly valuable because it includes analyses of trends in political recruitment since 1832. Two books provide detailed analyses of the careers of MPs: Austin Ranney, *Pathways to Parliament* (London: Macmillan, 1965), and, less successfully, P. W. Buck, *Amateurs and Professionals in British Politics, 1918–59* (Chicago: University Press, 1963). Useful sources of data on MPs can be found in J. F. S. Ross, *Elections and Electors* (London: Eyre & Spottiswoode, 1955), and in successive Nuffield election studies authored by D. E. Butler and others. R. K. Kelsall's *Higher Civil Servants in Britain* (London: Routledge, 1955) has the most statistical data on this category of public officials; its findings can be updated by successive reports of the Civil Service Commission, and related white papers. P. G. Richards' *Patronage in British Government* (London: Allen & Unwin, 1963) provides much valuable descriptive material about the maze of patronage appointments existing in the past and present. As the bibliography of this volume indicates, relevant journal articles are numerous. Note particularly the broad comparison of British and American career patterns by Ralph H. Turner, 'Sponsored and Contest Mobility and the School System', *American Sociological Review*, XXV v (1960).

Because the problem of political recruitment is common to all societies and because the offices to be filled are often similar in title, if not always in substance, data on Britain can readily be compared with findings from a wide range of other countries. Convenient introductions to findings in other countries can be found in Dwaine Marvick, *Political Decision-Makers* (New York: Free Press, 1961), and in *Decisions and Decision-Makers in the Modern State* (Paris: UNESCO, 1967). The controversy on the importance of social characteristics for policy-makers is classically presented in C. Wright Mills, *The Power Elite* (New York: Oxford University Press, 1956), and Nelson Polsby, *Community Power and Political Theory* (New Haven: Yale University Press, 1963). The argument is carried forward with considerable skill and important empirical data on French and German leaders by Lewis J. Edinger and Donald Searing in 'Social Background in Elite Analysis: a Methodological Inquiry', *American Political Science Review*, LXI ii (1967).

# THE SOCIAL BACKGROUND AND CONNECTIONS OF 'TOP DECISION MAKERS'

*By* TOM LUPTON *and* C. SHIRLEY WILSON

THE classic model of elitist government in Britain assumes that the men who govern are recruited from a socially unrepresentative background, tend to be similar to each other in their social characteristics and enjoy diffuse informal ties with persons in leadership positions outside politics. Potentially, these personal relationships may influence policy outcomes, but they are not, as many selections in this reader show, necessary or sufficient to determine policy choices. Therefore it is specially important to depend upon empirical evidence as well as inference in studying political recruitment. An unusual opportunity to do this arose from allegations made by Labour MPs in 1957 that information was improperly disclosed about the raising of the Bank Rate. A tribunal rejected these allegations; their published evidence provides a useful and unusual source of information about the activities of people whose work is usually conducted with little publicity. The resulting study by Tom Lupton and Shirley Wilson is distinctive in that the authors are able to combine analysis of social characteristics with some data about how the individuals studied acted in a concrete historical situation.

## I

OUR interests as sociologists have led us to make use of the Bank Rate Tribunal evidence as a convenient starting point for the analysis of some social connections between persons prominent in banking, insurance, politics, and public administration. Our choice of persons and categories was influenced by our starting point, and our enquiries were limited by considerations of time and space, and by gaps in the published sources of data. For these reasons our results are not statistically significant. But they will be of interest to

---

Reprinted in full from the *Manchester School of Economic and Social Studies*, XXVII i (1959) 30–52, where it was published along with two other articles: Ely Devons, 'An Economist's View of the Bank Rate Tribunal Evidence', and H. J. Hanham, 'A Political Scientist's View'.

sociologists, as representing the beginnings of an analysis of the social origins and interconnections of what we shall call the 'top decision makers'[1] in British society. We think that economists and political scientists will also be interested. To our knowledge, no such analysis has previously been made. Haxey[2] traced some family and business connections of Conservative MPs, but this was to support a political argument. Bloomfield made a study of certain aristocratic and middle class families.[3] But neither of these was part of a scientific investigation. To us, as sociologists, and as members of a Department of Social Anthropology, it was a natural first step to enquire whether the persons whose names appeared in the Tribunal evidence were linked to each other by relationships of friendship, kinship, affinity, common membership of associations, and so on. And the descriptions of behaviour given by witnesses in evidence revealed that some persons were so related. Reference to published sources revealed many more such relationships.

In attempting to interpret the behaviour they observe, sociologists look first at these 'networks' of relationships, and at the kind of training people receive to occupy positions within them. It seemed to us likely that there would be a 'structural' explanation for some of the behaviour described by witnesses at the Tribunal. This article is an attempt to map out some parts of the social structure of 'top decision makers'.

## II

Bagehot wrote:

> ... all 'city' people make their money by investments, for which there are often good argumentative reasons, but they would hardly ever be able, if required before a Parliamentary committee, to state these reasons.[4]

The statements from several witnesses at the Parker Tribunal justified this forecast. At one point, after varying attempts to explain

[1] The term 'top decision makers' is used as a makeshift. We are aware that not all the persons we consider are of equal prestige and authority. There are difficult problems of definition raised by this kind of investigation but we think it wise to postpone consideration of these. We shall presently state whom we have included in the category of 'top decision makers' for the purpose of this paper.

[2] S. Haxey, *Tory MP* (London: Victor Gollancz, 1940).

[3] Paul Bloomfield, *Uncommon People, a Study of England's Elite* (London: Hamish Hamilton, 1955).

[4] Water Bagehot, *Lombard Street* (London: Kegan Paul, Trübner & Co., 1892).

how Lazard's came to a decision to sell gilt-edged securities, Lord Kindersley interrupted counsel to say:

I have had a feeling — I have been here listening to the evidence in the last day or two — that there is some lack of understanding as to the way my firm works.[5]

The evidence of Lord Kindersley and others revealed that some important decisions were taken and others accepted because colleagues knew about, and relied upon, each other's beliefs and special aptitudes. Lengthy analyses were not a necessary prelude to decision making. This is not surprising. When decisions have to be made quickly most persons have to act according to precedent and 'hunch' and not in the light of detailed analysis of the current situation. The consequences of this process for economic decisions such as those which were described by Tribunal witnesses are the concern of the economist. As sociologists we were particularly interested *inter alia* in the influence of custom and precedent in defining roles and activities in the decision-making process. That influences of this kind were at work was indicated by persons appearing before the Tribunal. In his opening speech, the Attorney-General, Sir Reginald Manningham-Buller, referred to 'the time-honoured fashion' of announcing changes in the Bank Rate. He also stated that:

It would be a great departure from precedent and custom if the Chancellor of the Exchequer were to announce a change in the Bank Rate.[6]

When the Governor of the Bank of England, Mr Cameron Fromanteel Cobbold, was examined by the Attorney-General, he explained his 'normal practice' when considering 'a specific proposal'. He said that, depending upon the nature of the proposal, he would consult others in addition to the 'recognised sub-committee of the Court for that purpose'.[7]

In addition to the influence of custom and precedent in decision making, informality in relationships between decision makers came out clearly in the evidence. A good example of this came out during the examination of Lord Kindersley by the Attorney-General. The Attorney-General was asking Lord Kindersley why he, and not Mr Cobbold, had gone to see Lord Bicester about the possible effect of the Bank Rate rise on the Vickers issue and on relations between the 'City' and the Bank of England. Lord Kindersley replied:

[5] *Proceedings of the Tribunal appointed to inquire into allegations that information about the raising of the Bank Rate was improperly disclosed* (London: H.M.S.O., 1957) p. 187: Q. 7326.

[6] Ibid. p. 6.

[7] Ibid. p. 198: Q. 7733.

I consider it perfectly natural that I should be allowed to go and talk to a colleague in the Bank of England ... I do not think that Lord Bicester would find it in the least surprising that I should come to him and say to him: 'Look here, Rufie, is it too late to stop this business or not?';

and:

I have discussed this with Jim — with the Governor and I am coming on to see you.[8]

The same kind of informality was seen in the activities of directors of some City merchant houses as described before the Tribunal.[9]

The basis of informality in social relationships is often a shared social background, which promotes shared beliefs and confidence in customary procedures. It was this evidence of informality and custom which led us to look for common social background, and links between persons other than those arising from the formal needs of business life. There were pointers in the evidence itself and elsewhere that we might find connections of kinship and of affinity.[10] Ties of friendship and common interest were revealed by the description of a shooting party at which members of the Keswick family were joined by Mr Nigel Birch and others; and by the meetings of Messrs J. M. Stevens and D. McLachlan.[11]

Since it was clear that many of the 'top decision makers' whom the evidence mentions were interlinked in sets of relationships other than those directly arising out of business arrangements, we wondered whether the same kind of affiliations would be found in a wider sample of such persons, i.e., whether such affiliations tended to be typical of the social milieu of this particular set of 'top decision makers'. Our choice of a wider sample was influenced by our starting point, and the reader will find that it is biased. But we have included enough persons to make our findings of some sociological, if not statistical, significance.

8 Ibid. p. 191: Q. 7459 and 7462.

9 See, for example, the evidence of the Keswick brothers (*Proceedings*, pp. 94, 100, 103, 108).

10 Intermarriage amongst banking families has often been referred to. See for example:

L. S. Presswell, *Country Banking in the Industrial Revolution* (Oxford: The University Press, 1956);

R. J. Truptil, *British Banks and the London Money Market* (London: Jonathan Cape, 1936) p. 262;

H. Clay, *Lord Norman* (London: Macmillan, 1957);

E. Adlard (Ed.), *Robert Holland Martin* (London: Frederick Muller, 1947) p. 18.

11 See the evidence of Mr J. M. Stevens (*Proceedings*, p. 222) and Mr D. McLachlan (*Proceedings*, pp. 16 and 17).

III

The following are the six categories of 'top decision makers' we have chosen to study:

(A) Cabinet Ministers and other Ministers of the Crown;
(B) Senior Civil Servants;
(C) Directors of the Bank of England;
(D) Directors of the 'Big Five' banks;
(E) Directors of 'City' firms;
(F) Directors of insurance companies.

Category (A) includes all the persons named.[12] Category (B) includes the twelve senior members of the Treasury Staff and the Permanent Secretaries and their immediate deputies of twenty-one other ministries. Category (C) includes all directors of the Bank of England (as listed by Mr Cobbold before the Tribunal). Category (D) comprises all directors of the 'Big Five'. Category (E) includes the directors of fourteen merchant banks or discount houses, several of which were mentioned before the Tribunal. Some of these are private banks, others public companies, but all have an authorised capital of £2m. or more. We have taken the directors of only eight insurance companies, all with an authorised capital of over £3m., to make up category (F). The selection of these eight out of all insurance companies with authorised capital of over £3m. was not entirely random.[13] We made sure that the two large companies mentioned in the evidence were included. The analysis of the education, club membership, and connections of kinship and affinity, is based entirely on published data.[14]

Table 1 summarises the data on schools attended by members of the six categories. We have lumped together under the heading of 'other public and grammar schools' a large number of schools of diverse size and character. No single one of them had educated enough of the persons in our categories to justify being named

[12] *Her Majesty's Ministers and Heads of Public Departments* (London: H.M.S.O.) no. 60 (July 1958).

[13] The main reference was *The Stock Exchange Year Book, Vol. 1, 1958* (London: Thomas Skinner and Co. (Publishers) Ltd).

[14] *Who's Who 1958* (London: Adam and Charles Black);
*Burke's Landed Gentry 1952* (London: Burke's Peerage Ltd);
*Burke's Peerage, Baronetage, and Knightage 1956* (London: Burke's Peerage Ltd);
*Debrett's Peerage, Baronetage, Knightage and Companionage 1957* (London: Odhams Press Ltd).

separately. The Table shows that between one-quarter and one-third of the persons in each category except category (B) went to Eton College. Two-thirds of the Bank of England directors and a half of the Ministers went to the six named public schools, and in all categories except (B) nearly half were educated at these schools. Only three persons from all categories attended State elementary school only. The data on school education shows that the majority of persons in all categories shared the same kind of school education, with the exception of category (B).[15] We have not attempted to make anything of the totals in the right-hand column since they are distorted by the fact that many persons are members of more than one category and this applies especially to categories (C), (D), (E), and (F). We have 529 names, but not 529 persons.

TABLE 1

*Schools*

| | *Category* | | | | | | |
|---|---|---|---|---|---|---|---|
| | *A* | *B* | *C* | *D* | *E* | *F* | *Total* |
| Eton | 11 (32·4%) | 3 (4·1%) | 6 (33·3%) | 44 (29·7%) | 35 (32·7%) | 46 (30·9%) | 145 |
| Winchester | 3 | 3 | 2 | 9 | 4 | 7 | 28 |
| Harrow | 1 | 1 | 0 | 8 | 4 | 7 | 21 |
| Rugby | 0 | 5 | 2 | 3 | 2 | 4 | 16 |
| Charterhouse | 0 | 1 | 0 | 4 | 0 | 6 | 11 |
| Marlborough | 2 | 1 | 2 | 3 | 1 | 0 | 9 |
| TOTAL | 17 (50%) | 14 (19·2%) | 12 (66·6%) | 71 (48%) | 46 (43%) | 70 (47%) | 230 |
| Other Public and Grammar Schools | 15 | 54 | 4 | 53 | 13 | 26 | 165 |
| State Elementary School only | 1 | 0 | 1 | 1 | 0 | 0 | 3 |
| No data | 1 | 5 | 1 | 23 | 48 | 53 | 131 |
| TOTAL | 34 | 73 | 18 | 148 | 107 | 149 | 529 |

[15] It is interesting that category (B) is the only one of the six to which entrance is by competitive examination.

This last remark applies also to Table 2 which summarises the information on College and University education. A feature of Table 2 is the predominance of Oxford and Cambridge. Over 70 per cent of all Ministers went either to Oxford or Cambridge, and nearly 70 per cent of all senior civil servants, 50 per cent of Bank of England directors, 50 per cent of directors of the 'Big Five'. The financial categories (C), (D), (E) and (F) show the greatest proportion of persons with no university education.[16] It will be noted that in Table 2, as in Table 1, large numbers of category (D), (E) and (F) members are to be found under 'no data'. If our information were complete the picture might possibly be significantly different. Like Table 1, Table 2 shows that, for those persons in our six categories for which we have data, the majority shared the same kind of post-school education, although there are some differences in this regard between the first three and the last three categories. Similarity of educational background forms a link between many members of our six categories both within categories and across their boundaries.

TABLE 2

*College and University*

| | *Category* | | | | | | |
|---|---|---|---|---|---|---|---|
| | *A* | *B* | *C* | *D* | *E* | *F* | *Total* |
| Oxford | 18 | 30 | 2 | 46 | 24 | 30 | 150 |
| Cambridge | 7 | 20 | 7 | 28 | 13 | 27 | 102 |
| TOTAL | 25 (71·5%) | 50 (68·5%) | 9 (50%) | 74 (50%) | 37 (34·6%) | 57 (38·3%) | 252 |
| London | 2 | 5 | 0 | 1 | 1 | 2 | 11 |
| Other Universities | 1 | 10 | 2 | 10 | 2 | 8 | 33 |
| Sandhurst | 1 | 0 | 1 | 5 | 3 | 6 | 16 |
| Dartmouth | 1 | 0 | 0 | 1 | 1 | 5 | 8 |
| Woolwich | 0 | 0 | 0 | 1 | 1 | 1 | 3 |
| None | 4 | 9 | 7 | 36 | 13 | 21 | 90 |
| No data | 1 | 3 | 1 | 23 | 51 | 55 | 134 |
| TOTAL | 35 | 77 | 20 | 151 | 109 | 155 | 547 |
| No. in category | 34 | 73 | 18 | 148 | 107 | 149 | 529 |

16 Reflecting perhaps a tendency for persons to enter banking and finance as young men, and to forgo a university education

And there are also many shared directorships in the last four categories.

The only systematic information we have been able to collect about the leisure time activities of members of this sample concerned club affiliations. This is summarised in Table 3. Table 3 is less complete than Tables 1 and 2 because club membership was not always

TABLE 3

*Club Membership*

| | *A* | *B* | *C* | *D* | *E* | *F* |
|---|---|---|---|---|---|---|
| Athenaeum | 4 | 8 | 2 | 14 | 4 | 8 |
| Bath | 0 | 2 | 1 | 11 | 4 | 6 |
| Beefsteak | 2 | 0 | 1 | 3 | 5 | 8 |
| Boodle's | 0 | 2 | 1 | 4 | 2 | 8 |
| Brooks's | 4 | 4 | 2 | 24 | 11 | 20 |
| Buck's | 2 | 0 | 0 | 3 | 3 | 8 |
| Carlton | 18 | 0 | 1 | 23 | 8 | 16 |
| Cavalry | 0 | 0 | 1 | 5 | 4 | 4 |
| City of London | 0 | 0 | 1 | 13 | 8 | 5 |
| Guards | 0 | 0 | 1 | 5 | 1 | 3 |
| M.C.C. | 2 | 1 | 1 | 8 | 5 | 20 |
| New (Edinburgh) | 2 | 1 | 0 | 4 | 3 | 3 |
| Oriental | 0 | 0 | 1 | 6 | 3 | 2 |
| Pratt's | 5 | 1 | 0 | 7 | 4 | 5 |
| Reform | 1 | 15 | 0 | 6 | 0 | 2 |
| Services (various) | 2 | 1 | 0 | 5 | 3 | 5 |
| Sports (various) | 1 | 4 | 0 | 11 | 1 | 18 |
| St James's | 0 | 3 | 1 | 5 | 0 | 4 |
| Traveller's | 0 | 3 | 0 | 7 | 2 | 8 |
| Turf | 5 | 1 | 2 | 6 | 7 | 11 |
| University (various) | 0 | 15 | 2 | 6 | 0 | 3 |
| White's | 6 | 0 | 2 | 13 | 13 | 23 |
| Yacht clubs | 3 | 2 | 1 | 20 | 5 | 8 |
| Other clubs | 11 | 22 | 3 | 67 | 5 | 28 |
| TOTAL CLUBS | 68 | 85 | 24 | 276 | 101 | 226 |
| Number for whom data was collected | (31) | (63) | (14) | (119) | (53) | (90) |
| Number in category | (34) | (73) | (18) | (148) | (107) | (149) |

listed in the references we used. But many persons are members of more than one club. The totals at the bottom of the Table represent a count of all the clubs listed in published sources. Below this in brackets is given the number of persons for whom information was available, and the number of persons in the category. The clubs named in the list are those most frequently mentioned. Others have been counted under headings such as 'sports clubs (various)' which includes polo, fishing and golf clubs. Yacht clubs, have been named separately, and also the M.C.C. The various University clubs have been collected under one heading, and so have the various Services clubs, with the exception of the Guards and Cavalry clubs; these are separately named. A striking feature of the table is that the Civil Servants' club membership is confined largely to the Reform Club and to University clubs. There are few members of the other categories in these clubs. Amongst the other categories the clubs most frequently represented are the Carlton, Brooks's, White's, and the Athenaeum. The information we have shows that none of the Senior Civil Servants in category (B) belong to the Carlton club, or White's.[17] Again, in Table 3, a good number of the members of our six categories are shown to be linked by the sharing of a common activity, in this case club membership.

## IV

The evidence we shall assemble in this section is of a different order to that we have so far studied, and we shall say something to introduce it. It might occur to some readers that the most important feature of the diagrams we present below is the recurrence of certain long-established family names, and they might wish to read significance into this in the light of other knowledge and interests, or of preconceived ideas. Others might argue that the diagrams mean nothing because they do not include certain prominent families, or because they are incomplete and biased; and so on. That is why we want to make it clear at the outset that, for this analysis the diagrams are only intended to show the connections of kinship and affinity of some persons who are members of our six categories of decision makers. We used the following procedure: we began by taking persons who were prominent in the Tribunal proceedings, for example Lord Kindersley and Mr Cameron Cobbold. We traced the names of parents, siblings, spouses and children, and constructed a small

[17] We do not know how to assess the relative prestige or exclusiveness of the various clubs, but it is probable that the traditional impartiality of the Civil Service precludes its members from joining the Carlton, a club so clearly associated with one political party. Petrie says '... the great names in the Tory hierarchy down the centuries have always been found, and are still to be found, in the list of members of the Carlton' (*The Carlton Club* (London: Eyre & Spottiswoode, 1955) p. 15).

'family tree'. By following up the names of paternal and maternal kin it often proved possible to join the 'family trees' together into a kinship diagram.[18]

We have not been able to trace the kinship connections of all persons in the six categories; and it is only possible to present a limited amount of the material so far gathered. To include all connections of kinship and affinity for even a few dozen people would clearly require a great deal of space and demand greater resources of time and personnel than those available. There may be no kin connections between a great many of the people we have selected; and there are persons represented on the diagrams who belong to none of the six categories. This has partly arisen because we had already the kin and affinal *connections* of some people referred to at the Tribunal before we extended the scope of enquiry.

For ease of exposition the material is presented in a series of small abridged diagrams. The names of some persons who link one diagram with another are enclosed in heavy black rectangles with numbers of linked diagrams in small circles attached. Persons who are members of one or more of the six categories have the appropriate group letter or letters below their names.[19] The names of some persons who are directors of other concerns, industrial or financial and commercial, are indicated, where appropriate, with the letters 'G' and 'H'.[20]

We now trace some of the connections illustrated, indicating links between diagrams, links which would make one chart in reality. It would take too long to trace every connection on all the diagrams; the reader is invited to complete this task for himself.

Diagram 1 shows some of the connections of Mr C. F. Cobbold, Governor of the Bank of England and a member of a family of landed gentry. He is related on his father's side to the late Lt. Col. John Cobbold, who married a daughter of the 9th Duke of Devonshire. Lt. Col. Cobbold's sister married Sir Charles Hambro, a Director of the Bank of England. Lt. Col. H. E. Hambro, married the widow of the 5th Earl of Cadogan, whose grandson married a daughter of Lt. Col. Cobbold (*see* diagram 9).

Diagram 2 traces links established by the marriage of Sir Everard

[18] Properly speaking, a diagram of both kinship and affinity. Triangles represent males, and circles females. Unshaded signs represent living people. The equals sign signifies a marriage connection and the asterisk, a former marriage connection.

[19] For reasons of space we have had to shorten some names and titles; we trust no one will take offence at this.

[20] The source used for this information was *The Directory of Directors, 1958* (London: Thomas Skinner & Co. (Publishers) Ltd).

Hambro with a relative of Lord Norman, who was formerly Governor of the Bank of England. A cousin of Lord Norman married an uncle of the present Home Secretary, the Rt. Hon. R. A. Butler. A daughter of this marriage married Sir George Abell, a Director of the Bank of England, whose brother-in-law, Mr Nicholas Norman Butler, married into the Hambro family.

Diagram 3 illustrates the marriages of other daughters of the 9th Duke of Devonshire, among them that of Lady Dorothy, wife of the Prime Minister and sister-in-law to Lt. Col. John Cobbold. One of her cousins (father's brother's daughter) married the 28th Earl of Crawford, whose son, Lord Balniel, is Parliamentary Private Secretary to the Minister of Housing and Local Government (late P.P.S. to the Financial Secretary to the Treasury). The Earl is brother-in-law to the Attorney-General (*see* diagram 15), and also to the Marquess of Salisbury. This name takes us to the next diagram — No. 4 — which shows marriages of sons of Lord Eustace Cecil. One son married a daughter of the 10th Duke of Leeds, father-in-law of Lord Chandos, Chairman of A.E.I. (*see* diagram 12). Another son was Baron Rockley; his son, the present Baron, and Mr M. J. Babington Smith (a Director of the Bank of England and of A.E.I.) married daughters of Admiral Hon. Sir Hubert Meade Fetherstonhaugh, who is connected by marriage to the Glyn banking family (*see* diagram 21).

The 4th Marquess of Salisbury connects diagrams 4 and 5. His daughter, sister of the present Marquess, married Baron Harlech, the father of the Minister of State for Foreign Affairs, and father-in-law of the Prime Minister's son. Diagram 5 also connects with diagram 1, through the late Lt. Col. John Cobbold; he was related on his mother's side to the 7th Earl of Dunmore, whose granddaughter married Mr D. A. Stirling, a 'Big Five' director. Her brother, the late Viscount Fincastle, brings us to diagram 7. He married a daughter of the 2nd Baron Wyfold; another daughter is married to a son of Sir George Schuster, the brother-in-law of the Chairman of the Tribunal, Lord Chief Justice Parker.

Diagram 6 traces some of the connections of the Prime Minister's nephew by marriage, the 11th Duke of Devonshire, a brother-in-law of the writer Nancy Mitford; she married a son of Lord Rennell. Lord Rennell's wife is a sister of Lord Bicester, a senior director of Morgan Grenfell and Co. and a Director of the Bank of England. Lord Bicester, a witness at the Tribunal, was the 'Rufie' mentioned in the evidence. Lord Rennell links diagrams 6 and 22, for one of Nancy Mitford's sisters was married to Lord Moyne, grandson of the 1st Earl of Iveagh. Diagram 16 shows that Lord Rennell is also connected to the Keswick family by the marriage of his sister to a brother-in-law of J. H. Keswick. Mr W. J. Keswick, Director of the Bank of England, is related through his wife to Lord Lovat, brother-in-law of two Conservative Members of Parliament.

Diagrams 8 and 10 are joined by the name of the wife of Mr M. R. Hely-Hutchinson, whose brother is father-in-law to Mr J. M. Stevens, a Director of the Bank of England, who gave evidence at the Tribunal. Her father's family was linked by marriage to Baron Ashcombe, whose brother married a niece of Lord Norman. (Her later marriage is shown on Diagram 19.) Baron Norman's brother's wife was a daughter of the 4th Earl of Bradford, whose grandson, the 6th Earl, is a Crown Estate Commissioner. Another daughter of the Earl of Bradford married the 7th Duke of Buccleuch, brother-in-law to the 3rd Viscount Hampden. Viscount Hampden's son (now the 4th Viscount), managing director of Lazard's, was also a witness at the Tribunal.

The name of Viscount Hampden links diagrams 14 and 15, for the 1st Viscount's daughter was mother to Mr J. H. Bevan, brother-in-law of Earl Alexander of Tunis. Earl Alexander married a daughter of the 5th Earl of Lucan, whose wife was a daughter of Mr J. Spender Clay. This brings us back to diagrams 11 and 12, by-passed in the previous paragraph. A son of Mr J. Spender Clay married a daughter of the 1st Viscount Astor. Diagram 11 shows the Astor-Devonshire link; diagram 12 shows that the grand-daughter of Mr J. Spender Clay married the Hon. David Bowes-Lyon, and traces some other marriage connections of members of his family. A daughter of the Hon. Malcolm Bowes-Lyon married a son of the 13th Duke of Hamilton; another son is First Lord of the Admiralty. The 14th Duke is Lord Steward of the Queen's Household.

Mr H. C. B. Mynors, Deputy Governor of the Bank of England and witness at the Tribunal, is descended on his mother's side from a sister of Mr J. Spender Clay (*see* diagram 17). His brother, and the Earl of Home, Minister of State for Commonwealth Relations, married sisters, members of the Lyttleton family. The Earl's brother, William Douglas Home, son-in-law of the 4th Viscount Hampden, links this diagram with diagram 14. Further Lyttleton connections are shown on diagram 18. The son of Lord Chandos (Oliver Lyttelton) married a daughter of Sir Alan Lascelles (diagram 4), brother-in-law of the 1st Baron Lloyd. The first wife of Lord Chandos' father was a member of the Tennant family, also referred to in the last diagram. This repeats the name of the late Mr R. H. Benson. One of his sons married a daughter of the 2nd Earl of Dudley (diagram 21). The Earl's sister married the 4th Baron Wolverton and a daughter of this marriage became the wife of Mr Nigel Birch, MP. He was Economic Secretary to the Treasury at the time of the decision to raise the Bank Rate and also a member of the Keswick shooting party mentioned in the evidence, a party which also included a member of the Hambro Bank family.[21] Diagram 21 also shows two other members of the Government, the Secretary of State for Air, brother of the 3rd Earl of Dudley, and the Earl of Gosford, Parliamentary Under-Secretary of State to the Foreign Office. Their two families are linked by a marriage in the previous generation.

The next diagram (22) introduces Lord Kindersley, Director of the Bank of England and a prominent Tribunal witness. His brother married a niece of the 2nd Earl of Iveagh, father-in-law of the Rt. Hon. Alan Lennox-Boyd, MP, Minister of State for Colonial Affairs. The Earl of Iveagh is father-in-law to a sister of another Conservative Minister, the Rt. Hon. John Hare, MP, whose wife is sister to Viscount Cowdray, who was mentioned in evidence at the Tribunal in connection with the Pearson Group of companies.[22] These connections are shown on diagram 23. The final diagram refers to some further connections of Lord Kindersley.

Some of the diagrams, for example diagram 9, have not been referred to in the text. To have traced all the ramifications of kinship and affinity through all the diagrams would have been confusing, and would have obscured our main aim, that of tracing links between members of the six categories.

Seventy-three of the persons in the six categories appear in the kinship diagrams. We know that there could have been more had not the diagrams been abridged. Eight ministers are included in the diagrams; and 3 Senior Civil Servants. For the other four categories there are more names than persons, since there are multiple directorships. Nine of the category C names appear, 25 of the category D names, 20 of the category E names, and 32 of the category F names. The only category to be markedly under-represented in the diagrams is category B (top Civil Servants) with only 3 included of a total of 73 in the category. This may arise partly from the method used in compiling the diagrams.

Some estimate of the extent of multiple directorships may be gained if the number of names on the diagrams in categories C, D, E and F is compared with the number of persons: 86 as compared with 62. Finally, in comment on the diagrams, only about 18 per cent of all the names in the categories appear in the diagrams. On the hypothesis that all persons in the categories are linked by kinship or

[21] *Proceedings*, p. 98: Q. 3705 ff.

[22] *Proceedings*, p. 32: Q. 926; p. 33: Q. 946–9; p. 130: Q. 4886 ff.

affinity (one to which we do not subscribe) it would take a great deal more research to include them in a series of diagrams.

## IV

So far in this article we have presented facts baldly without attempting to assess their meaning and significance. It would have been unwise to have done so in view of the bias of the sample and the incompleteness of the data. Our study must be regarded, then, mainly as a contribution to the 'ethnography' of finance, politics, and administration. But we cannot conclude without attempting briefly to relate what we have said to one aspect of social structure which is of particular interest to us.

We have referred to the tradition of intermarriage between banking families. Also by tradition, some merchant bankers become directors of the Bank of England. It is not surprising then that the kinship diagrams show connections between directors of merchant banks, and between merchant banks and directors of the Bank of England. Nor is it surprising that we find that positions in certain firms are occupied by adjacent generations of the same family. The positions of chairman of Lazard Bros. and director of the Bank of England, for example, are now occupied by Lord Kindersley and were once occupied by his father.

What might seem surprising is that kinship connections of this kind have persisted through many changes in the scale and functions of banking, in the organisation of industry, and in the complexity of politics. Bagehot,[23] referring to the family basis of private banking at the end of last century, argued that it was inappropriate for modern large-scale organisation. Weber has also argued that bureaucratic, 'civil-service-type' structure, in which recruitment and promotion are based on specific technical qualifications, and in which authority vests in the office and not in the person, is the most appropriate to modern conditions, while traditional structures are unsuitable from the point of view of effectiveness. But Weber also argues that, for effectiveness' sake, decision making and execution ought to be separate. And he notes that: '... administrative structures based on different principles intersect with bureaucratic organisation'.[24]

Some of the organisations to which we have referred seem to have the separation of decision making and executive functions to which Weber refers. Possibly they incorporate both traditionalistic and

[23] Bagehot, op. cit. pp. 272 ff.

[24] H. M. Gerth and C. Wright Mills (trans. and ed.), *From Max Weber, Essays in Sociology* (London: Kegan Paul, 1947).

bureaucratic structure. They have both directors and the managers, generally different sets of persons, possibly of different social background and training. While there have been studies of the influence of kinship as a mode of succession amongst managers,[25] we are not aware of any study which has extended to boards of directors.

Weber's point about the intersection of different structural principles has not been followed up by empirical research in the area covered in this article. Gouldner's examination of some hypotheses derived from Weber in the light of facts about factory social structure could be taken as a model for such work.[26]

The intersection of different social principles has another, individual aspect, that of role conflict. Our evidence shows that many people occupy several social roles. For example, a person may have one role in a kinship system, be a member of one or more boards of directors, and a member of various clubs and associations.

The evidence at the Parker Tribunal referred in many places to this problem, but especially as it related to the dual roles of director of a merchant bank and of the Bank of England, which were occupied by Lord Kindersley and Mr W. J. Keswick. Commenting generally on this kind of problem, Mr Cobbold addressed the Parker Tribunal as follows:

> It seems to me that a similar position often arises both in business matters and, more generally, in other walks of life, where an honest man must often divorce one set of interests from another.... The position arises almost every day in banking, where a banker is not expected to use, for his bank's profit, secret information about a customer's affairs;

and:

> ... the existence of the problem (even if it arises infrequently) must pose the question whether the present arrangement is on balance best suited to the national interest. I am most strongly of the opinion that it is.[27]

Mr Cobbold seemed aware that there were disadvantages in a situation where individuals were faced, as a consequence of discrepancy between structural principles, with conflicts of loyalty or allegiance. But he was personally convinced that these were outweighed by the advantages. This raises a general problem of comparative social structure. The field we have ourselves surveyed

[25] R. Clements, *Managers — a study of their careers in Industry* (London: Allen & Unwin, 1958).
Rosemary Stewart, *et al.*, *Management Succession* (London: Acton Soc. Trust, 1958).

[26] A. W. Gouldner, *Patterns of Industrial Bureaucracy* (London: Routledge & Kegan Paul, 1955).

[27] *Proceedings*, p. 208.

provides extensive data relevant to this problem. These data suggest that 'top decision makers' as well as being linked by kinship, business interests and similar background, are also divided by competing, even conflicting interests. Indeed, kinship itself, in certain circumstances, may act as a divisive as well as a uniting force.

To carry out the research into the problems we have briefly outlined would require investigation of a wider field than we have surveyed, and the use of techniques other than those we have used. Interviews, direct observation of behaviour, complete quantitative analysis of such items as leisure time activities, as well as the construction of complete kinship diagrams would be necessary. This latter technique would close many gaps in knowledge of British social structure. Sociologists, including ourselves, have tended to concentrate on the study of working class groups or small local communities where there is much knowledge of the operation of kinship in social life. For our 'top decision makers' we have only biographical material, inspired comment, and little more. It is possible that sociologists have avoided the problem of kinship in 'higher circles' because of the formidable problems presented for empirical field research. We can see that there may be many problems of this kind but there is no reason why the published sources of data should not be fully used.

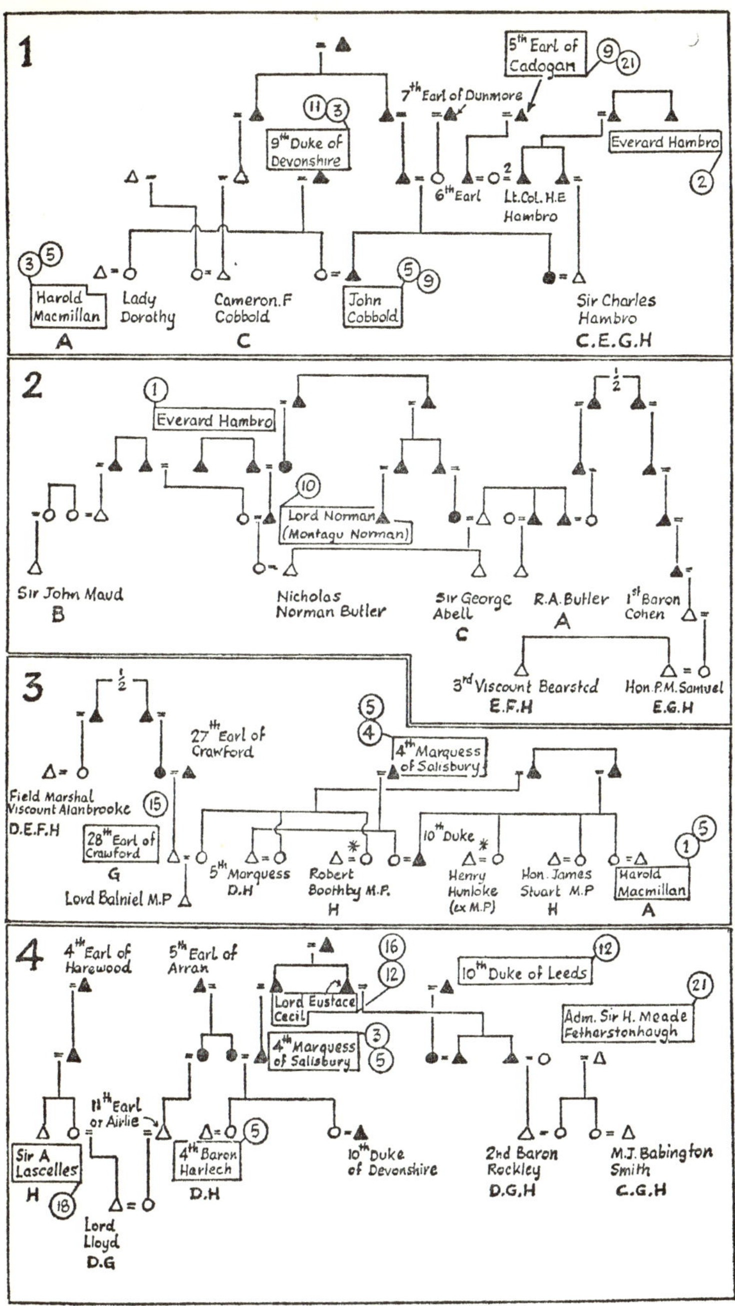
1
5th Earl of Cadogan
9
21
7th Earl of Dunmore
11
3
9th Duke of Devonshire
Everard Hambro
2
6th Earl
Lt.Col. H.E Hambro
3
5
Harold Macmillan
A
Lady Dorothy
Cameron.F Cobbold
C
John Cobbold
5
9
Sir Charles Hambro
C.E.G.H
2
1
Everard Hambro
10
Lord Norman (Montagu Norman)
Sir John Maud
B
Nicholas Norman Butler
Sir George Abell
C
R.A.Butler
A
1st Baron Cohen
3rd Viscount Bearsted
E.F.H
Hon.P.M.Samuel
E.G.H
3
27th Earl of Crawford
5
4
4th Marquess of Salisbury
Field Marshal Viscount Alanbrooke
D.E.F.H
15
28th Earl of Crawford
G
Lord Balniel M.P
5th Marquess
D.H
Robert Boothby M.P.
H
10th Duke
Henry Hunloke (ex M.P)
Hon. James Stuart M.P
H
1
5
Harold Macmillan
A
4
4th Earl of Harewood
5th Earl of Arran
16
12
10th Duke of Leeds
12
Lord Eustace Cecil
21
Adm. Sir H. Meade Fetherstonhaugh
4th Marquess of Salisbury
3
5
11th Earl of Airlie
Sir A Lascelles
H
18
4th Baron Harlech
D.H
5
10th Duke of Devonshire
2nd Baron Rockley
D.G.H
M.J. Babington Smith
C.G.H
Lord Lloyd
D.G

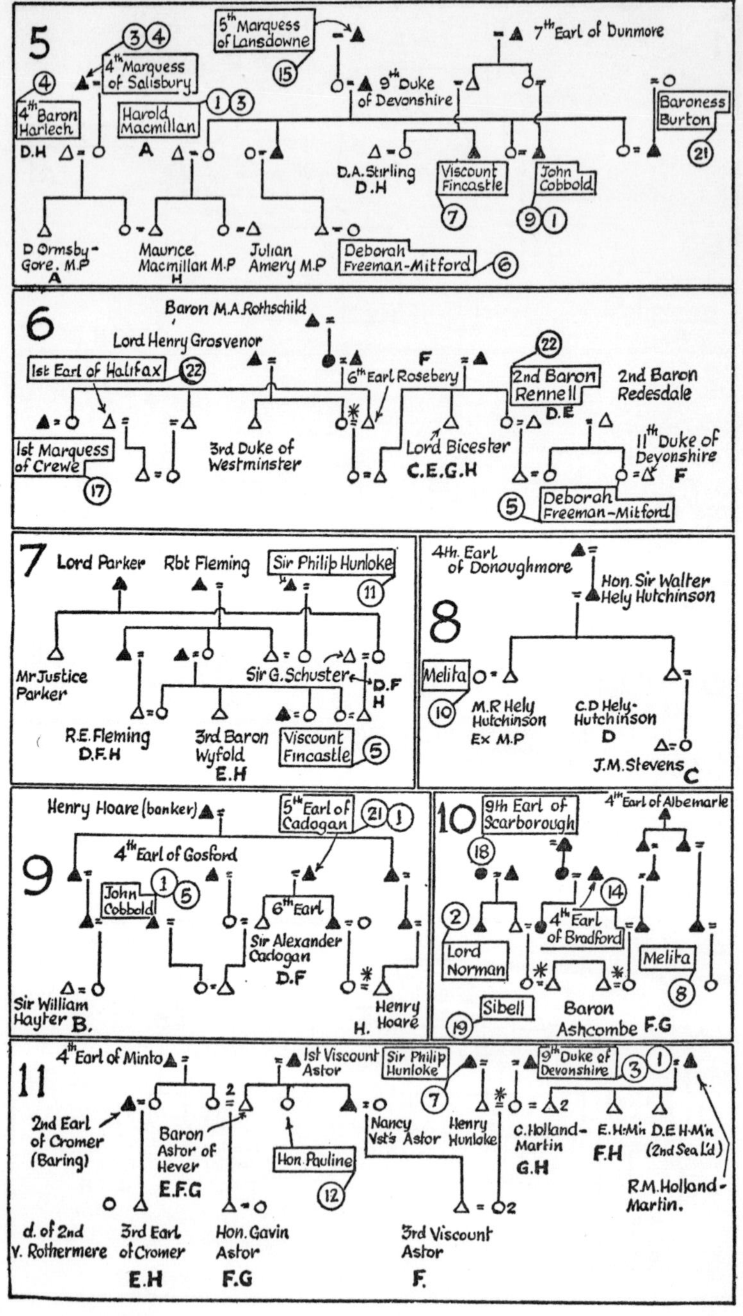
5
5th Marquess of Lansdowne
7th Earl of Dunmore
4th Marquess of Salisbury
9th Duke of Devonshire
4th Baron Harlech
Harold Macmillan
Baroness Burton
D.H
A
D.A. Stirling D.H
Viscount Fincastle
John Cobbold
D Ormsby-Gore, M.P A
Maurice Macmillan M.P H
Julian Amery M.P
Deborah Freeman-Mitford
6
Baron M.A. Rothschild
Lord Henry Grosvenor
1st Earl of Halifax
6th Earl Rosebery
2nd Baron Rennell D.E
2nd Baron Redesdale
1st Marquess of Crewe
3rd Duke of Westminster
Lord Bicester C.E.G.H
11th Duke of Devonshire F
Deborah Freeman-Mitford
7
Lord Parker
Rbt Fleming
Sir Philip Hunloke
Mr Justice Parker
Sir G. Schuster D.F H
R.E. Fleming D.F.H
3rd Baron Wyfold E.H
Viscount Fincastle
4th Earl of Donoughmore
Hon. Sir Walter Hely Hutchinson
8
Melita
M.R Hely Hutchinson Ex M.P
C.D Hely-Hutchinson D
J.M. Stevens C
Henry Hoare (banker)
5th Earl of Cadogan
9
4th Earl of Gosford
John Cobbold
6th Earl
Sir Alexander Cadogan D.F
Sir William Hayter B.
Henry Hoare H.
10
9th Earl of Scarborough
4th Earl of Albemarle
4th Earl of Bradford
Lord Norman
Melita
Sibell
Baron Ashcombe F.G
11
4th Earl of Minto
1st Viscount Astor
Sir Philip Hunloke
9th Duke of Devonshire
2nd Earl of Cromer (Baring)
Baron Astor of Hever E.F.G
Hon. Pauline
Nancy Vst's Astor
Henry Hunloke
C. Holland-Martin G.H
E.H.M'n F.H
D.E H.M'n (2nd Sea L'd)
R.M. Holland-Martin.
d. of 2nd V. Rothermere
3rd Earl of Cromer E.H
Hon. Gavin Astor F.G
3rd Viscount Astor F.

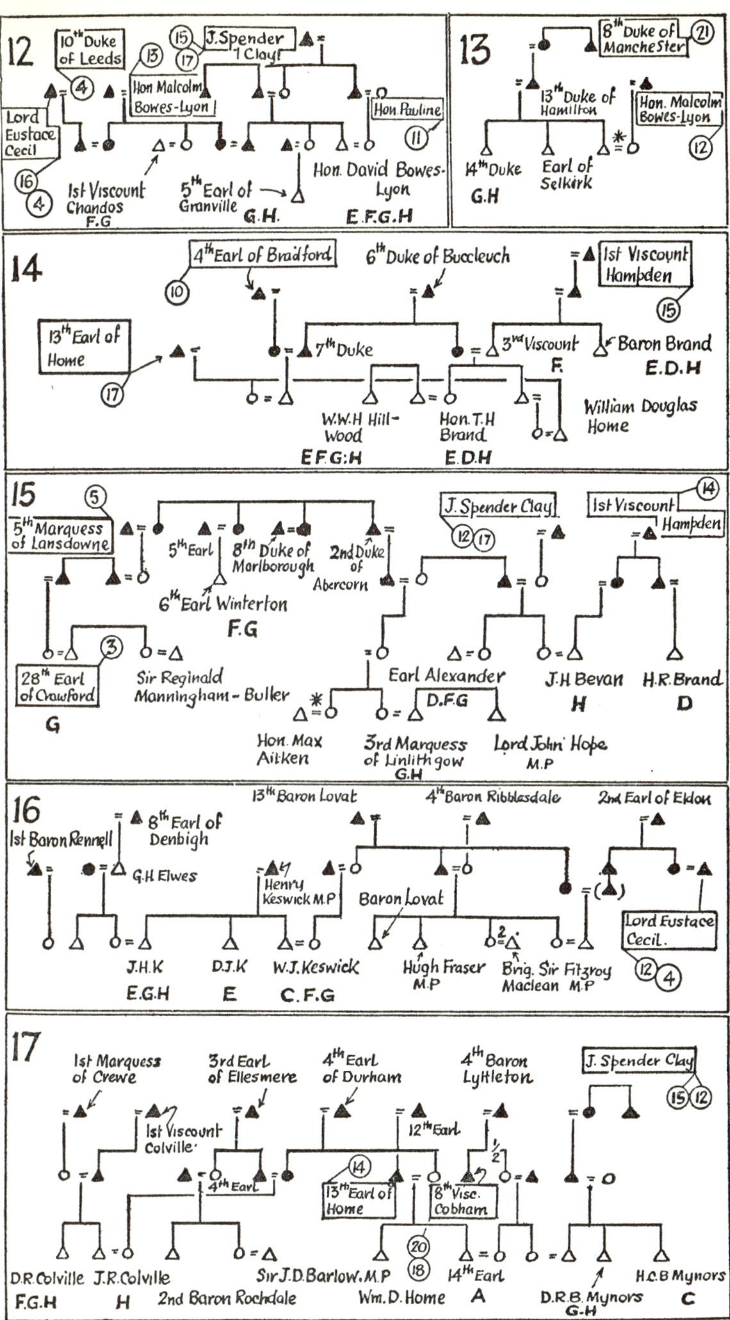

12
10th Duke of Leeds
J. Spender Clay
Lord Eustace Cecil
Hon Malcolm Bowes-Lyon
Hon Pauline
1st Viscount Chandos
F.G
5th Earl of Granville
G.H.
Hon. David Bowes-Lyon
E.F.G.H
13
8th Duke of Manchester
13th Duke of Hamilton
Hon. Malcolm Bowes-Lyon
14th Duke
G.H
Earl of Selkirk
14
4th Earl of Bradford
6th Duke of Buccleuch
1st Viscount Hampden
13th Earl of Home
7th Duke
3rd Viscount
F.
Baron Brand
E.D.H
W.W.H Hill-Wood
E.F.G.H
Hon. T.H Brand
E.D.H
William Douglas Home
15
5th Marquess of Lansdowne
5th Earl
8th Duke of Marlborough
2nd Duke of Abercorn
J. Spender Clay
1st Viscount Hampden
6th Earl Winterton
F.G
28th Earl of Crawford
G
Sir Reginald Manningham-Buller
Earl Alexander
D.F.G
J.H Bevan
H
H.R. Brand
D
Hon. Max Aitken
3rd Marquess of Linlithgow
G.H
Lord John Hope
M.P
16
13th Baron Lovat
4th Baron Ribblesdale
2nd Earl of Eldon
1st Baron Rennell
8th Earl of Denbigh
G.H Elwes
Henry Keswick M.P
Baron Lovat
Lord Eustace Cecil.
J.H.K
E.G.H
D.J.K
E
W.J. Keswick
C.F.G
Hugh Fraser
M.P
Brig. Sir Fitzroy Maclean M.P
17
1st Marquess of Crewe
3rd Earl of Ellesmere
4th Earl of Durham
4th Baron Lyttleton
J. Spender Clay
1st Viscount Colville
12th Earl
4th Earl
13th Earl of Home
8th Visc. Cobham
D.R. Colville
F.G.H
J.R. Colville
H
2nd Baron Rochdale
Sir J.D. Barlow, M.P
Wm. D. Home
14th Earl
A
D.R.B. Mynors
G.H
H.C.B Mynors
C

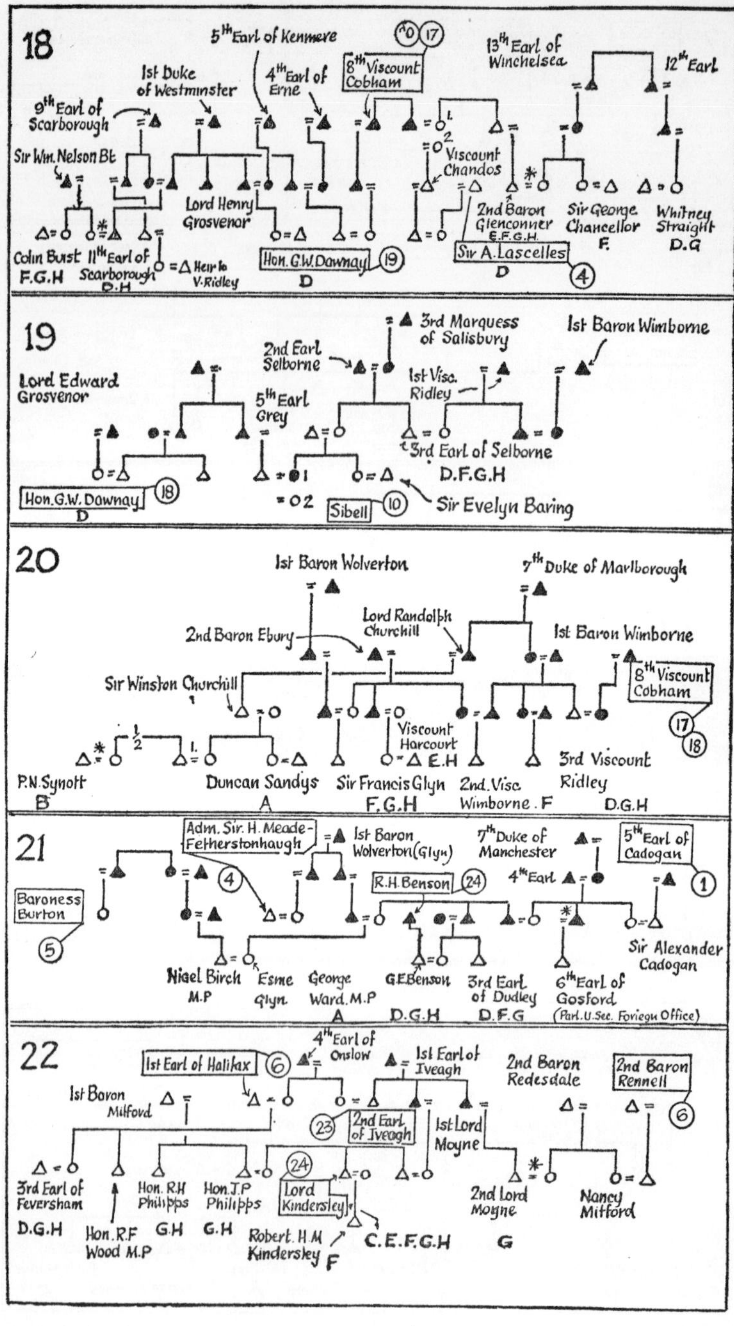
18
5th Earl of Kenmere
10 17
8th Viscount Cobham
13th Earl of Winchelsea
12th Earl
1st Duke of Westminster
4th Earl of Erne
9th Earl of Scarborough
Sir Wm. Nelson Bt
Viscount Chandos
Lord Henry Grosvenor
2nd Baron Glenconner E.F.G.H.
Sir George Chancellor F.
Whitney Straight D.G
Colin Buist F.G.H
11th Earl of Scarborough D.H
Heir to V. Ridley
Hon. G.W. Dawnay D 19
Sir A. Lascelles D 4
19
3rd Marquess of Salisbury
1st Baron Wimborne
2nd Earl Selborne
Lord Edward Grosvenor
1st Visc. Ridley
5th Earl Grey
3rd Earl of Selborne D.F.G.H
Hon. G.W. Dawnay D 18
Sibell 10
Sir Evelyn Baring
20
1st Baron Wolverton
7th Duke of Marlborough
Lord Randolph Churchill
2nd Baron Ebury
1st Baron Wimborne
Sir Winston Churchill
8th Viscount Cobham 17 18
Viscount Harcourt E.H
P.N. Synott B
Duncan Sandys A
Sir Francis Glyn F.G.H
2nd. Visc. Wimborne. F
3rd Viscount Ridley D.G.H
21
Adm. Sir. H. Meade-Fetherstonhaugh 4
1st Baron Wolverton (Glyn)
7th Duke of Manchester
5th Earl of Cadogan 1
R.H. Benson 24
4th Earl
Baroness Burton 5
Sir Alexander Cadogan
Nigel Birch M.P
Esme Glyn
George Ward. M.P A
G.E. Benson D.G.H
3rd Earl of Dudley D.F.G
6th Earl of Gosford (Parl. U. Sec. Foreign Office)
22
4th Earl of Onslow
1st Earl of Halifax 6
1st Earl of Iveagh
2nd Baron Redesdale
2nd Baron Rennell 6
1st Baron Milford
23 2nd Earl of Iveagh
1st Lord Moyne
24 Lord Kindersley
3rd Earl of Feversham D.G.H
Hon. R.F Wood M.P
Hon. R.H Philipps G.H
Hon. J.P Philipps G.H
Robert. H.M Kindersley F
C.E.F.G.H
2nd Lord Moyne G
Nancy Mitford

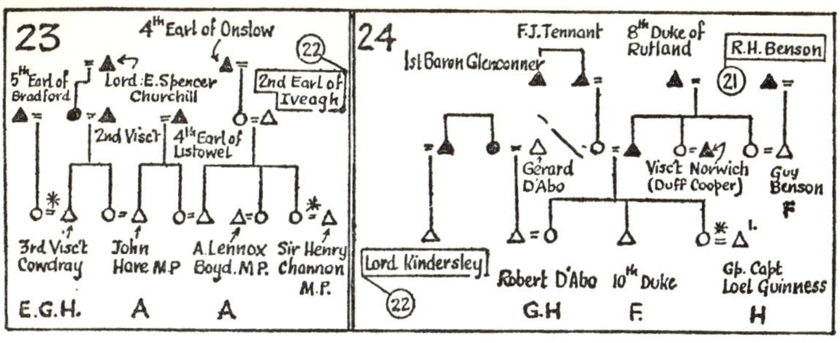
23
4th Earl of Onslow
22
5th Earl of Bradford
Lord E. Spencer Churchill
2nd Earl of Iveagh
2nd Visc't
4th Earl of Listowel
3rd Visc't Cowdray
John Hare M.P.
A. Lennox Boyd. M.P.
Sir Henry Channon M.P.
E.G.H.
A
A
24
F.J. Tennant
8th Duke of Rutland
R.H. Benson
1st Baron Glenconner
21
Gerard D'Abo
Visc't Norwich (Duff Cooper)
Guy Benson
F
Lord Kindersley
22
Robert D'Abo
10th Duke
Gp. Capt Loel Guinness
G.H
F
H

# PORTRAIT OF A LABOUR MEMBER

*By* ALAN WATKINS

GREAT changes in the importance of higher education and in the availability of educational opportunities since 1945 have greatly widened the catchment area from which politicians are recruited. This is particularly true in the Labour Party, for it has brought forward, in addition to manual workers and conventional upper middle-class politicians, men of middling social origins outside the traditional leadership sub-cultures of the Labour or the Conservative parties. The sweeping gains of the Labour Party at the 1964 and 1966 general elections helped bring about the return of dozens of such men to the House of Commons. Alan Watkins' sketch of one of these new types of politician is fictional; for this reason, it cannot be regarded as reliable in social science terms. It can nonetheless be valid.

LET us today consider the current situation and future prospects of Terence Collins, Labour Member of Parliament for North Bletchley. Collins? Terence Collins? Is he the man with glasses who is always defending the government on television . . . or the one with a twitch who is always attacking the government . . . or the one who has a bee in his bonnet about Rhodesia . . . or the MP who is in and out of trouble with his local party? No, no, madam, you must be thinking of someone else, for Collins does not exist, any more than his constituency exists. Or rather there are numerous Collinses, running well into double figures. Collins is a fictional character. At the moment he is not in the happiest frame of mind. But first, and principally, a look at his background.

Terence Collins was born in 1934 at Ipswich, the son of an executive-class civil servant. He attended the local elementary school and, having passed the scholarship examination (as it was then still called), one of the town's several grammar schools. His home life was happy and uneventful and not particularly political. Collins senior was, however, as he himself put it, 'a great reader'. The books in the small glass-fronted cases at home were mainly Penguins, Pelicans and Everyman classics, together with Chambers's encyclopedia and

Reprinted in full from the *New Statesman*, 12 Apr 1968, p. 470.

the collected works of Charles Dickens. There were also one or two Left Book Club editions picked up second hand from the stall in the market place, but the modest collection was in no way Left-inclined. The family took the *News Chronicle* and the *Observer.*

At school Collins did well. He was good at history and Latin and ended up editing the school magazine. He also discovered, rather to his surprise, that he had a talent for expressing himself when he was on his feet; he could always think up a quick and sometimes amusing answer to any question. One of the masters told him that this was something he would 'have to watch' as there was a danger he would 'neglect the hard work'. Collins did, however, work quite hard, and at the age of 17 won an exhibition to Lincoln College, Oxford. The examiners thought that he 'showed promise' (which, as they would frequently point out to one another, was what they were looking for) even if he did not exhibit the detailed knowledge of some candidates from public schools.

It was at around this time that Collins joined his local Labour Party. The step was in some ways a surprising one for him to take. His family, as has already been remarked, was not particularly political, and nor were his friends. There was intense disappointment with the performance of the defeated Attlee government; politicians, particularly Labour politicians, were generally despised by the intellectuals of the sixth form. Reaction was in the air; one of Collins's friends lent him several slim volumes by Professor Herbert Butterfield and advised him to read Eliot's essays; while one of the masters — it was the one who had warned him about his facility on his feet — told him about a 'chap called Oakeshott' who had, it appeared, a number of interesting and unusual things to say.

Collins dutifully read all these authors but remained unconvinced. He reasoned as follows: neither the world nor the society in which he lived was as he would wish it to be. Britain was in a bad way. It had, however, been in an even worse way. Improvement had been brought about by conscious human action, and this action had generally been initiated by men of the Left. Collins, though agreeing with Professor Butterfield about the imperfections of human nature and the limitations on human action, saw no reason why this process should not continue. He therefore went ahead and joined the Labour Party. This followed several months of trudging the rainy streets in search of an elusive ward secretary who did not seem particularly pleased to see him.

Before he could go up to Oxford he had to do his national service. This period he spent mainly in the equipment section of a flying-station in Essex; he finished as a senior aircraftman. It was not the happiest time of his life. But there was always Oxford to which to look forward. When at last he went up he joined all the clubs, but came to concentrate his attention more and more on the Labour Club. This in turn led him to the Union. Collins became chairman of the Labour Club and librarian of the Union. (He was defeated for the presidency by a right-wing Pakistani.) During this period he would describe himself as a Bevanite. He attended a Fabian summer school and literally sat at the feet of Mr Richard Crossman. Gradually, however, his views changed both because of the virtual end of Bevanism in 1956–7 and because he was much influenced, as far as domestic policy was concerned, by the publication of Mr Anthony Crosland's *Future of Socialism*. He worked hard in his last year and was awarded a second in P.P.E.

The problem now was what to do for a living. Collins had never devoted very much thought to this. A man at the appointments board had been highly discouraging when he had mentioned journalism, saying (incorrectly, as Collins subsequently discovered) it was essential to learn shorthand and typing. But Collins was sure of one thing: he did not want to join Shell or I.C.I. At this point he had a piece of luck. His old tutor wrote and told him of a research fellowship in politics being offered by an obscure university in the Middle West. Collins filled in numerous forms, produced several references to the effect that he was a young man of promise who was not a communist, was interviewed by a chain-smoking visiting professor at the Savoy Hotel and was later astonished to learn the fellowship was his. He spent 18 enjoyable and idle months in America. It was there that he met his wife, to whom he is still happily married, though they have had their ups and downs. They now live in a Wates house at Dulwich and have two children.

On his return from America Collins did not find it easy to get the job to which he thought his qualifications entitled him. There were, so it appeared, hundreds of young men who possessed seconds in P.P.E. and had been to America. Reluctantly, after several months of futile application and interview, he agreed to teach economics and current affairs at Bletchley Technical College. One of his fellow-teachers was the chairman of the local Labour party; and following the 1959 election (which Labour resoundingly lost at Bletchley as elsewhere) Collins became the new candidate for the northern division of the town. At about the same time he heard, also from a fellow-teacher, about the new University of Bucks, which was expanding rapidly and would shortly be advertising for additional staff. Collins anticipated the advertisement and wrote at once. Some months later he was appointed to an assistant lectureship in the department of politics.

Shortly before the 1964 election Collins wrote a Fabian pamphlet entitled *Technology — the Way Ahead.* Sections of it were quoted without acknowledgement by Mr Harold Wilson in his pre-election speeches. Mr Wilson did, however, briefly meet and congratulate Collins, asking him whether he could remember the line-up of the Huddersfield Town team of 1927. Collins could not. Also, he lost in the 1964 election by just over 1,000 votes. He remained as candidate, though he was less enthusiastic about the Wilson government than were some of his colleagues in the local party. In 1966 he won the seat by over 3,700.

Though proud to be in the House, Collins was infuriated by parliamentary procedure. As a gesture of protest he wore a sports coat on all possible occasions and grew a beard, which he later shaved off. His interests in technology, never very profound, had waned, and he decided to specialise more in economics. He voted for the measures of July 1966 but deplored them privately and said that Mr James Callaghan ought to go. Mr Callaghan obstinately stayed; Collins took to making speeches on devaluation. Though the speeches were clear enough, Collins's actual political opinions were becoming more confused. For years and years he had been of the Right (or, as he would prefer to put it, the Centre) of the party. Now he wondered whether revisionism was enough. Or was Wilsonism different from revisionism? He was not at all clear. He was clear that he did not approve of Mr Wilson, but could not think of anyone better. At the moment he is worried about his future. An old college friend, a B.B.C. producer, tells him that he would make a good T.V. interviewer. After the next election he is thinking of taking up the suggestion. It would of course mean giving up active politics, but Collins is quite prepared for this.

# THE IMPLICATIONS OF SAFE SEATS FOR BRITISH DEMOCRACY

*By* JORGEN RASMUSSEN

MANY theories about the influence of voters upon government posit that the desire of Members of Parliament to secure re-election is an important mechanism inducing attention to the views of the electorate in the course of policy-making. One could even hypothesise that the greater the number of seats subject to changing hands at a general election, the more Members of Parliament are responsive to popular influences. Determining whether a seat can be classified as vulnerable to electoral shifts is not a simple matter, as Rasmussen's article shows. Whatever the definition, however, the majority of Members of Parliament are recruited and sustained in office by a set of electoral mechanisms that makes them relatively invincible against normal swings in electoral favour; this fact has important implications for government in Britain.

DISCUSSION of safe seats is a prominent feature of both academic and journalistic analysis of the British electoral process. But no generally accepted definition of this term seems to exist. Hiram Stout in a standard text on British government refers to safe seats, but fails to define the term.[1] Roland Young qualifies the term by writing of 'relatively safe seats' and 'safer seats'. The latter are defined as 'those where one party predominates and customarily wins the election'.[2] His subsequent comments indicate that the first term includes any seat where the winner receives at least 55 per cent of the vote.[3] Even Richard Rose in his recent interpretive textbook on England comments only that safe seats are those 'unlikely to be lost by a sitting member'.[4]

Not only is there little agreement and precision on what constitutes

[1] Hiram Stout, *British Government* (New York: Oxford University Press, 1953) p. 209.

[2] Roland Young, *The British Parliament* (Evanston: Northwestern University Press, 1962) p. 46.

[3] Ibid. p. 47.

[4] Richard Rose, *Politics in England* (Boston: Little, Brown, 1964) p. 149.

Reprinted in full from *Western Political Quarterly*, XIX iii (1966) 516–29.

a safe seat, but little research has been undertaken to determine the extent of this phenomenon. Young, for example, simply comments that '[e]ach party has a number of relatively safe seats'.[5] Rose offers the very general estimate that two-thirds to three-quarters of the seats are safe.[6] The only estimate of any precision comes from Charles Jones. In his study of interparty competition in Britain, Jones found that over 87 per cent of 453 selected constituencies were won constantly by the same party over a four-election period.[7]

A more adequate definition of the concept of 'safeness' in terms of British electoral experience clearly is essential. And such a definition could be applied with profit to the British political system to ascertain the actual pervasiveness of safe seats. Even Jones's estimate was based on only one possible definition of safe seats, which he does not attempt to justify as being the only or the best definition.[8] Determination of the number of safe seats in Britain is desirable because widespread incidence would raise problems for the traditional conception of democratic government. If only one party consistently has any hope of winning a given seat, if the election result is for all practical purposes predetermined before the campaign even begins, can an election have any real meaning to the voters? Are the voters in a safe constituency presented with a genuine alternative; do they possess an effective choice? If not, how can they insure the accountability of their representative? Must the Marxian view that democratic elections are shams be conceded to be correct in its conclusions although not in its reasoning? The problem would be serious even if confined to only a few seats. Should, however, the great majority of a country's legislative constituencies be safe, then a nation would face the fundamental challenge that its entire governmental system was undemocratic. Certainly the line of responsibility to the public would have been short-circuited at its source, thus preventing the flow throughout the system of the popular consultation essential to democratic government.

In view of these considerations, this study develops an operational criterion of 'safeness'. Application of the criterion to the British political situation substantiates the current belief that the great bulk of parliamentary constituencies are safe. This definition of 'safeness' is tested in the General Election of 1964 and found to be highly

[5] Young, op. cit. p. 46.

[6] Rose, op. cit. p. 149.

[7] Charles O. Jones, 'Inter-party Competition in Britain — 1950–59', *Parliamentary Affairs*, XVII (Winter 1963–4) 52.

[8] Ibid. pp. 50–6. Jones does give some consideration also to margin of victory as an indication of the level of inter-party competition, but his discussion on this point is limited to the results of a single election.

accurate in identifying safe seats, despite a swing to Labour large enough to eliminate the Conservatives' 100-seat majority. The operational definition of 'safeness' then is modified to take account of the 1964 election results, so that it can be applied to the current political situation. The study concludes by discussing the implications for democracy in Britain of an electoral system providing few evenly matched constituency contests.

## *Definition of Safe Seats*

The simplest approach to defining safe seats is to employ Jones's method of repeated victory by the same party. Application of this approach is not as simple as it might appear, however, because of redistricting. If the boundaries of a constituency are changed from one election to another, the political situation within that constituency may be altered drastically. Thus what would appear to be a comparison of the same constituency at different times would in fact be a comparison of different constituencies. This consideration is especially relevant in the British context, for unlike the United States (at least until *Baker* vs. *Carr*[9]) Britain has attempted to construct and to maintain equitable constituencies by frequent reviews of the effect of population shifts. Thus the boundaries of a large number of constituencies were revised for the 1950 and 1955 elections. As a result, 220 of Britain's 630 constituencies have existed in their present form for four general elections. Since 43 of these constituencies underwent only 'minor adjustments' in 1955,[10] no more than 177 constituencies must be dated from that election. Of the remaining seats, 382 (including the 43 minor revisions just mentioned) date from 1950, thus having existed for six elections, while only 71 are unrevised for the whole postwar period or for seven elections.

In view of these boundary alterations, Jones chose to study only the 453 constituencies which had not been considerably revised in 1955. Only these seats had remained unchanged or relatively so over a period sufficiently long to provide reliable evidence about interparty competition. In over 87 per cent of these seats he found that the same party had won every election for almost a decade, having been victorious in the general elections of 1950, 1951, 1955, and 1959 as well as in any by-elections which may have occurred. So slight is the extent of interparty competition suggested by this figure that Jones felt forced to qualify his finding. He commented that the

[9] 369 U.S. 186 (1962). The United States Supreme Court ruled in this case that redistricting was a justiciable issue and could be required by the courts.
[10] *The Times House of Commons 1955*, p. 39.

period studied is one 'of steady Conservative dominance. There would be more changes if the 1945 election were included.'[11] In 1964 the Labour party reversed the long postwar trend to the Conservatives and in 1966 began their own period of dominance. This development combined with the opportunity to extend the period studied to sixteen years and six general elections calls for updating Jones's findings.

The most striking aspect of these updated results, which appear in Table 1, is how closely they correspond to what Jones had anticipated. He speculated that studying a period longer than he was able to do might obtain a result similar to American experience of 62 to 78 per cent of the seats in the House of Representatives being won consistently by the same party.[12] Following the 1966 General Election, 77 per cent of the 453 selected British constituencies had been won by the same party at every election held during the preceding sixteen years. Since elections for the House of Representatives occur more frequently on average than do elections for the House of Commons, Jones's American study does not include a period exactly comparable to the British case of six elections over sixteen years. For five elections over eight years Jones found that 78·2 per cent of the seats in the House of Representatives never changed hands, while for seven elections over twelve years, 62·1 per cent of the seats always were won by the same party.

Thus party competition, in terms of alternation in control of national legislative seats, would appear to be only about two-thirds as great in Britain as in the United States (23·0 to 37·9 per cent) although the comparable British period is four years longer, but one election shorter. Despite the fact that Labour held over 100 seats more in 1966 than it had in 1959, over three-fourths of the selected constituencies still are won by the same party at every election. Only 22 constituencies were won in 1964 by a party which had never won them since 1950 and only 24 shifted from the category of constant one-party victory to mixed results in 1966.

The low level of interparty competition confirmed by these updated figures forces questioning whether continued victory by one party in a constituency should be accepted as a trustworthy guide to identification of safe seats. Consider, for example, York, a constituency won by the Conservatives for five consecutive elections. Although in 1959 the Conservatives led Labour in York by 6·6 percentage points, their margin of victory in 1964 was only 1·9 and in their other three victories ranged from 0·1 to 1·8. Was York safe for the Conservatives? Hardly — in 1966 it fell to Labour.

[11] Jones, op. cit. p. 52.

[12] Loc. cit.

Investigating repeated victory by a party in a given constituency provides useful information on the degree of fluctuation in constituency control; as a criterion for distinguishing safe seats, however, it is questionable. Its utility as an index also is limited by the need to know a seat's past electoral history before it can be classified and by the problem of determining how much electoral experience is necessary to provide reliable information for classification. Are only two elections insufficient experience? Are four elections enough?

TABLE 1

*Number of constituencies won by the same party, 1950–66**
*(from 453 selected constituencies)*

| *Party* | *London* | *Eng. B.†* | *Eng. C.‡* | *Welsh B.†* | *Welsh C.‡* | *Scot. B.†* | *Scot. C.‡* | *N. Ire.* | *Totals* |
|---|---|---|---|---|---|---|---|---|---|
| Conservative | 6 | 43 | 103 | 0 | 2 | 2 | 13 | 9 | 178 |
| Labour | 19 | 61 | 39 | 8 | 16 | 13 | 13 | 0 | 169 |
| Liberal | 0 | 0 | 0 | 0 | 1 | 0 | 1 | 0 | 2 |
| TOTALS | 25 | 104 | 142 | 8 | 19 | 15 | 27 | 9 | 349 |

* Compiled from *The Times House of Commons* for the 1950, 1951, 1955, 1959, and 1964 elections and from the special election supplement to *The Guardian* for 2 April 1966.

† Boroughs or Burghs. ‡ Counties.

Rather what is needed is a measure which can be applied to the most recent electoral results in a constituency to determine whether the party presently holding the seat is highly likely to retain it at the next general election. Such determination turns not as much upon a party's ability to win a seat consistently as upon its margin of victory and the degree to which this margin can be expected to fluctuate.

The best way to ascertain the expected degree of fluctuation in the margin of victory is to investigate postwar British electoral experience.[13] Comparing the 1945 and 1950 elections, however, is not practical, since only 75 seats had the same boundaries for both elections. But with three exceptions,[14] all 613 seats can be compared from 1950

[13] The remainder of this study deals only with English, Welsh, and Scottish constituencies. The politics of Northern Ireland is *sui generis* with frequent huge majorities at times surpassing 90 per cent of the vote, unopposed candidates, election of imprisoned Irish nationalists, and widespread and fairly constant Ulster Unionist domination of elections. The 12 Irish constituencies are excluded, therefore, as being so atypical that they would tend to obscure the normal pattern of British politics.

[14] One exception is Hexham. Since it was held by the Speaker, only an Independent Liberal contested it in 1950. The Speaker's retirement before the

to 1951. The redistricting problem arises once again for the 1955 election, but not so severely as in 1950: 398 seats were unaltered from election, but not so severely as in 1950: 398 seats were unaltered from unchanged for the 1959 election and 612 are comparable.[16] Thus fluctuation in the margin of victory can be studied in 1,619 cases — 610 from 1950 to 1951, 397 from 1951 to 1955, and 612 from 1955 to 1959.

In 756 of these cases the winning party's margin of victory decreased from one election to the next. The magnitude of loss ranged from 0·1 to 26·9. Decreases of the latter magnitude were quite rare of course, and can provide no guide for generalisation about electoral experience. A more informative figure is the fifth percentile of all fluctuations in the margin of victory when ranked from greatest decrease to greatest increase. Such a measure avoids focusing on one or two extreme cases, but still allows discovery of the prevailing situation in the vast majority of cases. Specifically, the fifth percentile is a measure distinguishing the most extreme 5 per cent of a distribution. In effect it indicates what results are more rare than 95 times in 100. I propose that a seat should not be considered safe, if the winning party's margin is less than the fifth percentile of fluctuation in the margin of victory which past experience suggests can be expected in the next general election. Conversely, if a party holds a seat by such a large majority that the chances based on past experience are 95 out of 100 that it will not lose so much support in the next general election as to lose the seat, then that constituency should be termed safe.

---

1951 election made Hexham a political contest that year and thus not comparable to the result of the preceding election. The other exceptions are Bolton East and West where the electoral pact between the Conservatives and the Liberals formed prior to the 1951 election introduced an extraneous influence on the margin of victory.

[15] In this instance, unlike the procedure followed earlier in this study in investigating repeated victory in a constituency, the 43 minor revisions are excluded from the 1955 total. While a minor adjustment in boundaries would be unlikely to determine the victorious party, it quite possibly could affect each party's share of the vote by a few percentage points. Thus minor revisions could affect significantly any calculation of fluctuation in the margin of victory. The Speaker's seat need not be deducted from the 1951 to 1955 total number of cases, since his seat was among those undergoing a major revision and therefore already is excluded from consideration. But Sunderland South must be excluded since it switched from the control of one party to another in a by-election between 1951 and 1955.

[16] Again the Speaker's seat is an exception. Cirencester and Tewkesbury was fought by the Speaker in 1955, but by a regular Conservative in 1959. Thus this seat is excluded from the comparison of those two elections. In addition five other seats are excluded since they changed hands at by-elections between 1955 and 1959.

The fifth percentile for the total number of cases in this study is − 7·7. That is to say that in 95 per cent of the cases considered the victorious party either increased its lead over its nearest opponent or lost no more than 7·7 percentage points in its margin of victory. Or alternatively, in only 5 per cent of the cases did a winner experience a loss of more than 7·7 percentage points in his lead.

More informative than this gross figure, however, are the results obtained when the total number of cases is analysed by period, party, and type of seat, as is done in Table 2. To avoid consideration of groups too small for statistical treatment, London and English boroughs have been grouped together, as have all Welsh and Scottish constituencies.

TABLE 2

*Fifth percentile of fluctuation in margin of victory*

| Period | *English Urban* | | *English County* | | *Welsh & Scottish* | |
|---|---|---|---|---|---|---|
| | *Con.* | *Lab.* | *Con.* | *Lab.* | *Con.* | *Lab.* |
| 1950–1951 | −0·7 | −8·0 | −0·6 | −6·2 | −0·6 | −6·2 |
| 1951–1955 | * | −10·7 | −4·3 | −6·1 | −7·1 | −11·6 |
| 1955–1959 | −5·3 | −10·4 | −4·3 | −6·5 | −10·4 | −7·0 |

* Positive figure.

In English urban areas Labour's fifth percentile of fluctuation in the margin of victory levelled off in the two final periods after experiencing a marked increase from the 1950–1 period to the 1951–5 period. Labour's inability to reduce this figure justified application of the label 'safe Labour seat' only to those English urban seats in which it led its nearest challenger by 10·4 percentage points. Only in such cases, on the basis of recent electoral experience, were the chances 95 out of 100 that Labour would not lose so much of its lead as to lose the seat. The Conservatives, however, not only failed to improve in English constituencies, but experienced a great worsening of their position. For the 1951–9 period their fifth percentile was a positive figure. This indicates that over 95 per cent of the English urban seats won by the Conservatives in 1951 remained Conservative in 1955 with an increased margin of victory. In view of the Conservatives' sharp decline from this position in the 1955–9 period plus the impact of increased Liberal electoral intervention,[17] no Conserva-

[17] Most evidence indicates that a Liberal tends to draw more votes away from Conservative candidates than from Labour candidates. The difference is not large, but, on the basis of Butler and Rose's calculations for the 1959

tive English urban seat could be termed safe unless it was held by a margin of at least 6·5 percentage points.

In the English county seats it was the Conservatives who tended to level off after an earlier decline, while Labour's position remained fairly stable. The Conservative fifth percentile in the 1955–9 period was exactly the same as in the 1951–5 period. Therefore, again taking into consideration anticipated Liberal intervention, Conservative seats in the English counties required a margin of 5·3 percentage points to be considered safe. For Labour the margin necessary for 'safety' was 6·5. The worsening in Labour's position in 1955–9 compared to 1951–5 was too slight to suggest any trend towards further decline. In these constituencies a margin of 6·5 percentage points over the runner-up party should have been sufficient to ensure retention of a seat.

Labour apparently required a somewhat larger margin for safety in Welsh and Scottish constituencies. The incongruous figure for the 1951–5 period may be due to the reduced number of cases.[18] To compensate in part, however, for the possibility that it was the result of other factors which might be influential once again, a lead of at least 8 percentage points seemed necessary to distinguish a safe seat. The limited number of cases may be a distorting factor in the Conservative Welsh and Scottish seats in each period.[19] But the Conservatives clearly suffered a significant decline compared to the 1950–1 period. Taking into account strengthened Liberal efforts in the Highlands, Conservative seats would have needed to have been held by a margin of 11·5 or more percentage points to be labelled safe.

Thus the operational definition of a safe seat varies with the type of seat considered and the party holding the seat. No single definition is satisfactory because, as the previous discussion has shown, fluctuation in the margin by which a seat is held is not uniform throughout Britain. And since this margin fluctuates variously, a lead sufficient to ensure 'safeness' in one situation may not be adequate in different circumstances. To be considered safe, seats held by the Conservatives after the 1959 election required a margin of 6·5 percentage points for English urban constituencies, of 5·3 for English county seats, and of 11·5 for Welsh and Scottish seats. Labour seats could

general election, *The British General Election of 1959* (New York: Macmillan, 1960, pp. 233–4), would mean a reduction of almost 1 percentage point in Conservative margins of victory.

[18] Because of the boundary changes in 1955, the middle period includes only about three-fourths as many cases as either the 1950–1 or the 1955–9 periods.

[19] The greatest number of cases in any period, 41, is less than the number of cases in the middle Labour period.

be termed safe if they were held by a margin of 10·4 for English urban seats, of 6·5 for English counties, and of 8·0 for Wales and Scotland.

### *Application and Testing of the Operational Definition*

Application of the measures of safeness thus devised reveal that 64 per cent, 164 of 258, of the seats which Labour won in 1959 were safe seats, while 85 per cent, 301 of 353, of the Conservatives' were safe. Table 3 presents the detailed figures by type of seat. If the definitions offered in this study are accepted, 76 per cent of the seats in the House of Commons were safe.[20] A finding of this magnitude is not unexpected and thus serves to substantiate with rigorously obtained data the general impression which most observers of British politics already have formed regarding the limited degree of inter-party competition in Britain.

TABLE 3

*Safe seats* held following the 1959 General Election*

| *Party* | *English Urban* | | *English County* | | *Welsh & Scottish* | | *Total* | |
|---|---|---|---|---|---|---|---|---|
| | *safe* | *other* | *safe* | *other* | *safe* | *other* | *safe* | *other* |
| Conservative | 117 | 30 | 154 | 14 | 30 | 8 | 301 | 52 |
| Labour | 77 | 63 | 39 | 14 | 48 | 17 | 164 | 94 |
| TOTAL | 194 | 93 | 193 | 28 | 78 | 25 | 465 | 146 |

* As defined by the method discussed in the text.

But mere agreement with generally accepted belief is not sufficient to prove the value or the validity of this approach to 'safeness'. The operational definitions must be tested and be shown to be accurate before their acceptance is warranted. The 1964 General Election provides as severe a testing ground as could be devised.[21] The election

[20] Inclusion of the seats held by the Liberals would not reduce the proportion, while adding the Northern Ireland constituencies would raise the figure only very slightly.

[21] It should not be thought that I have devised the approach developed in this study only after I knew the results of the 1964 election and thus could suggest a method which I knew before-hand would prove successful. The original version of this study was written in the spring of 1963. It was then turned down for publication because the results of the then approaching general election might refute the predictive implications of the study to the embarrassment of both the publisher and the author. That version, for example, contained the following statement: 'How Labour, even in its moments

figures used in formulating the operational definitions come from a period of increasing Conservative dominance which saw the party barely lose one election and then win three. In 1964, however, Labour regained all of the ground lost during this period to win two seats more than a bare majority of the Commons' total membership. The extent to which the 1964 election represents a substantial shift in voting patterns can be seen from noting the proportion of seats which changed hands. Although during the 1950s the number of seats won from opponents ranged from only 3 to 6 per cent of the Commons' total membership, in 1964 11 per cent of the seats shifted from one party to another.[22] The General Election of 1964 clearly was atypical in including a large number of changes in constituency control. A greater number of shifts could be expected only in a watershed election like that of 1945 and in such a case most past voting patterns obviously are irrelevant. Successful testing of the operational definitions of 'safeness' in the 1964 General Election requires that a method devised when one party was in power prove accurate in an election when the opposition party returns to power and that an approach formulated during a period of slight or moderate turnover in control of seats be reliable in an election involving a large turnover.

That the method developed in this study of identifying safe seats proved highly accurate in 1964 for Labour-held constituencies is not surprising. Labour lost only 5 seats. None of these, however, could be termed safe according to this study's operational definitions. All 164 of the Labour seats identified as safe were retained by Labour.

The real test, given the direction of the 1964 results, is accurate distinction of safe Conservative seats. The criterion for safeness proved least successful in English urban seats. Sixteen[23] of the 117 presumably safe Conservative seats fell to Labour for an error of 14 per cent. In two[24] of these instances, however, the seat had been

---

of greatest fancy, can expect to win a majority greater than the hair-breadth one it obtained in 1950 is difficult to understand.' The study has been revised and updated, but the basic approach is unaltered since the 1964 results amply demonstrate the validity of this method.

[22] In 1951, 28 seats changed hands; in 1955, 15 of the seats unaltered or only slightly revised shifted in party control; and in 1959, 35 seats switched. Compiled from *The Times Guide to the House of Commons*, 1951, p. 215; 1955, p. 242; 1959, p. 226. For 1964, 70 seats changed hands. (*The Guardian*, 17 Oct 1964, p. 1.)

[23] These were Bury and Radcliffe, Darlington, Doncaster, Ealing North, Liverpool Kirkdale, Liverpool Toxteth, Liverpool Walton, Liverpool West Derby, Luton, Middlesbrough West, Preston South, Putney, Stockport North, Stockport South, Streatham, and West Woolwich.

[24] These were Luton and Middlesbrough West.

lost in a by-election between 1959 and 1964 and thus Labour was retaining an earlier success. By-election results often differ markedly from those produced by general election voting patterns. Therefore a margin large enough to ensure a seat's 'safeness' at a general election may not be sufficient in a by-election. But once the opposition party has gained a seat at a by-election, it may be able to entrench itself sufficiently to retain the seat at a general election. Fighting in the general election as incumbent certainly is a far stronger position than fighting as challenger. Thus had the two seats in question not been contested at by-elections, the Conservatives might have retained their control of the constituencies in 1964. Even this occurrence would have reduced the magnitude of error only slightly. While the error, then, for this group of seats is greater than expected, yet an 86 per cent correct identification of safe seats justly can be termed a qualified success.

Furthermore, for the other two categories of seats the criterion of safeness proved much more accurate. Only 3[25] of the Conservatives' 30 supposedly safe Welsh and Scottish seats were lost, an error of 10 per cent, and only 5[26] of their 154 apparently safe English county seats fell to opposition parties, an error of only 3 per cent. Two of the three Welsh and Scottish errors and two of the English county errors were losses to Liberals.[27] The Liberals are a somewhat anomalous element in British politics, so it is not too surprising that they should fail to conform to a general pattern in four instances. Also one of the English county seats (Orpington) won by the Liberals involves the distorting factor of an earlier by-election victory so that the Liberals were in fact retaining a seat previously gained. The comments in the preceding paragraph about by-elections apply here as well.

In total, then, only 24 of the 301 seats classified as safe Conservative seats by the operational definitions developed in this study failed to remain in Conservative hands in 1964, despite the complete elimination of the party's 100-seat majority. The total error of 8 per cent is only slightly greater than the expected 5 per cent despite the severe test afforded by the 1964 election. If the Labour seats are included as well, then the error falls to the anticipated 5 per cent — 24 incorrect classifications out of 465. Thus this study's approach to identification of safe seats proves to be highly accurate.

[25] These were Glasgow Pollock, Ross and Cromarty, and Inverness.

[26] These were Cornwall Bodmin, Dover, Epping, Hitchin, and Orpington.

[27] The Scottish cases were Ross and Cromarty and Inverness and the English county instances Cornwall Bodmin and Orpington.

### *Updating of the Operational Definitions*

Obviously the margins for 'safeness' calculated on the basis of the general election results from 1950 to 1959 are not immutable. Rather these figures must be revised following each general election to take account of the most recent electoral developments. Only such an updating will provide a set of figures permitting identification of safe seats in the current Parliament.

The major obstacle to such an updating after the 1964 election was the difficulty of determining the trend of political opinion in Britain. The Gallup polls at the close of 1964 showed that Labour had a lead substantial enough to gain another large block of new victories whenever another election was called.[28] Yet past British electoral experience suggested that this was unlikely; large shifts in the major parties' parliamentary strength are exceptional, to say nothing of such shifts occurring at two consecutive elections.

Also, the ability of the Labour Government to cope effectively with the severe economic problems which it faced was in doubt. Furthermore, Labour had threatened to nationalise steel — a step which might cost it electoral support. Finally, the Conservatives perhaps might refurbish their image in Opposition as successfully as they had after their 1945 electoral debacle. Such considerations suggest that public opinion might swing back to the Conservatives before the next election was called.

Therefore at the time (spring 1965) I concluded that estimating the margin requisite for 'safety' primarily on the basis of the 1964 election was inadvisable. Instead, the best course seemed to be to calculate the 'safety' margin on the basis of the electoral results for each of the four postwar periods (1950–1, 1951–5, 1955–9, and 1959–64) combined. Labour gains and losses in margin of victory in English urban constituencies for each of these four periods could be combined into a single distribution to determine a fifth percentile for the entire period. The same process could be followed for Labour results in the two other types of seats and for the Conservative results. This approach has virtue as well as necessity. Unlike the 1950–9 period, the 1950–64 period includes electoral success for both Labour and Conservatives. The latter period, unlike the former, includes both elections with little shift in party strengths and an election with substantial shift. Since the 1950–64 period encompasses a wide

[28] A mere shift of 500 votes from Conservative to Labour would result in Labour victories in 19 constituencies. (*The Times House of Commons 1964*, p. 249.) With a substantial movement of opinion to Labour the number would be increased greatly.

variety of electoral experience, it seems more likely to provide a reliable guide to the future than would a period of less diversified experience. It must be recognised that past electoral experience, however extensive and diversified, can never be considered a completely reliable guide to the future. Any election may prove to be a watershed election or a realigning election, to use the terminology of *The American Voter*. But as the authors of that study noted, elections in which 'popular feeling associated with politics is sufficiently intense that the basic partisan commitments of a portion of the electorate change . . . are infrequent'.[29] For the fact of political life is 'the persistence of partisanship . . . [the] evidence that identification with political parties, once established, is an attachment which is not easily changed'.[30] Although reliance on past electoral experience may result in erroneous conclusions in any single election, in the long run in most cases it should be a valid approach.

Calculation of the fifth percentile of fluctuation in the margin of victory for both major parties in each of the three types of constituencies for the combined four periods from 1950 to 1964 yielded the following figures: Labour English urban 8·8; Labour English county 6·3; Labour Welsh and Scottish 7·1; Conservative English urban 13·3; Conservative English county 10·4; and Conservative Welsh and Scottish 17·4. No additional loading was added to the Conservative figures to compensate for 'intervention' of Liberal candidates, because the results of the 1964 election demonstrated that estimating this effect has become so difficult as to be virtually impossible with existing data.[31]

Application of the preceding measures of 'safeness' produced the results presented in Table 4. Reversing the situation which obtained

[29] Angus Campbell, *et al.*, *The American Voter* (New York: Wiley, 1960) p. 534.

[30] Ibid. pp. 148–9.

[31] Richard Rose states that the figure for the over-all national swing to Labour in 1964 'is slightly misleading . . . because the increased number of Liberal candidatures cut into Labour votes in seats that it did not have a chance of winning. This reduced Labour's total vote.' But he also calculates that Liberal 'intervention' produced a 0·6 swing to Labour nationally. (*The Times House of Commons 1964*, pp. 240, 241.) *The Guardian*, using figures supplied by the KDF9 computer at the English Electric Leo Marconi computer centre, concluded however, that Liberals drew slightly more votes from Labour than from Conservative candidates where a Liberal 'intervened' in 1964 only and twice as many votes from Labour where both the 1959 and 1964 elections were three-cornered fights. (*The Guardian*, 19 Oct 1964, p. 2.) Obviously any conclusion about the origin or past partisan preference of Liberal voters is impossible on the basis of the gross election results alone. Only a national sample of Liberal voters can provide reliable information on this topic.

after the 1959 election, Labour had the advantage in safe seats. Not only did Labour hold almost one-third as many more safe seats as did the Conservatives, but also 77 per cent of its seats were safe whereas only 64 per cent of the Conservatives' were. Significantly, despite this shift in party control of safe seats, the proportion of safe seats in the Commons' total membership declined only slightly. After the 1959 election 76 per cent of the seats were classified as safe; after the 1964 election 71 per cent were.[32]

The manuscript reporting these findings was accepted for publication in May 1965: since then Britain has held another general election. This event provided an additional opportunity to validate the method I have proposed for identifying safe seats. The 1966 General Election was almost as severe a test of this method as was the 1964 election, for 54 seats changed from one party to another. None the less, the criterion which I proposed to identify safe seats proved even more accurate in 1966 than it had in 1964.

TABLE 4

*Safe seats* held following the 1964 General Election*

| Party | *English Urban* | | *English County* | | *Welsh & Scottish* | | *Total* | |
|---|---|---|---|---|---|---|---|---|
| | *safe* | *other* | *safe* | *other* | *safe* | *other* | *safe* | *other* |
| Conservative | 58 | 47 | 115 | 41 | 12 | 18 | 185 | 106 |
| Labour | 127 | 56 | 51 | 12 | 66 | 5 | 244 | 73 |
| TOTAL | 185 | 103 | 166 | 53 | 78 | 23 | 429 | 179 |

* As defined by the method discussed in the text.

This result is not surprising for the Labour party, since it lost only one seat and that to the Liberals. Since that seat had been held by less than one percentage point, all 244 of the Labour seats which I had classified as safe following the 1964 election were retained by Labour in 1966. (Labour did lose Leyton, which I had classified as a safe seat, at a 1965 by-election. The issues of race relations and clumsy intervention on candidate adoption by Labour national headquarters, however, made this result very atypical. At any rate, Labour regained Leyton in the 1966 General Election.)

As in 1964 the real test was whether my method could accurately identify safe Conservative seats. Although the Conservatives lost 51 seats in 1966, they were defeated in none of the 58 English urban seats or 12 Welsh and Scottish seats which I had classified as safe.

[32] Inclusion of the seats held by Liberals and the Northern Ireland constituencies would alter the proportion only slightly.

They lost only 1 of the 115 English county seats which I had labelled safe and that defeat was by a Liberal. Thus despite the Conservatives' dropping from only about a dozen seats behind Labour to 110 seats behind, my measures for safe seats were only 0·5 per cent in error in correctly identifying the seats which the Conservatives would not lose. If the Labour results are included as well, the error drops to 0·2 per cent, 1 error out of 429 cases.

Recalculating the measures for safe seats to determine how many strongholds each party can claim at the moment is not practical yet. As I noted earlier in this study, redistricting occurs much more frequently in Britain than in the United States. Under the House of Commons (Redistribution of Seats) Act of 1949 as amended in 1958 boundary commissions must submit reports no less than ten or more than fifteen years apart. Their next recommendations must come before November 1969. The Parliament elected this year can continue by statute until March 1971 and given Labour's majority, is not likely to be dissolved much more than a year in advance of that date at the earliest. Quite probably, then, many British constituencies will be redistricted before the next general election. The boundary commissions already are at work and have published several reports proposing changes in constituencies to correct the population disparities which have become marked in many instances because of the increased mobility of the British people.

Until Parliament approves the commissions' reports and Orders in Council are issued giving effect to the recommendation, no one can be certain which constituencies will retain their present boundaries or will be altered only slightly. Since substantial redistricting obviously may affect the margin by which a party holds a constituency, no classification of safe seats can be carried out until redistricting is completed. Therefore calculation of the measures for safe seats is purposeless now.

Since over 70 per cent of the seats in the House of Commons were classified as safe after both the 1959 and 1964 elections, however, I would not expect the proportion to alter greatly when redistricting is completed. Therefore, the problem raised at the beginning of this study remains: Do popular elections have any value under such conditions; are they simply shams or façades, the trappings but not the substance of democracy?

## *Implications of Safe Seats for British Democracy*

The evidence presented in this study indicates that in only a little more than a quarter of the parliamentary constituencies in Britain do elections make any difference. In the great majority of constituencies the victor in an election is preordained even before candidates are adopted. The electorate does not in fact choose a representative in these seats; the effective choice, the true political power lies with the local party organisation. This actually means that it is wielded by the small leadership group which controls candidate selection. To observe that nomination is tantamount to election hardly is new. This situation long has been recognised as a problem in the American South. In Britain, however, the problem is more serious. Primary elections in the United States offer the electorate an opportunity to play an influential role in the political process even in safe one-party areas. A genuine choice among alternative policies and candidates may still exist; the locus of this choice simply has shifted from the general election to the primary. Competition in primaries can be quite sharp with the result far from foregone.[33] In the United States an appreciable percentage of the electorate can participate effectually in the choosing of their representative, whereas in Britain only a handful of people have this power in the great majority of seats.

Another structural feature of the American system makes the incidence of safe seats less serious here than in Britain — the multiplicity of American elective offices. Even if party control over two-thirds or more of the seats in the United States House of Representatives rarely alters, as Jones's previously noted data suggest, competition for the Presidency may be quite lively during the same period and even in the same states where the majority of the legislative districts are safe. In addition, the election of governors involves a statewide contest which may be quite competitive despite the safeness of many congressional seats in that state.[34] In the United States the absence in any given area of genuine interparty competition for congressional office need not mean the virtual elimination of the voters from the electoral process. In Britain alternative means of participating in electoral control over some important level of government are not available. British voters denied a meaningful choice

[33] A study over a four-election period of primary elections for United States Representative found that in about a quarter of the primaries in safe districts the contest was close, that is, the winner got no more than twice as many votes as the runner-up. Furthermore, the proportion of close primary contests in safe districts tends to be relatively high in those states subject to long-term one-party domination. And when the contest involves choosing a new candidate to replace an incumbent not seeking re-election, 65 per cent of the primaries in safe districts are close contests. (Julius Turner, 'Primary Elections as the Alternative to Party Competition in "Safe" Districts', *Journal of Politics*, xv (May 1953) 197–210.)

[34] I am indebted to Leon Epstein for pointing out to me the significance in this context of presidential and gubernatorial elections.

in elections for the national legislature cannot participate at all in the essential democratic process of electoral control over the government.[35]

Attenuation of representative accountability to the degree ascertained in Britain obviously runs counter to the model of democratic government. Parties oppose each other in offering alternative policies and candidates, but in most cases their competition is irrelevant to the voter since one-party domination denies him a genuine choice. Even in these circumstances interparty competition remains a crucial aspect of democratic government. For were most of a country's legislative districts safe *and* were virtually all of them held by the same party, then democracy would be threatened. When the number of one-party legislative districts is divided fairly evenly among the leading parties, however, significant interparty competition is possible on a national or total seat basis even though viable competition may be absent in many districts. In Britain this is the situation since, as Table 4 shows, Labour holds only 57 per cent of the safe seats. Thus the high incidence of safe legislative districts in Britain and the United States does not force abandoning interparty competition as a democratic postulate, but merely entails modification. Genuine interparty competition on a widespread, subnational basis is not essential to democracy, while on a national basis it is crucial.

Furthermore, one-party electoral domination of an area eliminates only one democratic essential; it does not automatically destroy democracy entirely. If dissent can be expressed freely and alternative choices, however futile, legally are available to the electorate, the system can be characterised as democratic. Democracy does not require alternation of governing groups as much as it does the possibility of alternation. As long as a legal, organised opposition exists in a given area the possibility of shifts in control over governmental power exists in that area also. Especially is this the case in the long run. Where more than one party exists, safe seats may decline to marginality, as certainly happened to some of the seats which Labour won in 1945.[36] Electoral patterns are not so stable as to prevent constituencies from shifting into and out of the category of safe seats. The proportion of Labour-held seats which can be considered safe rose by 13 percentage points from 1959 to 1964, while the Conservatives' proportion declined by 21 percentage points. Be-

[35] Local council elections, of course, are held in Britain just as are city and county elections in the United States. But these hardly compare in importance to American election of governors and a President.

[36] Labour won North Kensington, for example, by 20·7 percentage points in 1945 but by only 2·5 in 1959.

cause of such changes only 57 per cent of Britain's parliamentary constituencies were classified as safe in both 1959 and 1964.[37] Significantly, party control over this group of seats is divided almost equally with Conservatives holding 53 per cent to Labour's 47 per cent. Such changes in classification of constituencies mean that genuine electoral alternatives are presented to a larger share of the British electorate than initially appeared to be true. The proportion of parliamentary constituencies providing no meaningful interparty competition constantly may remain at 70 to 75 per cent, but the cases included in this group will vary. The voter faced with meaningless alternatives at one election may find that his choice is a genuine one at the following election. The number of constituencies which remain safe for the same party for 20 or 30 years may be quite small.

Richard Crossman has observed that the 'election is the end of a long process'.[38] But is it not so much the end as a stage in an unending process of political competition and changing voting patterns, hence of shifting power? As long as these are characteristic of British politics, democracy will have a greater vitality in Great Britain than might be apparent at any single moment from the superficial application of the democratic model to its governmental system.

[37] Despite the movement of voting support away from the Conservatives in 1964, two seats classified as safe Labour seats in 1959 could no longer be so termed in 1964 and one seat not safe for the Conservatives in 1959 became safe in the 1964 election. Although the number is small, such movement indicates that the pattern of safe seats need not completely conform to the national trend of electoral opinion.

[38] Quoted in Butler and Rose, op. cit. p. 7.

# GOVERNMENT BY APPOINTMENT

*By* Political and Economic Planning

While the eighteenth-century patronage powers of British government have been curbed, new forms have flourished since the war in areas concerned with the problems of the mixed-economy welfare state. A variety of voluntary or paid appointments have been made to committees, councils and boards created in order to manage or advise the government in economic policy and the administration of the welfare services. There is no sign that the number will abate. The method of appointing these individuals raises substantial questions about the character of representative and responsible government in Britain; these issues are clearly delineated in the following PEP report. The number, dispersion and scope of the tasks which appointees are asked to undertake also raises questions about the institutional structure and boundaries of what is conventionally called British government. The following description of public appointees emphasises dramatically that British government involves much more than the choice of a single man as Prime Minister or 630 men as MPs.

## *Introduction*

Whether or not government by the people can exist, there is no escaping government by some people. Laws do not administer themselves, and government is not carried on merely through legislation. In modern times two main processes have been developed for choosing our rulers. Governing politicians, local and national, are elected by popular suffrage and civil servants are recruited impartially and promoted on merit. But this does not complete the picture. There has always been a number of people, not in the regular civil service, but carrying out governmental functions, who are appointed to their posts by a superior authority and not elected or promoted. This practice is not decreasing, and it is the purpose of this broadsheet to

Reprinted in full from *Planning*, xxvi cdxliii (1960) 207–25. For further discussion of these issues, see e.g. Political and Economic Planning, *Advisory Committees in British Government* (London: Allen & Unwin, 1960), and P. G. Richards, *Patronage in British Government* (London: Allen & Unwin, 1963).

examine its extent, and to describe what is known about the way appointments are made.

This growth of appointment amounts almost to a new patronage, for patronage has been defined as 'the recruitment of public servants by private recommendation',[1] and this is basically what is involved. There are vital differences, however, between current practices and some other forms of patronage. Many of the new posts are part-time and unpaid. They derive from the tradition of voluntary service in British public life, though the burdens of office may be accompanied by attractions in the form of prestige or influence. It is the quantitative aspect of the matter which gives rise to many of the problems nowadays. A Minister can devote care and attention to making a number of important appointments. But when there are considerable administrative structures to be built up (local and regional as well as central), then either some system of nomination and recommendation must develop, or the duty of selection and appointment must be delegated, higher authorities in a hierarchy appointing lower ones and so on.

It is common knowledge that the principle of administration by semi-independent boards, in abeyance between 1855 and 1906, has had a great revival since then.[2] From this situation — autonomy without complete independence — springs the need for appointed men in administrative jobs. Within an organisation positions are achieved by promotion. The top boards or councils of completely independent bodies can be elected or co-opted. But, where one authority — a Minister — retains some responsibility for an autonomous body, then he needs to control the general direction of the body in question and usually this is achieved by appointing those who run it. Non-administrative bodies like advisory committees and tribunals have added to the need for appointment for they require deliberately chosen — hand-picked — individuals.

In the last twenty years there have been many studies of the electoral process, in Britain as well as in other countries. Field investigations of elections in particular places have been carried out, and there have been thorough analyses of successive general elections under the auspices of Nuffield College. More recently the methods whereby candidates are chosen in the constituencies have been examined. The principles of civil service recruitment and organisation have also long been discussed; and there has been a notable series

[1] S. E. Finer, 'Patronage and the Public Service', *Public Administration* (Winter 1952) p. 329.

[2] See F. M. G. Willson, 'Ministries and Boards: some aspects of administrative development since 1832', *Public Administration* (Spring 1955) p. 43.

of reports from Northcote-Trevelyan to Priestley. The results of the system have been analysed in R. K. Kelsall's *Higher Civil Servants in Britain.*[3] In consequence a good deal is known about the two main governing groups, politicians and civil servants. Much less is known about this third group, the voluntary public servants and members of autonomous boards. They are certainly of less importance than the main groups, but they are not insignificant and in this century they have been relied on more and more. 'Patronage' is often regarded with suspicion, but, perhaps because the process of recruitment is personal and confidential, there has been little investigation of how these matters are conducted, and not a great deal of consideration of what principles might be involved.

The question is not one of academic interest only — it is not merely that we know very little about these matters. There is a practical issue too. Has the system reached the limits of its usefulness, or perhaps gone beyond them? Are, in fact, all the people suitable for these positions already recruited, or is there, on the contrary, a large quantity of neglected talent, ignored under present methods of recruitment?

The following pages describe the present situation in some detail, and the general problems are taken up again at the end of the broadsheet.

### *Extent of the Practice*

No problem can be understood if its extent is not appreciated. As stated, the main area where appointments are found is that of 'semi-independent bodies', though this expression should be widely interpreted. There is a particular problem where an extensive local or regional organisation is involved.

There are first of all the numerous advisory bodies — committees and councils attached to Government departments for purposes of consultation or expert advice. These often contain civil servants as well as outside members, and they may be either temporary or permanent. In 1949 it was stated that there were 700 of these bodies and in 1959 the figure of 850 was given. These figures only include national or central committees, but some temporary committees at least are included, as well as committees advisory to the Research Councils, the National Savings Committee and similar bodies. The number of national, standing advisory committees attached to the main departments of the central government was, in fact, in 1958

[3] R. K. Kelsall, *Higher Civil Servants in Britain* (London: Routledge, 1955).

about 500.[4] All these are appointed by the Minister concerned. Apart from civil servants the members include industrialists, trade unionists, university and industrial scientists, local government officials and councillors, and experts from many other walks of life. The term of service varies. Occasionally appointment is for an indefinite period. Three years is a common period, but usually reappointment is possible — though with some scientific committees rotation of membership is strictly enforced. Payment is rare, being confined to committees which involve a great deal of work.

The number of temporary advisory committees and Committees of Enquiry no doubt varies from time to time. However, the Prime Minister stated this year that there have been seventy Royal Commissions and Committees of Enquiry since 1955.[5] Royal Commissions are appointed by the Crown on the advice of the Prime Minister. There are usually only two or three of these at a time.[6] Other Committees of Enquiry are appointed by the Minister concerned. Members, usually unpaid, serve for the duration of the enquiry.

Secondly, there are the tribunals considered by the Franks Committee and now under the surveillance of the Council on Tribunals. There are over 2,000 of these in Great Britain. Among the most numerous are the 200 or so National Insurance Local Tribunals appointed by the Minister of Pensions and National Insurance. The National Assistance Board has about 150 Appeal Tribunals, whose members are also appointed by the Minister of Pensions and National Insurance. The members of both these sets of tribunals serve for three-year terms, with the possibility of renewal. The chairmen receive fees, but the members do not. There are many tribunals connected with the Ministry of Labour (though some of these will no longer be necessary with the ending of National Service). They include nearly 300 Disablement Advisory Committees where the Minister is responsible for the appointment of chairmen. There are still sixty-one Rent Tribunals in England and Wales and twenty-nine in Scotland, though their jurisdiction was curtailed by the Rent Act, 1957.

The administration of the National Health Service involved many part-time appointments. There are fifteen Regional Hospital Boards, where the chairmen and members are appointed by the Minister of Health (with 370 members in all in England and Wales) and 382 Hospital Management Committees (with about 20 members each), appointed by the Regional Hospital Boards. Members of the

[4] See PEP report, *Advisory Committees in British Government* (July 1960) p. 23.

[5] *Hansard* (15 Mar 1960) col. 1122.

[6] Fourteen Royal Commissions were appointed between 1945 and 1959.

Hospital Boards and of the Management Committees serve for three years, with the possibility of reappointment in both cases. The Boards of Governors of thirty-six teaching hospitals, each with about twenty-five members, are appointed by the Minister of Health. The Secretary of State for Scotland appoints five Regional Hospital Boards, totalling eighty-six members, and these appoint eighty-four Boards of Management. In each county and county borough area in England and Wales (except in a few cases where there are amalgamations) there is an Executive Council (138 in all) to supervise the family practitioner services — general practitioners, dentists, supplementary eye service, chemists. Five of the twenty-five members of each Council are appointed by the Minister of Health, for three years at a time.

The Ministry of Agriculture, Fisheries and Food has over fifty of the standing advisory committees already mentioned. But there are also sixty County Agricultural Advisory Committees, with not more than twelve members each, appointed by the Minister. Members serve for three years, one-third of each Committee retiring annually. Eleven similar Committees in Scotland are appointed by the Secretary of State.

The boards of nationalised industries are a special case. It is not clear that they belong to this class of appointment, for there is a widely accepted view that they should constitute the summit of a system of internal promotion. But it is the Minister who appoints, and in two corporations at least (the National Coal Board and the British Transport Commission) the Government has frequently undertaken reorganisation and reconstruction. So appointment from outside sometimes takes place, and the nationalised boards must be reckoned at present among the appointed bodies. The major national boards (airways, fuel, power, transport) have nine chairmen, eight deputy-chairmen, and twenty-five full-time members between them. There are over thirty part-time members at the national level (clearly always to be counted among 'appointed' men) and other gas and electricity boards need another 230 or so appointments, including part-timers.

Associated with the nationalised industries are many consumer and consultative committees. At the centre there are the Industrial and the Domestic Coal Consumers' Councils, and the Central Transport Consultative Committee. There are also in the regions fourteen Electricity Consultative Councils, twelve Gas Consultative Councils and ten Transport Users' Consultative Committees. All these have about 20–30 members each and are appointed by the Ministers concerned.

Ministers also make appointments to a variety of administrative boards. Some of these operate almost like minor Government departments: it is their ruling bodies that involve outside appointments, not the recruitment of their staffs. Thus the National Assistance Board (staffed by civil servants) consists of six members, appointed by the Crown and paid by a standing charge on the Consolidated Fund. The Medical Research Council (ten members) and the Agricultural Research Council eighteen members) as well as the Nature Conservancy (seventeen members) are appointed by a Committee of the Privy Council.

A full list of administrative boards cannot be given — it is doubtful if one has ever been made. But the following are among the bodies where appointment from outside (as distinct from election or regular promotion) is used, for some members at least. So far as agriculture and similar matters are concerned there are the Agricultural Land Commission (with five members), the Crown Estates Commission (eight members), and the Forestry Commission nine members). There are five members of the White Fish Authority and three of the Herring Industry Board. The National Parks Commission has fourteen members appointed by the Minister of Housing and Local Government. The War Damage Commission and the Central Land Board have the same eight members.

Industry, commerce, and finance have a considerable number of Government-appointed authorities, starting with the Bank of England (two Governors and sixteen Directors) and the Iron and Steel Board (three full-time and seven part-time members). Ministers appoint independent members to the Cotton Board and the Furniture Development Council. The Public Works Loan Board has twelve members appointed by the Crown and there are eight members of the Development Commission. The Monopolies Commission has nine members and there are seven lay members of the Restrictive Practices Court to be appointed, besides the five judges. There are also public corporations such as the Colonial Development Corporation and the National Research Development Corporation. There are, moreover, the National Savings Committee, the Sugar Board, the directors of Cable and Wireless Ltd, the Iron and Steel Holding and Realisation Agency, the Council of Industrial Design, and the British Travel and Holidays Association.

Other bodies where the method of appointment discussed here applies include the B.B.C. and the I.T.A., the British Council and the Arts Council, the Royal Fine Art Commission, the Royal Commissions on Historical Monuments, and the Historical Manuscripts Commission. Four members of the Racecourse Betting Control Board are appointed by Ministers.

Two further types of industrial body are relevant. First, there are the eleven Regional Boards for Industry, each with a chairman appointed by the Chancellor of the Exchequer, and about ten members appointed by him after consultation with industrial organisations. Secondly, there are several bodies concerned with trade disputes and wage negotiation. The Industrial Court has a president, four chairmen and eight members. There are about sixty Wages Councils or Wages Boards of varying size. All members are appointed by the Minister of Labour, but he has special responsibility for the three or five independent members on each Council — perhaps 180 appointments in all. The Minister also appoints arbitration bodies and Courts of Enquiry when they are needed.

The Government appoints directors to the boards of 104 public companies, registered as such under the Companies Acts.[7] These include some industrial firms like the British Petroleum Company Ltd, Short Bros and Harland Ltd, and Power Jets Ltd, and many research bodies like the Plant Breeding Institute and the Water Research Association. Over 350 persons are involved altogether. Some of these are civil servants, serving *ex officio*; others are industrialists and 'independent'. The term of service varies from case to case, and there are considerable differences in the extent of the duties involved. Directors are also appointed to some private companies, under the Distribution of Industry Acts, 1945–58.

The bodies so far considered probably involve something like 25,000 to 30,000 appointments. To these should be added 16,000 lay Justices of Peace whose method of recruitment is discussed in the following pages. The offices vary enormously in importance, of course; nevertheless it may be illuminating to find what is similar and what is different in the methods of recruitment.

Some other appointments which have not been counted might be mentioned for the sake of completeness. There are local advisory committees — bodies which rarely have very great power or influence, but which do meet and carry out some functions, and to which appointments must be made. They include the Ministry of Labour's Local Employment Committees and Youth Employment Committees, as well as the Disablement Advisory Committees already mentioned; the Advisory Committees in the Post Office areas; the Local Advisory Committees of the Ministry of Pensions and National Insurance; and the Advisory Committees in the Areas of the National Assistance Board. Most of these have about 15–20 members each.

The more traditional appointments need not be forgotten. There

[7] For a full list, see *Hansard* (22 Mar 1960) cols 193–204. Many of the companies are not trading concerns.

are forty-two Lords Lieutenant and forty High Sheriffs in the counties of England; and the Prime Minister's patronage would hardly be the same without the forty-one Bishops and the fourteen Regius Professors at Oxford and Cambridge.

### *How are Appointments Made?*

It is clear, then, that the practice of using appointed persons is widespread and that there are some fields where a large number of appointments need to be made. In these cases definite procedures leading to selection and appointment tend to establish themselves, though as customs rather than hard-and-fast rules. The practice, that is to say, is flexible and is rarely formulated in full, but something is known about some methods, and these examples illustrate what is involved.

### *Judicial and Quasi-Judicial Appointments*

The selection of magistrates is perhaps a classic case. The position of magistrate, unlike most of the others, does not arise from recent economic or social legislation. On the contrary, it is one of the oldest surviving offices in British government. In England and Wales all counties and county boroughs, and many non-county boroughs, have Commissions of the Peace, and, except in Lancashire, the Justices are appointed to the Commission by the Lord Chancellor. In Lancashire they are appointed by the Chancellor of the Duchy. The main work of selection is carried out by local advisory committees, who put forward names to the Lord Chancellor. These advisory committees have the Lord Lieutenant as chairman in the counties and a selected person in the boroughs. Their membership is highly confidential. They are themselves appointed by the Lord Chancellor. The way in which they make their choices is also confidential, though it is widely understood that since the Royal Commission on Justices of the Peace of 1948 the methods are more thorough. They do not necessarily involve interviewing candidates. Some conditions dealing with the retirement and residence of Justices are laid down in the Act of 1949. In Scotland, Justices of the Peace are appointed by the Secretary of State for Scotland, but the advisory committee system is the same.

The system, wrote a magistrate in the *Manchester Guardian*,[8] 'is essentially a grape-vine system, and . . . the strongest and most

[8] A Magistrate, 'Our Justices of the Peace', *Manchester Guardian*, 11 Nov 1958.

prolific of the vines have undoubtedly always been and still are the political parties'. In the last ten years there have been efforts to reduce this dependence on the local parties, but it is probable that they still have strong influence on the advisory committees. However, anyone may make nominations to the advisory committees, and the Lord Chancellor is by no means a passive appointing authority: Lord Kilmuir has been particularly active in promoting better standards of magistracy. The participation of local politicians helps to ensure a proper balance of political attitudes and perhaps of social class among magistrates; the dangers are that the politicians might be interested in little else, and that they might use the appointment as a reward for past services.

Some of the qualities needed for tribunal members are similar to those required for magistrates, since both positions involve making impartial judgements. For many tribunals, however, expert knowledge is necessary, and there is not the same emphasis in this field on the 'layman'. No general co-ordinated system of appointment has yet emerged. The Council on Tribunals, in its first report published in May 1960,[9] stated that it had not amassed sufficient knowledge to enable it to make general recommendations about the membership of tribunals; but it will no doubt be paying attention to methods of recruitment or selection, as did the Royal Commission on Justices of the Peace.

In the Oral Evidence given to the Franks Committee in 1956 some examples of how things used to be done came to light. A representative of the Ministry of Pensions and National Insurance explained how members of local tribunals were chosen.[10]

> There are some thousands of members of Tribunals throughout the country and we usually engage them through our Regional Controller acting through local advisory committees. The Act says the Minister may consult local advisory committees in choosing members of Tribunals and he in fact uses these committees. They are composed of people in the area representing employed persons, employers, local authorities, friendly societies and people generally interested in that sort of work; and they are called together when a Tribunal is to be reconstituted. The Regional Controller asks their advice as to which employers' associations in the area or large employers he should ask to submit names of suitable people. He also asks them which trade unions in the area he should consult about the employed persons' representatives. Then, when the invitations are sent out on the advice of the local advisory committees, and the replies come in, the committee sit down and between them they thrash out, say, that there shall be ten on one side and ten on the other.

[9] Council on Tribunals, *First Report* (London: H.M.S.O., 1960).

[10] Committee on Administrative Tribunals and Enquiries, *Minutes of Evidence* (London: H.M.S.O.) Second Day, p. 33, para. 273.

The secretary of the National Assistance Board, Sir Harold Fieldhouse, was asked about the appointment of members of National Assistance tribunals.[11] He replied:

> I am sorry if I do not seem to be very forthcoming about this, but you will understand the reasons. I gather that an enquiry has to be made in the localities for local people to act on local bodies. The Minister [of Pensions and National Insurance] has officers in the locality — his regional officers, and other local officers — and I have no doubt they report on likely persons. I believe the Advisory Committees are sometimes consulted about this, although I could not be absolutely sure. In looking round for local people to do the right sort of job, the Department uses its eyes and ears, i.e. its local staff.

In its Report the Franks Committee did not have a great deal to say about the composition of tribunals or about methods of choosing their members. Its chief concern was to ensure proper standards of procedure by having lawyers as chairmen. But it recommended that a supervisory council should be set up, and it is the function of the resulting statuory Council on Tribunals to review the constitution, as well as the working of tribunals. Perhaps the most interesting development is the establishment by the Lord Chancellor of a panel[12] from which the chairmen of many tribunals are chosen.

### *Local and Regional Administration*

Two examples of special-purpose organisations extending over the country offer themselves — the administration of the Hospital Service and County Agricultural Executive Committees.

It is a principle of the appointment of members of Regional Hospital Boards that they serve as individuals, not as representatives. Before appointing them, however, the Minister of Health consults universities, the British Medical Association, and other organisations representing the medical profession, local health authorities, and other bodies such as hospital associations and trade unions. Sometimes the chairman of the Board is consulted too. The Boards in turn appoint Hospital Management Committees. They consult (and in some cases they have committed themselves to consult) various interested organisations: for example, trades councils, the Royal College of Nursing, hospital contributory schemes, Women's Institutes, the British Red Cross, local medical committees, the St John Ambulance Brigade, business and professional women's clubs, chambers of

[11] Ibid. p. 46, para. 402.
[12] Under Section 3 of the Tribunals and Enquiries Act, 1958.

commerce and trade, branches of the BMA, women's standing conferences, the Women's Voluntary Service and women's co-operative guilds, and a miscellany of other bodies.[13] Management Committees may themselves make suggestions for the appointment of chairmen and perhaps about other members. Neither the Minister nor the Regional Hospital Boards are obliged to do more than consult, and in their appointments they are able to pursue their own policies on such matters as the proportion of lay to medical members, and overlapping membership between the Boards and Committees.

Each County Agricultural Executive Committee consists of a chairman, a deputy chairman and up to ten other members, all of whom are appointed by the Minister of Agriculture, with the advice of his regional officials. Seven of the members are chosen by the Minister from lists of nominees provided by the National Farmers' Union, the Country Landowners' Association, the National Union of Agricultural Workers and the Transport and General Workers' Union. The other members are chosen more directly by the Minister; one of these must be a member of the appropriate County Council appointed after consultation with the Council, and the others are selected to maintain a proper balance between the various interests on the Committee or to represent specialised forms of agriculture or interests closely associated with the agricultural industry within the county. The Minister has power of selection with nominated as well as directly chosen members, so he can ensure that all types and sizes of farms are represented and that the Committee is drawn from all parts of the county.[14]

### *Advisory bodies*

The standing advisory committees of Government departments are sometimes composed of nominees of national organisations and sometimes of individual experts. The majority of members are recruited by consultation with independent organisations, either by direct nomination or through the suggestion of names from which a choice is made. A minority is appointed on the recommendation of civil servants, existing members of committees and other personal contacts. The members of the National Production Advisory Council on Industry, for example, are put forward by the Trades Union Congress, the Federation of British Industries, and so on. In contrast the scientists on the Advisory Council on Scientific Research and Technical Development at the Ministry of Aviation are

[13] *Hansard* (2 Dec 1954) col. 461.

[14] PEP, 'Agricultural Executives', *Planning*, CCXCIV (31 Jan 1949) 223.

recruited through individual recommendations and university departments.[15]

The Regional Boards for Industry are advisory and consultative bodies associated with the National Production Advisory Council on Industry. They are appointed by the Chancellor of the Exchequer (though the central secretariat is at the Board of Trade). The chairmen are either industrialists or trade unionists and they help to select the other members, from names suggested by the British Employers' Confederation, the Federation of British Industries, the Trades Union Congress, the National Union of Manufacturers and the Association of British Chambers of Commerce. These organisations must in fact rely on their regional contacts or organisation, but nomination at the national level avoids the suggestion that members represent particular firms, union branches, or other organisations.

### *National Boards*

The methods whereby important national boards come to be selected are much more obscure. To some extent this is natural, for the Minister is likely to know many of the individuals involved and to exercise a much more personal choice. The more important the post, however, the more deliberate and considered the selection, with more time taken, if necessary, to reflect on the choices. One issue of significance at this level is how far the existing board or committee (or its chairman) should be consulted when new members are to be recruited. Though there is no precise information on the point it is scarcely likely that the situation recommended by Lord Simon of Wythenshawe — that nationalised boards should virtually appoint themselves, like private Boards of Directors — has been reached.[16] For appointments where specialised knowledge is not essential, such as committees of enquiry, Ministries may keep lists and panels of suitable people or they may have recourse to the central list in the Treasury.[17]

Though this section has not given an exhaustive account of methods of recruitment, enough has been said to indicate their general character — from the carefully built-up system now operating for Justices of the Peace to the informal suggestions prevalent in other fields. There is of course another, parallel, system of recom-

[15] These methods are discussed at length in *Advisory Committees in British Government*, ch. 3.

[16] Lord Simon of Wythenshawe, *The Boards of Nationalised Industries* (London: Longmans, 1957) pp. 28–9.

[17] See Committee on Administrative Tribunals and Enquiries, *Minutes of Evidence*, Fourth Day, p. 110, para. 931.

mendation in operation, which leads not to a new appointment but to an award in the Honours List. Perhaps some of the same channels are used.

### *The Problems*

What problems does this system raise for democratic government? It must first be asked whether the situation is avoidable — whether some other style of administration is possible, or whether (even if the administrative structure was much the same) the necessary office-holders might be chosen in some other way.

The description of methods of appointment in the last section showed the factors which had made appointed persons necessary. In some cases there is an overriding need for certain personal qualities, such as fair-mindedness, and appointment is a relatively certain method of getting people with these qualities. Similarly, the need for representative figures, for expert knowledge, and for a balanced team makes Ministerial selection necessary for most advisory committees. In other cases a specialised administration has been preferred to local authority control.

### *Could More be Elected?*

Could some appointments be replaced by some method of election? Three methods of administration involving elected persons are relevant to this question. One is for the duties to be undertaken by existing local authorities, controlled by elected councillors. Another is to arrange for the election of specialised authorities, like the old School Boards. The third is to elect the controlling bodies by special groups of constituents. The Marketing Boards for agricultural products, elected by registered producers, provide examples of this.

Obviously election is out of the question for some offices. The American practice of electing judges has never appealed to the British constitutionalist, and it is unlikely that the election of tribunals and similar bodies would ever be seriously considered. The objection to local authority control, where this might be practicable, is often more political than administrative. The medical profession was strongly opposed to allowing hospitals or other provisions under the Health Service to be directed by local councillors. The County Agricultural Executive Committees are believed to attract the support of the agricultural commmunity, by reason of their specialised nature, to a greater extent than would lay committees of County Councils. The objection to the election of specialised boards is that it involves the proliferation of elections, with the likelihood of very low polls and issues being determined by voters not greatly concerned with the subject. The third method, election by specialised functional constituencies, has not been much used in this country — it is difficult to delimit the constituencies and to register the voters. In practice such a system might well lead to the same results — the same persons in the same positions — as nomination by voluntary associations and similar bodies.

## *Career Officials*

On the other hand there are, in certain cases, possibilities of transferring functions from part-time laymen to regular officials. Thus, in a minority report of the Royal Commission on Justices of the Peace, Lord Merthyr envisaged the replacement of lay magistrates by a system of stipendiaries. Appointment would still be required, as with Recorders, but the employment of full-time, professionally qualified people would surely tend to bring about a discernible career structure. Such a system would at any rate be very different from the practices being considered here.

In other cases the functions exercised by appointed laymen may be absorbed by the civil service. An advisory committee of outside experts may become unnecessary if sufficient specialist or professional civil servants are recruited to do its job, or the detachment of the independent committee may no longer be thought necessary — the duties exercised by the Import Duties Advisory Committee in the 1930s have been left to the Board of Trade since the war. Dr Stephen Taylor advocated in 1951 the replacement of Regional Hospital Boards by small paid boards. The Council on Tribunals commends the tendency to have lawyers as chairmen of tribunals, and promises to give the question of remuneration further consideration. These trends perhaps do not make tribunal service into a career, but they indicate some measure of professionalism.

However, it is clear that outside appointment must remain for most of the positions where it is now used — certainly for advisory committees, Justices of the Peace, and tribunals, and for most of the national administrative bodies. The most practicable alternative for regional or local bodies would be transfer to local authorities, possibly to joint boards. But there may be good reasons for not doing this, and the practice of appointment ought to be assessed on the assumption that it will continue to be necessary. No amount of democratic emotion can conceal the fact that, if you want the best man for a specialist job, then appointment is more likely to find him than election. But is he the representative man? This raises the question of nomination by organised groups.

### *Nominations and Suggestions*

Clearly the great majority of the appointees being considered here have their names put forward in some way or other. The direct acquaintance of the Minister or other appointing authority can only be relevant for a few top national positions.

The mechanics of nomination, so far as they are known, were described in the previous section. The system has considerable advantages. It finds the necessary people. It makes use of the active and voluntary organisations of society — parties, associations, unions and so on — which have some claim to be regarded as the natural channels of community life. They nominate mainly their active members: but why should passive and inactive people expect to be appointed? Nevertheless, nomination by interest groups, national or local, also has disadvantages. Not all interests within the community are well organised — consumers, teenagers, and the sick, for instance, have in the past spoken little for themselves. Organisations that do exist, e.g., of tenants or of housewives, may be unrepresentative. Groups tend to put forward worthy and well-established figures rather than fresh and enterprising ones. When put forward by a group some people cannot shake off the mistaken belief that they are supposed in some way to act as representatives of the group. Where various interests are balanced on a committee, those with minor or intermittent (but still significant) concern are often ignored. An organisation's leadership, which makes the nominations, may be out of touch with its 'clientele'.

Names may also be suggested by civil servants (including local and regional officials), or by people already appointed to the position in question. This method may sometimes bring in people who would not be put forward by the groups; but if used extensively it is likely to produce the appearance (at least) of a narrow clique. Nomination by local authorities is also possible but in practice is difficult to distinguish from nomination by local political parties. Panels and lists of likely public servants, like those already mentioned, may be used; but this merely moves the problem one stage along — how do people get on the panels

The best solution, for any committee or set of offices, is usually to employ more than one method of recruitment — to have some suggestions from independent organisations, some from departmental or local officials and to take some from reserve lists.

### *Plurality*

But who gets appointed in the end to these various posts? Is it the same people over and over again?

Some evidence about plurality in the localities is given in the Statement of Evidence[18] by the Centre for Urban Studies to the Royal Commission on Local Government in Greater London. This includes, of course, elected councillors in its analysis. It states that:

> There are already far more posts of this kind — as members of councils, of their subsidiary agencies, of public boards and corporations, of government committees and as justices of the peace — than there are people who are able to occupy them. There is, therefore, already a species who might be described as the 'Public Person' or as the 'Ubiquitous committee man' (or woman).

The Centre has calculated that on the average each member of the London County Council holds nearly six other public posts; the county councillors of Surrey and Middlesex each hold nearly seven such posts.

> As might be expected, moreover, it is mainly the older, the retired or the wealthy people who are the 'Public Persons'; it is they who occupy the majority of the posts counted. They hold on the average ten public posts each.

The Acton Society, in its study of the Hospital Service, was apprehensive:

> At present very great dependence is being put on the part played by voluntary workers. . . . *A serious question for the future is whether this dependence can be permanently relied on.*[19]

PEP has itself contributed some evidence about national bodies. In *Government and Industry* it was shown that thirteen individuals occupied between them thirty-nine places on the six senior Government industrial committees; and thirty individuals were found who filled a total of 154 places (over five each) on Government bodies.[20] In *Advisory Committees in British Government* it is shown that there are twenty-two persons who occupy forty-six places on Board of Trade standing advisory committees, and there are thirty-four persons who have eighty-five places on such committees at the Home Office.[21]

18 *Statement of Evidence* (Centre for Urban Studies, University College, London, Dec 1959) p. 9.

19 *Hospitals and the State, 4; Regional Hospital Boards* (Acton Soc. Trust, 1957) p. 18.

20 *Government and Industry* (PEP, 1952) p. 131.

21 *Advisory Committees in British Government*, pp. 53–6.

These authorities, however, are each looking at part of the picture. It may well be that the full extent of plurality — or the small numbers available for service — can only be seen when a full range of posts is considered. To see the situation in its entirety not even the scope of this broadsheet is adequate. Not only Government appointments ought to be reckoned — local councils and voluntary bodies of all kinds should be considered. The range of availability often turns out to be surprisingly restricted. In an article in the *British Journal of Sociology* in 1957, Mr F. J. Bayliss showed that most independent members of Wages Councils were university teachers, lawyers or ex-civil servants, and that the appointment of people with other backgrounds was often not welcomed by either employers or workers.[22] It would be a mistake, of course, to assume that plurality is a bad thing in itself. In fact some repetitive appointments are deliberate. They facilitate administrative co-ordination. A doctrine of one man one job would hardly be practicable. It is excessive plurality that is an evil, for it indicates either a shortage of talent or an inadequate attempt to find it. The Acton Society expressed concern in case the supply of voluntary public servants diminished in the future. If the relation of persons to posts held could be calculated, would the existing supply be as great as supposed? Was it ever very great?

A serious shortage would limit the effectiveness of administrative reform, and blunt the impact of political change. On the analysis of the Centre for Urban Studies change of administrative structure or methods of appointment does not matter so much. As the Centre's *Statement of Evidence* says:

> Plus ça change, plus c'est la même chose. A good deal that might be new in name if such re-shuffling were to occur, would not be new in personnel.[23]

The problem, then, is whether the circles from which appointees are drawn can be widened. Before putting forward suggestions to this end, however, it must be stressed that so far very little is established about the present situation. It may well be that not only do a relatively small number of individuals share a large number of posts, but these individuals may be much of a type. The Centre for Urban Studies specifies 'the older, the retired or the wealthy'. The Council on Tribunals is considering 'age limits and the possible need for more women' in certain cases.[24] Here, in fact, is a promising sub-

[22] F. J. Bayliss, 'The Independent Members of Wages Councils', *British Journal of Sociology* (Mar 1957) pp. 22 and 17.

[23] *Statement of Evidence*, p. 10.

[24] *First Report*, p. 7.

ject for sociological enquiry. Studies of these matters might not only help with these immediate problems, but could also throw some light on the social bases of modern government.

### *Widening the Search*

In the meantime, can recruitment be widened? Three approaches suggest themselves. In the first place, something might be done by laws or regulations — by imposing fairly strict rules about plurality and rotation of office, so that Ministers and other appointing authorities had no choice but to search out new blood even more diligently than they do. Reliance on familiar figures arises not out of deliberate vice, but because it is easier and safer than enterprise. The standards applied need not be so stringent as those suggested by the *Manchester Guardian*:

> There can be no hard and fast rule, but in general, a man doing a full-time job ought to limit himself to one part-time appointment. . . . Part-time service to the State would be healthier for being more widely spread. And it is fairer to employers . . . that individuals should not expect to be released for more than one part-time activity, however meritorious socially it may be.[25]

Much depends, of course, on how much time is taken up by the part-time appointment. Restrictions need not be identical in all cases, but they should apply to all types of person; if they were applied only to those at work, an even greater burden would be thrown on the retired and the housewives.

Secondly, attention might be given to conventional limitations. Those connected with social class have diminished but have not disappeared. The working-class nominee is rarely other than a trade union representative. The middle-aged housewife has come to play a considerable part in local government, but women are still seriously under-represented in other fields, such as tribunals, advisory committees and national administrative bodies. Plurality of appointment (at least at the national level) among women seems to be even more frequent than among men. Maximum age limits would raise the rate of turnover and conventional ideas about the minimum age of suitability could do with revision. Definite rules about this are rare, but if recruitment to some posts started at 40 instead of 50, and to others at 30 instead of 40, the talent available might be multiplied. Too much service in public office begins after retirement.

Thirdly, the old issues about payment and release from employ-

[25] Leading article in the *Manchester Guardian*, 31 Mar 1959.

ment for part-time service might be given another airing. The virtues of the voluntary principle should be balanced against its possible limiting effect on recruitment. In fact, fees are already paid for service on certain scientific and other advisory committees, where considerable work is involved. The Council on Tribunals is examining the question of remuneration of tribunal members in detail. It notes that 'the reasons why salaries or fees are paid in some cases and not in others are by no means clear'. Nevertheless, if the 'voluntary principle' is retained, why not call for volunteers? For some bodies at least, like local advisory committees, it could do no harm if the need for new members were made known, and the initiative not left entirely to the appointing authority.

There may well be better means than these of widening the frontiers of availability. The main point is that the matter should not be regarded as a lost cause, and remedies should be the object of thought and action.

### *Conclusions*

The whole subject of appointment to the positions discussed in this broadsheet is sometimes regarded as one of great delicacy.[26] There is no doubt that privacy and discretion are necessary for the discussion of particular appointments. But as well as summing up the discussion in this broadsheet it may be useful to distinguish principles which could guide public policy in these matters.

The reasons for the growth of appointment are the need to secure people with particular qualities for particular jobs and for the Minister to exercise some form of remote control over administrative bodies. There is now a great range of appointments within the definition set out, from highly-paid members of nationalised boards to members of rarely-convened local advisory committees. There are perhaps 40,000 posts in all, national, regional, and local, not counting local advisory committees. The methods of appointment for the higher posts are obscure, perhaps necessarily so. For other bodies they involve consultation with interest groups, civil servants in the regions, and sometimes special advisory committees. There is some evidence that plurality is excessive, if the whole range of posts is considered, and it should be diminished if possible.

The first principle which might guide policy is that 'grape-vine' methods of recruitment should as far as possible be orderly and systematic, and they should be widely known, so that nominations may come from all quarters. Secondly, within the limits imposed by

[26] See, for instance, the remarks of the Secretary of the National Assistance Board quoted on p. 57.

the nature of the job to be done, as great a variety of persons as possible should be appointed. Thirdly, plurality should be treated as a general problem and not merely looked at in relation to a particular set of institutions. Until it has been fully examined on this basis, statements about the large numbers of people willing to give voluntary public service should be treated with reserve.

The new patronage, like other consequences of the twentieth-century revolution in government functions, has come to stay. The time has come to examine it, to document it, to regularise it and to establish for it public standards of propriety and good practice.

CHAPTER II

# POLITICAL ROLES

THE concept of 'role' provides a useful bridge between the biographer's concern with individual personality and the institutionalist's interest in formal political offices. A political role exists independently of the personality of an individual politician, for it is a set of expectations held by a large number of people. These expectations help shape what the person in the role expects himself to do, as well as what other people will recognise as acceptable behaviour. These expectations are strictly extra-legal. For example, before an individual enters the House of Commons he will have certain expectations of how he should act in Parliament; when he enters, he will find that his behaviour is judged in the light of commonly held criteria deemed appropriate by veteran MPs, lobby correspondents and other *habituées* of Westminster. One will find nothing in Erskine May's treatise on Parliament about the behaviour expected of a young man who aspires to move quickly to the front benches, of a trade unionist MP, or of the well-bred scion of an old landed family. Yet these expectations are important in determining how a new MP acts and, reciprocally, how others will react to what he does.

The institutional characteristics of an office are important in establishing limits upon what kind of behaviour can be expected of a politician. One can hardly expect, say, the Minister of Works to be an important influence upon foreign policy. When one does find an exceptional individual, such as Sir Horace Wilson, nominally chief industrial adviser to the Government, acting as a major foreign-policy adviser under Neville Chamberlain's Prime Ministership, then one can usefully distinguish between the office that Sir Horace held and the role he took in the policy process. Such an example is important as a reminder of the possibility of individual characteristics influencing political influence. Yet the long-run probabilities are such that the informal expectations and institutional characteristics of an office act as the prime determinants of what a single person can do in politics. A Prime Minister's behaviour can vary considerably, according to his personal characteristics; Clement Attlee's personality and style of leadership was very different from that of Winston

Churchill. Yet both men were compelled, by virtue of the expectations of others and by virtue of the institutional importance of the office, to perform a number of common tasks.

Political roles can be defined more narrowly than the characteristics of individual politicians, or political offices. Any politician, whatever his office, will have a number of political roles to perform, and he must be adept at recognising what behaviour is expected of him in different situations. A cabinet minister, for example, is expected to defend his department from criticism against Opposition MPs in his role as a spokesman for the government. He would not be expected to make the same type of speech in response to private criticism in a cabinet committee or in his own department; in the role of colleague or chief administrator he would be expected to reply more calmly and moderately, with none of the debating techniques appropriate to the Commons. The maladroit politician will fail to adapt himself, or continue to play the same role — proponent of party goals, expositor of administrative problems or platform orator — even when circumstances lead those around him to expect otherwise.

To say that a politician is expected to take many roles is not to say that he is a chameleon, changing his views with every change of audience. The need to play many roles arises from the complex nature of political offices. An individual MP is simultaneously a member of an old and distinguished club, the House of Commons, a political partisan, a constituency spokesman, and, perhaps a minister or an aspiring ministerialist. It is part of his job to perform a number of roles, and to perform them tolerably well. Moreover, as a human being, he is still involved in a variety of non-political role relationships with his family, friends and business or professional associates. Given the heterogeneous nature of their roles, it is hardly surprising that politicians sometimes find them in conflict. Role conflicts are almost infinite in their permutations. Sometimes they are avoided by the general acceptance of a hierarchy of obligations. For example, in Britain, a politician is expected to put his official obligations ahead of family roles and avoid giving jobs to friends and relatives on the basis of kinship claims. Other role conflicts are more uncertain in their resolution. For instance, it would be difficult to make categorical statements about the behaviour to be expected of a cabinet minister when his personal ambitions clashed with what was expected of him as an efficient administrator.

In theory, the language of role expectations is meant to be analytic, rather than moral or legalistic. Yet speaking about what people are expected to do has moral and legal overtones. In an ideal world of liberal political philosophers, we might expect voters and their representatives to act in the light of ideological formulae for realising social ideals. In a world of lawyers we would have very few expectations beyond the non-restrictive injunction that behaviour, whatever the end, should conform with the statute book. In some instances, we may find that our empirical observations of what politicians do differs in a morally neutral manner from what we might originally have anticipated. In the case of voters and of cabinet ministers, however, research has illustrated how great the conflict is between what we think ought to characterise people in these roles, and the physical and intellectual limitations which often frustrate these expectations.

## Bibliographical Note

Studies of British politics rarely make use of the formal language of role theory, although intuitive appreciation of its basic premises is often found in a wide variety of writings on the subject. Exceptions to this generalisation, besides articles printed in this volume, are few. The editor's own illustration of its use can be found in Richard Rose, *Influencing Voters* (London: Faber, 1967) chs 9–10.

The most substantial use of role theory in American political science has been in the field of legislative studies, and studies of the presidency. Heinz Eulau's *The Behavioural Persuasion in Politics* (New York: Random House, 1963) provides an outline of the place of the concept in relation to other more familiar political terms. The best-known example of legislative analysis is John C. Wahlke, *et al.*, *The Legislative System* (New York: Wiley, 1962). See also the anthologies edited by John C. Wahlke and Heinz Eulau, *Legislative Behaviour* (Glencoe, Illinois Free Press, 1959) and Robert L. Peabody and Nelson W. Polsby, *New Perspectives on the House of Representatives* (Chicago: Rand McNally, 1963). On the presidency, see especially Richard Neustadt, *Presidential Power* (New York: Wiley, 1960) and Clinton Rossiter, *The American Presidency* (London: Hamilton, 1957), ch. 1.

# ORDINARY INDIVIDUALS IN ELECTORAL SITUATIONS

*By* Richard Rose *and* Harve Mossawir

Studies of elections often imply that the role of voter is or ought to be very important to individual members of the electorate. Yet empirical studies of voters have consistently shown that the political awareness of the median elector is limited. Such studies have been variously interpreted by social scientists and by popular commentators. The following article is an attempt to relate the activities of individuals in their role as voter with their activities in other political and non-political roles. In this way, the meaning of voting — both for the individual and for the political system — can be seen in a proper multi-dimensional perspective.

Britain is a good country for intensive analysis of general theoretical questions about elections. Electoral institutions have traditional sources yet have proven adaptable, British procedures have often served as models for other countries, and a substantial mass of descriptive and survey material is readily available as a basis for further research. In order to explore the extent of voters' electorally relevant political demands, attitudes toward the electoral process, and the relationship between electoral attitudes and allegiance to the regime, a survey was undertaken in the Stockport North constituency in February–March 1964.

The constituency was chosen for a number of reasons. On key variables such as social class, housing and population growth, Stockport consistently ranks near the middle among towns in England and Wales.[1] Politically, the constituency was marginal, and was won by Labour from the Conservatives at the 1964 election. Last and not least, it was relatively convenient to our former University. A total of 889 names were drawn from a fresh electoral register by systematic random sampling methods. Student interviewers conducted

[1] See C. A. Moser and Wolf Scott, *British Towns* (Edinburgh: Oliver & Boyd, 1961) pp. 112–13.

Reprinted from pp. 182–9, 192–4 of a lengthy comparative study by Rose and Mossawir, originally published as 'Voting and Elections: A Functional Analysis', *Political Studies* xv ii (1967).

all but two dozen interviews, which were undertaken by the senior author. The response rate was 77 per cent of all names drawn; non-respondents included refusals, 6 per cent; moved or absent for a prolonged period, 6 per cent; sick, senile or dead, 6 per cent; not at home after three or more calls by an interviewer, 4 per cent; house demolished, 1 per cent. The research cost of £91 was met by a grant from the Faculty of Economics of Manchester University. Interviewing occurred at a time when an election had to take place within the next eight months. Yet respondents were not interviewed during the election campaign, when an abnormally high interest might have been temporarily generated in the questions. Stockport North was chosen as a marginal constituency with a reasonably representative social structure; moreover, it had been systematically exposed to pre-election propaganda by both parties for more than six months in advance of interviewing. One survey of this type can, of course, only provide illustrative evidence. But in present circumstances, it is highly desirable that general theoretical problems should be considered in relation to data which provides some empirical bearings, and gives suggestions for more special surveys 'around' elections.

In order for an election to have the function of voter choice or influence upon policy as well as office-holding, an individual voter must be aware that government influences his life, he must have demands seen as relevant to politics, and he must be willing to consider altering party preferences in response to changes in policies. In addition, a large proportion of voters would be expected to show interest in politics and believe that they possessed political influence.

When Stockport respondents were asked how much effect government had on the lives of people like themselves, 48 per cent attributed a lot of influence, 28 per cent a little influence, and 11 per cent no effect; an additional 13 per cent said they did not know. Among those perceiving some government influence, evaluations of influence were mixed or positive. A total of 44 per cent thought the value of the impact depended upon the situation, and 37 per cent that government usually made things better; 13 per cent replied that government usually made things worse, and 6 per cent said don't know.[2]

When asked to give some examples of the influence of government on their lives, among those perceiving influence, 30 per cent did not

[2] Similar answers for Britain, America and Germany were obtained in *The Civic Culture* survey by G. A. Almond and S. Verba, but that survey reported far higher proportions unambiguously seeing government as improving conditions, since the question employed offered a polarised choice: '31b. On the

offer any example, and only 18 per cent offered more than one example. Reference was most often made to economic policy, welfare measures and taxes.

The relatively low salience of government to the central concerns of the majority of voters is evidenced by answers to the question: 'What would you say is the main concern of you and your family today?' (Table 1.) Few of the respondents mentioned a problem that

TABLE 1

*Main concern of respondents*

| *Subject* | *Per cent* |
|---|---|
| Economic (standard of living, job, pension, housing) | 40 |
| Personal (health, happiness, lead a decent life) | 16 |
| Family (children, relatives) | 13 |
| War | 5 |
| Miscellaneous | 5 |
| None | 21 |

was unambiguously personal, such as ill health, or one that was unambiguously political, such as nuclear war. When asked what group outside their family could help them with their chief concerns, the great majority of respondents (71 per cent) saw themselves reliant strictly upon family resources, and could think of no other group to provide assistance. Even though this question was asked immediately after a series about government and 40 per cent had referred to economic concerns, only 15 per cent of persons with a problem referred to obtaining assistance from a government or other political source. To assess the existence of latent demands which could be crystallised by campaigners, individuals were asked whether or not they were satisfied with six things for which governments accept responsibility — their standard of living, job, housing, education today, welfare services generally, and the condition of pensioners. On five of these points, the proportion reporting themselves satisfied ranged from 61 to 75 per cent. Only the condition of pensioners showed a majority of voters dissatisfied, notwithstanding the very intensive criticism of the state of England at the time in the media and among party activists.

When Stockport respondents were asked point-blank what they thought were the most important things the government *ought* to do something about, virtually everyone could give voice to some com-

whole do the activities of the national government tend to improve conditions in this country or would we be better off without them?' (Princeton University Press, 1963, pp. 80 ff., and p. 529.)

plaint which they wished government action to remedy. The apparent discrepancy between this response and other evidence of the low salience of politics to the ordinary voter can best be explained by the fact that for the respondent to state a political demand in response to explicit questioning it is only necessary for him to have a minimum cognitive awareness of public affairs, and less than 100 per cent satisfaction with things as they are. It does not necessarily reflect interest or knowledge comparable to that of candidates, political scientists and newspapers that commission public opinion polls. For example, only 45 per cent of Stockport respondents described themselves as 'interested' or 'very interested' in politics, 41 per cent knew the name of their MP (Sir Norman Hulbert had sat for Stockport since 1935), 10 per cent considered themselves members of a political party, and only 9 per cent described themselves as 'very interested' in politics. These figures are consistent with other findings suggesting that no more than one-sixth of the British electorate is in any meaningful sense actively involved in politics.[3]

Voters are also aware that they are not the only members of society seeking to influence government, and that the deference paid them by politicians during election campaigns may not be lasting. In the Stockport survey, 52 per cent said that they thought the pledges made by party leaders during campaigns were sometimes sincere and sometimes not, and 26 per cent thought campaigners usually insincere. Similarly, only 14 per cent claimed that people like themselves had a lot of influence upon the way the country is governed, and 12 per cent some influence; 38 per cent said people like themselves had little influence, and 27 per cent no influence, with the remainder don't know. Attribution of political influence is pluralistic, inasmuch as more than half the respondents credit five groups with substantial, i.e. 'a lot' or 'too much', impact on government (Table 2). But voters see people like themselves in the lower half among influential groups; only the Queen was thought less likely than voters to have 'a lot' of influence and only the Church of England and the Queen were more often said to have no influence Thus, while recognising what Dahl calls 'dispersed inequalities',[4]

[3] See Richard Rose, *Politics in England* (London: Faber, 1965) ch. 4. See also G. Almond and S. Verba, op. cit. p. 188, showing that only about 15 per cent of all British respondents claim ever to have tried to influence local government. Germany, Italy and Mexico have fewer activists, when those claiming activity are taken as a percentage of all adult respondents.

[4] *Who Governs?* (New Haven, Conn.: Yale University Press, 1961) p. 228. Attributions of influence were similar in a nation-wide Gallup Poll survey on the same theme, reported in *Gallup Political Index* (London) no. 37 (Jan 1963) pp. 15–16.

voters seem to think that in the dispersion of inequalities, some people are more unequal than others.

TABLE 2

*Influence of groups upon government*

| | *A lot* (%) | *Too much* (%) | *A little* (%) | *None* (%) | *Don't know* (%) |
|---|---|---|---|---|---|
| Prime Minister | 62 | 5 | 22 | 5 | 6 |
| Members of Parliament | 54 | 4 | 31 | 8 | 3 |
| Big business | 52 | 29 | 11 | 2 | 6 |
| The Press | 46 | 11 | 27 | 9 | 7 |
| Trade unions | 39 | 24 | 24 | 2 | 11 |
| Television | 36 | 6 | 30 | 18 | 10 |
| Senior civil servants* | 30 | 6 | 30 | 12 | 22 |
| Church of England | 17 | 2 | 39 | 31 | 11 |
| The Queen | 13 | 2 | 35 | 43 | 7 |

* Piloting the questionnaire showed that many respondents had no conception of the title or duties of administrative class civil servants; the chief referent for 'civil servants' appeared to be a local clerical officer. The term 'senior civil servant' was employed as more meaningful to respondents. The Don't Know group was twice as high for civil servants as for any other group.

Given the foregoing attitudes, it is hardly surprising that voters do not see a general election as a time at which a choice of some importance can be made between parties. In fact, the majority of voters do not see it as a time of choice. Only 12 per cent of persons who had voted in the 1959 general election reported altering their party preference in Stockport by March 1964. The reason most often given was the intervention of a Liberal candidate. An additional 19 per cent said they could think of things that the other parties could do that might make them change their vote, e.g. modify welfare policies. But 69 per cent of the voters declared that they could not think of anything that could make them think of voting differently from their established party preference. Moreover, data from the Civic Culture survey shows that only 1 to 7 per cent of respondents in the five nations volunteered references to changing a vote as a means of influencing government.[5] In short, for most individuals the

[5] Op. cit. pp. 203 ff. For detailed discussion of changers defined in this article as individuals switching support from one party to another, see R. S. Milne and H. C. Mackenzie, 'The Floating Vote', *Political Studies*, III i, and, more generally, H. Daudt, *Floating Voters and the Floating Vote* (Leiden: Stenfert Kroese, 1961). The definitive account of voting shifts in British elections should appear in the forthcoming study by D. E. Butler and Donald Stokes of the 1964 and 1966 British elections.

function of voting at a given general election is not that of calculating and registering a fresh choice, but rather reaffirming an allegiance established long ago. To speak of the majority of voters at a given election as 'choosing' a party is nearly as misleading as speaking of a worshipper on a Sunday 'choosing' to go to an Anglican, rather than a Presbyterian or a Baptist church.

Notwithstanding the relatively low salience of elections as instruments of choice, they do appear to have some meaning to electors, for turnout of voters is consistently high in Britain, with well above three-quarters of persons physically able to do so casting their votes. Particularly in a country where free elections have been a highly valued symbol for generations, one might posit that an individual's participation in elections is primarily motivated by a commitment to the electoral process itself, rather than by expectations of choosing or influencing government. Yet in recent years, the mass media have increasingly discussed the extent to which voters may be manipulated by politicians. Such discussion may influence or reflect considerable cynicism among voters about the electoral process. Alternatively, one might suggest that most voters are as apathetic about the electoral process as they are about other features of politics that command the attention of the opinion elite.

To explore the values and beliefs of voters about the electoral process, Stockport respondents were asked four questions, each of which offered a statement consistent with liberal doctrines of representation and one representing disaffection. The first point to note in the answers is that voters are not apathetic or confused. The maximum expressing no opinion or uncertainty on any question was 8 per cent, and only 4 respondents in 684 had no views on at least three of the four questions (Table 3). Secondly, a clear majority of voters endorsed each of the liberal alternatives, with support ranging from 57 per cent to 73 per cent. Thirdly, the median voter endorsed liberal values and beliefs. A total of 56 per cent of respondents opted for the liberal alternative at least three out of four times, and only 12 per cent opted for a disaffected alternative at least three times.[6] Moreover, cross-analysis by conventional demographic variables showed that endorsement of these values is found in all strata of the electorate.

The voters' support for the electoral process on grounds that appear to be more symbolic and expressive than instrumental[7]

[6] The position of the liberal and disaffected alternatives were reversed on questions 2 and 4 in order to avoid response-set bias.

[7] Elections are not the only political institution capable of analysis for symbolic meaning, See e.g. Thurman Arnold, *The Symbols of Government* (New

TABLE 3

*Attitudes of voters towards the electoral process*
*(L=Liberal alternative; D=Disaffected alternative)*

| | | | *L* (%) | *D* (%) | *No opinion* (%) |
|---|---|---|---|---|---|
| 1. | (L) | Voters have a *big* influence on the way the country is governed, OR | | | |
| | (D) | Voters *don't* have much influence on government . . . . . . . | 60 | 35 | 5 |
| 2. | (L) | Most people *do* think about how they vote, OR | | | |
| | (D) | Most people *don't* think about how they vote. | 57 | 35 | 8 |
| 3. | (L) | There *is* a real difference between the parties, OR | | | |
| | (D) | There's *no* real difference to choose from between the parties . . . . . . | 73 | 23 | 4 |
| 4. | (L) | Voters should vote for the *party* they think best, OR | | | |
| | (D) | Voters should vote for the *men* they think best without regard to party . . . . | 68 | 28 | 4 |

suggests the best possibility that voting may be an end in itself, providing emotional gratifications for those who participate in elections. The important question then becomes whether elections have a strong or a very limited emotional function, and whether emotional responses are favourable or unfavourable. The Stockport survey found that 54 per cent said that elections had no emotional effect at all upon them, as against 31 per cent who enjoyed elections, and 8 per cent reporting annoyance. Similarly, Almond and Verba found that a majority of their respondents did not report a feeling of satisfaction when voting.[8] Interestingly, on all five comparative measures American respondents showed markedly higher emotional response to elections than respondents in Britain, Germany, Italy or Mexico. One might speculate that the enthusiasm of American social scientists for voting studies reflects among other things, a general cultural orientation, and that in America elections as well as election studies are more important than in other countries.

York: 1935) and, more recently, Murray Edelman, *The Symbolic Uses of Politics* (Urbana, Illinois: University Press, 1964).

[8] Op. cit. p. 146. The published table reports that 71 per cent in America showed satisfaction when going to the polls, but this percentage is calculated only in relation to recent voters, and they are much fewer in America than elsewhere. The proportion of total respondents expressing satisfaction is only about 44 per cent.

The low emotional effect of elections suggests that for most voters the gratification obtained from voting is a result of having done a necessary but not particularly pleasurable duty. The duty of voting is the only act of political participation expected of a majority of persons in Britain, and stressed in pre-adult socialisation. When an election is at hand, an individual can hardly avoid awareness of polling, because of intensive and extensive publicity through the mass media; for example in Stockport in March 1964, 89 per cent were already aware an election would be held some time later in the year. On election day, the social norms internalised by the individual will make him feel impelled to cast a vote. The cost of voting, in terms of time and effort, is usually low in highly urbanised Britain. By voting, an individual may achieve a sense of emotional gratification from doing a duty or he will at least avoid tension and possible guilt feelings which could have arisen through failure to do his duty. The sense of duty may, of course, be reinforced or counteracted by either personal and social pressures, e.g. a sense of party identification making it a duty to vote for a particular party whether it has a chance of victory or not in the constituency, or a sense of social solidarity, making it important to vote if one's family, friends and fellow-workers are voting.

Evidence in support of this line of analysis is found in the Stockport survey. When asked whether you don't have to vote unless you feel like it, or whether voting is a duty, 82 per cent replied that they thought voting a duty. Many surveys of turnout have consistently shown that as the importance of voting varies, so does the propensity to vote, whether variations be caused by differences in individual political involvement, in types of elections (e.g. national and local government) or in differential socialisation into prevailing cultural norms.[9] In Britain and other free societies, the duty to vote, through a process of socialisation, becomes a response to an internal compulsion. In many countries, however, an individual may vote primarily because he fears external sanctions may be brought to bear upon him if he fails to support the party organising the election. In both types of situation, voting is not so much behaviour freely undertaken by an individual seeking to initiate or advance interests, but rather a

[9] See e.g. Angus Campbell, *et al.*, *The American Voter* (New York: Wiley, 1960) ch. 5; Angus Campbell, 'Surge and Decline: A Study of Electoral Change', *Public Opinion Quarterly*, XXIV iii (1960); and R. E. Lane, *Political Life* (Glencoe, Illinois: Free Press, 1959), especially pp. 350 ff.; and, on London local government, L. J. Sharpe, *A Metropolis Votes* (London School of Economics: Greater London Papers, no. 8, 1962) pp. 18 ff. Cf. Dilys M. Hill, 'Democracy in Local Government' (University of Leeds: Ph.D thesis, 1966), especially chs 3–4.

more-or-less passive response by an individual to continuing social pressures, whether the demands are manifested overtly by mobilisation through a single party or transmitted more subtly through a diffuse process of socialisation.

Voting has much greater significance for the political scientist or the candidate than it has for the voter. For individuals, the chief functions of voting are emotional or allegiance-maintaining. Only a limited fraction of the electorate seems able or willing to act so that their votes can consciously have for them the function of choosing governors or influencing government policy. Within the field of social science, a model from social psychology would seem best suited to the data. In democratic and non-democratic societies alike, voting is a norm. When this norm is internalised by an individual and/or supported by strong social pressures, a majority of individuals will vote, even if lacking in partisanship, anticipating a one-sided result, expressing not much interest in the campaign, having no concern about the election outcome, and a low sense of political efficacy.[10] For such individuals, voting may provide a mild gratification, or simply dissipate tension arising from failing to act according to established norms. In such a model, motivations to vote are not to be evaluated as 'rational' or 'irrational', but rather as 'compelling' or 'failing to compel'.

It is important to emphasise that this argument does not mean that politics is relatively less important for an individual than participation in other more-or-less voluntary social organisations. A key finding of comparative studies of associational life is that only a minority of the adult population participates in formally organised social groups. The Civic Culture study, for example, found the figure varied from 26 per cent in Mexican urban areas to 57 per cent in America. Except in America, the great majority of individuals belonged to only one organisation and had never held an office in it. While not exactly comparable between nations, figures for 'civic-political' group membership showed that it was neither among the highest nor the lowest of the eleven types of organisations categorised.[11] Intensive studies of religious behaviour and of trade union activities confirm that low levels of active participation in social organisations are not specific to politics. In religion and, by analogy in trade unionism, it is clear that the great majority of

[10] The proportions ranking lowest on these indices who nonetheless voted ranged from 52 to 70 per cent in American elections in 1952 and 1956, according to data in Campbell, *et al.*, op. cit. pp. 97–105.

[11] Almond and Verba, op. cit. pp. 302 ff. For a more general discussion of organised groups in political life, see William Kornhauser, *The Politics of Mass Society* (London: Routledge, 1960).

individuals do have a group identification, as is the case in politics; yet there too, only a small minority go beyond identification and regularly participate in activities of the groups with which they identify.[12] Depending upon criteria employed, the politically important activists are seen to be minorities of a few per cent to about one-sixth of their society.[13] The great bulk of individuals are much more concerned with primary group relationships outside or even inside formal organisations than they are with the larger, society-wide goals of institutions of which they are aware, but with which they are only intermittently and superficially involved.

The non-political significance of a formally political act is better understood if one follows out the full implications of the Michigan dictum: 'Our approach is in the main dependent on the point of view of the actor.'[14] The language of political science unfortunately leads us to narrow our attention from the multiplicity of an individual's roles when we speak of him in terms of one relatively minor and intermittent role, that of 'voter'. The word 'voter' refers to an abstraction, just as much as does the term 'economic man'. The chief social roles of an individual are those of spouse, parent, relative, wage-earner, friend, etc. For most individuals, though not for activists, the role of 'citizen or 'subject' is likely to be of little significance; the very limited obligation of his role as voter exhausts his commitment to activity within the political sub-system of society. It would thus be much more accurate and only a little cumbersome if, instead of writing about voting behaviour, we wrote about the behaviour of ordinary individuals in electoral situations.

[12] Cf. data in Michael Argyle, *Religious Behaviour* (London: Routledge, 1958), especially chs 2–4, and Martin Harrison, *Trade Unions and the Labour Party Since 1945* (London: Allen & Unwin, 1960), ch. 3, with Richard Rose, *Politics in England*, ch. 4. Roman Catholics are an exception to this generalisation, but it is worth noting that the Church like some political parties determined to secure very high voting turnout, claims influence upon the totality of an individual's social relationships.

[13] For comparative data, see the special issue on political participation of the *International Social Science Journal*, XII i (1960).

[14] Angus Campbell *et al.*, op. cit. pp. 27 ff.

# THE BUREAUCRAT AND THE ENTHUSIAST

*By* John P. Roche *and* Stephen Sachs

The familiar statement that it takes all kinds of people to make a political party would be better stated in the following form: many different political roles must be filled within a political party. There is a need for different and complementary styles of behaviour within a party, rather than a need for random variations in behaviour. This is particularly true of an organisation such as the Labour Party, which has sought to combine many of the emotionally arousing characteristics of a movement and the pragmatic features of an election-winning, office-holding organisation. Roche and Sachs' study clearly shows how individuals in the contrasting roles of bureaucrat and enthusiast have interacted during the first fifty years of the party's history.

The quest for historical uniformities is a dangerous game, and one which generally reveals more about the preconceptions of the observer than about the historical process. The historian, alas, is denied even the camouflage of numbers, which so often permits the social psychologist to portray his hunches as 'science', and he is fair game for countless safaris of cultural anthropologists who are prepared to fire instantly at any suggestion that, say, Zulus have anything in common with Japanese, or Americans with British. Historical speculation, unless cloaked with the rites of numerology, has clearly been consigned to the province of journalists, mystics, and fakirs.

To say this is not to endorse for a moment all that has been done in the name of history. On the contrary, it is patent that historians have brought much of this obloquy upon themselves by their oracular pretences, by their unfortunate tendency to confuse insight with 'fact'. Yet, admitting both the uncertain nature of the data and the imperfections of the analyst, the student of politics can learn much from the perusal of history. The specialist in public administration who neglects — to use but one example — Philip Woodruff's superb *The Men Who Ruled India*, deprives himself of an invaluable fund of information and insight, and the student of social theory can simi-

Reprinted in full from the *Western Political Quarterly*, VIII ii (1955) 248–61, where it appeared with the sub-title 'An Exploration of the Leadership of Social Movements'.

larly find in historical and biographical studies an enormous body of significant data.

It is in this spirit that we have prepared this brief analysis of leadership types. The technique applied deserves explanation: we have in the text advanced a series of generalisations which are largely, though not exclusively, based on an intensive case-study of the history of the British Labour party. Because we have attempted to keep the generalisations in the text general, the footnotes are unusually elaborate — constituting, in effect, another article. We should like to make it clear that the hypotheses suggested here are not put forth under the *imprimatur* of science, although we feel that they may have utility in the examination of organisations as different as political parties, churches, and labour unions, we make no claim to universal validity. Furthermore, we assert no copyright on the ideas incorporated herein; other scholars, better equipped than we, have conducted forays of a similar type into the nature of organisational leadership, and we have profited from their explorations. Moreover, the classic exposition of our thesis is Dostoevski's symbolic *tour de force*, 'The Grand Inquisitor'.

The examination of social movements which seek public support for their political, social, or religious objectives suggests that there is a tendency for two major leadership types to emerge. Their specific characteristics may vary greatly with the cultural context or with the type of goal towards which the organisation is oriented, so that precise definition is elusive. Yet, granted this elusiveness, we feel that a meaningful typological distinction can be made, and we have designated the two leadership types the 'bureaucrat' and the 'enthusiast'.[1] To forestall the criticism that we are indulging in psychological monism, we should state at the outset that one individual can, in varying social situations, display the characteristics of both, i.e., he can perhaps be a bureaucrat in his union and an enthusiast in his religion. But in any one context, the pattern of behaviour tends to remain constant and is thus subject to generalisation.

The bureaucrat, as his name implies, is concerned primarily with the organisational facet of the social movement, with its stability, growth, and tactics. To put it another way, he concentrates on the organisational means by which the group implements and consolidates its principles. He will generally be either an officeholder in the organisation or interested in holding office. While he may have

[1] Our 'bureaucrat' is a first cousin of Max Weber's bureaucrat, sharing many of the latter's characteristics. Our 'enthusiast' is on loan from theological studies where he has had a long and tumultuous career; cf. Mgr Ronald Knox, *Enthusiasm* (London: Oxford University Press, 1950).

strong ideological convictions, he will be preoccupied with the reconciliation of diverse elements in order to secure harmony within the organisation and maximise its external appeal. He seeks communication, not excommunications.

In contract, the enthusiast, seldom an officeholder,[2] and quite unhappy when in office, concerns himself primarily with what he deems to be the fundamental principles of the organisation, the ideals and values which nourish the movement. No reconciler, he will concentrate on the advocacy of these principles at the risk of hard feelings or even of schism.[3] While the bureaucrat tends to regard the organisation as an end in itself,[4] to the enthusiast it will always remain an imperfect vehicle for a greater purpose. Whereas

[2] The British Labour party's bureaucrats generally centre in the party Executive and the Parliamentary Labour party, notably in the contingents supplied to each of these bodies by the trade-union movement. The enthusiasts formerly rallied around the standard of the affiliated Independent Labour party (I.L.P.) and upon its disaffiliation migrated to the Socialist League. Since the latter was disbanded, there has been no nesting place organisationally, but functionally the enthusiasts can always be located in the Constituency Labour parties and can be spotted ideologically by their vigorous support for Aneurin Bevan. They constitute the readership of the journal *Tribune* and of the *New Statesman & Nation*, and are at present busy learning Chinese.

[3] For instance, Stafford Cripps' work for the constitution of a popular front with the Communists and other 'anti-fascist' organisations which led in 1939 to his expulsion from the party. Cripps, of whom Churchill once observed: 'There, but for the grace of God, goes God', never faltered for a second in his labours for this cause and, secure in his conviction that it was just, accepted expulsion as the stigma which proved it.

[4] The bureaucrat *par excellence* of the Labour party was Arthur Henderson, longtime party secretary and foreign minister in the 1929–31 government. A good example of the bureaucratic preoccupation with organisation and reconciliation was the preparation by Henderson of the 1918 party constitution, a masterpiece of organisational ingenuity; see G. D. H. Cole, *A History of the Labour Party from 1914* (London: Routledge, 1948) pp. 44 ff. Henderson was severely criticised for not leading opposition to Ramsay MacDonald during the 1929–31 period, when it appeared to many that the Prime Minister was ignoring party policy, but to do so would have run contrary to Henderson's bureaucratic loyalty. As Cole puts it, Henderson 'in that crisis . . . made . . . too many . . . concessions in the hope of holding the Party together' (Cole, op. cit. p. 305). Henderson, of course, never dreamed that MacDonald would desert the party. Postgate's description of Henderson after that sad event is illuminating in this context: 'Henderson seemed shrivelled and bowed, and his usually ruddy face was yellow. Disloyalty was a thing he could not understand. He had given his most unswerving support to the handsome, eloquent leader who had helped him build up the movement; he had never allowed himself to be influenced by the fact that he had not in his heart liked MacDonald and had more than once received discourtesy from him. Now that man had deserted the people in its greatest misery. He could not understand, though he would try to forgive; he looked like a man who had been given a mortal wound.' Raymond Postgate, *George Lansbury* (London:

the bureaucrat is likely to equate 'The Cause' with its organisational expression, the enthusiast, with his fondness for abstraction, identifies it with a corpus of principles.[5]

Several other typical characteristics emerge from this fundamental difference in outlook. Outstanding among them is the varying attitude towards compromise in policy matters. The bureaucrat approaches a policy question with a predisposition towards harmony; he is prepared to compromise in order to promote unity and cohesion within the organisation and to broaden its external appeal. He considers policy, if not a mere expedient with which to build up organisational strength, no more than a flexible expression of intentions which can be modified as required by 'practical' needs.[6] However, to the enthusiast policy is far more than a 'political formula'. far more than a sonorous exposition of attractive, organisation-building slogans; on the contrary, he insists that policy must be the undiluted expression of first principles.[7] The bureaucrat specialises in studied ambiguity; the enthusiast, in credal precision. In short, while the former looks upon policy statements as something less than ex cathedra pronouncements of the whole 'Truth', the latter views policy as the living Word and considers compromise as not only wrong, but also evil.[8]

The same approach to compromise is evident in attitudes towards

---

Longmans, Green, 1951) pp. 271–2. Cole elsewhere notes Henderson's identification of the cause and the organisation (op. cit. p. 305).

[5] To understand this approach, a reading of the various studies by Archibald Fenner Brockway is invaluable. See his *Socialism over Sixty Years* (London: Allen & Unwin, 1946); *Inside the Left* (London: The New Leader, 1942); and *Bermondsey Story* (London: Allen & Unwin, 1949). Brockway was a paladin of enthusiasm and his various crusades, and those of the men he chronicles, against the party leadership make exciting reading. One is struck with the resemblance to *Pilgrim's Progress*, for he is transported to a world populated by moral 'forms', and the perils of Socialist (the Christian of Brockway's epics) are frightful to behold.

[6] For an exhaustive treatment of this theme see Robert Michels, *Political Parties* (Glencoe, Ill.: The Free Press, 1949), and Gaetano Mosca, *The Ruling Class* (New York: McGraw-Hill, 1939). It is also discussed by Max Weber in his essay on 'Bureaucracy' in H. H. Gerth & C. W. Mills, eds, *From Max Weber: Essays in Sociology* (New York: Oxford University Press, 1946).

[7] For example, George Lansbury's 1926 motion to 'abolish the Navy by discharging 100,000 men', Postgate, op. cit. pp. 236–7 as distinct from the regular Labour motions in favour of disarmament in the abstract. See also the I.L.P. position on 'the cruiser issue' in 1924 (Brockway, *Inside the Left*, p. 156).

[8] The I.L.P. split from the Labour party on precisely this point. The I.L.P. Members of Parliament demanded the right of private judgment, asserting that an MP should vote on the merits of a proposal rather than under party instruction. The Labour party, operating on the maxim *ex nihilo nihil*, refused to permit this and the I.L.P. disaffiliated. (Brockway, *Inside the Left*, p. 215;

membership: the bureaucrat is inclusionary, and holds a quantitative emphasis, while the enthusiast is exclusionary, desiring to limit the body of saints only to those full of grace.[9] That this problem of membership has plagued social movements from time immemorial hardly needs elaboration here; suffice it to say that the struggle between the inclusionists and the exclusionists, which inspired St Augustine's polemics against the Donatists as it does those of the Bevanites against Attlee, is a constant feature in ideologically oriented groups.[10] In particular, it plagues political organisations, for the bureaucrat here is characterised by an acute hypersensitivity towards the marginal voter,[11] while the enthusiast, with full confidence in the truth of his convictions, operates on the principle that if the people refuse to share his vision, so much the worse for them. To the latter, defeat at the polls means nothing; a moral totalitarian, his slogan is 'Damn the electorate! Full speed ahead!'[12]

---

Postgate, op. cit. p. 278.) The I.L.P. saw the MacDonald defection as the logical conclusion of moderation: 'Truly the policy of compromise has brought its reward.' (Brockway, *Socialism over Sixty Years*, p. 294.)

[9] This is a function of the perfectionism of the enthusiast and is a common feature of all enthusiastic political, social, or religious movements. A man can not be saved by 'good works', but only by true inspiration, which may or may not lead him to good works. The bureaucrat, essentially Niebuhrian in outlook, is prepared to settle for less on the assumption that while good works may be badly motivated, they are still preferable to bad works, however motivated.

[10] For a discussion of this aspect of the Donatist heresy, see Knox, op. cit., ch. iv. Actually the Donatists were never officially ruled heretics, but they were treated as such by Augustine and his bureaucratic descendants.

[11] According to Cole, MacDonald objected to the I.L.P.'s 'Socialism in Our Time' programme because 'it would only frighten the electorate and ensure a crushing Labour defeat' (op. cit., p. 198). In contrast the official 1929 programme was, according to the same authority, 'a moderate social reform programme, in which socialism found neither place nor mention. It was evidently drafted in contemplation of a result to the Election which, at best, might enable Labour to take a minority office with a stronger backing than in 1924.' (Ibid. p. 213.) Following the 1931 defeat, Lansbury wrote Cripps that Henderson wanted to 'trim our sails so as to catch the wind of disgust which will blow [MacDonald] and his friends out and that he is not anxious for us to be too definite about Socialist measures as our first objectives. Put them in our programme but be sure when we come to power we keep on the line of least resistance. . . .' (Postgate, op. cit. p. 208.)

[12] For instance, in both 1924 and 1929, in each case when the Labour party became a minority government, the I.L.P. sought to implement a radical programme, knowing that it would bring defeat in Commons. Such a defeat, they urged, would put to the country in stark terms the issue of socialism versus capitalism, and would arouse the working class to full militancy in the class struggle. See Cole, op. cit. pp. 157 ff., 210 ff., 218, 246, 281 ff.; Postgate, op. cit. pp. 225–6, 224; Philip Snowden, *An Autobiography* (London: Nicholson & Watson, 1934) II 592 ff.; Brockway, *Socialism over Sixty Years*, pp. 206 ff., 214, 229 ff., 253, 259 ff.

It is perhaps, therefore, valid to suggest that the bureaucrat seeks to extend the area of compromise; the enthusiast, the area of principle.[13] Although we are not asserting that the bureaucrat always flees from principle, nor that the enthusiast is inevitably a moral totalitarian, there is in our view sufficient evidence to justify the establishment of these positions as typical.[14] David Riesman, drawing on the insights of Ortega y Gasset[15] and Erich Fromm,[16] has suggested a similar hypothesis in different language.[17] Following his typology, we might say that the bureaucrat, conditioned and moulded by his intense awareness of, and concern for, the opinions of others, both within and without the organisation, is 'other directed'; whereas the enthusiast, whose actions and beliefs stem from a set of a priori principles, is 'inner directed'. In fact, bureaucratism and enthusiasm are the 'other directed' and 'inner directed' facets of the organisational personality.

However, there is one important qualification to the last generalisation which, while it narrows the scope of the thesis, serves also to highlight the fundamental difference in orientation of the bureaucrat and the enthusiast. The bureaucrat, a genial eclectic with respect to policy questions, becomes an uncompromising fighter when he feels that the sovereignty or organisational integrity of the group is menaced. The enthusiast, in his pounding pursuit of principle, is often prepared to compromise organisational integrity, to form 'Popular Fronts' or 'United Fronts' with those who share his ideological assumptions. Against this form of eclecticism, the bureaucrat will wage ruthless war, as he will against the common tendency of the enthusiast to build a faction, a party within a party. As the history

[13] As, for instance, when Jowett and Wheatley, ministers in the 1924 government, refused to wear morning dress on a visit to the King; Brockway, *Socialism over Sixty Years*, pp. 208–10; or when Brockway himself, on principled grounds, refused to attend a party given by Lady Astor (*Inside the Left*, p. 201). Surely the high point of this symbolic rejection was achieved by Dr Salter, a republican, who kept his hat by his bed so he could quickly put it on when the chimes of a nearby church played 'God Save the King' at seven in the morning. (Brockway, *Bermondsey Story*, p. 14.)

[14] That is to say, definable types. Obviously, a man may have a mixed personality, may be enthusiastic with respect to some things and passive about others. But this differentiation is not important for our purposes; we are solely concerned with the relationship of these types to the operation of social movements. How an individual integrates the different facets of his personality is a problem for the psychiatrist and psychoanalyst.

[15] The distinction between 'mass man' and the 'aristocrat' developed in *The Revolt of the Masses* (New York: W. W. Norton & Co., 1932).

[16] The quest for autonomous personality which is the central theme of *Escape from Freedom* (New York: Rinehart & Co., 1941), and *Man for Himself* (New York: Rinehart & Co., 1947).

[17] *The Lonely Crowd* (New Haven, Conn.: Yale University Press, 1950).

of the Catholic Church's dealings with heresy will indicate, the bureaucrat is prepared to tolerate a wide range of viewpoints within the organisation so long as the viewpoints do not become organised factions, but once the enthusiasts raise the standard of organisational autonomy and attempt to institutionalise their ideas, tolerance ends and is replaced by war to the knife.[18]

To say this is not to impugn the motives of the bureaucrat, to assert that he is a self-seeking Machiavellian who consciously manipulates men and ideas in the effort to gain and maintain power. On the contrary, the significance of this typology lies in large part, at least in our view, in the fact that the bureaucrat *does not* deliberately plan his course. In fact, he often plans very badly what little he does plan, permitting enthusiasts to put organisational integrity in great jeopardy before he realises that a threat exists, and taking counter-action long after an effective Machiavellian would have gone into action. Thus, it is a cast of mind, a psychological pattern of reaction, rather than counsels of greed and guile that supplies the bureaucrat with his direction.

It is with this difference in fundamental attitudes that we must concern ourselves now. We make no attempt to discuss the factors that influence human behaviour in the directions of enthusiasm and bureaucratism except to note a dissent from any monolithic theory, any rigid determinism. What we are concerned with is not the 'Why?' but the 'What?' — and we shall limit ourselves to an exploration of the objective aspects of the problem, i.e., the pattern of action and belief that seems to be associated with our two types. Again we must caution that our remarks and definitions will not be applicable to all situations; rather, we are making probability statements which, although they may not subsume each individual case, have aggregate validity.

'Respectable, conventional, orthodox religion', wrote Emrys Hughes, an outstanding Labourite enthusiast, 'is something very different from the living faith. And that is also true of politics.'[19]

[18] This may be true even if the bureaucrat is in ideological agreement with the factionalists, a fact which greatly hindered certain C.I.O. unions in their struggle against communist domination. When an anti-communist district or local decided that secession was their best programme, no one could be more ruthless in fighting them than anti-communist bureaucrats who put their organisational loyalty above ideological considerations. See Vernon Jensen, *Nonferrous Metals Industry Unionism, 1932–54* (Ithaca, N.Y.: Cornell University Press, 1954), *passim*, for some classic examples of this manifestation in the Mine, Mill & Smelter Workers. For a similar French experience, see Val. R. Lorwin, *The French Labor Movement* (Cambridge: Harvard University Press, 1955) pp.125–7.

[19] Emrys Hughes, *Keir Hardie* (London: Lincolns-Prager, 1950) p. 5.

Following this line of demarcation, the bureaucrat is the 'respectable, conventional', and 'orthodox' churchman. The organisational structure, from which he gets profound satisfaction, and with which he identifies himself, exists concretely — he need only look about him or open his desk drawer to appreciate its reality. His patient, untiring, and probably publicly unrecognised labour has gone into its creation, and the stable security that it offers acts as an antidote to his insecurity. Like the men and women who refused to leave slum hovels during intense wartime bombing because these were 'home', the bureaucrat has a psychological commitment to the organisation that far outweighs any economic attachments. Thus, it may be predicted that the bureaucrat will be reluctant to depart from habitual and tested practices which have fostered the past growth of the organisation; he will assuredly take a dim view of experiments, although he will seldom oppose them frontally. He is the past master of the motion to delay.

In part because he is tradition-oriented, and in part because of the psychological make-up of his opposition, the bureaucrat tends to be anti-intellectual. The proportion of intellectuals among enthusiasts is often quite high, although it must be added that in situations where organisation and intellectualism have gone hand in hand, for example, in the Church of England, the enthusiasts may rally around anti-intellectualism and anti-rationalism of the crudest sort. But even given this qualification, the man who causes trouble in an organisation must attempt a respectable intellectual case for his position — indeed, in the twentieth century we have seen the irony of intellectuals building an intellectual foundation for anti-intellectualism![20] — and so the bureaucrat grows to look with suspicion on people who think too much, who are always popping up with new ideas. He is likewise suspicious of oratory and big meetings, where his hard-built discipline may tumble before the charismatic charm of an enthusiast-demagogue; his natural habitat is the committee room where even if a Messiah should reveal himself, he would not recruit more than half-a-dozen disciples. In short, the bureaucrat detests and fears unpredictability and the flamboyance with which the unpredictable often gird themselves; the road to his affection and trust is through hard work, patiently and undramatically executed, and acceptance of hierarchical decision-making.[21]

[20] Some of the German and Italian justifications for fascism, notably those of Schmitt and Gentile, fall into this category, as do certain contemporary French apologies for communism.

[21] The respect for 'channels' is very great in bureaucratic circles; indeed, one of the main complaints made against the enthusiast is his disregard for

Unlike the bureaucrat, the enthusiast has no tangible symbols to supply him with satisfaction and security; almost by definition, he must believe in the ultimate value of things unseen, and he is likely to scorn institutions as snares set to draw men from the paths of righteousness.[22] While the bureaucrat is an instinctive collectivist, holding as he does an almost Burkean view of the presumptive validity of tradition, the enthusiast is a militant individualist, prepared like Nietzsche's 'Super Man' to achieve self-fulfilment at whatever cost to the social fabric. If the bureaucratic personality is dominated by caution and fear of the unorthodox, the enthusiast is a captive of *hubris*, of cosmic egotism, and of blindness to the fact that 'Humanity' is not humanity. He lives in a world peopled by abstractions rather than by human beings, and it is quite possible for him to contemplate, in Koestler's phrase, 'sacrificing one generation in the interest of the next'.[23]

The ideals which the enthusiast seeks to realise, whether a glorious vision of heaven on earth, the resurrection of a romanticised past, or less ambitious versions of both, are hardly capable of attainment in this imperfect world; indeed, such is the nature of ideals. Yet, gripped by his Promethean quest, the enthusiast never ceases in his effort to storm heaven. Against the sceptical patience of the bureaucrat, he pits his passion and his chiliastic dedication; his is indeed a 'living faith'.[24]

---

them, his willingness to 'appeal to the movement' or to the 'people' against unpleasant decisions instead of patiently appealing to the various hierarchical bodies in the apparatus, through 'channels', for recourse. Much of Aneurin Bevan's unpopularity in the Labour party, notably among the trade-union potentates, was an outgrowth of his lack of respect for decisions collectively made, and his effrontery, as they see it, in appealing these to the wider constituency.

[22] This is particularly true of religious enthusiasts, who generally distinguish between true religion and the Church much as Jesus contrasted Judaism with the religion of the Pharisees. See Knox, op. cit. *passim*, and for some rather unFriendly polemics in this vein, *The Journal of George Fox* (Everyman ed.; New York: E. P. Dutton & Co., 1924).

[23] Koestler used this figure of speech in an address in New York some years ago. We have not seen it used in any of his works.

[24] Eric Hoffer observes: 'It is the true believer's ability to "shut his eyes and stop his ears" to facts that do not deserve to be either seen or heard which is the source of his unequalled fortitude and constancy. He cannot be frightened by danger nor disheartened by obstacles nor baffled by contradictions because he denies their existence. Strength of faith, as Bergson pointed out, manifests itself not in moving mountains but in not seeing mountains to move. And it is the certitude of his infallible doctrine that renders the true believer impervious to the uncertainties, surprises and the unpleasant realities of the world around him.' *The True Believer* (New York: Harper & Bros., 1951) pp. 78–9.

In the light of this analysis of the two polar types, it might be suggested that each makes a major, and vital, contribution to the organisation. Enthusiastic cadres supply it with its ideological dynamic, attempting to make it into a 'living faith', while the bureaucrat injects organisational stability and a sense of realism. In the same sense that each type contributes its assets to the group, each also donates its liabilities. From the viewpoint of sound organisation, let us now examine their respective contributions in the effort to ascertain what relationship between the enthusiast and the bureaucrat provides the firmest foundation for group success and organisational effectiveness.

The faith of the enthusiast may have negative consequences for an organisation in two significant regards. First, his firm belief in the basic articles of his credo may lead him to be dogmatic and doctrinaire and into unfortunate excesses. He frequently offends his non-enthusiastic brethren by the rigidity of his viewpoint,[25] as well as by his semblance of sanctimonious piety.[26] The enthusiast specialises in denouncing organisational shortcomings, falls from grace, so to speak, and this role, no matter how reluctantly or humbly it is performed, creates in the minds of listeners the impression that the speaker considers himself pure and uncontaminated, a saint calling upon sinners to renounce the wicked and their ways. Such homilies can arouse great resentment, and sometimes lead to internecine conflict and schism.[27] Externally, the enthusiast's inability to compro-

[25] When MacDonald entered the Dawes Plan negotiations, the I.L.P. demanded that he insist on the total abolition of German reparations and protested vigorously when all that emerged was a lightening of the German load. Brockway, *Inside the Left*, p. 152. Later, after MacDonald's defection while the regular Labour MPs were seething with hatred towards their former leader, the I.L.P. members aroused much indignation by their attitude of 'good riddance'. Brockway records that the others were 'indignant [at the I.L.P.] because we remained cool amidst their heated denunciations'. (Ibid. p. 217.) This attitude of 'we knew it all along' is calculated to win few friends, particularly since there was good reason to believe that the I.L.P. had been right for the wrong reasons.

[26] While Stafford Cripps was probably the leading candidate for canonisation, Aneurin Bevan has also been characterised as a 'Jeremiah, Cassandra, and guardian of the Holy Socialist tablets'. Vincent Brome, *Aneurin Bevan* (London: Longmans, Green, 1953) p. 202. The I.L.P.'s conspicuous asceticism and its refusal to participate in the gayer side of Parliament irked many Labour MPs, who looked upon these enthusiasts much as a well-fed Benedictine monk probably reacted to a flagellant friar in an earlier epoch. (Brockway, *Inside the Left*, ch. 22.)

[27] Thus, the I.L.P. attitude towards MacDonald, and their self-congratulatory pose when he 'sold out', led to a hardening of relationships between the I.L.P. and the Labour party. The fact that the enthusiasts had been objectively 'right' in their analysis, far from bridging the schism that had been

mise his principles, and the vigour with which he presses them, is likely to alienate potential organisation supporters of moderate views, even if the organisation does not accept his doctrines.[28]

A second unfortunate consequence of the enthusiast's 'living faith' is that it warps his own judgement. With his fervour and sense of righteousness, he can easily become a prisoner of his own presuppositions with the result that the actual world becomes a handmaiden of his abstractions.[29] Moreover, the more tenaciously the enthusiast embraces his a priori's, the more he loses sight of the pluralism, the diversity, and the complexity of the universe, and the more likely will he be to subscribe to a conspiracy theory which will ascribe his failure in rallying public support to a sinister plot, to a devil.[30] The consequences of such flights from reality can be quite serious, for not only do they hinder the enthusiast from fulfilling his proper calling, but they also lead to a weakening of public confidence in the organisation.[31]

But, while he creates great problems for an organisation, the enthusiast can make an enormously significant positive contribution. In the first place, he suplies a vigour, stemming from his convictions,

widening throughout the 1929–31 Labour government, made them absolutely unbearable in the view of the average Labour member. Indeed, the I.L.P. fought the 1931 election as a separate party, although it did not formally disaffiliate until 1932. See Brockway, *Socialism Over Sixty Years*, chs 15–17; *Inside the Left*, chs 20–2; Cole, op. cit. pp. 274–5.

[28] The Labour party Executive, for instance, went to great lengths in the late '30's to 'disassociate itself' from certain radical positions taken by the Socialist League which the anti-Labour press had characterised 'as revealing the "real mind" of the Socialists'. (Cole, op. cit. p. 298.)

[29] This is particularly true of the enthusiast's approach to war, and to international relations in general. Rejecting concrete alternatives, he may generally be found clinging to a 'third position', which, if only implemented, would avoid the dangers of war, oppression, starvation, misery, etc., latent in the other viewpoints. Thus, in recent years, Labour enthusiasts have raised the slogan: 'Neither Washington nor Moscow', and have attempted to build 'third force' sentiment around Jugoslavia and, more recently, India. See Leon D. Epstein, *Britain: Uneasy Ally* (Chicago: University of Chicago Press, 1954), *passim.*

[30] A classic instance of this devil theory in action was the enthusiast's explanation for the failure of the General Strike of 1926. Although it is quite clear that the strike was a failure because the average worker was unprepared to become a revolutionary, and or display a willingness to start a revolution and the strike had no place to go, the enthusiasts claimed that the 'revolutionary will of the Proletariat' had been betrayed by the union leadership. (Brockway, *Inside the Left*, pp. 192–3.) MacDonald's 1931 defection was, in similar fashion, attributed to Wall Street machinations. (Postgate, op. cit. pp. 270–2.)

[31] See John P. Roche, 'The Crisis in British Socialism', *Antioch Review* (Winter 1952–3) for a discussion of the consequences of Bevanism on the public view of the Labour party.

which is the *sine qua non* of effective organisation. Paradoxically, it is this vigour and willingness to work for 'The Cause' which forms the foundation of the bureaucratic apparatus. Beyond this, his originality, initiative, and flamboyance, the characteristics which frighten and unsettle the bureaucrat, serve as a stimulant and tonic to the whole movement, and act as an effective and necessary antidote to the traditionalism of the bureaucrat.[32] His idealism and faith contribute an *élan* and a courage, encouraging the movement to expand its horizon and strike out boldly for new worlds to conquer. Indeed, if we believe with Max Weber that only by reaching out for the impossible has man attained the possible, it is the enthusiast who may bring the movement to the fullest realisation of its own potentialities.[33] Thus, the enthusiast injects idealism into hard organisational reality and brings to the movement a priceless leaven.

The second, and equally significant, contribution of the enthusiast is the moral tone which his presence lends to organisational action. His fundamentalism, his very refusal to come to terms with immorality, his frequently prophetic assertion of basic values and aspirations, make him the conscience of the movement, the voice which calls it back to the ways of righteousness.[34] It is this Messianic function of the enthusiast which can serve to counteract the ideological myopia of the bureaucrat, and the latter's tendency to compromise his ideals to the point of extinction.[35] Furthermore, the spirit of self-sacrifice which is characteristic of the 'true believer', to use Eric Hoffer's phrase, is a wholesome antidote to the opportunism of the bureaucrat.[36]

While anyone who has read widely in the history of enthusiasm tends to sympathise with the bureaucrat in his endless conflict with

[32] The valuable function that the I.L.P. played in creating and stimulating the Labour party is emphasised by G. D. H. Cole, *British Working Class Politics, 1832–1914* (London: Routledge, 1946) pp. 250 ff. Henry Pelling, in his excellent study *The Origins of the Labour Party, 1880–1900* (London: Macmillain, 1954), credits the energy of the Socialists with much of the success in creating an independent working class party.

[33] Max Weber in 'Politics as a Vocation', op cit.

[34] This was manifestly the outstanding contribution of George Lansbury to his beloved party, as Postgate's excellent biography makes clear.

[35] As, for instance, was the case with the French Socialist deputies who voted *pleins pouvoirs* to Pétain in 1940, or with the German Socialists who became militant chauvinists in 1914 and turned the *Freikorps* on the *Spartakusbund* after the war. See the bitter critique of the latter by Eduard Bernstein, discussed in Peter Gay, *The Dilemma of Democratic Socialism: Eduard Bernstein's Challenge to Marx* (New York: Columbia University Press, 1952).

[36] For a discussion of this spirit of self-sacrifice and its ramifications, see Hoffer, op. cit. ch. 13.

'wild men', it must be realised that the bureaucrat too has his limitations. Caution and moderation can easily become sluggishness and inaction, and the bureaucrat's dedication to the organisational structure can lead him to an almost paranoidal suspicion of all proposals which involve change.[37] In addition, the collective anonymity of the bureaucracy can encourage an assembly-line approach to the problems of the membership, a depersonalisation of the group's function which it is extremely difficult to counteract. 'Rank and file' protests he dismisses scornfully as the work of disgruntled, disappointed office-seekers because he is incapable of spontaneous action himself and projects his own personality upon the organisation.[38]

But probably the bureaucrat's greatest drawback is his inability to dream the enthusiast's dreams, his fundamental lack of empathy. His concentration on organisational problems may lead him to ignore policy and particularly to overlook the relationship between policy and principle.[39] Although, as was suggested earlier, this attitude is seldom founded on conscious Machiavellianism, he often comes to the point where he considers a policy question essentially as an organisational gambit: 'What do we stand to gain from it?'

[37] Robert Michels has given this ample treatment in his *Political Parties*, cited earlier. The German Social Democrats, who have always suffered from an acute case of over-bureaucratisation, supply the best examples of this mentality in action. Of course, because he feels that the bureaucracy is not representative of the true feelings of the movement, the enthusiast is perpetually crusading for structural changes that 'will increase grass-roots democracy'. The French Socialists have been so successful in this that they have fallen off the other side of the bed; see Philip Williams, *Politics in Post-War France* (London: Longmans, Green, 1954) pp. 60–76.

[38] As is usually the case in a trade-union under similar circumstances, the bureaucrat, faced with 'rank and file' opposition, inquires cynically, 'Whose rank and file?' Similarly, the possibility that two or three people could arrive spontaneously at the same viewpoint never enters his head; his immediate reaction is 'They have a caucus'. As a projection of the bureaucratic personality, with all its paranoidal trappings, upon a society, the Moscow Trials have never been equalled. Arthur Koestler implicitly makes this point in *Darkness at Noon* (New York: Macmillan, 1941) when Rubashov, a bureaucrat, is hoist by his own bureaucratic petard. See also Victor Serge, *The Case of Comrade Tulayev* (Garden City: Doubleday, 1950).

[39] Cole suggests that the Labour government was deluded in its notion that it had triumphed in its defeat of the Mosley manifesto in 1930–1; it might have given this statement far more serious consideration and profited from some of its suggestions. Cole, op. cit. p. 258. As it was, the party's handling of the unemployment crisis bore no visible relationship to the principles advanced by socialists; a capitalist government would probably have acted no differently. See Adolf Sturmthal, *The Tragedy of European Labor* (New York: Columbia University Press, 1943), for a discussion of the socialist dilemma of whether to ameliorate or to eliminate capitalism.

Similarly, his dislike for policy formulations which may offend potential supporters can lead to wishy-washy pronouncements which, far from assuaging discordant elements, only aggravate them further and leave nobody happy.[40] In short, the bureaucrat, preoccupied with organisational politics, may treat policy much too lightly and, in his willingness to compromise both policy and principle for the sake of organisational strength, may destroy the ideals and values which the movement was formed to advance, its very *raison d'être*.[41] If the dangers of enthusiasm stem largely from a rigid maintenance of principle regardless of organisational consequences, the abuses of bureaucratism flow from its hyperconcern for organisational consequences and its callous disregard for the movement's fundamental spiritual values.

Yet, with all his defects, the bureaucrat, too, makes a precious contribution to the success of the movement. First, by his scepticism about the authoritative nature of the enthusiast's revelation, he provides psychological ballast; his assumption, in George Orwell's brilliant phrase, 'that Saints must be presumed guilty until proved innocent'[42] helps to keep reason in control and inhibit potential Peter the Hermit's from dragging the group into some disastrous charismatic crusade. Against the monism of the enthusiast and the devil theories that so often accompany it, he raises the standard of common sense, asserting that men are men and not abstractions of good and evil. Where the enthusiast is optimistic about man in the abstract, but pessimistic about man in the concrete, the bureaucrat takes the world as he finds it and judges men as men, rather than as 'Man', whom he has never met and probably never worried about.

Second, the bureaucrat's agnosticism and nominalism — his rejection of the enthusiast's true faith and abstract man — combine to make him profoundly suspicious of short-cuts; he is likely to be satisfied with piecemeal progress, scorning as fatuous and unrealistic the 'all or nothing' approach which is so characteristic of the enthusiast. 'Half a loaf is 50 per cent better than no loaf,' he submits,

[40] The history of the Italian Socialist party supplies superb examples of the failure of this tactic; the centrists, known variously as 'integralists' or 'unitarians', regularly worked out compromises which aggravated both the left and the right wings and, if anything, exacerbated internal tensions. See W. Hilton-Young, *The Italian Left* (London: Longmans, Green, 1949).

[41] See, for instance, the flip-flops, rationalised in terms of principles, which various socialist leaders performed on the war issue in 1914; Merle Fainsod, *International Socialism and the World War* (Cambridge, Mass.: Harvard University Press, 1935).

[42] In his 'Reflections on Gandhi', in *Essays by George Orwell* (Garden City, N.Y.: Doubleday-Anchor Books, 1954).

'and tomorrow we can go after the other half.'[43] To this end, he builds his cadres, convinced that ideals are no stronger than the organisation engaged in institutionalising them, and that organised pressure, not doctrinal purity, is the key to success.

Indeed, it is this dedication to technique, to means, which is the bureaucrat's supreme gift to a movement. It is he who builds the instruments of social action, the structural machinery necessary to channel, concretize, and implement the group's aspirations, and it is he who puts organisational flesh on the bones of theory. Denied the vision of the enthusiast, sneered at by the high-flying intellectual, he spends his life in the quagmire of detail, and in so doing renders a unique and invaluable service to his cause. While the enthusiast is out exploring the nature of the cosmos, the bureaucat is repairing the mimeograph machine; yet, who will deny that a well-working mimeograph is as essential as correct doctrine to the effective operation of a social movement?

Thus, both the bureaucrat and the enthusiast supply a movement with vital components. Each by himself works badly; left alone, the bureaucrat simply goes in concentric circles around his precious organisation, while the enthusiast rushes unsheathed from one ideological orgasm to another. Consequently, a healthy vital social movement needs both, and profits from their complementary assets. True, there will always be conflict, for to the bureaucrat, the enthusiast—'impatient', 'emotional', 'dogmatic', 'sanctimonious' —will always *ipso facto* remain a threat to the organisation; and to the enthusiast, the bureaucrat—'timid', 'opportunistic', 'cynical', 'manipulative' —will always seem indifferent to, if not subversive of, the very ideals and values from which the enthusiast draws his inspiration. But this conflict, inevitable as it is, is by no means a mere disruptive influence; on the contrary, it is a life-giving dialectical process in which each force counters the weaknesses of the other and from which a movement can emerge with both dynamism and stability.

The history of social movements is the history of this conflict. On the one hand, we find groups, such as the German Social Democratic party of 1900–14, or the American Federation of Labor of 1900–37, which have been stricken with bureaucratic paralysis and have lost all power to move. On the other, we see those movements, such as the French Socialist party of our era, or the Puritan left of Cromwell's time, which disintegrated, or are in the process of disintegrating from the unchecked centrifugal force of enthusiasm triumphant.

[43] This conflict between the 'possibilists' and the 'impossibilists' has been endemic in socialist movements (see Sturmthal, op. cit. *passim*) as well as in religious organisations (see Knox, op. cit. *passim*).

These are the extremes, for we can also find organisations which have moved on from generation to generation, expanding their horizons as they go, because they have attained a proper balance between these two forces. How this balance is struck is the subject of another analysis; suffice it here to conclude that the struggle between bureaucratism and enthusiasm is part of a larger canvas on which similar battles, between security and freedom, realism and idealism, means and ends, passion and perspective, are waged, and in which the outcome is likewise determined by the extent to which factors which are logically irreconcilable are reconciled.[44]

[44] 'Passion and perspective' are the criteria submitted as central to political analysis by Max Weber in his 'Politics as a Vocation', in Gerth and Mills, op. cit.

# SEVEN CHARACTERS IN COMMITTEE WORK

*By* Sir Kenneth Wheare

Committees are of great importance in co-ordinating the work of different government departments, and in bringing together people in government and representatives of interests outside the ranks of established public officials. Formally, most committee members occupy statuses within a group lacking the well-defined offices and titles characteristic of cabinet government and of the civil service everywhere. Informally, as Sir Kenneth Wheare's study shows, these committees involve a number of recognised roles. Experienced committeemen become adept at recognising the varied role expectations suited to committee members, just as those who appoint committee members recognise the need to provide a roster of men who collectively can fill all the roles important in making a committee work. The committees also illustrate the importance of distinguishing between the *ex officio* identity of committee members and wide variations in their observable behaviour in political roles.

## I

Before we look at the way in which the different types of committee do their work, it is important to have some ideas of what the seven characters in committee work are like. It should be explained at the outset that a member of a committee may well combine in himself more than one of these characters; they are by no means mutually exclusive. A chairman may well be an official and an expert; a layman may be also a party man and an interested party. It is necessary none the less to distinguish the capacities in which members of committees may be acting, if we are to understand clearly the influences at work in committees. It should be emphasised also that these characters, or people acting in one or more of these capacities, may have influence upon or take part in committee work without actually being members of the committees. Their influence must be studied whether it is exercised in or upon committees.

Reprinted in abridged form from chapter II of *Government by Committee: an Essay on the British Constitution* (Oxford: Clarendon Press, 1955) pp. 12–42.

As we are studying committees which form part of the machinery of government in Britain, it is convenient to say a word first about the official. It is rare to find a committee in which the official is not concerned. He may be a member of a committee; he may be its secretary; he may be the servant through whom its decisions are executed; he may be a responsible officer of a department whose work a committee is to scrutinise and control; he may be the adviser of a minister in charge of a bill which a committee to legislate is considering; he may be a witness before a committee to inquire; he may be the means through which a department is seeking the assistance of a committee to advise. In any of these capacities we recognise the official who is a civil servant in central or local government. But officials are found outside the government service and these non-governmental officials take part also in committee work, whether as members or witnesses or chairmen or the like. Their status and responsibilities differ in some obvious ways from those of government officials, but they have also certain common characteristics which must be kept in mind. It is well to say a little about them at this point.

An official is, as a rule, an administrator, an organiser, a manager. He is engaged in running something. He is usually doing this as part of an organisation, for, as his name implies, he is part of an 'office'; he is an office man. One characteristic of an office is hierarchy. It is an organisation of people on the principle of superiors and subordinates, each with his allotted sphere of work, each reporting above and overseeing below. It involves the notion of a disciplined organisation, with loyalties inside itself, between chiefs and subordinates and within one division or section as against another, and to the whole office as against the outside world. The official has a place in this hierarchy. He is responsible to his superiors and for his subordinates. He has his allotted area of responsibility and his loyalty to the office. He has prospects of promotion.

From this hierarchical nature of the office a second characteristic tends to show itself. The work of offices comes to be organised into certain prescribed procedures or modes of operation or routines. This is unavoidable if the proper duties are to be performed at each level, if those above are to be enabled to take decisions upon matters when they are ready for decision and not before, and if some relationship is to be kept between decisions. This predilection for working through prescribed procedures is a characteristic of any office where more than two or three people work. It often irritates those who have to do business with offices and more particularly with government offices. It is a feature of office work which can be carried to excess, so that the forms of work are placed before the work itself. An excessive devotion to prescribed forms and procedures is described as 'red tape' and it is an occupational disease to which officials are always liable.

A third characteristic of the office is that we think of officials as appointed and not as elected. This characteristic also is linked with the notion of hierarchy, for the principle of election would work against hierarchy. The whole idea of hierarchy depends upon superiors having the powers to appoint and promote their subordinates. If people held office by virtue of being chosen by some outside body to whom they were responsible and to whom they looked for reappointment, the relationship between people in an office would be changed fundamentally from what we understand by an office. When, as in this country and in others where representative or popular government operates, the heads of offices or departments are elected or are chosen from elected persons, they are always regarded as distinct from officials and their function is commonly supposed to be the control of the officials.

If officials are appointed and not elected, it is natural that their tenure should be conceived of as more secure than that of elected persons. A part of the idea of the official in Britain is that his tenure is determined by his capacity and industry and not by his party affiliations. This principle, already taken for granted in business and industry, is accepted in government service also. The official, whether civil servant or not, is a 'career man'. Being a career man and being engaged full-time upon his work, he is supposed also to have some skill and knowledge in his subject. He is indeed a professional in both senses of that word — he is in the work as a career, and he is also not an amateur.

Finally, the official has, as a rule, a characteristic which he shares with committees — they are both sedentary institutions. Committees sit to carry out their work; there is no clearer sign that a committee is out of order than that some of its members are standing up or wandering about. So also with the official. We picture him, rightly, as at work in his office chair. He works at his desk; he manages and administers from his bureau. Perhaps from their sharing this common characteristic of being sedentary workers, committees and officials find it natural to work together.

It is obvious that not all officials possess all these characteristics or exhibit them all to the same degree. But it may be said that what is likely to strike non-officials on a committee in their dealings with officials are characteristics of this kind — their sense of hierarchy, of proper procedures and modes of doing business, their being appointed and not elected, their being permanent and not transient, their being professionals and not amateurs.

## II

When Walter Bagehot came to consider the official in his *English Constitution* he made this observation. 'The truth is', he wrote, 'that a skilled bureaucracy is, though it boasts of an appearance of science, quite inconsistent with the true principles of the art of business. . . . One of the most sure principles is that success depends on a due mixture of special and non-special minds — of minds which attend to the means and of minds which attend to the end.'[1] For this man of non-special mind Jeremy Bentham had a name. He called him 'the lay-gent'.[2] The word 'gent' is nowadays become facetious and in the plural peculiarly specialised, but we may occasionally use Bentham's term, with its quaint charm, to describe what is normally called in modern time the layman. Good administration, in Bagehot's opinion, was the product of co-operation between laymen and experts. He considered officials to be experts in this context and he claimed therefore that if we were to get the best out of officials, we must associate laymen with our officials.

The terms 'layman' and 'expert' need some explanation at the outset. They are essentially relative terms. They are relative to a subject or a field or part of a field of knowledge and they are relative to persons. Most people are expert in a few things; everyone is a layman in regard to most things. The mere notion of an expert, implying a specialised knowledge or skill in a limited field, carries with it the implication of the non-special mind in relation to other fields. The status of layman or expert will be accorded to an individual in relation to a given subject in a given situation. Thus a committee of experts may appear, from one point of view, to be a committee of laymen, for though each member is an expert in his own field, he may be a layman in regard to the field of the men sitting next to him. It is proper to ask then: Who are the experts and where are they to be found? And we shall be interested particularly in those experts who find a place on or around committees in British government.

It is commonly assumed, as Bagehot evidently assumed, that the official is an expert. The assumption arises from the fact that the relation we think of most, in considering the role of the official in

[1] p. 174 (World's Classics ed.).

[2] *On the Art of Packing Juries* (1821). See *Collected Works of Bentham* ed. Sir J. Bowring (11 vols, 1838–43) v 159.

committee work, is that between the ordinary elected person — the member of the House of Commons or of the local council — and the official. It is true that, as a rule, the elected person in this relation is usually a layman and that the official, considered in this relation, is not a layman. But must it follow that, if he is not a layman, he is necessarily an expert? An analogy from the terminology of the medical profession may help us here. Doctors are not all experts. Most of them are general practitioners, some only are specialists. Now it is true that, in relation to all doctors, be they general practitioners or specialists, most people are laymen; but we do not conclude from this that all doctors are experts.

When we look at the way in which offices are organised, both in the government and outside it, we find that, as a general rule, officials at the top or head of the office are not experts; they are usually general practitioners. This is in most cases a consequence of necessity, for those at the top must deal with a wider range of questions than those lower down and they are bound to be less expert. In British government and in a good part of British commercial and industrial organisations, it is indeed positively asserted that the officials at the top should be general practitioners and not experts. It is not thought odd or unusual to move the permanent head of the Ministry of Supply to be head of the Colonial Office or of the Ministry of Health. A high official of the Treasury is regarded as fit to be head of any department of government. It is general capacity — not specialised knowledge — which is encouraged by the recruitment and promotion policies of the British civil service. In local government, too, a town clerk, a chief education officer, or a treasurer are general practitioners. It is with officials at this sort of level that committees are usually associated and it will be common for them to find that they are dealing not with experts but with general practitioners.

If experts are rarely at the top of offices, they are rarely also at the bottom. Citizens who have been brought into contact with officials in the years since 1939, when so much of the economic life of the country has been subject to control by officials, have formed the opinion at certain times that they know a great deal more about these things than do the officials that deal with them. Even if officials higher up may have some technical knowledge of the subject under control, those lower down, dealing with the public at the office counter, are almost certain not to be expert. They are most likely to be laymen in relation to those with whom they have to deal. These subordinate officials usually concern committees only in so far as their work is carried out under the administration or the scrutiny and control of a committee, but it is none the less important to notice that they can usually lay no claim to the title of expert.

Which officials, then, are the experts? They fall into a number of groups. First of all there are those who may be called expert because they have committed to their charge a part of a department's work.

But there is another group of experts which is of a rather different kind. They are expert in some skill or technique or branch of knowledge which may have a reference to more than one section of the department's work and may be needed anywhere. The legal adviser is the best example of this kind of expert.

The work of some departments requires that the scientific and technical experts should be more than advisers to officials and should actually undertake administration themselves. The service departments, for example, and the Ministry of Supply staff certain of their branches with experts in armaments, surveying, building and construction work, and engineering, to name only a few. Most of these administrators would be unable to perform their tasks unless they had a specialised knowledge of the fields with which they deal.

Most of the experts of whom we have been speaking so far are administrative officials. But it would be misleading to suggest that the experts in the civil service are always administrators. On the contrary many thousands of those employed in the civil service who could be classed as experts are not engaged in regulatory work at all. They are in the civil service because the state has taken over direct responsibility for certain types of research and for the production of certain goods. The Atomic Energy Research Establishment at Harwell is a good example of this kind of organisation. It is predominantly an organisation of experts, some of whom are responsible for running it, but most of whom do not perform the administrative function. It is these scientific employees of the state who make up the greater part of the scientific civil service.[3] They far outnumber now the specialised inspectorial staffs or professionally qualified regulatory staffs which for a long time constituted the bulk of the technical experts in government service.

From the point of view of committee work it is apparent that these scientific experts who are not administrators are likely to be called upon for their services and should not therefore be disregarded in our analysis. They present special problems also, for in their contacts with laymen and with officials, more particularly with the general practitioners among officials, they find difficulty in presenting their views in sufficiently non-technical language or in the appropriate form to be effective. One of the problems in committee

[3] See Cmd. 6679 of 1945, *The Scientific Civil Service.*

work is to make the best use of the expert and in particular of those experts in the scientific civil service.

But let us remember in conclusion that not all experts are in the civil service. Experts outside government service are to be found, for example, on the various committees to advise that are associated with British government. Scientists, economists, statisticians, philosophers and historians, antiquarians, educationists, lawyers, doctors, architects, chemists, sit along with experts in, say, the retail trade, in the affairs of some trade union, or in the problems of some industry or branch of agriculture. These later types of expert belong also to the category of 'the interested party' of which more is to be said later in this article. It will be our concern when we study the layman in committees to consider how far Bagehot's judgement is still true that the co-operation of laymen with experts is essential to successful administration. The layman who sits upon committees concerned with British government is often an elected person, and the committees of the House of Commons and of local authorities contain laymen of this kind. But they may be appointed, like justices of the peace or certain lay members of committees to inquire or to advise; they may be co-opted, as certain members of local government committees are, or they may, like the laymen in the House of Lords, be partly elected (like the Scottish representative peers), partly appointed (as are peers when first created), and partly hereditary. Again, the layman on committees is usually unpaid (though his out-of-pocket expenses may be met) but sometimes he is paid, as are, for example, members of the House of Commons. The layman usually, too, is a part-time worker. Though he may, like some members of Parliament or town councillors, spend all his time at committee work, he will be obliged to cover so wide a field that he will be able to devote only part of his time to any one. This is usually why he is or remains a layman.

One mark of the good layman in church circles is that he is interested and concerned with church and religious matters. It is this characteristic which may first be mentioned as a mark of the good layman in committee work. A good layman on a committee is one who is, first of all, interested and concerned with the work of the committee. In this respect he must resemble the good layman in the church.

A second mark of the good layman has links with a second common use of 'layman'. This is not the ecclesiastical use of the term but the legal use. Just as there is a distinction between layman and clergyman, there is a distinction between laymen and lawyers, expressed in the House of Lords in the distinction between lay lords and law lords. But whereas the ecclesiastical distinction is not now based upon the distinction of learned and unlearned — though it was originally derived from it — the legal distinction is so based. It is the distinction between those who are unlearned in the law and those learned in the law. The layman is unlearned. But if that is all he is, he is not a good layman. He must be capable of understanding the issues put to him and of giving a judgement upon them. He may be ignorant but he must be educable. Lawyers do not expect justices of the peace to be experts in the law, but a good justice of the peace is one who can grasp the point of law which applies to the case before him and can apply it. It is recognised that he must be advised upon the law by one learned in the law — a legally qualified clerk — but to be a good lay justice he should be capable of understanding and following that advice. So also in committee work, the layman is not expected, by definition, to be the expert, but the good layman must be capable of grasping the issues as presented to him by the expert or the general practitioner. He must be capable of learning or of being taught.

A third mark of the good layman is suggested by experience in the world of business. It is the common practice for many undertakings in private enterprise and in public hands to associate lay directors with expert directors or administrators on the directing boards of these organisations. Not only banks and insurance and shipping companies but also a great technical undertaking like Imperial Chemical Industries Ltd.[4] find a place on their boards deliberately for lay directors. These lay directors, then, are often chosen because they have had experience and indeed are often experts in some other walk of life, whether in politics or in some allied field of industry or commerce. In other words it is thought that a good layman ought to be an expert in something and preferably in something relevant. This mark of the good layman may be expressed by saying that he ought to be knowledgeable. By definition he is not expert or even knowledgeable on the matter concerning which he is a layman, but he should know something or even a good deal about other matters and preferably cognate or connected matters. So in committee work the layman who is used to doing something thoroughly, is a master of some trade or business or profession or subject, is usually qualified thereby to learn and make judgements about matters upon which he is a layman. A Jack of all trades seldom makes a good layman in committee work.

[4] See *Large-Scale Organisation*, ed. by G. E. Milward (London: Macdonald & Evans, 1950), chapter by R. A. Lynex, Secretary of I.C.I., pp. 154–156.

It is not so much knowledge, however, which a layman is expected to bring to his work in committees as sense, common sense. He is to check the excesses of bureaucratic and expert nonsense by the application of his own common sense. It is not enough for the layman to be interested, to be educable, or to be knowledgeable. He cannot make the best use of these qualities unless he has qualities of mind and temperament which mark him out as the sensible or reasonable man. The 'reasonable man' is a well-known figure in English law. What he considers to be excessive, negligent, slanderous, or dangerous is decisive. He is an equally important figure in British public administration. This man of good sense and moderate views is part of the idea of a good layman in committee work.

But though reasonable and moderate, he must not be passionless. He must provide some of that questioning temper of the outsider, some of that impatience of rigid procedure and accepted methods which is expected of the lay-director in private business. He must approach his committee work with an original and a critical mind. He must animate or galvanise. It is difficult to get one word to describe this quality of a good layman. It is rather like saying that he must have all the virtues of the reasonable man and also all the virtues of the unreasonable woman. Indeed, some of the best laymen are women and unreasonable women at that. It is the quality — often associated, by men at least, with women — of being unable to see the sense in what is being done, of questioning the whole basis of organisation, of brushing difficulties aside, of ignoring logical argument, and of pressing a point beyond what most men consider a reasonable limit, which is required as part of the make-up of a good layman. It is against criticism of this kind that officials and experts should be required to justify their proposals and procedures in public administration. The reasonable man is not enough; we need the unreasonable woman also.

## III

It is important to say a word about the party man, one whose position in or around a committee is that of speaking and acting as a member or supporter of a party. When a man acts in that capacity he is a party man for the purposes of our discussion. He may have other capacities; in other situations his character as a party man may be irrelevant or unimportant. It is clear that a party man may be a layman; he may be an expert; he may be a chairman or he may be a partisan or interested party. In some situations one of these capacities of his may be of no less or of more significance than his capacity as a party man. In committee work the party man is not a separate and isolated character. He is often an aspect of the nature and function of a committee member, who may exhibit also other functions, as a layman or an expert or a chairman, and so on.

But it is necessary to pause for one moment and ask what is the relation of the party man to one other character in particular — the official. Here a more qualified answer must be given. In the first place it may be said that an official in private employment may be a party man. Managers, trade union officials, and the like take part in party politics and sit in Parliament or on local councils as party men.

When we come to consider the officials in the government service, more complicated considerations arise. Let us begin first with those employed by the central government, the servants of the Crown. Here the official is affected by a rule which applies generally to all civil servants whether they are officials or not. Civil servants are disqualified by statute from sitting in the House of Commons.[5] The statutory prohibition upon sitting in the House of Commons goes only a short way, however, towards regulating the activities of an official who might want to behave as a party man. Might he not stand for Parliament and resign if elected, or might he not campaign for the election of others? The proper behaviour of the official is not regulated by statute but by rules made by the Treasury or by departments. It is not easy to summarise the position,[6] but broadly speaking it may be said that certain officials — particularly those who work in the spheres where policy is determined and those who work in local offices of central departments and deal directly with the individual citizen in relation to his personal circumstances — are required in effect to abstain from political activities in the national field, though they are given permission where possible to take part in local government activities, subject to the exercise of discretion.[7] The officials with whom the committees we study are concerned are for the most part within the category of those excluded from political activities in the national field but permitted, subject to discretion, to take part in local politics.

This prohibition of party political activities to certain officials in British central government is well known. Let us consider just what it means. It does not mean that the official is expected to have no

[5] There are inconsistencies and obscurities in the law on this subject, but the general principle is undeniable.

[6] See *Report of the Committee on the Political Activities of Civil Servants* (Cmd. 7718 of 1949), presided over by Mr J. C. Masterman, and Cmd. 8783 of 1953, *Political Activities of Civil Servants*.

[7] The terms in which discretion is described are in Annex 2 of Cmd. 8783.

personal preference between political parties. He has a vote and he is assumed to be able to express his preference with no less ease than other men. Nor should it be assumed to mean that in his work he will have nothing to do with party. In a narrow and personal sense that is true, of course. He must not be working for a political party on his own account. But let it always be remembered that the official in the higher ranges of the civil service is always working, professionally and in his official position, with a party, the party in power. Most of what he touches has party implications. He shares in the formulation of the policies of a party government. His Minister is a party man. The official in Whitehall is expected to do all he can to make his Minister's policy successsful. His mistakes may lead to party troubles and even to the defeat of the party in power. He spends a great deal of time thinking of ways of answering the Opposition's criticisms, and many of these criticisms are party criticisms. He tries to protect his Minister, support him, and extricate him from difficulties. He is on the government side; he is out to help that side against the Opposition side. All this must be stressed when we say that the British civil service is outside party and that the official is not a party man.

What is really meant, perhaps, by saying that the official is not a party man is that he is not a one-party man. He is a government party man. He offers his best services to the party in power, to the government of any party. How far this is possible or desirable is a question often discussed. The record of the British civil service in this century shows that it has achieved this object to a very considerable degree. What is important here, however, is to stress that while the official in the civil service cannot be a party man, he works very closely with party men, and all that he touches is capable of party interpretation and party consequences. He is not above party. He is in the midst of parties and he is working in alliance, though only for the time being, with the party in power. The party man and the official are very closely associated and not least in committee work in modern British government.

This is not the place to ask whether the doctrine of British government that the party man must not be an official in the central and local government service is good or even whether it is found to work in practice. It is proper to point out, however, one limitation upon its working. It works on the assumption that the divisions between party men are such that people of ability, of power, and influence, in the higher civil service, can feel no sense of impropriety, futility, dishonesty, or disloyalty either to the state or to their party (if they have one) or to their consciences by working as hard as they can to execute the policy of one party and defend it against the Opposition and then reverse the roles completely when the Opposition becomes the government. It means that they must believe that party differences, though important, are not as important as all that.

## IV

To adopt the term 'interested party' to describe a wide and varied class of people has certain dangers. To begin with, it is a term which has a narrow and fairly well-defined connotation in the law, more particularly the law relating to local government, in the procedure of the courts, and in the procedure of Parliament. The rules of local councils provide, for example, that if a member is interested financially, directly or indirectly, in a matter before a council or its committees, he must declare that interest and take no part in the proceedings upon that matter. In the standing orders of the House of Commons on private bills a member whose constituency is locally interested or who is himself personally interested in a bill may not sit upon a committee dealing with that bill. So far as public bills are concerned, a member may not vote upon them if he has a direct personal pecuniary interest, but this is narrowly interpreted.[8] The existence of the interested party is thus recognised and in these particular cases certain steps are taken to see that his position as a member of a committee does not give rise to an abuse.

But although the idea of the interested party as embodied in the rules of local councils and of Parliament is fairly limited, it does not seem inappropriate to use it in an extended sense in this essay to cover all those who are closely identified with an organisation or a point of view and who, in this capacity, take part in British administration. The whole category of interested party will range from the man who is concerned in a contract to supply meat to a civic restaurant to the woman who is secretary of the parish branch of a pacifist society. Their position as interested parties is, like that of the expert, a relative position. The interested party raises special problems and questions. It would be foolish to act as if he did not exist. While it is not necessary to go to the length of regarding all interested parties as sinister, it is necessary to consider how best they can be made use of in public administration and what special opportunities or special obstacles should be placed in their way.

When we come to describe the nature of the interested party, we find that, like the expert, the members of this class fall into a num-

[8] See Erskine May, *Parliamentary Practice* (15th ed., 1950) pp. 418 ff.

ber of groups. The first kind of interested party is the man with the financial interest in, say, a government contract. Often he does not represent any organisation or association, though he may represent a firm. In many cases he is himself the interested party and his interest is clearly and demonstrably financial. There are, however, many cases of doubt in this relationship, where the interest is so indirect that it is not easy to say whether a man is an interested party or not. But the category itself is clear enough.

From this relatively simple case of personal or financial interest, we can pass to that large collection of organisations whose sole or primary object is the economic welfare of their members, the trade unions and other associations of employees. With them may be considered the associations of employers who are concerned with them in discussions about economic and financial affairs. There are, as is well known, thousands of associations of employees in Britain, organised locally, regionally, and nationally, and they are to be found in every industry, profession, and calling.

These organised interests are accepted in Britain and recognised as part of the constitution. Their right to express their views and to speak on behalf of their members is freely admitted and what is more is made full use of by government departments. One of the ways in which they are associated with administration is through committees, either by membership or by presenting their views. It must be emphasised that this is only one of their ways of being used by the government whether central or local. There are formal consultations and informal day-to-day dealings which are even more important than what is done through committees. Yet their value in relation to committees is very great. There is hardly an occupation upon which a committee could deliberate in this country for which there could not be found some union or association to represent and advocate the interests of those engaged in it.

It is well to add, perhaps, that an interested party may be an expert in his own affairs or in the affairs of the organisation he represents. There is nothing surprising in that, for almost by definition he cares very much about the matter in which he has an 'interest'. What is more significant, however, is that where organised interests are concerned, it is very common for them to be represented by officials, their own officials. In the trade unions and associations, both of employers and employees, in the professional associations and institutes, in the associations of local authorities with each other, in the voluntary bodies advocating some cause or opinion, there are officials as there are in the government. It is their job to maintain and strengthen the organisation of the interest concerned, and they deal with governments, local and central, as one official with another.

## V

No committee can do business without a chairman and a secretary. These two characters are its essential officers. The secretary, in the committees with which we deal, is usually also an official in the sense in which we are using this term. In committees to inquire, to advise, or to negotiate he is usually an official of the central government departments concerned; in committees to administer in local government he is the town or county clerk or some similar administrative official; in the committees of the House of Commons to legislate or to scrutinise and control he is an official of the House. In all these cases, however, he has a distinct function to perform as secretary of the committee and he must take care that his other loyalties and duties as an official do not overbear or distort his loyalty and duty to the committee. A secretary has indeed a distinctive and important position in relation to a committee. He is concerned to see that its business is transacted efficiently. He has a primary responsibility for preparing its agenda and for seeing that the material it needs for its deliberations is available to it at the right time and in the right form. He should be concerned to see that matters appear on its agenda when they are ready for consideration — not before and not after. He records and transmits a committee's decisions — a most important function. He is the channel through which people outside the committee deal with the committee. In all these functions he is the servant of the committee. He is not the servant or the subordinate of the chairman. The secretary and the chairman must work in co-operation, for there are many matters in which both are entitled to have a say, but they are co-ordinate officers of the committee. As a rule, in the committees with which we deal, while the chairman is a member of the committee, the secretary is not. Yet he has his own peculiar function as guardian and adviser of the committee, and on occasion indeed, as we shall see, he may be called upon to assert the rights of the committee or some of its members even against the chairman. That is why it is seldom wise for the same person to hold the office of chairman and secretary of a committee.

So far as the chairman is concerned he may well be one of the remaining five characters in committee work — an official, a layman, an expert, a party man, or an interested party. And, of course, he may be more than one for, as we have seen, they are not all mutually exclusive capacities. As a rule there is some reason in a particular type of committee why a chairman should or should not belong to one of these other categories. It is seldom a matter of complete indifference. If a committee is set up to adjudicate, for example, it will usually be right that the chairman should not be an interested party.

The status and influence of the chairman varies greatly from one type of committee to another and even within different examples of the same type. His position will be affected by a variety of factors — the function of the committee, the method of the chairman's appointment, where the responsibility for the leadership of the committee rests, and so on. Many illustrations of these variations will be encountered in later chapters. At this stage, however, it is interesting to see from what origins a chairman's authority comes.

The function of the office of chairman, put at its irreducible minimum, is to promote and maintain order. To this end it is agreed that, in a numerous body like a committee, the chaos that would come if members addressed each other at will or at random can be averted by providing that all remarks will be addressed to one person. Simple and obvious as it appears, this is the very foundation of order. The most elementary and elemental form of being 'out of order' is to direct one's remarks to someone other than the chairman. 'Please address the chair' is the cry both of those who love freedom of speech and of those who love order.

It is from this primary function of being responsible for order and from this unique position of being the target of all remarks in the course of a committee's work that a chairman's opportunities of leadership spring. To begin with, all questions are addressed to or through him. Soon he may find himself answering the questions, justifying the actions of the committee, perhaps justifying the actions of its officials, if it is an administrative committee. Soon the officials are supplying him with the answers to questions and criticisms and he may find himself acting almost like a minister defending actions which he comes to feel are his responsibility. Now it need not work in this way of course. A chairman can treat himself as no more than a channel through which questions pass to chief officials. But if he wishes to influence his committee, the opportunity often presents itself when questions are asked.

A chairman, too, is usually in a position to take the initiative. In a sense, and within very wide limits, he is never 'out of order'. A chairman thus has opportunities for intervention in a discussion which are denied to other members. He can always catch his own eye and he can choose his own moment for intervention. While the ordinary member of a committee may find it difficult to get an opportunity to speak more than once on a subject, a chairman, without actually making a set speech, may comment frequently as a discussion proceeds and in effect guide and influence the discussion. This influence flows naturally from the chairman's position as moderator or traffic policeman of the discussion, as its guardian of points of order.

A chairman's influence over discussions and decisions may be exerted also in his regulation of the proceedings. By his interpretation of what is in order and what is not, of what may be raised on a certain item of the agenda and what may not, of what line of argument is to be encouraged or discouraged, what questions pressed and what allowed to fade away, what motions and amendments accepted and what discouraged, deferred, or declined, a chairman can, within limits of course, influence the line of a committee's discussion. In the same way he has a certain discretion in calling upon other members of the committee to speak at an appropriate moment, and by allowing a member to open a discussion or to wind it up, or by calling upon a succession of speakers all of whom express the same views, he can influence the opinions of the committee as a whole. How often we hear the comment: 'Fortunately the chairman encouraged me', or 'Unfortunately the chairman gave me no help' — illustrations of the fact that, quite legitimately, a chairman may by the use of his discretion assist or retard some particular course of action. And it is for reasons of this kind that members of committees who have something to say — and officials also — are keen 'to have a word with the chairman beforehand'. Needless to say, what a chairman can do in this respect depends in the last resort — as do most actions of a chairman — upon what a committee will stand. They can limit or nullify him at any time if they have the will to do so.

A chairman's actions in the sphere of order will be influenced, too, in many cases by the advice of the secretary. It is commonly a secretary's function to be something of an expert on points of order — in standing committees of the House of Commons or in local government committees — and since many chairmen are not expert in those matters, a secretary's advice may have great weight. In this respect sometimes a secretary is defending the rights of committee members or is intervening on the side of the efficient conduct of business, and may have to assert his opinion against the wishes of the chairman. But here again, the chairman gives the ruling but the last word will be with the committee.

A chairman has an opportunity to lead his committee also because of the desire, natural in a presiding officer, to bring a discussion to a close and get the question settled. This desire is often strong in members of a committee also, and chairmen are urged to get a decision and 'give a lead'. It is undoubtedly part of a chairman's function to bring a discussion to a conclusion and not merely to allow it to come to an end. But it happens often that after a discussion, and quite a valuable discussion, no decision can be taken unless someone can draw out some acceptable proposal from the course of the discussion and place it before the committee for acceptance or rejection. This is an opportunity which a chairman may and indeed very often should take. He can bring the issue to a point and suggest a line of action. In some cases where it is not clear what course of action will commend itself to a committee, almost any proposition from the chair is valuable because it will help to clarify issues and indicate where an acceptable solution may lie. Action of this kind is not and of course need not be confined to chairmen. In many cases an ordinary member of a committee may act even more effectively than a chairman, or a chairman may intervene with his proposal more effectively after other members have tried their proposals. What is apparent, however, is that from his function as the conductor of the discussion a chairman may suggest solutions and in this way affect the course of policy.

This influence which the chairman exercises may be seen round the other way when a chairman who wishes, for some reason and conceivably for some good reason, to avoid or postpone a decision is able to use all his powers and influence to prevent the discussion being brought to a conclusion and to achieve an adjournment or a stalemate or a truce. A chairman's opportunities for leadership may be used with equal effect both in construction and in obstruction.

A chairman's readiness to exploit his opportunities of bringing the committee to a decision is increased by certain other factors. A chairman tends to get himself identified with his committee not only in his own eyes but in the eyes of his colleagues and of the public. Advisory committees and royal commissions tend to be known by the name of their chairman and their report is spoken of almost as his report — the Haldane Report, the Simon Report. Their success or failure is his success or failure. If they are not doing their work well, people say: 'What is wrong with the chairman? He should not allow his committee to go on like that.' It is 'his' committee. He will be anxious, therefore, that what they do or decide or advise should be something which he can approve and support and defend. His influence in this direction is assisted, too, by the practice, common in committees or commissions which are set up to produce a report, of the chairman producing a draft report for discussion by his colleagues.

A chairman's tendency to regard a committee as 'his' committee is increased by the fact that he acts for the committee on various occasions. He represents them, if they need representation. He is speaker on their behalf, whether it be in words of congratulation or condolence or whether it be in negotiation or in opposition to the claims or demands of other committees. In times of emergency, too, he usually acts on their behalf, seeking their confirmation for his actions later, while in normal times it is common for them to authorise him to act for them upon routine or even upon exceptional matters. In these and in many other ways the one is made to speak or act for the many.

It may be suggested, finally, that a chairman has an opportunity of influence from the fact that he is entitled to have some say in the drawing up of the agenda for a committee meeting — usually an important matter. There is often some argument about who should determine what shall and what shall not go on the agenda. There can be no doubt surely that the last word on this question must rest with a committee. It must decide whether or not it will deal with a particular topic. This is not universally admitted by all secretaries. But what is more important in practice is not who has the last word upon the construction of the agenda but who has the first. The sound practice would seem to be that the secretary should prepare the agenda; but that he should consult the chairman at the earliest stages on all but routine items so that the chairman may have an opportunity of giving his views. If a chairman wishes to add an item to the agenda, that item should be inserted by the secretary. If the secretary objects strongly to the inclusion of the item, it will be the chairman's duty to see that the committee, having heard the facts of the case, decides whether to proceed with the item or not. The last word here should be with the committee. A similar procedure should be followed if a secretary desires to insert an item on the agenda and the chairman objects. The item should be inserted and the committee invited to express its views and to decide the point. Similarly, any question or dispute about the order in which the items of the agenda should be taken — a question, sometimes, of considerable practical importance — must be determined in the last resort by the committee. A secretary may give his advice, a chairman may give his ruling, but the committee has the last word.

# ON BEING A CABINET MINISTER

*By the* Rt. Hon. Patrick Gordon Walker, MP

The pyramid structure of British government concentrates much governmental responsibility upon the individual cabinet minister. This is a double-edged feature of political life. A minister has considerable formal authority within his department, and, as a member of Cabinet, upon general considerations of government policy. Yet, by virtue of his several and important roles he is also expected to undertake many and varied time-consuming activities that do not directly relate to the work of his department. Patrick Gordon Walker, holder of four different cabinet posts, provides a first-hand account of how the roles of a cabinet minister — both political and non-political — bear upon the life of a minister.

## *Of Pounds and Pence*

It is still true — perhaps truer than it has ever been — that a Cabinet Minister with private means finds his job a good deal easier to do. The means *must* be unearned. Earning is strictly forbidden, whether as a journalist, employee, or company director. Dividends alone are above suspicion — even should the shareholding constitute a controlling interest in a concern.

In the eyes of the state (which applies very different standards from business, private or public) a Minister has all his proper financial needs taken care of. He has a car and driver at his disposal. Since he lives so near the edge of physical exhaustion, and has to be in so many places at once, any reasonable comfort of transport is rightly assumed to be in the public interest. After a brief, brave show of economy, the Conservative government has quietly restored a Minister's right to a car. But this right is by no means unrestricted. Parliament and the Treasury together make a very fussy employer. If a Minister uses his official car to go to the theatre or to a political meeting, even if his official engagements have kept him till the last moment, the cost is recovered from him at so much a mile at the end of the month. It is one of the jobs of his secretary to make out a proper return.

Reprinted in full from *Encounter*, no. 31 (Apr 1956) pp. 17–24.

It is also assumed — this time quite wrongly — that the public purse looks after all the entertainment that a Minister need engage in. Government hospitality arranges and pays for dinners and parties that he gives in his official capacity. And he is himself the subject of a great deal of entertainment. He has privileged access to splendid events and occasions in superbly appropriate settings. He meets the great ones of the world (amongst whom he is temporarily reckoned to figure) in palaces and great houses of state. He has also to attend innumerable cocktail parties and diplomatic functions and a series of practically identical annual dinners appropriate to his office — maybe of Commonwealth Clubs, Trade Associations, Local Authority Organisations, professional bodies, or City Companies. One of his problems is to frame an eating and drinking policy that is compatible both with courtesy and survival.

But there is one important segment of entertainment for which there is no provision — a quiet evening where one can talk over problems with one or more people of importance — perhaps even a visiting Commonwealth Minister. Government hospitality has certain minimum standards of lavishness: a meal must be on a scale appropriate to the dignity of the person entertained. Other Ministers, civil servants, members of the Opposition must all be asked. Moreover, Government hospitality is necessarily limited by its own rules. Only certain visiting personages qualify for official entertainment: and even these can only be entertained every so often according to their degree.

A Minister soon finds that his job demands that he must do some entertaining on his own that falls outside the scope or under the scale of Government hospitality. It is here in particular that the lack of private means becomes a painful matter. For a Minister is not allowed to claim *any* expense whatever against tax. He is treated by the tax authorities as a unique creature — he is the only person in the land who cannot even lodge a claim. No matter what rights in this respect have been established by apparently similarly situated people, the Minister is simply told that no claim whatever can even be considered. The official justification is that, despite all appearances, a Minister's proper needs are covered by the Treasury.

Since his salary is deemed to be solely in respect of his office, he is not even allowed to make the normal claims of an MP for certain constituency expenses, although all these expenses continue unchanged: a Minister must not use his office for the despatch of his parliamentary business. And out of his fully taxed income he must make running provision for next year's super-tax, when his salary may have suddenly dropped from £5,000 to £1,000, or even to nothing.

Thus a Minister has to mix on equal terms, but in unequal circumstances, with lots of people who are much better off than he is and most of whom use expense accounts as a matter of course. This applies equally to his encounters with most visiting Ministers from Commonwealth and foreign countries.

Of somewhat graver import is that the top civil servants whom the Minister must command will soon be getting up to £1,000 a year *more* than he does, quite apart from valuable pension rights. This may not amount to a great deal in terms of cash, after taxation; but, as is well known in business, a man's authority is subtly weakened when he has to give directions to men who are substantially better off than himself.

In practice, in the rush, anxiety, and honour of his occupation all these financial considerations only occasionally enter a Minister's mind. After all, he is first and foremost an MP. He will have got his training as a back-bencher and junior Minister and will be soaked in the ways of Parliament. Amongst other things, he will have grown accustomed to being the worst paid and provided Parliamentarian in the world.

### *Christian Names*

A British Cabinet Minister can be pretty certain to find himself in charge of a Department of State he knows nothing about. He is the personification of the ambivalent British attitude towards experts — trust and respect them, but leave decisions to the layman. If a Minister has been a teacher, that is reason for *not* putting him at the Ministry of Education. It is also often considered a good ground for moving him to another Department that he has been three or four years in the same office — he may have become too much of an expert himself and therefore lost touch with the rough good-sense of the man in the street (or on the back-bench).

In his Department the Minister represents one side of that distinction between Minister and civil servant which is fundamental to the British concept of parliamentary democracy. There must never be any doubt that the civil servant advises and executes policy whilst the Minister makes it. One of his trickiest personal problems this provokes is how far he should translate this distinction into terms of his personal relations with his civil servants. Should he, for instance, get on to Christian-name basis with them?

When a Minister first goes to his Department he is always

addressed by his official title — 'Minister', 'First Lord', 'Secretary of State'. But so close and friendly do Ministers become with their top officials, that many of them quickly slip into Christian names on both sides. I was perhaps too rigidly constitutional, but I always resisted the temptation. It was not easy: over and over again it seemed the most natural thing in the world to let a Christian name slip off the tongue. But the time might always come when one had to overrule the strongest advice, post an official where he did not want to go, pass someone over in promotion, or even consider his removal. And there was the general need to remember that a Minister and a permanent official are different sorts of constitutional creature.

I have found, since I have been in opposition again, that I naturally call by their Christian names men with whom I became very friendly in office but whom I then always called by their surnames.

### *The Hidden Hierarchy*

This probem of Christian names in the Department is part of the curious system of hidden hierarchy in which a Cabinet Minister lives his official life.

In the first place, he is himself in the first eleven. The Cabinet is made up of some fifteen members out of a total of about thirty full Ministers. All these have equal legal status; they are all Ministers of the Crown, all collectively responsible for the actions of the Administration, all charged with the execution of some part of the royal prerogative. Indeed the Cabinet itself is unknown to the law — it has no rights, no corporate means of proclaiming or enforcing its decisions. Its powers are merely the sum total of those inherent in Ministers of the Crown or conferred upon them by Statute. Yet it makes a vast difference whether or not a Minister is a member of the Cabinet. As such he is, whatever the law may say, part of the effective sovereign authority of the United Kingdom.

Within the Cabinet, the equality of all members, one with another, is an important principle that has many practical applications: but here, too, there is something like the 'pecking order' that is said to prevail amongst hens. In the antechamber outside the Cabinet room where Ministers gather before meeting, there is a row of coat-pegs. Under each peg is the name of a great office of state — Lord Chancellor, Chancellor of the Exchequer, Foreign Secretary, etc. Only Cabinet Ministers hang their hats and coats here — and only in the prescribed order.

When the time for the Cabinet meeting arrives, the Prime Minister himself opens the door from within, to the minute, and invites in his waiting colleagues. At this stage they are still merely personal friends and party colleagues. They smoke and exchange gossip and banter as they take up their set places round the large oblong table covered with green baize. The Prime Minister always sits in the middle of one long side of the table, his back to the fireplace and facing the large windows that give on the garden and the Horse-guards Parade beyond. On his immediate left (at least in my day) is the Lord President and beyond him again the Chancellor: opposite sits the Foreign Secretary. Other members sit in an order arranged by the Secretary to the Cabinet. If the Chiefs of Staff are in attendance, they sit in uniform to the Prime Minister's right along the narrow side of the table, which is just large enough to accommodate the three of them not very comfortably.

Directly Ministers are seated, have opened their despatch boxes and arranged their papers, the Prime Minister calls them to order. In my day, smoking was prohibited till one o'clock and the signal for the formal opening of business was when the Prime Minister knocked out his pipe.

At once the whole atmosphere changes. Here is no longer a set of individual men, but the collective sovereign power of the state. During the meeting Ministers address all their remarks to the Prime Minister, as they do to the Speaker in the House. They refer to him and all their colleagues by their official designation. 'Prime Minister, I can't go all the way with the Secretary of State for Scotland....' 'Before we leave this question, Prime Minister, may I make this point?...'

A great deal turns on the proper timing of an intervention. You can speak too early or too late in a discussion; too often or too little; and certainly too long. Cabinet discussion is highly skilled conversation. Underlying the quick and free exchange of equal opinions is a tacit respect for precedence. Certain Ministers by virtue of their office or seniority are accorded a right to longer speech.

Every Prime Minister, too, has a sort of 'inner Cabinet' that is even less known to the law than the Cabinet itself: he may discuss informally with three or four close associates in high office tricky matters before they come up in Cabinet. They may concert their views on questions of such secrecy or confidence that the Cabinet willingly leaves them to the Prime Minister — perhaps concerning counter-espionage and security, the timing of a General Election, or possible Cabinet changes. In such matters the Prime Minister may consult whom he chooses or no one at all. The opinions of these close associates of the Prime Minister naturally carry added weight. The Minister who has departmental responsibility for the subject under discussion is also entitled, whatever his seniority or standing, to special respect for his views.

It is all too easy to give a false impression about the nature of Cabinet discussion. Despite the hidden hierarchy, all members are really equal: all are expected to express their views with the utmost frankness. The Prime Minister may change or dismiss his Ministers; but at any given moment the Cabinet is the master. No decision setting in motion the whole elaborate machinery of the state can be taken save by the Cabinet; and all Cabinet Ministers share equally in the making of these decisions. The youngest and most junior member can sometimes get his colleagues to change their minds.

Here again the word 'decisions' may mislead. There are no resolutions or set propositions before the Cabinet; no voting system — just talk. Members discuss until a consensus of opinion is arrived at. When he thinks fit, the Prime Minister will sum up the views of his colleagues as they have emerged — a summary which may not altogether coincide with the opinions that he has himself expressed. Silence signifies assent — not necessarily precise agreement, but acceptance of the prevailing view. If contrary argument is still advanced, the discussion goes on again and may even be carrried over to another Cabinet meeting. Occasionally a small group of Ministers may be invited to try and thrash out and settle some stubbornly unresolved point. But this sort of thing is extremely rare: it calls for great and persistent conviction to hold out against the impatient unanimity of colleagues eager to get on with the never-finished work of the Cabinet. On even rarer occasions — perhaps never at all in the life of a Government — the Prime Minister may 'collect the voices': ask each member in turn to say 'yes' or 'no' and count up the result. This can occur on a matter about which opinions are equally divided but which is agreed to be of secondary importance; a vote may cut off time-consuming argument. Or on some tremendous issue, maybe involving threatened resignation. A Cabinet that has to resort to this sort of voting is in all likelihood near the end of its days.

The regular and hardly ever broken pattern is that, perhaps with some minor amendment, the Prime Minister's summary of the consensus of opinion is accepted and the Cabinet turns immediately to its next item of business. It is the job of the Secretary to the Cabinet to translate into 'decisions' this never very precise consensus of opinion, by recording it in the Cabinet Minutes.

These Minutes are an essential part of the machinery of modern British government — the transmission belt that converts the views of the Cabinet into executive actions throughout the sprawling and world-wide apparatus of servants of the Queen, civil, diplomatic, and military. But they will prove a sad disappointment to historians when at long last they come to be published; for they do not set out a record of the proceedings in the usual way of minutes. Their purpose is to enable the will of the Cabinet to be instantly understood by the Departments concerned: they are in reality designed as instructions, not as a reflection of Cabinet proceedings, still less of any divisions of opinion. Once it has made up its mind the Cabinet is unanimous. The Secretary reduces the consensus of opinion to a number of tabulated 'decisions'; only as much of the preceding discussion is set out as is necessary to elucidate and clarify these decisions — normally with exemplary brevity and hardly ever mentioning the names of those who took part in the discussion.

The Secretary is the servant of the Cabinet and any member may challenge the Minutes at the next meeting: but the work is done with such dutiful skill and in so practised a form that this scarcely ever occurs.

### *The Cabinet Network*

The Foreign Secretary's weekly verbal report on foreign affairs is the only relic of the primeval form of the Cabinet, when it not only included all Ministers, but these brought up issues without notice. This is still the rule in New Zealand. But in modern Britain, if all Ministers sat in the Cabinet it would turn it into a meeting instead of a conversation. The rush of affairs is so tumultuous that the fine machinery of the Cabinet is in constant danger of getting clogged up with a surfeit of business.

In relatively recent times a number of devices have been elaborated to keep the Cabinet's head above water; and these greatly affect the daily life of a Minister. The main development has been the paper-preparation of all Cabinet discussions. Cabinet papers, in which Ministers set forth their views, are continually circulated by a staff of confidential messengers who carry red boxes all over Whitehall. Some of these papers are for information — perhaps a report of a journey abroad or a statement of long-term policy. The great majority relate to matters that a Minister wants to bring before his colleagues. The means by which they are reduced to orderly and manageable proportions is the Cabinet Agenda. It sets out, with elaborate cross-references to papers that have been circulated and to previous Cabinet decisions, the business which fifteen or sixteen men can reasonably hope to despatch in three hours or so.

Ministers often jockey to get a good place on the Agenda, fairly close to the rails if possible; for Cabinets often do not get through a whole Agenda. Ministers (whether or not in the Cabinet) propose items to the Prime Minister, sometimes by personal representation. He alone decides the composition and order of the Agenda. Some matters, like parliamentary business or foreign affairs, are standing items.

Non-Cabinet Ministers are called to the Cabinet for questions that touch their departmental competence. This can be a testing ordeal. You are invited to attend at a stated hour when your business is expected to be reached — your appearance is nearly always premature; though occasionally, if the Cabinet goes unexpectedly fast, you may have to rush over from your office on a sudden summons. Usually you have to wait outside the Cabinet room, alone in the antechamber, which is the only place I know bleaker than a dentist's waiting-room. When the Secretary calls you in, you enter a Cabinet in full swing; find an empty chair where you can; hurriedly open your papers; and, at the Prime Minister's invitation, embark on an exposition of your case. When the point is settled, you rise and leave the Cabinet to get on with its remaining business.

Matters that do not at once get on the Agenda or which are not reached may just have to wait their turn till later. But Cabinet questions cannot be left like letters to answer themselves. The Cabinet has shown its extraordinary flexibility by evolving the so-called Cabinet Committees for the delegation of business. These Cabinet Committees are as secret as once was the Cabinet itself: they have no warrant in law: it is not even publicly known what Cabinet Committees exist nor which Ministers sit on them. Yet to these Committees is given the power of the Cabinet itself to set in motion the wheels of the State.

Committees of the Cabinet may be set up and disbanded in an instant as occasion demands. It is not unknown for the full Cabinet to charge a few of its members to deal with some difficult problem that may require minute-by-minute decisions. But the relentless demands of modern society have imposed a certain fixity of pattern upon this easy and fluid capacity of the Cabinet to propagate by splitting. A Defence Committee, an Atomic Energy Committee, a Home Economic Committee, a Future Legislation Committee — these have practically become parts of the constitution.

These Committees, which are nominated by the Prime Minister, consist of a few members of the Cabinet together with all the Ministers, whether or not in the Cabinet, who are departmentally concerned with their subject-matter. The Prime Minister himself may be chairman of some of them, the Lord President or Chancellor of others.

Cabinet Committees are an exact replica of the Cabinet. Each has its secretariat, agenda, and minutes; papers circulate beforehand; other Ministers are invited to attend as required. There is no very precise line of demarcation between the business that goes to these Committees or direct to the Cabinet: it is settled by the Prime Minister and the chairmen. The Committees have concurrent and equal jurisdiction with the Cabinet. A matter of very high import may occasionally come first before a Committee and then the Cabinet. If a Committee cannot agree on some matter it goes for final settlement to the full Cabinet. Otherwise the 'decisions' of Cabinet Committees as recorded in their minutes are carried forthwith into effect with the full authority of the state.

This interconnecting and somewhat overlapping network formed by the Cabinet and its Committees largely dominates a Cabinet Minister's life. There seems to be one or another of these meetings at almost every hour of the day; and, by their nature, they consume time: if one is to have government by talk, there must be adequate time to talk things out.

In my day, Cabinets met twice a week in the morning from ten o'clock to one o'clock. Sometimes an extra Cabinet would be called, when engagement calendars had to be cleared at however short notice of any other encumbrance. Cabinet Committees usually met at fixed times every week, often after Parliamentary Questions — about 4 p.m. They, too, would sometimes hold extra meetings, for which time might have to be found, say at nine o'clock in the evening after dinner. Then there might well be special *ad hoc* committees that would meet weekly for a month or two. One way and another, a Cabinet Minister would be lucky to have less than half-a-dozen such meetings to fit into his weekly programme.

This incessant press of meetings has an important but little remarked effect upon the nature of modern government. *It sets a strict upper limit upon the extent of democratic planning.*

Planning presupposes the careful co-ordination of policy between those men who have the powers to carry the plan into effect. There can only be a relatively few such men, or administrative confusion will result. But co-ordination of policy consumes much of the time and energy of these few men. Every hour spent in meetings must be subtracted from the exiguous ration of hours that a Minister has left for the task of direct administration. Beyond a certain point — the more you plan, the less you do.

Ministers conceive a deep distaste for embarking upon projects that will entail more and longer meetings with their colleagues. This means that even Socialist Ministers are selective about the sectors of the national life that they can attempt to plan. They are the first to realise that in a democracy you cannot plan everything; nor, for that matter, with efficiency, under any system however totalitarian.

Even in matters that require planning, Ministers develop a strong inclination to find methods of administration that will leave them free to concentrate on the really decisive tasks. It is no accident that bodies like the Arts Council or the University Grants Committee have been evolved in the age of planning for the independent administration of public funds for social purposes. There is not the least danger of overburdened Ministers being tempted to follow up financial aid by state intervention in these fields.

## *In the Minister's Office*

In some ways a Minister's Department is his refuge. Here he is master in his own house. He is given every aid by his officials and armed with the best arguments for his own policies, whether for use in Parliament or Cabinet.

He is wonderfully served by his private office, which is the link between him and all spheres of his public and even his private life. His Principal Private Secretary, a promising young member of the Department, is his main prop, aided by one or two assistant secretaries and a staff of typists. The Private Secretary keeps a free flow of state papers, arranged in the most intelligible form, moving across the Minister's desk; sees that officials in the Department are instantly available at the right moment; keeps time free for necessary appointments, often rationed out in five- or ten-minute periods; constantly rearranges engagements; finds people at the other end of the country; makes elaborate arrangements for travel without bothering the boss; compiles his box or boxes of papers to take home at night; and does a hundred other things, including the sustenance of Ministerial morale.

The Department may be a refuge; but it is no place of rest. The Minister has his hardest decisions to make in his office because he is on his own. However able the advice he receives, the decisions are his; it is he and not his officials who are shot if they are wrong. The better the civil servants, the more will they put up problems to the Minister in the form of arguments pro and con; it is amazing how often these seem exactly in balance, with the direst consequence liable to flow from any decision. He must decide whether to settle matters on his own authority or to trouble his Cabinet colleagues with them. He must as far as possible compose his own Cabinet papers — alas, a task that is getting more and more beyond the compass of his time.

Somehow the Minister must manage to deal with the immense mail that reaches him, in some Departments in great sacks. It will have to be sorted for him and much of it answered in standard form. A good Private Secretary will bring the right letters to his personal attention, including any letter from an MP, and frame suitable replies out of the briefest and most cryptic comments, scribbled perhaps in the middle of the night.

A Minister's relations with the press present one of his most difficult problems. In the House of Commons he will often get into usually rather casual conversation with Lobby correspondents, many of whom will be personal friends of long standing though they may have to criticise him severely in the course of duty. They have the highest standards of discretion, but a Minister must watch his words. His head is packed with information from all sorts of sources and it is not easy to remember which are communicable. Lobby correspondents, too, are adept at putting together into a coherent story stray words dropped by different people.

Outside the House other correspondents will seek him out. Some may be dangerous to see because their disclosures of secret information are so incessant that as likely as not something concerning your own Department may come out, and then everyone will think it was you who imparted the information. You must be careful about discrimination between newspaper men and it may be best to hold an occasional press conference in the Department, at which you can safely give information for quotation or off the record.

In general a Minister will tend to become more conscious of individual journalists and less conscious of particular newspapers. The effect of having the entire daily and weekly press laid out for one's perusal is that one skims through it and has often only the haziest idea of the headlines or views of one paper rather than another. Your Private Secretary sees to it that you have cuttings concerning yourself and your Department. Moreover a Cabinet Minister tends not to rely on the press for information; he has access to Foreign Office and Commonwealth Relations Office telegrams from every capital in the world.

### *Running to Stand Still*

It is in Parliament that a Minister has his roots, and his duty to it comes first. The answering of Parliamentary Questions must take precedence over everything else. I recall once when Questions went much faster than usual, and my Question, low down on the Order Paper, was reached whilst I was still in my room upstairs; I was saved only by the fact that a colleague of mine for the same reason was absent for the Question that came just before mine: the Opposition made such play of his absence that the time ran out before my Question was actually reached. Sometimes, after a weary day, a Minister may have to come down to the House late at night to answer a critical attack upon him. Cabinets held in Parliament time often meet in the Prime Minister's room at the House, so that Ministers may be instantly available.

Apart from the Chamber itself, a Minister must find time to meet his colleagues in the dining-room, smoking-room, tea-room, and about the lobbies; for it is here that much of Parliament's life goes on and many of its opinions formed. A Minister who is too much about will be noticed as much as one who is too often absent: Members of Parliament expect him to get on with his job as well as to be reasonably available.

All Ministers are heavily overworked: but it is membership of the Cabinet that makes the real difference. It not only adds to the meetings that must be attended but to the sea of papers that threaten to submerge one. Besides mastering his Departmental papers, a Cabinet Minister must prepare himself for intelligent discussion on all matters that come before the Cabinet: he must also read a very wide selection of Foreign Office and Commonwealth Relations Office telegrams.

He must run to keep standing still. There is always something to do somewhere else. Whilst he is sitting in the Cabinet or a Cabinet Committee there are papers piling up on his desk; a meeting to arrange with the Prime Minister, perhaps about an important telegram that must be quickly sent or about a matter that should perhaps come before the Cabinet; a meeting to fit in somehow with two or three of his colleagues; a debate to attend and prepare for; an MP to have a word with. All the time his Private Secretary will be postponing and rearranging engagements. At the end of the day, perhaps after an official dinner at which he has made a speech, he always takes home one or two red boxes stuffed with papers that must be read before he retires. Very rarely did I get to bed before 2 a.m.

Yet when a Minister loses office the sense of let-down is far more incisive than the sense of physical relief. Indeed, lacking the drive of power and high occupation, he may discover for the first time how tired he really is.

From being at the very heart of affairs and among the few dozen best-informed men in the world, faithfully served day and night, he suddenly reverts to obscurity. The invitations which had a short time before seemed to flow in embarrassing numbers, thin to a trickle. Workmen arrive to remove the direct line which linked him to his Private Office and by which he could control a great Department of State.

For a month or two, perhaps, the carry-over of the information that he carries, pressed down and overflowing, in his head may make him more knowledgeable than his successor in office — a period of grace which gives him just about time enough to learn again to make speeches and marshal his arguments without the best briefing that any public man anywhere in the world could have.

# A DOG'S LIFE IN THE MINISTRY

*By the* RT. HON. ERNEST MARPLES, MP

WITHIN the limitations of the role of cabinet minister, the behaviour of individual politicians varies. Ernest Marples, an unusual and energetic cabinet minister, developed a distinctive personal style and a daily routine atypical of his Conservative colleagues while he held office from 1951 to 1964. His article not only emphasises the problems of working in the midst of constant official engagements expected of a minister, but also, the advantages accruing to politicians with great physical stamina and adaptability.

WAS it really such a dog's life? In terms of challenge the answer must be 'No'. To be put in charge of Transport, as I was for five years, is to be presented with a most teasing, a most complicated and one of the most dangerous problems of our day.

It is teasing because the answer to it is elusive. It is complicated because one has to deal with railways, roads, ports and cities that were originally laid out for nothing faster than the horse and cart. It is dangerous because any Minister of Transport who does his duty risks the enmity of the motorists — the most powerful lobby in Britain.

'Marples must go' was the slogan I used to see dangling from the back windows of the cars in front of me. Their mudguards, I noticed, were usually dented or bashed about — evidence of their ability as drivers. Fortunately, I was sustained by an enormous postbag which showed that the public was overwhelmingly on my side.

In any other sense the job was indeed a dog's life. I do not mean by this that I objected to the hours, crushing though they were. Indeed, odd though it may seem, no Minister in my experience has ever complained about hard work.

The point is that these exhausting hours are largely taken up with trivialities and are therefore wasted. Under our present system a Minister is at the beck and call of every Tom, Dick and Harry from Land's End to John o' Groats. Instead of being able to sit back and

---

Reprinted in a slightly abridged form from the *Sunday Telegraph*, 22 Nov 1964.

concentrate on the major problems, he finds himself immersed in the minor ones.

Let me underline the point by quoting from my diary of 1963. Here is a typical page:

5.0–8.30 a.m. Work in study.
8.45. Tennis.
10.30 Standing Committee on Harbours Bill.
2.45. Mr Nicholas Ridley, MP
3.0 To receive petition from the Gibson Square Protection Society.
3.45. Mr Peter Utley.
4.15. To receive the Japanese Ambassador.
4.45. Nationalised Transport Policy.
5.30. Dr Beeching.
7.30 for 8.0. Dinner — Guild of Motoring Writers, R.A.C.
9.40. Speech to the Guild.
10.5–11.20. Questions after the speech.

This is almost shorthand, and to understand what it means I must still explain what a Minister's life is like. First of all he is not only a grand member of the Government: he is also a humble Member of Parliament. He has a constituency and therefore he must continually break off from his preoccupations in order to make himself known and manifest to those who returned him.

If he is in a controversial job, he has the public perpetually clamouring at his door. When I was Minister of Transport I had to reply to a thousand letters a week. Most of the answers, of course, were drafted by my staff. But they still had to be read and they had to be signed.

The members of an important County Council are incensed by a proposal to widen a road, and they insist on seeing the Minister. Nobody else will do. Any of my three Parliamentary Secretaries could quite easily deal with most of these problems or, if there were complications, they could refer the matter to the Minister. But if a Minister dealt with a Council in this way there would be an immediate uproar. The Minister might soon have to defend himself in the House of Commons. What is more, he would probably be humiliated.

Then every MP claims the right to see the Minister. Here again one cannot refuse. Never mind that the point may be trivial and could be dealt with by almost anybody on his staff: the tradition is that a Minister must keep open house for every member of the Commons.

Taking all this into account a fair average summary of my busy day might be as follows:

5.00–8.30 a.m. Paper work. At home all papers would be read, all letters signed, all speeches prepared. For the rest of the day I reject paper work.
8.45–10.00. Exercises plus one hour's tennis, singles at that, and all with a sweat.
10.00–13.00. Meetings, discussions, Cabinet, etc.
13.00–13.30. Light lunch (unless I had to have a five-course banquet in the way of duty).
13.30–14.30. Sleep — in a horizontal position.
14.30–18.30. Discussions, deputations, arguments and House of Commons.
1830–20.00. Dinner ($\frac{1}{2}$ hr) and sleep (1 hr).
20.00–22.30 p.m. Sometimes a dinner and a speech, sometimes a House of Commons debate.
Total — 17$\frac{1}{4}$ hours. Summary: Exercise 1$\frac{1}{4}$ hours; Sleep 2 hours; Meals 1 hour; Work 13 hours.

All the same we must not fall into the mood of thinking that efficiency is everything. These continual deputations, interviews, consultations, letters and protests may often be a waste of time, but they also create a curious and intangible intimacy between the rulers and the ruled. The public must never be given an excuse for thinking that the members of its Government inhabit a superior and impenetrable world where it can knock but never enter.

What is more, the democratic process is not just a one-way traffic. A good Minister is a Minister who can lead but is always going back to the grass roots. He should remember that he is not dealing with ruthless profit and loss, but with the lives of ordinary men and women.

Having said this, the fact remains that a controversial Minister — and there are few Ministers who are not in a controversial department — is not given a fair chance. By the time he has finished his democratic chores, his day, if it is a normal trades union day, is almost over. Policy and thought inevitably come last on his agenda, and they clearly ought to come first. I am not forgetting the long summer recess, though the idea that a Minister can then completely relax is a delusion.

Let me try to illustrate the point by comparing the life of a Minister with that of a high executive in industry. A business tycoon chooses whom he will see and whom he will not see. The initiative is his. His diary will not remotely resemble mine while I was at the Ministry of Transport. Whereas his will be almost virginal in its vacant spaces, mine had every moment filled.

Or let me give a practical example. It never occurs to anybody who buys a faulty shirt at a shop to insist on an interview with the managing director. He will flap the offending garment in front of the salesman. But not in Government.

While Dr Beeching was at I.C.I. no member of the public ever thought he had a right to see him about a faulty piece of Terylene. Now Dr Beeching is seen as a public servant, he is in a very different position. Anybody who has a stale sandwich at a station buffet wants to talk to him about it. 'We pay him, don't we?' is the attitude.

How does one retain the democratic process and at the same time reconcile it with the needs of a modern society? There seems to me to be only two solutions.

The first is to reduce the democratic chores — a dangerous mode of thinking, in my opinion. We do not want to end in a position where a man with a legitimate grievance has no way of making his views known to those in the highest authority. The alternative is to protect the Minister from the full blast and turmoil and distraction of his present democratic duties. Perhaps we could have the top man who does the executive work in the Lords, plus a second in command who explains and obeys our democratic urges in the Commons. If they made a mess of it, then both should resign.

I believe that this, if we want efficient Government, is the most urgent problem that faces us.

# PERMANENT UNDER-SECRETARY

*By* LORD STRANG

THE heavy burdens of departmental business, the diffuse role-expectations of political heads and the limited number of ministers in each department inevitably give senior civil servants an important role to play in policy-making. These are the men who see that the minister's department is running smoothly and that papers are prepared for his attention while the minister is engaged in extra-departmental pursuits. As Lord Strang's memoir makes clear, the pressures of work that threaten to overbear individual ministers also weigh heavily upon their civil service advisers, notwithstanding the fact that these men have by comparison with their political directors specific and relatively limited role-expectations. Since Lord Strang's retirement, it is possible that the decline in Britain's world role has lessened the difficulties of a Permanent Under-Secretary at the Foreign Office. The expansion of the economic and welfare commitments of other government departments has, however, kept the average work-load of a senior civil servant high.

I HELD the office of Permanent Under-Secretary of State for Foreign Affairs for nearly five years, from 1 February 1949, until 30 November 1953. Before that I had been Joint Permanent Under-Secretary for the German Section from 20 October 1947. My two immediate predecessors, Sir Alexander Cadogan and Sir Orme Sargent, had held office for eight years and three years respectively. The Secretaries of State whom I served were the late Ernest Bevin, in his last tragic two years; Mr Herbert Morrison; Mr (now Sir) Anthony Eden, and, during Mr Eden's illness in 1953, Sir Winston Churchill and the Marquess of Salisbury.

The duties of the Permanent Under-Secretary in the Foreign Office are in essence three: he is the chief adviser to the Foreign Secretary on the conduct of foreign affairs; he is responsible to the Foreign Secretary for the good administration of the Foreign Service and for the smooth functioning of the Foreign Office and Her Majesty's Embassies, Legations and Consular Establishments abroad; and, as Accounting Officer, he is personally responsible to Parlia-

Reprinted from ch. 10 *Home and Abroad* (London: Deutsch, 1956), pp. 269–86.

ment through the Public Accounts Committee of the House of Commons, before whom he appears for examination, for ensuring that funds voted by Parliament for the Foreign Service are expended with due economy for the purposes for which they are voted, and for no others.

It may be asked how one person, within the space of a day's work, can perform all these tasks, together with other extensive duties of a special character which need not be treated here.

Those who enter upon the charge of a great public department find an elaborate and highly developed mechanism ready to their hand, which is the less difficult to master if they have been for long years familiar with its methods and organisation and with the subject-matters with which it deals. The art and science of public administration in all its branches is directed towards the expeditious, exact and wise performance of public business; and in particular to the orderly handling, the accurate recording and the ready availability for reference, of the papers upon which the major part of public business is carried. The two chief devices adopted for the achievement of these ends are the sub-division of subject-matter and the hierarchical organisation of staff. The direct responsibility to Parliament of Ministers in charge of departments of the Government for the official acts of all their subordinates imposes a certain uniformity of pattern upon the organisation and methods of public departments, however great the variety in the subject-matter of their operations; but each department, in the light of its own long experience, has developed for itself the structure and rules of procedure best suited to its own function. Departments whose main duty is the administration of statutes will differ in their organisation and ways of working from those whose main function is to conduct business with other governments in Commonwealth and foreign countries. There will be a similar differentiation between those departments in which the great mass of decisions are taken by subordinate officials under general directives from the Minister, and those in which the principal matters for decision are of their very nature disparate, and require to be examined each on its own merits and to go for decision to higher officials or to the Minister himself. The Foreign Office falls within the second category in each case.

This is not the place to describe in detail the organisation and working of the Foreign Office and of Her Majesty's Missions abroad. An account of these, and of other aspects of the Foreign Service, will be found in a volume[1] prepared by members of the

[1] *The Foreign Office* in The New Whitehall Series (London: Allen & Unwin, 1954).

Foreign Service and published under the auspices of the Royal Institute of Public Administration. But some general indications may be given.

The rules of procedure for the conduct of business in the Foreign Office are laid down in detail in an Order Book; and this, together with the traditional practices passed on from seniors to juniors down the years, determines the methods by which work is done and the spirit in which it is done. The Order Book is a comprehensive compendium which contains a body of instructions ranging from the rules of draftsmanship formulated by Sir Thomas Sanderson, Permanent Under-Secretary at the end of the nineteenth century, to the latest circular issued by the Permanent Under-Secretary of the day to make some modification in organisation or method called for by the changing character of the work, or to correct some fault in existing procedure that has revealed itself in practice. The Order Book also on occasion embodies the personal predilections as well as the weightier injunctions of Ministers. Sir Winston Churchill, when Acting Foreign Secretary, decreed that dates on official documents were to be quoted as 'January 1, 1954' (this is the practice in the press) or 'the 1st of January, 1954' (as in the Order Papers of the House of Lords) and not otherwise — not e.g. '1st January' or '1 January' or 'January 1st'; and this rule will continue to govern the Foreign Office and indeed the whole Foreign Service unless abrogated by some succeeding Foreign Secretary with other predilections. The importance of neatness and orderliness in the presentation of work cannot be over-estimated. The Order Book is one of the instruments in the hands of the Permanent Under-Secretary for the achievement of this purpose. The Book is under constant revision to meet the frequent variations in the demands made upon the Office; only so can the Office be kept responsive and alert. It must be a burden to the juniors, who are apt at any moment to receive a slip of paper from the Permanent Under-Secretary observing that in this or that minute or draft that has reached his hands they have disregarded this or that injunction of the Order Book: but provided that such reproaches are not over-frequent and are couched in terms proper from one colleague to another, both engaged in the same enterprise, they can promote efficiency without provoking exasperation or discouragement. Sir Eyre Crowe, a bureaucrat if there ever was one, but much else besides, was a great circulator of reproachful remarks to juniors. We once received from him a red slip to which a bedraggled length of pink tape had been pinned, with the words: 'To send a dirty piece of tape like this to the Secretary of State is really quite wrong.' And his constant complaint on receiving bulky files was: 'Too many previous papers. Always too many previous papers.'

Unless papers are submitted in neat and orderly fashion, with minutes or memoranda concisely drafted and recommendations clearly stated, and (if not typed) written in a legible hand, and unless all necessary consultations have been completed and their results shortly set down, the burden falling upon the senior officials, and especially upon the Permanent Under-Secretary, becomes intolerable. It is a mistake to think that the latter confines his attention to matters of high policy or major problems of administration. It may well happen that the subject-matter of the paper which lies before him and which is to go to the Secretary of State, important though it may be, is not the most immediate or pressing of his preoccupations. His problem will be to make sure first of all that the paper is in a fit state to be placed before the Minister for a decision. If it is not, and if time presses as it so often does, he may have to put the file right himself, adding his own endorsement or amendment of the recommendations it contains. Then there may be the problem of where to find the Secretary of State. He may be in his room at the Foreign Office, in which case the Private Secretary will be warned that the paper (if it is a very important one) is on its way up; but the Secretary of State may well be elsewhere — in the House of Commons, or at his house, or out at dinner, or in his constituency, or even on business in a foreign capital while still remaining in charge of the Foreign Office. The Permanent Under-Secretary must make it his business to know where the Minister is to be found, day and night, and how papers are to reach him in case of need. If papers cannot be got to him in due time, the P.U.S. has to decide whether to take the decision himself, or to seek the authority of another Minister, if one can be found.

I have digressed somewhat from the rules for the presentation of papers, but the observation of those rules is one of the indispensable conditions for the prompt conduct of affairs. Another indispensable condition is rapidity, accuracy and security of communications. Man is essentially a communicating animal, and he is necessarily so in his foreign relations. Reports and recommendations must come by telegram from Ambassadors, and instructions must go out to them from the Foreign Office. Time usually presses. The precise language used is often of the highest importance. The content of such telegrams must not be open to be read by other governments. This involves an elaborate and rather expensive organisation, since the volume of telegram traffic is very heavy, and rapidity and security are costly commodities. The Ambassador dictates his telegram or writes it in manuscript. It is passed to his Chancery for despatch and by them to the Embassy telegraph room. There it is put into cipher and despatched by cable or by wireless. At the London end it is delivered to the Communications Department of the Foreign Office, deciphered, copied, duplicated and circulated to those in the Foreign Office whose business it is to see it. To govern all these operations there is a Communications Handbook which is the counterpart, in this sphere, of the Order Book, and like the latter, subject to revision in the light of experience.

One of my preoccupations was to reduce the volumes of telegrams passing to and from the Office which, as well as costing a lot of money, threatened to choke the communications machine. Two measures were adopted: first, a system of scrutiny under which, if a telegram was judged to be too prolix or completely unnecessary, a letter of gentle remonstrance was written to the originator in the Foreign Office or at the post abroad; and secondly, the circulation of quarterly statistics, post by post, showing increases or decreases in the number of telegrams sent, the total number of cipher groups carried, and the average length of telegrams. At the end of two years, the average daily volume of telegrams had been reduced by nearly half.

As I have said, the machine is there, ready to the hand of the new overseer, apt for its purpose and familiar to him in its movements. Yet still the question remains: how is he to meet all the day's obligations within the day? The Foreign Office receives hundreds of thousands of papers a year. There is a staff of all ranks of something over 10,000 to be administered at home and abroad. There are some eighty British diplomatic missions in foreign countries with which the Foreign Office has to correspond. There are some eighty heads of foreign missions in London who are entitled to wait upon the Permanent Under-Secretary. And there is his own Minister, for whom he must be at call at any hour — and Minister's hours are necessarily irregular. However smooth and flexible the official machine may be, however well-regulated the system of delegation of responsibility, however skilful and speedy he himself may be as a craftsman, however discriminating in his choice of what to read and what not to read, there must always fall upon the P.U.S., unless he takes resolute steps to spare himself, a burden greater than any man could be expected to bear. The problem for him to settle, either deliberately or by trial and error, is how much he can sustain and what steps he can take to limit the load to what is bearable. He obviously cannot work twenty-four hours a day, but is it to be eighteen or sixteen or twelve or how many? The theoretical upper limit is the limit of his own physical and mental tolerance. The theoretical lower limit is the degree of his own sense of duty or the limit of tolerance of his chief. If he strictly worked his official forty-four hour week, say, from ten to six, and from nine to one on Saturdays and not at all on Sundays, he would not be able to get through the work which, whatever shifts he might resort to, would inescapably fall upon him. He would not, for example, be available if his chief urgently required him at night or on Saturday afternoon or on Sunday. Sir Winston Churchill's hours are well known. When he was acting as Foreign Secretary, I was often at Downing Street till midnight or even one in the morning, or was called to Chartwell or Chequers on Saturday afternoons or Sundays. Very exhilarating these vigils and expeditions were: never was there a more stimulating, if unpredictable, chief or a more charming or more courteous host.

Experience tends to show that, if the job is to be done with due conscientiousness, the hours must normally be twelve or upwards a day. In practice, I found that I could, if need be, do fourteen for a good while without undue strain, if there was some easing up on Saturday afternoons and Sundays. I was usually able to keep it down to between twelve and fourteen. When I had no house in the country to go to, I found it more restful to stay in London during week-ends, and to do whatever urgent work there might be, than to pack up and displace myself to stay with friends or at hotels. When, in my last year of service, I established a house in the country, I used to take one clear week-end off in three, and place papers firmly in the hands of one of the Deputy Under-Secretaries. But even this had the disadvantage that there was a tiresome accumulation of work to read on Sunday evening or Monday morning.

This kind of existence calls for a deliberate concentration of energies on public duties and a discarding of much that makes life agreeable, the cultivation of friendships, social commerce with congenial companions, or the leisurely savouring of art and nature. It was rare for us to dine out with friends or to have them in to dinner in a purely personal way: there were so many diplomatic dinners to attend as a matter of duty that on the evenings we were free of them it was a relief to stay quietly at home and get on with one's papers. Abnegation became a habit, more galling for one's wife than for oneself.

Since in this book I am talking about myself, I make no apology for now going on to describe how I ordered my day. I usually awoke about seven-thirty and read *The Times.* I breakfasted in bed about eight-thirty and rose about nine. By then there might be a telephone call from the Secretary of State about some item in the newspaper or about some file I had sent to him the evening before, and some instructions from him for action to be taken as soon as I arrived at the Office. I left home about nine-thirty and walked to the Office, which was about ten minutes away. To live near one's work was to save much wear and tear. At the Office the first duty was to dispose of the papers I had worked on at home the evening before. Then to read, or at least to run over, the file of telegrams which had come in since the last evening: these would already have been selected and classified by my private secretary. These telegrams set the stage for the morning's work. There were usually some important and urgent questions raised in them on which decisions would be required during the day, and on which instructions would need to be sent to posts abroad or action taken in London as soon as possible. My usual course was to have a brief word on the telephone with the Deputy or Assistant Under-Secretaries severally concerned, who would also by then have read the telegrams. I would seek their first reactions and find out when they thought they would be ready with recommendations or whether they wished for a meeting with me first, in which case I then fixed a time, generally later in the morning. It was important to make this immediate contact, but without any appearance of pestering, since the Secretary of State would himself also have read the telegrams and, if he were of an impatient cast of temperament, would want to know what I thought of the telegrams and what I was doing about them. I had to be in a position then and there to let him know the plan on which we were moving and the way in which, at first impulse, our minds were working. This colloquy would either confirm or amend the preliminary line we were following; or conceivably the subject might be so urgent or important that the Secretary of State would wish to hold a meeting about it himself, in which case other engagements had to give place. Until the solution of the morning's problems was thus set in train, my mind was not at ease. I look back on my mornings as times of stress, when the day's work loomed up like a mountain in one's path. Meanwhile, the routine files would be arriving on my desk, the urgent and the less urgent duly distinguished one from the other, and the more immediate brought to my special attention by my private secretary. These were disposed of in the intervals between interviews and other consultations. I would ask an Under-Secretary to come and bring me up to date on some aspect of his business which the Secretary of State might wish to raise; or he in his turn might want to come and report progress and get approval and guidance for his operations. I might also send for a head of department or a junior to brief me for an interview requested by a foreign

Ambassador, whose business one had either been forewarned of, or had to guess at. I seldom went to lunch before one-thirty. I walked to the Travellers' Club and if possible relaxed for half an hour, returning about two-thirty. That is, unless I had an official lunch to attend, in which case my working time might well be eaten into from a quarter-to-one to three. I tried to keep my early afternoons for visitors, whether foreign Ambassadors or Foreign Service colleagues from abroad, or for more formal Office meetings such as those of the Senior Promotions and Appointments Board.

Vernon Bartlett once roundly reproached me in the *News Chronicle* for not being forthcoming enough in my dealings with the press. It is one of the protections established for the P.U.S. that relations between the Foreign Office and the press are channelled through the Foreign Office News Department, which is directly responsible to the P.U.S., and that it is only on special occasions that the P.U.S. himself will have to receive a press representative; but what, I think, irked Vernon was that at the Travellers' Club, of which he was also a member, I was reluctant to sacrifice my precious few minutes of midday relaxation in order to talk about current foreign problems with him or with anybody else.

One other encounter with the press should be recorded. On 19 October, 1952, the *Sunday Express* came out with a full-dress article attacking my administration of the Foreign Office, casting blame upon me for the outcome of certain ventures in our foreign policy, and suggesting that the Foreign Secretary (Mr Eden as he then was) should not delay my retirement from the public scene beyond my sixtieth birthday which would fall early in January, 1953, a few weeks later. Reading the article again now with a cool mind, I think (as in fact I did think at the time) that, while it made some fair points, it was, in general, to quote from a letter addressed by an authoritative correspondent to *The Times*, 'ill-informed, inaccurate and ill-mannered'. Some other writers in the press used stronger language about it. Several newspapers referred to the need to maintain the generally accepted practice that criticism of policy should be directed against Ministers and not against civil servants. This point was made by Mr Eden on a public occasion a few days later when, after referring to 'this most unjust and unworthy attack', he said that if anyone wanted to attack our foreign policy, they should attack the Foreign Secretary direct. And he did, in fact, ask me to stay on after my sixtieth birthday.

It was some little while after this that I found myself seated next to Lord Beaverbrook at an official luncheon at No. 10 Downing Street. I did not think the occasion a proper or fitting one for a remonstrance. At one point, Lord Beaverbrook remarked, somewhat ominously I thought, that he had been looking into the papers about the European Advisory Commission, which had been one of the counts against me in the article; but the talk then slid off into other channels. We found that we shared a taste for John Galt's *Annals of the Parish*, though, unlike myself, Lord Beaverbrook was familiar with all Galt's other works as well as with his successes and misfortunes as one of the early builders of Canada. He also confessed, and I could not but agree, that neither age nor experience could dispense from the extreme care and attention which ought to be devoted to the launching of business or professional enterprises, nor from the anxiety, the flutter in the stomach, with which one watched their development.

Much of the P.U.S's time is taken up with interviews. In this matter, I was grateful for the forbearance shown by my foreign colleagues in London in their official relations with me. They seldom took my time unless they had something specific to ask or to communicate; they arrived punctually; and they did not linger. As for my colleagues in the Foreign Service employed abroad, the Heads of Mission always came to see me on their visits to London; and some of their juniors came if they knew me well. These personal contacts were of great importance in helping to hold the Service together and to mould it into a team. However heavily pressed or however weary I might be, I never felt tempted to be sparing of the time or care given to these talks.

By about five o'clock the back of the most arduous part of the day's work was usually broken. I found that, by early afternoon, my engine was thoroughly warmed up and I worked easily and confidently and with zest. I could look forward to a relatively undisturbed period in which to dispose of papers — to take decisions on them, or send them up to the Minister, or send them back to the department for further treatment, or merely to read and note them. These papers — as the Under-Secretaries themselves came to the end of their own day — began to flow in from about six o'clock onwards. From then until about seven-thirty I was usually working at speed, either to take such decisions as I could on my own, or to get the more urgent of the files into the box that would go to the Secretary of State that evening, to be read by him if possible before morning. At about seven-thirty or a little later, I went home in a Foreign Office car, with my black box of papers. Shortly after the nine o'clock news, I usually went to bed, and there, quiet and rested and relaxed, finished off my papers, whatever they might be, political, economic or administrative. There might be a telephone conversation with the Secretary of State, himself similarly occupied. This comfortable routine was broken into when there was an official dinner to attend. There was first the scurry to clear off the urgent papers in the Office before coming home to dress. Then the effort to make conversation at dinner; the being buttonholed by an importunate Ambassador who might want to talk politics; and the nagging consciousness of that black box waiting at the Office to be picked up on the way home. My good friends, the Foreign Office drivers, were only too familiar with this routine.

To show the kind of day that had sometimes to be faced, I quote my engagement list for 24 March, 1953, which I have kept as a matter of curiosity:

11.15 a.m. Assistant Under-Secretary and Head of Department (Middle East).
12 noon Deputy Under-Secretary (Germany).
12.15 p.m. H.M. Ambassador to Siam.
12.30 Greek Ambassador.
1.15 Assistant Under-Secretary and Head of Department (Egypt).
2.45 Private Secretary to the Secretary of State.
3.00 Representative of an industrial firm.
3.30 Representative of a commercial firm.
3.45 Assistant Under-Secretary (Information).
4.15 Brazilian Ambassador.
5.00 Egyptian Ambassador.
6.00 Chilean Ambassador.
6.15 Private Secretary to the Secretary of State.
6.30 Parliamentary Under-Secretary.
6.45 Assistant Under-Secretary (Intelligence and Security).

When I first became Permanent Under-Secretary, I asked my two immediate predecessors whether there was any way to avoid having to take papers home at night. They both said without hesitation that there was not. The day was so broken into by interviews and meetings and urgent operational papers that anything that required concentration or leisurely perusal or even just a rapid exploratory scrutiny had to be reserved for the evening, not to speak of any surplus of urgent papers remaining over at the end of the day. I made it a rule, only rarely to be broken, to finish off each day's work that day so as to start clear in the morning. It was less of a strain to spend an extra hour or two quietly working at night than to face an accumulated residue in the morning, in addition to the pressing problems of the new day. This, and a capacity to shut up official cares in the black box and sleep soundly and wake refreshed, carried me through the five years' occupation of the chair in which one of my predecessors, so he told me, had spent so many agonising hours.

As a result I have, I hope, come to retirement with health unimpaired and zest unblunted.

Nevertheless, there have been occasions when it was necessary to overwork. At such times I used to watch the effect of prolonged fatigue upon powers and methods of work. In order to protect itself, the mind (if it is permissible to speak of such a thing) sought to bring about a progressive restriction of the area in which it might be called upon to operate. The major restriction was naturally the concentration of one's waking attention almost exclusively upon one's job. Even in the sphere of foreign affairs, the mind revolted against the reading of discourses or articles that had no immediate bearing on day-to-day problems. The next resistance erected would be against aimless discussions at large about foreign affairs, whether inside the Office or outside. In all this, the mind was attempting to shed all but the inescapable task of dealing with essential interviews or with the flow of papers and of reaching decisions on the matters of business carried by them, and protecting its capacity to perform these functions, come what might. However tired I was, I never lost the will or the power to put pressing official business through, or wholly lacked the zest which would provide the spur; though I confess that, when very tired, I turned more willingly to administrative than to political problems. There were times, happily very rare, when the bare minimum residual field was all that the mind could compass, and when to turn to any other task was intolerably painful. I was brought to this state in the five months' crisis in Moscow in 1933 over the arrest and trial of the Metropolitan-Vickers engineers: I do not think I was ever so tired or so angry.

It is plain from what I have said that the work of civil servants is essentially that of dealing with papers. But we obviously do not deal with papers as such: they are the vehicles of public business, the indispensable instruments for the preparation and consummation of decision and action. There is a knack of handling papers that can be acquired as a professional technique. Civil servants are not much use if they do not acquire it; but this, once mastered, becomes second nature, a well-established habit, and can be exercised without much effort. What imposes a strain is the reality behind the papers, the need for decision and action, the call upon one to make up one's mind, often upon inadequate information, often at short notice with scant time for thought. This is where experience and the garnered fruit of reflection come into play. When the inescapable moment for decision comes, one gathers oneself together and commits oneself to one's judgment as a swimmer commits himself to the water. When one has done that, the technique resumes its role, and one sets down one's conclusions as shortly and clearly and quickly as one can, in the hope that the Minister will deduce the whole picture from the sketch which is offered to him.

In explanation of the last foregoing few words, I would, by way of digression, say this, Ministers are very busy and harassed people. Some of them encourage their staff, when presenting their work to make what is complex appear to be simple, to draft papers composed of short sentences and cut up into short paragraphs, so that they can be taken in almost at a glance. This process (which has its dangers) is as far removed as it is possible to be from the deliberate and exhaustive methods of formal scholarship. That is why the proceedings of bureaucrats appear to the academic mind to be so superficial. Between the official and his Minister there is a wide area of common ground which, in their communications, they can take for granted and need not bring formally into question.

In the process of coming to decisions, the burden that weighs, the strain that tells, is not so much the responsibility of taking a decision or of making a recommendation. Once the decision is taken or the recommendation made, the mind can be at ease and turn to its next task. The real burden is the burden of making up one's mind what to decide or what to recommend. This can be an agonising experience when arguments are strong for and against this or that course, and the more so when the conflicting arguments are disparate and not comparable in origin, scope or point of impact.

A day's work may appear formidable, indeed insuperable, in prospect: but experience shows that the most mountainous accumulations can be cleared before the day is over. A day, for purposes of paper-work, is a long period of time and it usually takes fewer minutes than one fears to dispose of even a complex and tricky file, if one has the necessary skill and power of concentration. The secret is to concentrate and to work as quickly as one tolerably can. Once having taken up a paper, don't send it away or put it aside until you have finished with it so far as you can; if you want more information, set down what it is you want, and why; if you want to sleep on it, set down precisely the decision you will take or the recommendation you will submit next morning, subject to such counsel as the night may bring. Work is done best when there is rather too much work to do and rather too short a time in which to do it. A department is most likely to be efficient when it is slightly (but only slightly) undermanned. The staff should be on their toes and happy to be on their toes. Human beings, being what they are, seldom work at a maximum tolerable *tempo* unless they are constrained to it, but tend (at any rate, if they are civil servants) to suit the rate of work to the time available. During the war, at a time when the air-raids came shortly after nightfall, the order was given that staffs should so far as possible be clear of the Office before the siren might be expected to sound. In winter this meant that quite early in the evening there were neither registry clerks nor typists available, except a skeleton staff for emergencies. We found that by setting to work with determination at high speed we could complete by five or five-thirty what in normal times would have taken us till seven or later. Undoubtedly there were many occasions when, as P.U.S., I could, by working all day at top speed, have finished my papers by seven or so. But this would not necessarily have released me, since I could never be sure that the Secretary of State would not send for me before leaving the Office, or that one of my colleagues would not have an urgent matter to put to me at the end of his day. And in any event, however fast one may work, there are parts of one's occupation that are not under one's own control, to determine their duration or the speed at which they are to be performed. It would not have been for me to curtail a meeting with the Secretary of State; and if a foreign Ambassador called it would be necessary to hear him out, however long he might be.

But I have not yet explained, as I set out to do, how the P.U.S's work can be performed within a tolerable number of hours per day. The first essential is to see that the Office is rightly staffed; the second is to be quite ruthless in seeing that work is properly prepared and presented; the third is so to organise the Office that, while the P.U.S. is always kept informed of what is going on, he can at need be by-passed by a Deputy or Assistant Under-Secretary in seeking a decision from the Minister. The P.U.S. ought rarely to have to draft: and if he has relations of friendly confidence with his fellow Under-Secretaries and confers freely with them, he will find that he need write no more on quite a number of important papers which he sends up to the Minister than: 'I agree' or 'I support the department's recommendation'. He will, on occasion, have to write memoranda on matters of major policy, but his influence will more normally be exercised in prior informal discussions with his colleagues during the process of formulating recommendations.

The first step towards this happy end is to choose the right men as heads of departments — these correspond to what are usually called 'divisions' in other government offices. Departments are either territorial (e.g. Far Eastern Department) or functional (e.g. Economic Relations Department) or administrative (e.g. Personnel Department). The department is the basic unit, and each department has a quota of duties sufficient for one man — the head — to supervise in detail. If the work grows beyond the limit, some of it is re-allotted to other departments or the department is made into two. If it falls far below the limit, departments may be amalgamated. The organisation of the Office is readily responsive to such changing pressures. A head of a department must know how to make his staff work smoothly and happily as a team; he must see that their work is turned out in the right form; and he must have the judgment to make wise recommendations. He must, for example, be able to draft at short notice a Cabinet paper required by the Secretary of State for circulation to his colleagues. It will be an advantage if he is an expert in at any rate part of the work of his department, but the prime function of a civil servant is to know how to conduct public business, and the possession of this quality is in general to be more highly prized than brilliance of intellect or originality alone. The qualities required in a head of department are curiously rare. He stands at a nodal point in the traffic of business, the point at which instructions from above meet recommendations from below. It is his duty to see that there is no conflict between orders from above and action below, to ensure that the subordinates execute approved policy. He must be alert to note, and to warn his superiors, if policy is getting out of harmony with the facts. For this reason it is much harder to find a Counsellor to head a busy department of the Foreign Office (and there are always some that are very much busier than others) than to fill a vacancy in a post abroad. I kept a questing eye open for likely candidates for these posts and laid plans for their transfer in due season.

Above the heads of departments are the Assistant Under-Secretaries and the Deputy Under-Secretaries, about a dozen in number. When I was young and serving in a department, we juniors used to wonder what was the use of an Assistant Under-Secretary. We knew about heads of departments and we had an inkling of the functions of that august personage, the P.U.S., and even of his Deputy. But we did not see why our head of department, who was as a chieftain to us, need pass his work through any intermediate officer. In fact, as we learnt later, the Under-Secretaries are the chief mechanism for that canalisation and delegation of work which alone enables a great Office to work smoothly at high speed and under great pressure, as the Foreign Office has to do. Each of them supervises a group of departments and may have special tasks as well. One of them is in charge of all the administrative departments; two of them share the economic work of the Office; one takes all the Far Eastern and South-East Asian questions; another, the Middle East and Africa; and so on. As I see it, it is the Under-Secretary who must be made responsible for formulating recommendations of policy within his sphere, and for co-ordinating such formulation with other Under-Secretaries who may be concerned. He must take hold of his subjects and act as though he alone had to make the recommendation to the Secretary of State. He will normally send in his papers through the P.U.S., and will usually confer with the latter before making his recommendation, but if the P.U.S. is hard pressed or otherwise occupied, the Under-Secretary will report direct to the Minister, informing the P.U.S. that he has done so. The problem before the P.U.S. is at one and the same time to keep his eye in a general way on all that is going on, so that he can answer to the Secretary of State, and yet not to be borne down with work. His only salvation is to ensure that the Under-Secretaries are adepts at getting official business done; that they are capable of assuming full responsibility; and that they recognise that in case of need they will have to assume it. Here again the most careful choice of staff is necessary, for the Under-Secretaries can make or mar the Office. I believe that the best course is to appoint as Under-Secretaries keen young men with previous experience of the Foreign Office, on first promotion to this rank. A sprinkling of them can with advantage be heads of departments promoted direct. To appoint young men in this way ensures that they will work with a will and carry cheerfully and resiliently the heavy burden placed upon them. To be promoted to these posts early in their career ensures that they will not be held back from further promotion or from transfer abroad on the plea that they cannot be spared from the Office, since they are in the normal course likely, after three or four years, to be transferred abroad, perhaps with promotion, by the time they are ripe for it. Indeed there is no better training for the headship of a Mission abroad than a tour of duty as Under-Secretary in the Foreign Office. The latter is near enough to the centre of things in London to acquire a close insight into the principles and operations of government, and he who knows how his own government works will be well qualified to observe and report upon the working of a foreign government and to profit by that knowledge in negotiating with it.

This emphasis upon the responsible role of Assistant Under-Secretaries will induce an increased sense of responsibility in heads of departments also, and this is all to the good; for though a young man, too ready to assume responsibilities out-running his judgment and experience, can cause great trouble and confusion, it is better that a few mistakes should be made through over-confidence than that the flow of business should be stemmed by over-caution.

The qualities which a Secretary of State will most prize in his Under-Secretaries of all ranks are drive and good judgment. He cannot himself attend to everything: and he will often be absent from the Office. He will wish to be secure in the confidence that his most responsible subordinates will, whether he is there or not, get on with the work of the Office and bring it to conclusions and, subject to normal human fallibility, to the right conclusions. They will know his mind, will correctly interpret his wishes and will have a just sense of the point at which their discretion reaches its limit and they have to return to him for instructions. If with all this, they have a touch of the daemon, so much the better; the highest posts should not be filled by 'grannies'.

With this foundation and superstructure soundly planned and established, there can be a distribution of pressure that will make it possible to avoid major distortion or disequilibrium; and while no device of organisation can relieve the Minister and his chief adviser from the duty to take the whole field of foreign affairs and Service administration within their purview, or the Minister from sole responsibility for all acts of policy, they can at any rate count upon a staff which has the necessary skill, imagination and judgment to bring major matters of business with a sure touch up to the point of final decision, which lies with the Minister alone. In these conditions, the Permanent Under-Secretary, if he is strong-minded enough, can save himself from being overwhelmed: but the same liberty is not so easily enjoyed by the political chief, who has other compulsions upon him than those of departmental life.

Soon after I took over the German Section of the Foreign Office, I read a memorandum by the Secretary of the Cabinet on the duties of senior civil servants. One thing which he said was that the Permanent Under-Secretary should make his presence and influence felt in every corner of his department. I tried to apply this advice both in the German Section and later in the Foreign Office. On appointment, I visited every department of the Office and tried to see every member of the staff from the highest to the lowest in the place where he or she worked. After that, the technique was, on selected occasions when I came across an error or a breach of procedure, either to address a brief and mildly reproachful minute to the department concerned or to send for the young man himself and talk the point over with him. The watchful but not unkindly eye is a good stimulus to good work; but this watchfulness is even more necessary on the part of the Minister himself, though what he will watch for will be political trouble rather than professional solecism. He must be sensitive to the potentially explosive item of business, and will induce a corresponding alertness, not to say unsleeping circumspection, on the part of his subordinates, senior and junior. If he is inert, his subordinates may, as civil servants have been known to do when left too long to themselves, by force of habit exercised unthinkingly on the unaccustomed occasion, land him in a political storm. The Foreign Secretary is no more immune from this danger, and is perhaps less so, than other Ministers. It is one of the Permanent Under-Secretary's prime functions to ensure that he and his juniors act as the eyes and ears of their Minister and reconnoitre the ground for the pitfall and the snare.

# COMPLEXITIES OF PARTY LEADERSHIP

*By* RICHARD ROSE

THE party leader, whether or not Prime Minister, holds a unique political office, but his solitary position in British politics does not emancipate him from the problem of reconciling role conflicts and official responsibilities. While the literature on party leaders is extensive, much of it concentrates upon description and historical analysis. Important as an understanding of historical precedent is, the meaning of particular incidents can only be generalised within some kind of conceptual framework. The article that follows discusses carefully the importance of defining terms such as 'leader' and 'power', if one is to assess how much a British party leader is affected by the difficulties that affect individuals in other roles and offices described in this chapter.

STUDYING party leadership is almost as difficult as exercising it. This is because party leaders have strengths and limitations resulting from a variety of governmental, party, sociological and psychological pressures. Relevant studies of party leadership in Britain have usually emphasised only one dimension of the job. In order fully to understand party leadership, it must be studied in all of these contrasting dimensions. When this is done, it appears that a party leader is less powerful than often claimed; he must also be a good follower. And he must be prepared to be checked by those whose authority rests upon foundations outside the structure of the party.

### *The One, the Few and Sociology*

Robert Michels' study of political parties remains relevant nearly half a century after it was written because he pioneered brilliantly the study of oligarchy in nominally democratic party organisations. Writing at a time when 'direct democracy' was a concern of political reformers, he sought to confound their efforts by showing how only oligarchy was possible in theory and practice. The argument is best read; it is unfair to sum up its complex development in a single iron law.

---

Reprinted from *Parliamentary Affairs*, XVI iii (1963) 257–73.

Michels was particularly concerned with the growth of parties with national mass-membership organisations. He argued, 'as a result of organisation, every party or professional union becomes divided into a minority of directors and a majority of directed'. Oligarchy, the rule by the Few, is 'a matter of technical and practical necessity', 'the inevitable product of the very principle of organisation'.[1] This is true notwithstanding the fact that party organisations, especially those of Socialists, may claim to be democratic. Leaders, whether party bureaucrats or parliamentarians, will inevitably develop vested interests different from rank-and-file members due to their high position in the party organisation. Rank-and-file members will, individually and collectively, lack power in the organisation; furthermore, psychological feelings of gratitude and deference will tend to make them submissive.

Throughout his analysis, Michels emphasised that party leadership was normally in the hands of a plurality of politicians. The Few who form in each party the leadership stratum were not mistaken for the One, the individual who holds the office of Leader in the party. In fact, Michels devoted relatively little attention to the One. Instead, he concentrated upon the power of the Few in comparison to the Mass of party members. He asserted: 'When there is a struggle between the leaders and the masses, the former are always victorious, *if only they remain united.*' (Italics supplied.) But he immediately went on to catalogue at considerable length inherent tendencies within a party making for disunity among the leadership: differing institutional ties, as with trade union and party leaders; national and regional differences; conflicts among old members and new recruits; age differences; social differences; and last, but hardly least, ideological differences. In addition, he catalogued a number of things that can cause conflict among leaders as the result of personal frictions.[2] The resignations and reshuffles of Conservative cabinets and the open factional conflicts between Labour leaders show that in the past decade (and earlier) both British parties have not had unity among their Few.

Michels describes two major ways in which conflict within the leadership stratum may be handled. On the one hand, those engaged in controversy may decide to amalgamate in order to reduce the weaknesses caused by disunity. Thus, in 1957, Hugh Gaitskell and Aneurin Bevan agreed to stop the warfare of the previous six years in hopes of greater gains for both. Alternatively, or at a prior stage,

[1] *Political Parties* (Collier ed., New York, 1962) pp. 70–2. The introduction by S. M. Lipset provides a good brief account of Michels' life and influence

[2] Ibid. pp. 167–87.

disputes may take the form of an appeal by the minority of the leadership stratum to larger and subordinate bodies in the party hierarchy. The minority in the Cabinet or Shadow Cabinet may appeal to a full party meeting in Parliament,[3] and, if defeated there, may continue the fight by appealing to the mass membership of the party. This phenomenon is taken for granted in America, where the built in obstructiveness of Congress *vis-à-vis* the President makes it necessary for him to regard an 'appeal to the people' as one of his most important resources. The simultaneous involvement of the Few and the rank-and-file Mass in disputes which divide the party on policy lines is the classic form of controversy within the Labour Party. The debate on German rearmament from 1951 to 1954 involved joint action by linked sections of the rank-and-file and the leadership stratum against other vertical groupings. The same sort of combinations, cutting across the Few/Mass distinction, were also in evidence during the debate on nuclear disarmament from 1957 to 1961. The preference of the Conservatives for keeping disputes private and the lesser position of the Conservative Party Annual Conference have reduced the number of occasions on which a section of the Conservative leadership stratum has appealed to those outside Parliament. The interwar and the pre-1914 conflicts on tariff reform show that this can sometimes happen. Michels granted that the rank-and-file and auxiliaries could, in instances of disunity, be decisive in their power. Furthermore, he recognised the influence which the *anticipation* of conflict might have upon the actions of the leadership stratum, citing as a profound psychological truth the dictum: 'He who wishes to command must know how to obey.'[4] For instance, one might speculate that the Commonwealth Immigration Act had its genesis in party leaders acting in anticipation of demands from their rank-and-file to restrict coloured immigration.

Because of the simple antithesis between 'direct democracy' and oligarchy, Michels' conclusions are pessimistic, and he ended his life a supporter of Benito Mussolini.[5] But today, our expectations of democracy are more narrow, and can be satisfied even if one grants that individual parties themselves are controlled by the Few. Schumpeter, for instance, treats democracy as a byproduct of electoral competition between competing party élites. Dahl has argued that inequalities exist, but that they are dispersed among a range of

[3] MPs may appear as members of the leadership stratum from the perspective of rank-and-file members. From the vantage point of the Front Bench, they may appear to be outside the leadership. In this analysis, the bulk of MPs are regarded as auxiliaries, intermediate between rank-and-file members and the leadership.

[4] Ibid. p. 173.

[5] Ibid. pp. 32–3.

leaders, whose actual ability to exercise leadership varies from situation to situation. Schattschneider has described democracy as existing as long as disunity among party leaders results in appeals to the mass of party members and electors. Elsewhere, I have argued that the existence of competing factions and tendencies within British parties at all levels, from that of the Front Bench in the Commons to the mass of a party's voters, itself provides important restraints upon the dominance of the One or of a Few. But Michels, with higher expectations of democracy, was disinclined to find satisfaction in scaling down expectations. For instance, he thought that conflict within the leadership stratum tended to produce the repressive discipline of factional conflict and contributed 'practically nil' to democracy.[6]

R. T. McKenzie's *British Political Parties* is a modern[7] landmark in British political studies, because he analyses both the theory and practice of party leadership. Historical in emphasis, the study gains in significance — and in controversiality — because it is also a book with a thesis. Although dealing with the same sort of problems as Michels, it differs in concentrating exclusively upon Britain, in a concern with the impact of constitutional offices upon party leadership, and in the greater attention paid to the One who is official leader.

McKenzie's analysis distinguishes between the One, the Few, the parliamentary auxiliaries, the extra-parliamentary party membership, and the electorate. It runs together a constitutional dictum and historical data, for the author is concerned to argue, *contra* believers in intra-party democracy, that it is unconstitutional for members of the extra-parliamentary membership to attempt to control the parliamentary leadership, who owe their primary allegiance to the electorate.[8] Furthermore, he demonstrates that 'direct democracy' cannot work within the Conservative and Labour organisations. The Mass of the party ought not to attempt to control the leadership (though misguided members of the Labour Party might ignore this

[6] Ibid. p. 187. Cf. J. A. Schumpeter, *Capitalism, Socialism and Democracy* (London: Allen & Unwin, 4th ed., 1952) ch. 22; Robert Dahl, *Who Governs?* (New Haven, Conn.: Yale University Press, 1961); E. E. Schattschneider, *The Semi-Sovereign People* (1960) chs 1, 8; Richard Rose, 'Parties, Factions and Tendencies; The British Example', *Political Studies*, XII i (1964) 33–46.

[7] Here it is appropriate to note that limitations of space prevent a discussion of that earlier classic, M. Ostrogorski, *Democracy and the Organization of Political Parties* (London: Macmillan, 1902).

[8] See e.g. *British Political Parties* (London: Heinemann, 1955) p. 583. Cf. Ralph Miliband, 'Party Democracy and Parliamentary Government', *Political Studies*, VI ii (1958).

dictum); the mass of the population can, however, exercise power by means of deciding between competing teams of party leaders at general elections.[9] Here McKenzie follows Schumpeter. Elsewhere, he introduces the possibility of individuals exercising political power between elections through pressure groups.[10]

The key term in the analysis is 'leadership by consent'. The analysis of the Conservative Party is intended to show that '*there is ample precedent for the withdrawal of that consent*', normally by activity within the 1922 Committee of backbench Conservatives in Parliament.[11] Thus, the Conservative Party is not so dominated by the Leader as it might appear. The Labour Party, nominally controlled by its membership, is also said to differ in practice from its dignified façade. But McKenzie then goes on to argue quite another point, that the two parties are in an essential feature alike: 'the distribution of power within the two parties is overwhelmingly similar'.[12] It is at this point that McKenzie begins to get into trouble. The cause is the under-emphasis given to the role of the trade unions in the Labour Party. For instance, Ernest Bevin receives fifteen indexed references compared to thirty-three for J. R. Clynes; similarly, Walter Citrine is indexed only twice, and David Kirkwood five times. But, although the author might think that the trade unions *ought* to play a part no more important in the Labour Party than that which the extra-parliamentary members of the Conservative Party play,[13] it does not follow that his preference matches that of leading trade unionists. And the constitution of the Labour Party, which assigns considerable formal authority to the trade unions in Annual Conference, in the National Executive Committee and in paying for sponsored MPs, is fundamentally different from that of the Conservatives.

The confusion caused by this attempt to ignore the *unique* position of the trade unions in British party politics is indicated in an important sentence in the text:

'Each element in the controlling group wields great authority; but each is composed of the accepted leaders of a voluntary democratic organisation (in one case the Parliamentary Labour Party, in the

[9] But compare Michels on Bonapartist tendencies in this process (op. cit. pp. 212–23).

[10] 'Parties, Pressure Groups and the British Political Process', *Political Quarterly*, xxix i (1958).

[11] Italics in the original. *British Political Parties*, pp. 22, 58. The phrase is quoted from Nigel Birch.

[12] Ibid. p. 582.

[13] See e.g. 'Policy Decision in Opposition: A Rejoinder', *Political Studies*, v ii (1957).

other the trade union movement), and, like the Conservative Leader, they exercise their authority *only with the consent of their followers.*'[14] Subsequent studies have indicated that in the making of *political* policy trade unions are hardly voluntary democratic organisations and may even be more dominated by the Few than a political party.[15] The machinations concerning block votes for and against nuclear disarmament between 1959 and 1961 provide striking evidence of how political policy is made there. More important is the ambiguity of the idea that both unions and the Parliamentary Party wield 'great authority'. McKenzie usually argues that the 'great authority' here attributed to unions must be and is overshadowed by the greater authority of the Parliamentary Party. Alternatively, one might suggest that the authority which each independently possesses can only be exercised jointly, like the authority of the Senate and the House of Representatives in America. In the words of Morgan Phillips, 'The Parliamentary Party could not for long remain at loggerheads with Annual Conference without disrupting the Party. . . . None of these elements can dominate the others. Policy cannot be laid down: it must be agreed.'[16] In requiring consent, the Labour and Conservative parties may be said to resemble each other and all other non-totalitarian parties. But a single resemblance at this level of generality does not make for 'overwhelming' similarity.

The subtitle of McKenzie's study is: 'the distribution of power within the Conservative and Labour Parties'. The book does a good job in stating where power does *not* lie — it does not rest exclusively with the One Leader of the Conservative Party, nor does it rest with the mass membership of the Labour Party. But while this knowledge is necessary, it is not sufficient, if one is to locate power in British parties. Many questions remain unanswered. We are not told why it is democratic for the electorate to be offered a choice between two and only two teams of leaders, and whether a choice between Tweedledum and Tweedledee would deny democracy. The effect of the differences in the social psychology of the parties and, for that matter, in their myths of internal government, are not explored. Nor does the author measure power in relation to making party policy so much as in relation to retention of office. Finally, the relative strength of the One and the Few is left unclear. In one sentence,

[14] *British Political Parties*, p. 507. Italics in the original. Cf. pp. 520–1.

[15] See e.g. Martin Harrison, *Trade Unions and the Labour Party Since 1945* (London: Allen & Unwin, 1960); Leslie Hunter, *The Road to Brighton Pier* (London: Arthur Barker, 1959); B. C. Roberts, *Trade Union Government and Administration* (London: Bell, 1956) ch. 4.

[16] *Constitution of the Labour Party* (1960) pp. 3–4.

McKenzie can speak of the Leader, by virtue of being actual or potential Prime Minister, as enjoying 'enormous authority over his followers'; the Cabinet is presumably included with the followers. Such remarks may shortly be followed by references to the Prime Minister and his Cabinet jointly sharing enormous powers.[17] Any contemporary discussion of leadership in British parties starts with McKenzie but cannot end with him.[18]

### *The Social Psychological Dimension*

The emphasis of sociologists such as Michels and McKenzie upon the structure of parties and government stands in sharp contrast to the approach of those journalists and academics who focus upon the psychology of party leaders and upon the relationship of a Leader or leaders with followers, i.e., the social psychology of leadership.

Any search for a single psychological set of characteristics necessary for a party leader is illusory — even though one may find commentators whose remarks presuppose that only one kind of personality is suitable for leadership. First of all, the personality most suitable for leadership may differ as the political situation changes. The Labour Party could hardly have been built so quickly if its leaders before 1914 had all been as undramatic as Clement Attlee. In the 1930s the Conservatives rejected Churchill as a peace-time leader, but turned to him later in wartime. Secondly, a survey of modern party leaders indicates that no one type predominates. Some individuals, such as Lloyd George, Ramsay MacDonald and Churchill, represented standards of behaviour far from those of the average party member. On the other hand, Bonar Law, Stanley Baldwin and Attlee appeared to enjoy a measure of appeal because of their very ordinariness; they did not stand far above their followers. It would certainly be false to history to argue that Keir Hardy, Attlee, Neville Chamberlain and A. J. Balfour all had the same type of personality and appeal. One might just as well argue that Woodrow Wilson, Warren Harding, Franklin D. Roosevelt, Dwight D. Eisenhower and John F. Kennedy 'essentially' have the same type of personality.

There is no guarantee that a party leader will necessarily enjoy psychological good health. In America, a school pioneered by Harold Lasswell has explored the idea that those who seek political power

[17] *British Political Parties*, p. 55.

[18] At this point it would be appropriate to mention the author's own indebtedness to R. T. McKenzie for starting him on his study of British politics in an extremely stimulating seminar at the London School of Economics, 1953–4.

are neurotic. In Lasswell's view, men may be said to go into politics as a means of sublimating their own neurotic disturbances by rationalising a desire for authority over others in terms of pursuit of the public interest.[19] Such an approach cannot be dismissed out of hand in a study of Hitler's Germany or Stalin's Russia. Research findings in America present conflicting results. In a study of Anton Cermak, mayor of Chicago in the early 1930s, Alex Gottfried concluded that Cermak's neurosis was 'negative from the point of view of human intercourse' but 'useful in the career of a political power-seeker'. But John McConaughy found that a group of South Carolina legislators were 'decidedly less neurotic than the general male population'.[20] In Britain, it remains unusual for a political biographer to attempt an intensive analysis of personality along conventional psychiatric lines.[21] Yet it would appear that this dimension of the life of Lloyd George, Churchill or Aneurin Bevan would be as important in understanding their political behaviour as it would be in the case of Theodore Roosevelt, Woodrow Wilson, or Franklin D. Roosevelt. Personality is not formed or altered overnight.

Less controversially and more clearly, psychological considerations are involved in the motives of party leaders. McKenzie's analysis often suggests that all members of the leadership stratum have a common motive — office-seeking, both for themselves and for their party collectively.[22] Yet his historical analysis notes instances in both parties when motives were very different. MacDonald in 1914, Austen Chamberlain in 1922 and Lansbury in 1935 all left the post of Leader because they put policy ahead of office. The careers of Churchill, Eden, Macmillan and Harold Wilson all indicate that the power of the Leader to give promotion to those within the leadership stratum cannot keep individuals from resigning — and that such resignations need not be political handicaps. Some members of the leadership stratum seem to have been motivated by a desire to avoid long periods in office — and others, such as Arthur Henderson, appear to have preferred secondary posts. The complexities of moti-

[19] See especially his *Psychopathology and Politics* (Cambridge: The University Press, 1930) and *Power and Personality* (London: Chapman & Hall, 1948).

[20] Alex Gottfried, 'The Use of Psychosomatic Categories in a Study of Political Personality', *Western Political Quarterly*, VIII ii (1955) 247. J. B. McConaughy, 'Certain Personality Factors of State Legislators in South Carolina', *American Political Science Review*, XLIV (1950) 903.

[21] An exception is R. W. Thompson's *The Yankee Marlborough* (London: Allen & Unwin, 1963) which attempts to illuminate Churchill's relations with his political colleagues by analysing his relations with his nanny, mother and wife.

[22] See e.g. *British Political Parties*, pp. 55, 585.

vation can be illustrated in the case of the Labour Party in the 1940s, when Attlee was strengthened by Bevin's preference for a nominally subordinate position in the party hierarchy[23] as well as affected by Aneurin Bevan's unwillingness, apparently partly on temperamental grounds, to stick the routine of office.

Much attention is often given to the purported impact of the personality of the party Leader upon the electorate. But the preponderance of evidence shows how *little* direct impact the personality of an individual party Leader has upon a general election result.[24] Party loyalties are remarkably stable in Britain, between elections and through an individual's lifetime. When a party gains a new Leader he is not evaluated so much in terms of his intrinsic personality as in terms of the partisan loyalties of electors. In other words, lifelong Conservatives will tend to like any man made Leader of their party, and lifelong Labour voters to like any man made Leader of their party. As Graham Wallas noted, between every politician and his audience there is interposed 'the party mask, larger and less mobile than his own face'.[25]

The Gallup Poll in this country does show that satisfaction with the Leaders of the two parties undergoes marked fluctuations. But these fluctuations are not reflected in the voting intentions of respondents. For instance, between January and August 1959, the number indicating satisfaction with Harold Macmillan rose from 53 to 67 per cent on the Gallup Poll — but the number of intending Conservative voters only rose from 37 to 41 per cent. In America, too, short-term fluctuations in the personal popularity of the President are not accompanied by similar movements in voting intention. As Richard Neustadt emphasises, popular impressions of a President's personality remain relatively constant; what fluctuates is the extent to which the public regard these constant traits — imagination, calmness, firmness, conciliatoriness — as salient to particular and pressing problems.[26]

Personality traits which may enhance an individual's recruitment into the leadership stratum cannot easily be specified — and they may be so numerous as to exclude only the certifiable lunatic from leadership. More readily documented, however, are the socially ap-

23 Due to the humble circumstances of his birth.

24 I have summarised this in 'People behind the Party Masks', *New Society*, no. 16 (17 Jan 1963).

25 *Human Nature in Politics* (London: Constable, 4th ed., 1948) p. 91.

26 *Presidential Power* (1960) p. 95. Neustadt's book, which deals with the *years* a President is in office, has been sadly neglected in Britain; too much emphasis is placed upon the presidential campaign — though it is far shorter in time and less important in its effect upon policy.

proved characteristics particularly appropriate to membership in the House of Commons. At one time, many thought these traits were inherited, and deferred to the House of Lords on this ground. In 1959, 35 per cent of the 258 Labour MPs elected listed their occupations as manual workers, and undoubtedly, in some instances, having a personality recognisably working-class facilitated nomination. In the Conservative Party, 72 per cent of MPs had attended public schools, and in more instances, having recognisably public school characteristics facilitated nomination.[27] Possession of such characteristics may or may not be an asset in terms of leading a political party; they can, however, be assets in getting into the House of Commons and beginning to rise up the career ladder in the party.

Though factors of personality are often stressed in writings about party politics, it is noteworthy that when social psychologists study leadership as a general phenomenon in society, they find them of little importance. The work of social psychologists is worth considering because they have explored the complexities involved in the theory and practice of social leadership to a far greater extent than have students of politics, even though in very different circumstances.

The most striking feature of this literature is the emphasis placed upon the reciprocal flow of influence between the Leader and followers. On balance, most writers emphasise the limited personal influence of leaders, especially of an individual Leader. This is because followers have a set of expectations concerning the behaviour of a Leader. In order to maintain the confidence of followers and their consent to his commands, the Leader must frame his commands so that they are in accord with what his followers expect. In other words, the Leader must conform to the already established expectations of his followers.[28] A Conservative Party Leader, taking office in 1957, could hardly have survived if he had repudiated the Suez intervention, which he was expected to support. In 1963, he would risk his leadership if he suggested, say, nationalising road transport. In the Labour Party, Hugh Gaitskell demonstrated that a Leader could not get his followers to repudiate the symbolic commitment to Socialism enshrined in Clause IV. The virtual absence of public discussion in the leadership stratum of conscription as an alternative to a British H-bomb suggests that Labour MPs expect such a policy

[27] See D. E. Butler and Richard Rose, *The British General Election of 1959* (London: Macmillan, 1960) pp. 127–30.

[28] See e.g. Ferenc Merei, 'Group Leadership and Institutionalization', in E. E. Maccoby, T. M. Newcomb and E. L. Hartley (eds), *Readings in Social Psychology* (3rd ed., 1958).

to be a non-starter and do not canvas it, anticipating that they could not gain a following for such a cause. A major difference between the Conservative and Labour parties is this: Conservative followers give overwhelming emphasis to expecting success at elections. A Leader is allowed much leeway on policy if he is electorally successful. In the Labour Party, expectations about policy are quite important to followers, and these expectations are likely to be harder to fulfil. A section of the Labour Party, as the post-1959 election debate demonstrated, has been prepared to reject electoral success as its object, expecting a leader to choose Socialism and defeat rather than Revision and possible electoral victory.[29] To turn Michels upside down, one might say that as long as followers remain united in their expectations, they are always victorious. One of the arts of leading a party is to know when one can conquer due to divisions and when one must bow before clear expectations of united followers.

The expectations of followers influence the behaviour of a party Leader long before he occupies the office, in the years when he is serving his apprenticeship as an auxiliary and a member of the leadership stratum. At this point he will be measured by expectations and standards which pre-date his arrival on the scene. As McKenzie emphasises, the Leader of a party emerges before he is elected. A man such as Anthony Eden or Hugh Gaitskell emerged because he lived up to the expectations of those who choose the Leader. In a reciprocal fashion, men with years of party service, such as Curzon, Morrison, Bevan (and individuals still in the House) have failed to become Leader because they did not fit the expectations of followers. The intrinsic character of an emerging contender for the Leadership may alter standards to a limited degree, but most important of all seems to be the closeness of the fit between followers' expectations and the perceived characteristics of individuals.

Once in office, especially the office of Prime Minister, a party Leader may begin to shape new expectations among followers, just as the expectations of followers may change due to the impact of external events. In other words, there is a dynamic element in the leader-follower relationship; it is not fixed through an individual's term of office. In America, this can be easily recognised in the 'honeymoon' which a newly elected President may enjoy with Congress; this is followed by a period of conflict as his policy preferences emerge, and subsequently, by a relationship in which the ups and downs of the partners are as frequent as in a turbulent marriage. In England, the virtual certainty of a Leader winning a vote on the

29 See e.g. R. H. S. Crossman, *Labour in the Affluent Society* (Fabian Tract 325, 1960) especially pp. 4–5.

floor of the House or a party meeting makes it harder to trace ups and downs because one is dealing in intangible measures of confidence. It seems that Harold Macmillan's influence upon his party has not been constant. When he took office in 1957 many things were unclear. By 1959 he had established a considerable measure of personal authority, but this has waned in the past eighteen months, and in the spring of 1963 one could speculate whether his career would end with his influence high, or nearly bankrupt. Neville Chamberlain provides an example of a Leader who rose to the heights and then abruptly fell. Stanley Baldwin, by contrast, gradually gained increasing influence over his followers, and reached a crest shortly before retirement — only to suffer a severe devaluation retrospectively. On the Labour side, Attlee began as a chairman so weak that he would not risk his influence by seeking to have the party end its opposition to service estimates in 1937.[30] As deputy Prime Minister during the war he gained a firm hold on the office. During most of his time as Prime Minister, however, he still showed some deference to Sir Stafford Cripps and Ernest Bevin. Perhaps the height of his personal authority was reached in 1951 when those two had left office. But by the time of his retirement in 1955 his authority within the party had again declined.

Individual leaders may have their ups and downs in office. Equally important, the office of Leader may itself have its ups and downs, when held by men who have differing conceptions of the job. In America, one may readily observe the dramatically different conception of the office which Dwight D. Eisenhower and John F. Kennedy have had. The contrast was as deliberate as that between many earlier holders of the office, such as Franklin D. Roosevelt and Herbert Hoover, or Woodrow Wilson and Harding. Richard Neustadt has succinctly described the position of President as one in which an individual may be functionally a leader or clerk, though the formal powers of the office are the same in both instances.[31] In Britain, as in America, a party Leader's image of his job will greatly influence the kind of relationship he seeks and attains with followers. At one extreme, Lloyd George stood free from stable ties with followers, building *ad hoc* coalitions of supporters. At the other extreme, J. R. Clynes saw himself as tied by the restrictions which followers placed upon a Labour Leader.[32] Baldwin's approach to the Leadership-Prime Ministership was that of a man who gave high priority to

[30] See Hugh Dalton, *The Fateful Years* (London: Frederick Muller, 1957), p. 133.

[31] Op. cit. ch. 1.

[32] See remarks quoted in McKenzie, *British Political Parties*, p. 306.

maintaining party (and national) unity, even if this meant that in policy terms he was often a do-nothing. Neville Chamberlain by contrast, appeared to see the office as one in which a man was judged by what he got done, and he pursued an active interventionist course in domestic and foreign policy. Hugh Gaitskell, in his approach to leadership, appeared not only to believe in policy intervention, but also to believe in settling intra-party disputes by rational discourse, as well as by steamrollering opponents through the prearranged mobilisation of trade union votes. (This, it might be noted, is never something a Labour Leader can personally command, but from the early 1930s onwards, a Leader who enjoyed Ernest Bevin's confidence could usually enjoy the benefit of this steamroller.) It remains to be seen whether Harold Wilson will take an active part in attempting to stamp his personal policy preferences upon the party, or whether he will often adjust his views in deference to others.

Because a Party Leader, like a President, stands at the centre of several different political institutions and networks, he will inevitably be involved in conflicts of roles; behaviour appropriate in one role may conflict with that suited to another co-existing leader-follower relationship. Clinton Rossiter, writing of the Presidency, lists possible conflicts between the President's roles as chief of state, chief executive, chief diplomat, commander-in-chief of the armed forces, chief legislator, chief of party, voice of the people, manager of the economy, and leader of the free world coalition. Rossiter notes that the President 'is all these things all the time', and 'several of these functions are plainly in competition, even in conflict with one another'. Neustadt comments on this multiplicity of roles: '*The same conditions that promote his leadership in form preclude a guarantee of leadership in fact.*'[33]

In Britain, the conventions of unified power through Cabinet government somewhat simplify matters. But conflicts nonetheless exist. A Prime Minister is, by turns and often simultaneously, chief partisan, head of a policy faction within his party, symbol of party unity, head of government and administration, supplicant for votes, bargainer and possible persuader of pressure group leaders, subordinate leader in the North Atlantic alliance, senior Prime Minister in the Commonwealth, ambitious of retaining office, and concerned with safeguarding the 'public interest'. The potential for conflict is considerable. Of particular importance is the tendency for actions as a party Leader appealing to partisans to conflict with actions as a national Leader appealing to those without partisan attachments

[33] C. Rossiter, *The American Presidency* (English ed., London: Hamish Hamilton, 1957) p. 25; Neustadt, op. cit. p. 7, italics in the original.

and those with attachments to party opponents. Macmillan, for instance, may recommend a national incomes policy to the nation in his role as national leader. But in seeking to make it work he must succeed as a persuader of trade unions, although he is also Leader of a party viewed suspiciously by them. At great moments of crisis in British party history, individual Leaders have sometimes resolved role conflicts by abandoning their party: this has been true from the days of Peel through the time of Ramsay MacDonald. Given the varied expectations from different groups of followers (and, perhaps, from conflicting allegiances in his own mind) a Leader can only hope to minimise conflict; he cannot eliminate what is inherent in his position.

The analysis of leadership from the vantage point of psychology and social psychology does not provide any simple formula by which to explain leadership or to assess leaders. These disciplines do provide wider and deeper insights into the complexities of party leadership. But no single factor will account for all the influence which a Leader may exercise upon followers, or followers upon a Leader. As Sidney Verba has written, in concluding a wide-ranging summary of the literature: 'There is no one "best" leadership structure. What structure is best must depend upon the group setting, task and membership — in short, upon the total situation.'[34]

### *Leadership and Political Power*

In order to assess the power of the party Leader and of the leadership stratum, we must go beyond the concern with retention of office, and focus upon the party as a policy-making body. Policies represent, as it were, the output of government. A Leader who cannot affect this output is no more than a figurehead, or a puppet. A leadership stratum that is severely limited in its influence upon this output is far from the potent oligarchy described by Michels.

It is here that the limitation of McKenzie's approach is most notable. In the second sentence of his preface he rules out any concern with 'party ideologies or programmes'.[35] But it is impossible to study the distribution of power within a political party — especially one controlling the Cabinet — without reference to these programmes, McKenzie's emphasis is upon retaining office as an index of power. The motives of the leadership stratum are taken to revolve around the party gaining office through a general election victory and indi-

[34] Sidney Verba, *Small Groups and Political Behavior: a study of leadership* (1961) p. 243.

[35] *British Political Parties*, p. vii.

viduals within the stratum receiving office, or promotion. There is a suggestion that the Conservative Leader may have trouble securing allegiance from the Party 'when its members are deeply stirred on an issue of principle'.[36] Conflicts on principle and policy within the Labour Party are treated curiously. For McKenzie, the 'basic issue' between the I.L.P. and the Labour Party in the 1920s and 1930s concerned the relationship of the party in Parliament with the party outside.[37] This writer would interpret it as primarily a conflict on policy; McKenzie's constitutional dictum would have been irrelevant if one held the views of the I.L.P. One might also ask whether the most important point at issue within the Labour Party in 1960 was a question about parliamentary and extra-parliamentary relations. One might assert the main conflict was between two conflicting foreign policies, one of which was dangerous and one of which was not.

A Leader who cannot influence policy is little more than Neustadt's 'clerk'. As Neustadt indicates, the President can so reduce his influence upon policy that the very suggestion that he has a programme is enough to send Congressmen into fits of public laughter.[38] When one focuses upon party (and government) policy-making, perspective abruptly changes. The mass membership is largely ignored — but the Leader loses his pre-eminence. He becomes (as in Saul Rose's analysis of the Labour Party, 1952–5) only one of a number of possible sources of policy decisions.[39] Most theoretical analyses of decision-making in politics emphasise the difficulties of assigning pre-eminent political power to one individual.[40] The question is an empirical one, to be answered empirically by investigating the particular circumstances in which policy decisions are made in Britain. Because Americans believe that they have a right to find out how decisions are made in government before all concerned are dead, it was possible for Richard Neustadt to analyse the President's influence upon policy through case studies. This is not permitted here. Because of official restrictions, any analysis is bound to remain a sketch. But a sketch is preferable to leaving an important area blank.

This sketch will concentrate attention upon the power of the party Leader when he is Prime Minister as well as head of a majority party

[36] Ibid. p. 103. [37] Ibid. p. 444.

[38] Op. cit. pp. 64–5. The incident cited occurred during President Eisenhower's second term.

[39] Saul Rose, 'Policy Decision in Opposition', *Political Studies*, IV ii (1956) 129.

[40] Most conveniently, see the summary by R. C. Snyder, 'A Decision-Making Approach to the Study of Political Phenomena', in Roland Young (ed.) *Approaches to the Study of Politics* (London: Stevens, 1958).

in the House of Commons. (The latter assumption is one that Asquith, Lloyd George and Ramsay MacDonald could not, of course, make.) This is because the machinery of British government gives supreme influence to the majority party at the expense of the minority, a situation different from America, where the existence of competing leaders in Congress complicates matters. It might be argued that just because a Prime Minister has so many role conflicts he is weaker rather than stronger in terms of personal influence on decisions. But because the decisions in which he is involved are government decisions, and not shadow decisions taken in Opposition, his potential power is the greater.

J. P. Mackintosh's *The British Cabinet* has outlined in some detail the historical and contemporary factors working to place the Prime Minister on a different level from his Cabinet colleagues, in terms of involvement in many areas of decision-making. But the pressures of modern communications, technology and an increased load of business weigh upon the Prime Minister individually as well as the Cabinet collectively. We have eloquent testimony from ministers and civil servants of the strenuous pace of departmental life, where simply keeping up with day-to-day work is difficult enough. Richard Neustadt has given us a picture of a President in office as a man whose time 'remains the prisoner of first things first. And almost always something else comes first'. It is difficult to conceive of a Prime Minister remaining sufficiently abreast of the complexities of foreign affairs, economics, defence, depressed areas, colonial affairs, education, housing, security, etc., to be able to exert personal influence when major decisions are to be made in all these fields. (One may avoid this problem by adopting a tautological criterion of major decision: one made by the Prime Minister.) If, as Professor Finer has shown, the responsibility of a minister in fact is somewhat different from the connotations of the term in some theories, then the responsibility of the Prime Minister for 'his' government is also not meant to be taken as personal involvement in all that is done in his name. A strength of British central government is that it simultaneously provides a dignified concentration of authority in the Cabinet, while dispersing efficient decision-making power to a wide variety of disparate groups.[41]

It would be misleading, however, to regard the expressed personal

[41] Cf. J. P. Mackintosh, *The British Cabinet* (London: Stevens, 1962) pt. 5; Neustadt, op. cit. p. 155; Lord Strang, *Home and Abroad* (London: Deutsch, 1956) ch. 10; P. C. Gordon Walker, 'On Being a Cabinet Minister', *Encounter*, no. 31 (1956); S. E. Finer, 'The Individual Responsibility of Ministers', *Public Administration*, XXXIV iv (1956).

preference of a Leader or Prime Minister as necessarily his own independent view. Attlee has neatly put the importance of a Leader anticipating what subordinates will expect:

'He has got to collect the voices of his Cabinet. He's got to reflect the views of his party. He's also got to some extent to reflect the views of the country as a whole. That does not mean he does not lead, but he leads in such a way, if he's wise, that he carries either his party or his country or his colleagues with him.'[42] For instance, a decision of the Attlee Government to nationalise the coal mines presumably represented the personal wish of the majority of the Cabinet, including the Prime Minister. But here, the leadership stratum was acting as the agent for a section of the party, rather than deciding independently. One might argue that the decision of the Prime Minister since 1957 to rely upon a British H-bomb is a sign of weakness, for it is simply going along with the prevailing sentiment of the party. A strong, McKenzie-type Leader might have shown his strength by abandoning the H-bomb and maintaining conscription. In practice, Macmillan has not sought to test his 'enormous authority' by exposing such a personal preference. In some circumstances decisions might be said to be taken by events. For instance, when Neville Chamberlain announced that Britain was at war with Germany in 1939, he had no alternative — and the decision represented his weakness in the face of external pressures, rather than independent authority over events or over followers.

When one surveys the major areas in which the British government is active — foreign affairs, defence, colonial policy, economics, and social welfare — it readily becomes apparent that there is little to fear from concentration of power in the hands of a Party Leader-Prime Minister or in the hands of one or two cliques in a leadership stratum.[43]

In international affairs and defence, the Prime Minister and his associates must bargain with other sovereign states in order to reach common goals. The failure of Britain, with France's aid, to sustain independent activity at Suez in 1956 dramatically indicated the limits of Britain in this field. The abrupt and unexpected switch of Britain's defences from reliance upon Skybolt to Polaris is a more recent example of the way in which the Prime Minister's policy in defence can be decided in Washington rather than London. The Cuban crisis last autumn demonstrated that this diminution in the independent authority of Her Majesty's Government has not been

[42] Quoted in *The Guardian*, 21 Apr 1963.

[43] This interpretation is developed at length in a forthcoming book by the author.

accompanied by a share in making decisions of greater impact.[44] In colonial affairs, the Prime Minister and Cabinet are again taking decisions in a climate which is determined outside Britain, and continuously facing the consequences of unilateral action taken by independence parties and illegal organisations. It would be misleading to say that Cyprus gained independence through a Cabinet decision. It gained independence primarily as the result of waging a guerrilla war. The British Government could influence the timing of such a decision more than its substance.

Economic policy involves decisions which are dependent in some measure for success upon international economic developments. These market factors are beyond the control of the British government, and to some extent, beyond the control of any national government, or any combination. Some economic arrangements can be concluded by bargaining. But the failure of the Prime Minister to enter the Common Market indicated spectacularly that what may have been the personal decision of one Englishman could be frustrated by the countervailing action of one Frenchman. Within the domestic economy, policy involves bargaining between the Government, business pressure groups and trade unions. The creation of the National Economic Development Council may be regarded as a formal recognition that important decisions about the economy are *de facto* taken outside Cabinet.

In the social welfare field the decisions of the Prime Minister and his colleagues are often binding. The decision to hang, or to reprieve, a convicted murderer is atypical; most welfare decisions involve prolonged bargaining with pressure groups, and changes in society may change the consequences of decisions. This for example, is happening in education, where the failure of the birth rate to conform to official projections has created difficulties in maintaining established policy for primary schools, just as the increasing numbers of qualified candidates for university education is having a major impact upon education (and government decisions) at the university level.

The foregoing sketch indicates that the restrictions upon the power of the party Leader which so concerned McKenzie, and of the leadership stratum, which so concerned Michels, are not located within the party organisation but outside it. In a democratic society such as Britain, by contrast to a party-dictatorship along Soviet lines, party leaders must work in conjunction with extra-party institutions and influences if they are to make decisions of consequence for their society.

[44] See e.g. 'Backbenchers Shed Some Illusions', *The Times*, 29 Oct 1962.

It thus no longer seems accurate to regard Britain as enjoying the type of *simple* constitution which Bagehot credited it with, one 'in which the ultimate power upon all questions is in the hands of the same persons'. Rather, the distribution of power is what Bagehot termed *composite*, 'in which the supreme power is divided between many bodies and functionaries'.[45] The latter type of government he described as characteristic of America. It is still characteristic of America and, because of the relative diminution of the influence of Cabinet in terms of the widened responsibilities today placed upon it, it is increasingly characteristic of Britain. The patterns of party and governmental leadership in the two countries are drawing closer together, not because of the increase in the power of the Prime Minister, but because his power is weakening. The dignified parts of British parties and of party government give the impression of great strength in the hands of leaders or a Leader; the efficient working of the political system contradicts this. The most important competition which confronts the party leadership stratum (Schumpeter's élites) comes not from within a party or from the opposition party, but from leadership based upon power rooted in other sections of British society, or outside it.[46]

45 *The English Constitution* (World's Classics ed., 1955) p. 201.

46 This article was written before the outbreak of the Profumo scandal, an extraordinary example of the complex social psychology of leader-follower relationships. *Editor's Note:* See pp. 172–82.

## CHAPTER III

# CASE STUDIES IN PUBLIC POLICY

THE simplest way to observe the policy-making process is to study it in terms of a single case. This is true whether the observer is a participant lobbying on behalf of a cause, or a student sitting in a library reading about some constitutional crisis of the past. Case studies show how seemingly disparate parts of a political system can be influential in the resolution of a particular matter of controversy. The concreteness of cases provides an excellent test of the meaningfulness of generalisations that rapidly proliferate in the social sciences today. Examining a general idea in terms of a relevant case may also lead to a more careful and precise definition of a concept, or to a reassessment of empirical assumptions that fail to hold true in the case at hand. In a complementary fashion, the study of individual cases may lead inductively to the development of new insights into politics, and concepts that can be generalised from the *aperçus* of close observation. Last and not least, case studies are true to life: properly done, a case study is an historically correct account of a sequence of events; it reveals the character of individual politicians as well as of more general social and political forces, and it is written in sufficient detail so that a good picture is drawn of policy-makers in action.

Notwithstanding their considerable value, case studies suffer from severe limitations. Precisely because such accounts concentrate upon specific, and sometimes idiosyncratic features of a situation, they can give the impression that every political event, as well as being unique unto itself, is also the result of laws unique to one situation. It is platitudinous but important to insist that the exposition and explanation of every political event involves influences which are generic to a significant class of cases, as well as influences that are presumptively unique to the case at hand. For instance, the Profumo scandal of 1963 involved many unique happenings, yet the basis of the government's difficulties lay in the fact that gentlemen are expected to tell each other the truth when lies could have dangerous consequences. A second and more serious limitation is that it is dangerously easy to generalise conclusions from a single case. The influences at work in a specific situation, because they are clear in themselves and plausibly relevant elsewhere, can be summarily stated as general propositions at the conclusion of an investigation into one event. Logically, such conclusions can only be valid for the situation from which they were extracted. In practical terms, generalisations usually have meaning in some other situations. The awkward fact is that it is difficult to stipulate which features of the given case must necessarily be found elsewhere for the generalisations to hold, and which factors need not remain constant. The problem can be overcome by generalising across time and space. For instance, Richard Rose's study of political public relations, *Influencing Voters*, involves case studies of public relations activities across a range of parties and pressure groups in two different general election campaigns in Britain. By analysing a number of cases, the author is then able to state conditions causing the rationality of campaign policy-makers to vary from election to election within a party, and from party to party and pressure group to pressure group at a given time.

When reading a case study, the most important and most difficult question to answer is: What range of problems is this particular case typical of? Contemporary social scientists have been disinclined to analyse carefully what differences, if any, exist between the way in which a government makes policies concerning the economy, the administration of justice, and pensions and welfare benefits. On *a priori* grounds, one might distinguish policy areas in terms of government policies now common to all modern states — foreign affairs, defence, the management of the economy, the provision of welfare services, and the maintenance of internal law and order. There are *prima facie* reasons for considering that the total influence of government varies and the particular role of governmental institutions also varies according to whether the problem at hand is, say, the punishment of a murderer or an international balance of payments deficit threatening currency devaluation. The variations in the role of government in the policy process reflect to a considerable extent the strength of the groups — within society and outside its boundaries — that are called into play by the type of problem at hand. Defence and foreign exchange crises by definition involve the government and citizens of other states. Even when all concerned are citizens of a single state, government domination is not certain; student protests involve extreme and overt challenges to law and order by persons consciously repudiating their legal obligations as citizens.

The familiarity of a problem and the time available to deal with it are additional features distinguishing cases confronting policy-makers. In a situation such as the administration of the National

Health Service, policy-makers are dealing with continuing and recurring problems of providing services; they respond to demands which are, within limits, capable of estimation. In a Royal Commission, members usually deal with a problem infrequently considered by governments, yet the members have the advantage of considerable time in which to obtain evidence and reach conclusions. In the Commonwealth Immigration Bill of 1963, the Home Office and MPs were faced with a novel piece of legislation, drafted and debated under severe (and self-imposed) pressures of time; the issue then proved to be recurring. The later activities of policy-makers in this field have shown that the initial pattern of confused and hasty activity is recurrent. Foreign policy and defence are most likely to present novel problems requiring immediate solution. The Suez War of 1956 was, however, the last major foreign-policy crisis in which Downing Street played a central role. The Profumo affair, involving key decisions taken and taken wrongly after midnight in anticipation of a deadline of the following morning, represents here the performance of government in an 'urgent' crisis.

## Bibliographical Note

Studies of particular political problems can be found in many contexts, from the Sunday papers to the memoirs or biographies of long-dead politicians. In the field of foreign policy, the most conveniently studied case is that of the Suez crisis, as discussed in Anthony Nutting, *No End of a Lesson* (London: Constable, 1967), Leon Epstein, *British Politics in the Suez Crisis* (London: Pall Mall, 1964), Peter Calvocoressi (ed.), *Suez — Ten Years After* (London: B.B.C., 1967) and Hugh Thomas, *Suez Affair* (London: Weidenfeld & Nicolson, 1966). Defence problems generally are discussed in R. N. Rosecrance, *Defense of the Realm: British Stategy in the Nuclear Epoch* (New York: Columbia University Press, 1968). The best known and most controversial study of wartime policy is C. P. Snow's *Science and Government* (London: Oxford University Press, 1961). The most uninhibited study of economic policy-making is Samuel Brittan's *The Treasury under the Tories, 1951–1964* (Harmondsworth: Penguin, 1964). George Ross's *The Nationalization of Steel* (London: MacGibbon & Kee, 1965) is a careful study of a conflict between big government and big business. *The Trial of Lady Chatterley*, ed. C. H. Rolph (Harmondsworth: Penguin, 1961) illustrates, as does the Profumo affair, how public policy and private morality can be intermixed. Nigel Nicolson's *People and Parliament* (London: Weidenfeld & Nicolson, 1958) is a first-hand account of the author's own problems in dealing with his parliamentary colleagues and his constituents. Richard Rose's *Influencing Voters* (London: Faber, 1967) extends studies in party politics to include party headquarters and pressure groups in the 1959 and 1964 general election campaigns.

Generalisations from case studies are most typically found in the literature of British pressure groups. Harry Eckstein's *Pressure Group Politics* (London: Allen & Unwin, 1960) has the broadest theoretical context. Other book-length case studies include James Christoph, *Capital Punishment and British Politics* (London: Allen & Unwin, 1962), Peter Self and Herbert Storing, *The State and the Farmer* (London: Allen & Unwin, 1962), Graham Wootton, *The Politics of Influence* (London: Routledge, 1963), H. H. Wilson, *Pressure Group: the Campaign for Commercial Television* (London: Secker & Warberg, 1961) and Frank Smallwood, *Greater London: the Politics of Metropolitan Reform* (Indianapolis: Bobbs-Merrill, 1965).

# SCANDAL 1963: THE PROFUMO AFFAIR

*By* Clive Irving, Ron Hall *and* Jeremy Wallington

The drama and sensational disclosures arising from the admission of John Profumo, Secretary of State for War, that he had lied to the Commons in 1963 about his relationship with a model, Miss Christine Keeler, attracted much more public attention than social science reflection. While the Profumo affair differed greatly in its superficial characteristics from many problems facing politicians, the events of the crisis do illustrate persisting characteristics of policy-making. These are well delineated in a study conducted at the time by three journalists then on the *Sunday Times*: Clive Irving, Ron Hall and Jeremy Wallington. Throughout their book on the Profumo affair, the authors draw attention to the importance of trust — and of misplaced trust — in British government. The excerpt printed here also underlines the problem of co-ordinating information dispersed among government departments, and the difficulties subordinates have in selecting what information is appropriate and necessary to tell a Prime Minister.

Until the beginning of April, the inquiries into the Profumo case had been conducted through three basic channels: by politicians, the Security Services and the newspapers. All three by then knew about the same amount: the Press had detailed but unsubstantiated accounts from Miss Keeler, Miss Rice-Davies and lesser versions from Dr Ward and others; the Security Services knew about Ivanov, Dr Ward and Mr Profumo's association with them, and of Miss Keeler's part; the Prime Minister and his staff knew about the rumours but felt that they had been effectively answered by Mr Profumo's denial; and Mr Wigg and Mr Wilson had their dossier. There remained to be added a fourth pressure. This began its course on 2 April, when Chief Inspector Samuel Herbert and Det. Sgt. John Burrows, two officers attached to Marylebone Lane Police Station, began investigations into Dr Ward's activities.

---

Reprinted from *Scandal '63* (London: Heinemann, 1963) pp. 119, 131–42. For the official account, see *Lord Denning's Report*, Cmnd. 2152 (London: H.M.S.O., 1963). See also Wayland Young, *The Profumo Affair: Aspects of Conservatism* (Harmondsworth: Penguin, 1963).

Then, after nearly eight weeks' work, the separate strands began to come together, or, to put it another way, the left hand was about to learn what the right hand had known for some time. It is now necessary to recapitulate and survey the whole machinery of inquiry and political communication, for somewhere there had been a serious breakdown in communications. This was the comparative state of knowledge up to 28 May:

*The Prime Minister* knew from 4 February that rumour alleged that Mr Profumo and Miss Keeler were lovers; that the *News of the World* had a story which alleged that Mr Profumo was sharing his mistress with the Soviet naval attaché; from 27 March he knew from the letter Mr Wilson had given to him that Dr Ward, who presided over whatever kind of relationship Miss Keeler had with Mr Profumo, had acted as an 'honest broker' in unofficial approaches by the Russians to the Foreign Office; from 10 April he had had Mr Wigg's dossier with its detailed description of the activities of Dr Ward and Ivanov, and its picture of the lurid world into which Mr Profumo had apparently strayed, and the relationship Dr Ward claimed with the Security Services; from 7 May he knew that Dr Ward was saying that Mr Profumo had not told the truth in his statement to the House of Commons on 22 March; and he knew that the Leader of the Opposition felt strongly that there had been a security *risk* in Mr Profumo's relationship; he knew all this and he knew that Mr Profumo had strenuously denied that he and Miss Keeler were lovers and that security had in any way been prejudiced.

*The police* knew from 26 January, as a result of their inquiries into the Edgecombe case, that Miss Keeler alleged that she had been asked by Dr Ward to pump Mr Profumo for military information, and that she said she had not done so; from 24 March that Miss Keeler's mother had been approached by Mr Eddowes about her relationship with Mr Profumo and Ivanov; from 29 March that Mr Eddowes alleged that Miss Keeler had been asked by Ivanov to question Mr Profumo about nuclear warheads; and from 2 April how Mr Profumo fitted into Dr Ward's life and what that life consisted of.

*The Security Services* knew from June 1961, as a result of their surveillance of Ivanov, that the Russian saw a lot of Dr Ward; from July 1961, from Dr Ward himself, that Mr Profumo was a friend of his; that on 9 August 1961, Mr Profumo had been warned of the dangers of associating with Dr Ward; from late in 1962 that Ivanov and Dr Ward had made approaches on behalf of the Soviet Embassy during the Cuban crisis; from January 1963 about Miss Keeler allegedly being asked to obtain nuclear secrets and the subsequent statements repeating this; from 10 April, according to the dossier compiled by Mr Wigg and passed on to them by the Prime Minister, that Dr Ward had been evasive about his interest in Ivanov and sympathetic to Russian interests during both the Berlin and Cuban crises.

*Mr Wilson* knew from 10 March of Mr Wigg's growing dossier; from 26 March of Dr Ward's activities during the Cuban crisis and all that he had told Mr Wigg; from the middle of May that Dr Ward was ratting on Mr Profumo and making allegations to the Home Office and the newspapers.

This was the situation on 28 May, while Mr Macmillan was reassessing the facts. By that evening he had decided that there would have to be an inquiry, and that Lord Dilhorne, the Lord Chancellor, should conduct it. Mr Profumo's days as a Minister were now numbered.

The information about Miss Keeler's 26 January statement reached Mr Macmillan from the Security Services on 29 May, having taken 123 days to do so. This would probably in itself have been enough to set off an inquiry; in the event the Prime Minister had already done so. Mr Wilson could claim some of the credit for that... and, of course, Mr Wigg, whose long, wearing and much-criticised investigation was about to be vindicated.

The Prime Minister communicated his change of attitude to Mr Wilson on 30 May. He wrote: 'I have been thinking about our talk on Monday. I am sure in my own mind that the security aspect of the Ward case has been fully and efficiently watched, but I think it important that you should be in no doubt about it.' And he disclosed the Lord Chancellor's inquiry.

This was the last full day of Parliament before Whitsun recess. When Mr Macmillan's note was delivered to Mr Wilson both of them were at Westminster, and both were in the chamber at question time. Mr Wilson scribbled a note to the Prime Minister asking that the Lord Chancellor's inquiry should be announced, in view of the fact that so many people then knew of Dr Ward's allegations. The note was slipped across to Mr Macmillan, but he did not react. Later that evening it was formally acknowledged by the Prime Minister's secretary; Mr Macmillan himself was going to Scotland for a holiday.

There was another incident in the Commons that afternoon, which seemed meaningless at the time. Several MPs noticed that in the shadow behind the Speaker's Chair Mr Profumo was in a huddle, first with the Prime Minister and then with Mr Redmayne, the Chief Whip.

The Prime Minister was later criticised for not doing what Mr Wilson had requested: revealing the Lord Chancellor's inquiry when it began. The reason was that, as Mr Macmillan had said in his note to Mr Wilson, he was still confident about the security aspect, and at that stage the inquiry was confined to within the administration itself, for the private consumption of the Prime Minister and Mr Wilson.

Mr Wilson had anyway decided to continue the psychological warfare. Mr Parkin had finally returned to Westminster from his country seat on Tuesday, the 28th. His question and his immediate absence after tabling it, had created something of a panic. As soon as he got back he was met by a Whip's runner, literally panting. Mr Wilson, he was told, wanted to see him at once.

Mr Wilson explained to him that the part of his question which had referred to 'expensive call-girl organisations' was against his policy of tackling the case from the sexual side. He did not want to institute an inquiry into vice, but into security. He asked Mr Parkin if he would mind withdrawing his question, and Mr Parkin agreed. There was no question of a *diktat*; it was done for the sake of consistent tactics. Mr Wilson then told Mr Wigg that he wanted a question put down, and he felt that it should have the maximum authority behind it. He suggested that it should be tabled by an elder statesman of the Party, Mr Chuter Ede, a former Home Secretary and the man who had set up the Lynskey Tribunal in the Sidney Stanley case. Mr Ede had a reputation for maintaining the highest standards of Parliamentary and public life. He agreed to the idea, and the new question was drafted in Mr Wilson's office.

All this was happening on 30 May; and since the House was about to go into recess there was little time left. Another pressure intervened: it was also the day of the Coronation Cup race at the Epsom meeting (the Derby was run the day before) and Mr Wigg, a considerably experienced student of the turf, had arranged to drive Mr Chuter Ede and his sister down to Epsom for the afternoon.

As they left Westminster Mr Ede gave Mr Wigg a copy of the question as it had been drafted, but since they were anxious to get to Epsom Mr Wigg pushed it into his pocket without looking at it. This had bizarre consequences. Mr Wigg, Mr Ede and his sister were in the grandstand when a message was relayed over the entire loudspeaker system and consequently over all of Epsom Downs. The voice boomed its incongruous message: 'Would Mr George Wigg please go to the weighing-room?' Somewhat embarrassed, Mr Wigg headed for the weighing-room to find there was a phone call for him from Mr Wilson's office. There, among the saddles, the jockeys and the weighing machines, high Parliamentary business was discussed. But the din was too much, and Mr Wigg went to the telephone in the office of the Clerk of the Course and phoned back. He was told that the Chuter Ede question was out of order, and he was asked to consult Mr Chuter Ede on the redrafting. Having done so, he decided to drive straight back to Westminster and check the final version when it was put down.

The original question had said: '. . . to ask the Secretary of State for the Home Department what information he has received from Dr Stephen Ward in connection with inquiries carried out by the Metropolitan Police; and what action he proposes to take.' It was the mention of the police inquiries which put the question out of order. The revised question was tabled at 4.50 p.m. It said: '. . . to ask the Secretary of State for the Home Department what information he has received from Dr Stephen Ward *about a Ministerial statement made to the House on 22nd March 1963* and what action he proposes to take thereupon.'

This question was intended to harry the government and to step up the war of nerves. The tactics had been approved by the Shadow Cabinet. They were certainly effective.

Mr Macmillan took the night sleeper to Inverness on 30 May leaving Lord Dilhorne to begin his inquiry. On 31 May Lord Dilhorne told Mr Profumo that he would want to see him on the following Thursday, 6 June. Soon after learning this, Mr and Mrs Profumo left London to spend Whitsun in Venice. They intended to return on 5 June. Over the Whitsun weekend, which brought the first spell of warm weather since the severe winter, there was the first holiday exodus of the year. But Lord Dilhorne was not taking a rest — he was a tireless worker — and he made better progress than he had expected. He sent a telegram to Mr Profumo, via the War Office, saying that he would want to see him a day earlier on Wednesday, 5 June.

Mr Profumo had gone to Venice clearly realising that the forces of truth were closing in on him. The lie was becoming impossible to live with. Lord Dilhorne's cable indicated that escape was now impossible. He knew that the Labour Party were pressing for details of Dr Ward's allegations, and he realised that if the cornered Dr Ward was prepared to rat on him his own fate was ineluctable. The first person he had to tell demanded the most painful confession of all: his wife. Until then she, like all Mr Profumo's colleagues, had not known. And so, that weekend Mr Profumo's burden became lighter by one person. The crisis made the beauties of Venice incongruous; the Profumos cut short their holiday and arrived back in London on the Golden Arrow on Whit Monday.

That evening Mr Profumo telephoned Mr Bligh, the Prime Minister's Principal Private Secretary, and said that he wanted to see the Prime Minister because there had been 'a serious development'. It was pointed out that the Prime Minister was in Scotland, and that if the matter was urgent it had better be dealt with at once in London. It was arranged that Mr Profumo should see Mr Bligh at Admiralty House at 10.30 a.m. the following day. When Mr Profumo arrived for this meeting Mr Redmayne, the Chief Whip, was also present.

The 'serious development' was that Mr Profumo had decided to confess that for four months he had been lying to his colleagues, to his wife and to the Law Officers of the Crown. He had lied on the floor of the House of Commons and had so betrayed the display of loyal trust provided by the Prime Minister. He had taken legal action and recovered damages on the basis of those lies.

He tendered his resignation and said that he would apply for the Chiltern Hundreds, the archaic procedure by which he immediately ceased to be a Member of Parliament. His political career was finished and his reputation ruined. Later that day, on the next pre-arranged phone call to the Prime Minister, Mr Bligh told him of Mr Profumo's confession and resignation. When the Prime Minister had left for his holiday he had still felt that the incident, as he then knew it, raised no security issues, and he was convinced that Mr Profumo had been telling the truth all along, a conviction fortified by the successful legal action which had been taken. Now the deception cut deep into the Prime Minister's instinct of trust, the blow was personal and severe. He said that he wanted time to consider his reply, and would dictate it the following morning by telephone.

At Admiralty House, meanwhile, the statement announcing the sensation had to be prepared. This involved Mr Profumo's solicitor, Mr Clogg, and Theodore Goddard & Co., who had been deceived by their client. They were anxious that the statement should clearly absolve them from complicity in the deception. By the morning of Wednesday, 5 June, the form of the statement had been settled, and the Prime Minister's reply had been received from Scotland. All that then had to be done was for copies of the confession and reply to be duplicated and released to the world.

While this revelation was on the brink of disclosure Sir William Haley, as if by some clairvoyant urge, was making an uncannily apposite speech at the annual lunch of the Automobile Association. The Press, he said, lived by disclosures, and a healthy society should also live by disclosures: 'We have to fight for more freedom. We need a new attitude on the part of the makers of news — officialdom, Government departments, parish councils, institutions, big business and trade unions — any or all of whom will try to withhold news if they can.'

The message was an echo of Sir William's 'It *is* happening here' leader: 'It is easy to understand the reluctance of people in any kind of body to reveal information which will disclose error or weakness, and how they at once hastily arrange a Press conference to sidetrack any real inquiry.' Mr Macmillan's Press secretary, Mr Harold Evans, was at that moment arranging a Press conference for an opposite purpose.

At 2 p.m. the political correspondents had been called to the Conservative Central Office to hear an outline of a report on the health of the Conservative Party machine, which had been a labour of love over many months for the ex-Chancellor of the Exchequer, Mr Selwyn Lloyd. At the end of this conference the lobby correspondents were told that Mr Evans would make an announcement to them at 6 p.m. By 4 p.m. some of them had phoned their editors and told them that their hunch was that announcement concerned Mr Profumo.

At 6 p.m. Mr Evans released Mr Profumo's statement. It said:

Dear Prime Minister,

You will recollect that on March 22 following certain allegations made in Parliament, I made a personal statement.

At that time rumour had charged me with assisting in the disappearance of a witness and with being involved in some possible breach of security.

So serious were these charges that I allowed myself to think that my personal association with that witness, which had also been the subject of rumour, was, by comparison, of minor importance only.

In my statement I said that there had been no impropriety in this association. To my very deep regret I have to admit that this was not true, and that I misled you, and my colleagues, and the House.

I ask you to understand that I did this to protect, as I thought, my wife and family, who were equally misled, as were my professional advisers.

I have come to realise that, by this deception, I have been guilty of a grave misdemeanour, and despite the fact that there is no truth whatever in the other charges, I cannot remain a member of your Administration, nor of the House of Commons. I cannot tell you of my deep remorse for the embarrassment I have caused to you, to my colleagues in the Government, to my constituents and to the party which I have served for the past 25 years.

Yours sincerely, Jack Profumo.

The letter was dated 4 June and sent from 3 Chester Terrace, Regent's Park, N.W.1, the Profumos' home.

The Prime Minister's reply, dated 5 June, was sent from Ardchattan Priory, Connel, Argyll, the home of Lieut.-Colonel and Mrs R. Campbell-Preston, where he was staying. It was more brief:

Dear Profumo,

The contents of your letter of June 4 have been communicated to me, and I have heard them with deep regret. This is a great tragedy for you, your family, and your friends.

Nevertheless, I am sure you will understand that in the circumstances, I have no alternative but to advise the Queen to accept your resignation.

Yours very sincerely, Harold Macmillan.

### *Who Was to Blame?*

When the truth about Mr Profumo was revealed, the reaction to it was so violent that it obscured the real issue: how had he got away with it all this time? The rumour had been breeding for so long that elaborate fantasies were created, some of them wilfully, others the product of misunderstanding. Many adult, mature men of great political experience were prepared to believe the wildest inventions. The sinister and the grotesque found ready ears.

Underneath, interred by mounting deposits of absurdities, somewhere lay the truth.

The first fantasy was the gravest charge of all: that the Prime Minister had known about Mr Profumo's sad affair all along and had, for some lunatic reason, decided to bluff it out. This was quite seriously suggested by some senior members of his own party — if they suggested it without being serious it somehow would have been worse. They believed it. The kindest interpretation that can be put on this story is that it resulted from them receiving only half the information: that they knew that in February the Prime Minister had been told about the rumours, but because no overt action followed he had connived to conceal the truth. Many of Mr Macmillan's enemies saw him as the cartoonists caricatured him: as an Edwardian recluse, remote from reality with government somehow being conducted by others who trouble him as little as possible. And yet they saw the same man capable of compromising his honour, prejudicing his future and jeopardising his government solely to protect an adulterer. Did that fit the Edwardian code? One illusion cancels the other.

In the end the charge against the Prime Minister was just that nobody had told him. A failure of communication. But it did not end with not being told — how anxious was he to *be* told? It is not an entirely passive responsibility. What, then, should have activated his curiosity? The failure was really created by two things: a system and an attitude.

To get the attitude right, it is necessary to recall the time when Mr Macmillan became Prime Minister, just over six years before. He followed, in Eden, a man who had not only been unseated by the political disaster of Suez but a man whose health had been broken by the job. Eden, in turn, had succeeded in Churchill a man of abnormal, Herculean constitution. When Eden broke down it was said the Prime Ministership had grown too big a burden for one man; that it was, in fact, a killing job. It was certainly a wounding one in the way that Eden did it; nobody else could be *his* Foreign Secretary.

Mr Macmillan appraised this argument, that the job was lethal, and saw its flaw: that it depended on the philosophy of the man. He then made a decision that was fundamental to his whole subsequent performance: he would rely absolutely on delegation. He constructed the pyramid of command, carefully chose the men who would form it, laid down the lines of responsibility, and left himself clear for the essence of Prime Ministership: decision-making.

This system seemed to work, and it suited superbly his own abilities and character. It kept his mind uncluttered, and it ensured his physical survival. Where it broke down was in the one area where there was no minister to delegate to: security. Delegation was a sound enough philosophy, and the only viable one. But it required that each department should have not only its administrators but its political heads: men able not only to operate the machine but who knew also the wider canvas of the Cabinet and pressures external to their own ministries.

Mr Macmillan's government had been accident-prone in its handling of security (though it is fair to add that the Labour party had had similar troubles when it was in power). Each spy incident had been followed by an inquiry of some form, and each time communications failure had played some part, notably in the failure to record and pass on the glaring character defects of Houghton, the Portland Base traitor. Each case had led to some minor tightening up, but it was always the policy of the stable door. The Profumo case, involving not a security leak but a security risk, made the security issue a political one more than one of actual security techniques (though it suggested that the resources for surveillance were not all that they might have been). There was a great deal of confusion in the way of seeing the new security problem clearly: many people mixed it up with external intelligence. But it was a defect of *political structure*.

Certainly, the head of the Security Services had direct access to the Prime Minister. But this meant that he went to see Mr Macmillan only when he felt that there was need to: that depended on his own evaluation and judgment, yet he was unaware of what political pressure there might be. It was plainly a one-dimensional role, which anyway carried enough administrative burden without requiring political instincts as well. Mr Macmillan's Achilles heel was that he had no Minister of Security. This was a controversial idea, but it had been around for years. Mr Wilson subscribed to it. Yet Mr Macmillan was wary of it. There was in his make-up a genuine fear, perhaps a little old-fashioned, of creating within the executive a monolith security organisation which, by reason of its essentially covert nature, might become a law unto itself. He was always at pains to emphasise that a free society had to be wary about how much rope it allowed its Security Services. He said, after the Profumo revelation: 'There is, of course, unfortunately under modern conditions, where so much is known of the ways in which private weaknesses can be played upon, a wide range of behaviour which is properly a matter of security. But if the private lives of Ministers and of senior officials are to be the subject of continual supervision day and night, then all I can say is that we shall have a society very different from this one and, I venture to suggest, more open to abuse and tyranny than would justify any possible gain to security in the ordinary sense.' This may be admirable sentiment, but it was only sentiment. The point which it avoided was that anybody whose office or responsibility in any way involved the security of the state must accept, surely, that their freedom has to be circumscribed by degrees appropriate to their responsibility. This is far from being the creed of McCarthyism, which Mr Macmillan rightly feared.

In any case, Mr Macmillan's case could hardly hold water as an argument against having a Minister of Security: this would give him more of a safeguard rather than less.

But there was another, more practical obstruction to the idea of a new Minister. It was that whichever politician was chosen for the job, he would have to commit virtual and instantaneous political suicide, or at least a form of self-denial extremely rare among politicians. He would have to submerge completely from public life. He could not go before the House of Commons and brag about his department's successes. His appearances would be confined entirely to answering criticisms of failure. Wherever this man of advanced humility was to be found, it seemed that it was not among Mr Macmillan's colleagues.

The Prime Minister's dependence on *ad hoc* contact with the head of Security Services introduced two entirely subjective conditions: the will in the Prime Minister himself to question and to seek the answer; and the will in the head of the Security Services to tell. Each would decide independently. The Security man would, for example, obviously trouble the Prime Minister only with items which he thought he should know — yet he could not possibly foresee all the situations when this would be necessary. From a day or so after 26 January the Security Services had had Miss Keeler's statement, but obviously decided that there was no reason for it to go to Admiralty House. Sir Norman Brook had made a minute of his warning to Mr Profumo in 1961 and he, only a door away from the Prime Minister, had not felt that it merited passing on. With the information they had, they were probably right. Had they been in the Prime Minister's chair they might have seen it differently, certainly after the events of 4 February.

There was no question of dereliction of duty; there was simply not the channel of communication which enabled each fully to appreciate the other's problem. When Mr Macmillan was, on 27 May, finally provoked into instituting an inquiry, the results came soon enough. But the machine had to be kicked.

# THE GENESIS OF THE RACE RELATIONS BILL

*By* KEITH HINDELL

LEGISLATION on race relations in Britain has been characterised by a series of *ad hoc* and hasty government responses to specific and immediate political controversies. The public controversy surrounding such legislation has made it peculiarly amenable to close examination. Whatever one thinks of the outcome of such measures, the process of their birth is far more complex and messy than that which is usually presented as characteristic of policy-making in modern British governments. Because much legislation is drafted in a different tempo, in a situation reflecting years of bargaining relationships, policy-making on race need not characterise the whole of British government. Yet the behaviour shown is sufficiently general in its implications so that Hindell's study raises questions about the over-all performance of what is often described metaphorically as the smoothly oiled machinery of British government.

AT the end of October the present Parliament will complete some purely formal stages of the Race Relations Bill and one month later it will become law. This article is an account of its origins, the stages of evolution and the process of enactment.

Soon after Sir Frank Soskice took up office as Home Secretary in October 1964 he gave instructions to his staff to prepare legislation on racial discrimination and race hatred. He was honouring a pledge made by the Labour Party in its election manifesto:

> A Labour Government will legislate against racial discrimination and incitement in public places....

This followed closely the National Executive Committee's emergency pronouncement on the subject in September 1962, although the Party had been committed to make discrimination illegal since 1958.[1] But it seems that the Party did not make any preparations for

[1] Labour Party, *Report of Annual Conference 1962*, p. 197, and *Racial Discrimination — Statement by the Labour Party* (1958) p. 4.

Reprinted in full from *Political Quarterly*, XXXVI iv (1965) 390–405. For a long-term analysis of the situation, see Nicholas Deakin 'The Politics of the Commonwealth Immigrants Bill', ibid. XXXIX i (1968) 24–45.

legislation until after Harold Wilson incorporated it in his speeches on immigration from November 1963 onwards.[2]

Individual members of the Labour Party had been advocating legislation along these lines at least since 1950. At that time Mr Reginald Sorensen (now Lord Sorensen) introduced a Colour Bar Bill to make discrimination in public places a criminal offence. Two years later the Commonwealth Sub-Committee of the N.E.C. asked two experts to give them advice 'on the advisability of sponsoring such legislation'. Dr Kenneth Little of the Department of Social Anthropology at Edinburgh University and author of *Negroes in Britain* advised that there was

> a good case both in principle and in fact for the enactment of colour bar legislation . . . as a means of stirring the national conscience and of creating a new standard of public behaviour in relation to coloured people.[3]

He also urged that administrative machinery similar to the American Fair Employment Practices Commission, be set up to deal 'both practically and positively with the wider implications of the Colour problem'.

Sir Lynn Ungoed-Thomas, MP (now a judge), examined the legal aspects of Little's memorandum and advised the sub-committee against any colour bar legislation 'for purely propaganda value'. Instead he recommended that it should be confined to specific abuses such as discriminatory clauses in leases, discrimination in inns, public-houses, lodging-houses, dance halls and employment. He also thought that administrative action could be of value especially in dealing with landladies who discriminated against coloured students.

The Labour Party did not act upon either of these briefs and in the circumstances of 1953 when the problem was one principally of hundreds of students rather than one of hundreds of thousands of immigrants it is not surprising. It might have been wiser to advocate such legislation then, but it was hardly a matter of practical politics.[4]

Three years later when the first waves of immigrants were arriving Fenner Brockway, MP (now Lord Brockway), introduced a Racial Discrimination Bill which clearly owed a great deal to Ungoed-Thomas' earlier suggestions. It sought to prevent the keepers of inns, lodging-houses, restaurants, public-houses and dance halls from discriminating on the grounds of 'colour, race or religion'. It also

[2] House of Commons debate, 27 Nov 1963.

[3] Unpublished paper (1953) p. 6.

[4] See Cedric Thornberry, 'Commitment or Withdrawal? The Place of Law in Race Relations in Britain', *Race*, VII (July 1965) for a somewhat different interpretation.

sought to make it illegal for an employer of more than fifty people to discriminate in hiring and firing and to make discriminatory covenants in leases void. Anyone found guilty of discrimination was to be liable to a maximum fine of twenty-five pounds and withdrawal of his licence or registration if any. In addition any person who suffered damage as a consequence of discrimination could also recover such damage by a civil action.

Fenner Brockway's Bills on discrimination became almost an annual event as between 1956 and 1964 he introduced eight more. As time went by the original syllabus was enlarged in some directions and reduced in others. Discrimination in the paying of wages was included in three Bills but then omitted and the Bill published in November 1960 dropped the employment clause. The final change was in December 1961 when a clause was added which sought to make racial incitement, either in speech or in writing, an offence and it increased the maximum penalty to £100.

Brockway's Bills were never taken up by the Parliamentary Labour Pary and were never allowed a second reading but as the racial situation became more serious and more obvious they did attract support from all parts of the House. At the start the co-sponsors were mainly left-wing members of the Labour Party but the sixth Bill in December 1960 was signed by three Conservatives, one Liberal (Jo Grimond) and four right-wing members of the Labour Party including Ungoed-Thomas. The three subsequent Bills all had support from members in all three parties.

### *Labour Prepares for Office*

Six years after it had first made a definite commitment the Labour Party began to make detailed preparations. At the beginning of 1964 the Shadow Cabinet and the Society of Labour Lawyers were both asked by the National Executive Committee to draft proposals for legislation.[5]

Three members of the Shadow Cabinet (Sir Frank Soskice, Douglas Houghton and Gilbert Mitchison) drafted a Bill and a memorandum which Soskice presented to the N.E.C. Study Group on Race Relations in June 1964. The Committee concerned itself mainly with the question of incitement — what was the best way of defining it? what was the best method to use to control it without infringing too much on the rights of free speech? how could the law

[5] On 15 Feb Wilson said Labour 'would take the Bill over, with whatever minor amendment that may be necessary and turn it into a Government measure and legislate it'. (*The Times*, 17 Feb 1964.)

best catch a major fascist figure and yet not be too irritating to the general public? where was a suitable law whose general principle Parliament had already accepted? After a great deal of careful and erudite thought the committee concluded that the Public Order Act of 1936 should be enlarged to make it illegal to publish a defamatory libel of an individual or a group with the intention of provoking hatred or disorder. In effect they sought to return to an old common law definition of seditious libel whereby it was illegal to excite ill-will between different classes of the King's subjects. This doctrine had been effectively struck down by Mr Justice Birkett in the case of *Rex* v. *Caunt* (1947). In Birkett's view there had to be an intention to provoke violence. The maximum penalties proposed were made deliberately severe in order to deal with the major fascist figure — three years and £10,000 — but all prosecutions had to be referred to the Attorney-General in order to prevent trivial or factious proceedings.

The Soskice Committee agreed with Brockway that discrimination in public places was a real problem but it gave far less attention to it and made no original contribution to the debate as it had to the incitement question. The Committee's draft Bill roughly followed Brockway's definition of public places. On the other hand, it deliberately omitted to ban discriminatory leases or to provide for right to civil suit or to include as an additional penalty loss of licence. All of these omissions were made on the grounds that they would have been difficult to enforce.

The Soskice Committee concluded their memorandum with a disclaimer to the effect that their Bill was only a draft working model which could be improved. It seems that the Soskice Committee had not considered the possibility of legislation to cover anything other than racial incitement and discrimination in public places and in leases. At least they did not tell the Study Group that they had considered discrimination in employment and housing, for instance, nor did they indicate any awareness of foreign experience or legislation. The problems were considered conscientiously but narrowly, strictly according to the brief given them by the N.E.C.

The Society of Labour Lawyers set up a Sub-Committee on Racial Discrimination under the chairmanship of Andrew Martin, Professor of Comparative Law at Southampton University, to draft proposals for the N.E.C.[6] The Martin Committee worked inde-

[6] The other members were Cedric Thornberry, Peter Beneson, F. Ashe Lincoln, Anthony Lester, Evi Underhill (all barristers), Michael Zander (Lecturer in Law at London School of Economics and Legal Correspondent of *The Guardian*) and two co-opted members — E. J. B. Rose and Nicholas Deakin (Survey of Race Relations in Great Britain).

pendently of the Soskice Committee but there was some contact and cross-fertilisation and some suggestions from each were identical.[7]

On the whole, however, the Martin Committee's ideas were far different from those of the Soskice Committee, with Brockway's Bills somewhere in between. In contrast to Soskice, the Martin Committee thought the Public Order Act to be inadequate and explicitly rejected the common law approach (seditious libel) on the grounds that racial problems were totally new to this country. Instead of paring down Brockway's conception, the Martin Committee tried to produce the strongest possible Bill to deal with incitement and discrimination in public places. On incitement it proposed that whoever promoted race hatred would be guilty of a new statutory offence regardless of whether he intended to provoke hatred or violence. Discrimination it dealt with in much the same way as Brockway and Soskice — i.e., criminal penalties, except that it expanded the coverage to public transport and to *all* places of public resort maintained by a public authority. In a subsequent memorandum Martin's Committee explained that it thought discrimination a much more intractable problem than incitement. Consequently it argued that as this was the first legislation in this field it must be designed to set an example to show that 'authority' disapproves. This being the case it was essential that no publicly operated place should discriminate.

> Unless discrimination is eradicated from the whole public sector as a whole, the educational and example-setting effect of the whole legislation will be destroyed. You cannot convict a publican for refusing to serve a negro if at the same time you tolerate discrimination at the employment exchange or at the municipal housing office.[8]

In view of a lively but inaccurate account published a year later in *The Observer*,[9] it must be emphasised that the members of the Martin Committee were in agreement that a criminal law would be suitable to deal with discrimination in public places. However, they were of the opinion (as the Soskice Committee was not) that discrimination in other areas was of more importance and that there the criminal law was not everywhere suitable. They acknowledged that it was not strictly in their brief but they drew attention to the American practice of dealing with discrimination by using administrative means and incorporating some element of conciliation.

[7] e.g. both suggested maximum penalties for incitement of three years and £10,000 and both suggested no prosecution without the Attorney-General's consent.

[8] Martin Committee, unpublished memorandum, 7 July 1964.

[9] 30 May 1965.

The Study Group was not very enthusiastic about either Bill and was most worried about the possible infringements to free speech. It did not come to a decision on their respective merits, but later developments rather suggest that the concept of conciliation aroused some spark of interest. The drafts were passed on to the N.E.C. who took no action. It was the July before a certain election in October and the Labour Party was keeping extremely quiet about anything to do with immigrants.

### *Smethwick and After*

The election result at Smethwick where Peter Griffiths defeated Patrick Gordon Walker underlined the importance of the race issue and had a crucial effect upon the history of the Race Relations Bill.[10] The national political parties had all tried to avoid the fact that racial antagonism was an issue which seriously concerned the British public. But when Gordon Walker was defeated once at Smethwick and again at Leyton it seemed desperately important to a number of people in the Labour Party that something be done quickly before race became a monster which devoured British politics.

One of these people was Anthony Lester, who had been a member of the Martin Committee. He now brought together a group of like-minded and well-placed people who thought that in the aftermath of Smethwick the Labour Party's election promise and Soskice's draft proposals to the N.E.C. were quite inadequate.[11]

The Lester group was greatly influenced by Canadian and American experience and practice and they spent a great deal of time studying it and drawing lessons from it.[12] In particular an article by Professor Bonfield on the operation of various kinds of state civil rights laws convinced them that criminal laws would be a failure and administrative procedures a success.[13]

Early in 1965, after two previous drafts, the group came to the following conclusions:

[10] See analysis of Smethwick election and of other constituencies where race was a factor in Nicholas Deakin, editor, *Colour and the British Electorate 1964* (London: Pall Mall Press, 1965).

[11] The group consisted of four practising lawyers (Lester, Jeffrey Jowell, Ian MacDonald, Roger Warren Evans), an academic lawyer and journalist (Michael Zander) and a lecturer in Government (Bernard Donoughue) and an expert in race relations.

[12] See, for instance, Jeffrey Jowell, 'The Administrative Enforcement of Laws against Discrimination', *Public Law*, Summer 1965.

[13] Bonfield, 'States Civil Rights Statutes: Some Proposals', *Iowa Law Review*, XLIX (1964).

1. Britain needed a Statutory Commission to deal with discrimination in employment, housing, public facilities, advertising, education including private schools, insurance and credit, Government departments and bodies receiving Government grants.

2. The first aim of the Commission should be to achieve compliance with the law without formal proceedings but it should have full powers of investigation and subpoena and authority to enforce its decisions through the courts.

3. The Commission should also conduct research on problems of discrimination.

These proposals which were sent to the Home Secretary, the law officers, the Prime Minister and selected contacts in Parliament were by far the most comprehensive and strongest put forward in the whole long genesis of the Bill.

In support of their proposals the Lester group argued that legislation must tackle the main problems and not just the fringe problem of public places. Moreover, transatlantic experience indicated that the criminal law was ineffective because of the reluctance of local law officers to prosecute and of local juries to convict. The group also dismissed the idea of a non-statutory commission with powers of investigation but with none of enforcement (which it had itself suggested in an earlier draft entitled 'A Citizen's Council') because experience in Kansas showed it to be useless. On the other hand, in those states and the province of Ontario which have Statutory Commissions the vast majority of legitimate complaints were dealt with without the need for a public hearing or enforcement in the courts.

At the same time as they were evolving their proposals, the members of the Lester group began sowing the seeds of their ideas in influential quarters. They talked to people they knew in Parliament and at the Bar, they wrote or stimulated favourable Press comment in *The Guardian*, *New Society*, *Socialist Commentary* and the Fabian journal *Venture* and Lester broadcast on the Third Programme. More important, they won over four specialist organisations. The Campaign Against Racial Discrimination (set up to unite the efforts of all the immigrant organisations) was persuaded by Lester and three of his confederates to support the proposals for a Statutory Commission.[14] Some members of CARD were at first unwilling that discrimination should not be made a criminal offence, but they were won over. CARD then sent its proposals to a large number of MPs in all three parties and a delegation went to see

[14] Lester, Zander, Jowell and MacDonald were all members of CARD's legal committee.

George Thomas, Minister of State at the Home Office. The British Caribbean Association actively canvassed in Westminster and Whitehall and the Institute of Race Relations also sent briefs to MPs, including Bonfield's article. The Society of Labour Lawyers' Racial Discrimination Committee was revived with a new Chairman, Philip Kimber, and this also urged the establishment of a Conciliation Commission to deal with the sensitive areas of employment, housing, insurance and credit.

The outcome of all this lobbying activity was that most of the MPs who had a geniune interest in the subject were now convinced that the criminal law should not be used for discrimination. In the debates and committee stages that followed the publication of the Bill it was obvious that many speakers were talking from the same brief, using the arguments and often the same words of the CARD (alias Lester group) proposals.

### *The Bill*

On 7 April, 1965, the day after CARD's delegation had been at the Home Office, Sir Frank Soskice published his Race Relations Bill. By and large he had not been convinced by the lobbyists. Discrimination in hotels, public-houses, restaurants, theatres, cinemas, public transport and any place maintained by a public authority was to be a criminal offence punishable with fines up to £100. Prosecutions under this section were only to be undertaken with the authority of the Director of Public Prosecutions. Discriminatory restrictions on sub-letting were made unreasonable and therefore unenforceable. Incitement to race hatred in speech or writing was made illegal, with a penalty of up to £1,000 or two years in prison.[15] Lastly, the scope of the Public Order Act was extended so that it would be illegal to publish threatening or insulting material with intent to provoke a breach of the peace.

The publication of the Bill brought forth a wave of Press criticisms and intensified the behind-the-scenes activity. A number of newspapers echoed CARD in saying that the Bill did not really tackle the main problems, but none of them openly supported a full-scale Statutory Commission. Most of the critics not already immersed in the subject seized upon the simple notion that conciliation was more appropriate to deal with discrimination than the criminal law. Contrary to Soskice's expectations far fewer showed

[15] This section extended the law as it then existed in the Public Order Act by making incitement an offence even where there was no likelihood of a breach of the peace and even though it did not occur at a public meeting.

much concern that the incitement provisions might also be used for censorship.[16]

In the month that elapsed between publication and the Second Reading on 3 May, Soskice decided to scrap his proposal to use the criminal law to deal with discrimination in public places. He began his opening speech in the debate by saying that this Bill was merely part of the Government's overall policy for immigrants and that he might reduce the inflow still further.[17] He said that he had already given thought to proposals for conciliation made by the Opposition and by various pressure groups and by the Press and he showed he was about to yield by saying: 'We will take careful note of what is proposed in that regard in argument in this debate.' It is a phrase that Ministers often use but rarely mean. This time was an exception.

Inevitably, one must ask the question, why did the Home Secretary change his mind at such a late stage in full view and change in a direction with which he ought to have been familiar for some months. The Home Office rationalised it this way to the author. Their spokesman said that it was seen from the beginning that there were two possible ways of dealing with discrimination: one by making it a criminal offence and the other by making it only a civil offence and attempting to use conciliation in the first instance. The arguments in favour of each were finely balanced but in the end the Home Secretary decided in favour of using the criminal law on the grounds that it was more in line with our own legal tradition and it dealt with the offence in a quick and exemplary fashion. (As I have shown above, Sorensen, Ungoed-Thomas, the Martin and Soskice Committees had all recommended using the criminal law.) When, however, it was seen that most people favoured using the other method of conciliation, the Home Secretary said, in effect, all right, it doesn't matter much either way, let us change to suit the popular feeling; after all it is a new area of legislation and we do not want it to be unpopular right from the start.

Many critics of the Home Office do not believe this explanation. In their view the Home Office is ignorant of foreign practice and did not think seriously about using anything but the criminal law until it was forced to. Whether or not this criticism is justified, the Home Office explanation underplays the activity which went on in Cabinet and Whitehall in April. The Government soon realised that it had sponsored a Bill which pleased no one and as it was feeling the strain of governing with a slim majority of three there were

[16] *The Times*, 8 Apr 1965, was an exception.

[17] The debate is in *Hansard*, vol. 711 (3 May 1965) cols 926–1060.

good tactical reasons for bending with the winds of criticism. Moreover, it was very short of parliamentary time and did not wish to risk a protracted battle over an issue that certainly would not win any votes from the electorate and might even lose some.

The whole thing is cloaked in Cabinet secrecy, but one person is known to have played a part — Maurice Foley, then newly appointed co-ordinator of policy on immigrants. After he had been bombarded by memoranda and button-holed by the interest groups he became completely convinced that criminal penalties for discrimination were wrong. Such evidence as there is suggests that Soskice was persuaded to change his Bill by a Cabinet committee and on that committee Foley was the most ardent advocate of conciliation.

As a result of Soskice's opening concessions the rest of the Second Reading misfired because the main target had already been scuttled. The Conservatives led by Peter Thorneycroft were quick to exploit Sir Frank's discomfiture at having to admit that he had brought forward such unsuitable proposals. First of all Thorneycroft attacked the Bill because it failed to tackle the areas of most importance: namely, housing and employment. Later on he pointed out that the Home Secretary had offered no evidence that cases of discrimination were so widespread as to justify legislation.[18] Thorneycroft was accused of trying to have it both ways — of wanting to please both CARD and his own right wing who wanted total opposition to the Bill. The Conservative Home Affairs Committee had in fact met twice to consider the Bill prior to the Second Reading debate and a clear division of opinion had resulted in a compromise motion which, like Thorneycroft's own speech, also wanted to have it both ways. The motion was rather muddled but did say that as it thought conciliation more appropriate to discrimination than criminal sanctions the Conservative Party would oppose the Bill as published.

Two other Conservative speeches were significant. Henry Brooke, a former Home Secretary, showed that his views had not changed since he rejected Brockway's earlier proposals.[19] He said that he thought such legislation against discrimination to be unnecessary and might even be provocative. In fifteen years in his constituency (Hampstead) he had never heard of it. He also attacked the proposal to deal with race hatred on the grounds that it bit into 'free speech' unnecessarily. He said that while he was Home Secretary, the Statutory Advisory Council on Commonwealth Immigration had

[18] There is in fact plenty of evidence available; see, for instance, *Report of the Committee on Housing in Greater London* (Milner Holland Report), Cmnd. 2605, pp. 188–96.

[19] *Hansard*, vol. 680 (9 July 1965).

never suggested to him that a law against racial incitement was needed.

Peter Griffiths, in a short speech Selwyn Lloyd later described as 'admirable', opined that the real intention behind the Bill might be to act as a gag if there was continuing mass immigration. He also said that the Bill would encourage extremists and that in any case much discrimination was really imagined by coloured people.

The strangest thing about the debate was that although many Labour members supported the Bill in principle, none spoke in favour of Soskice's actual proposals on discrimination. David Ennals made a straightforward plea for a Statutory Commission, arguing word for word from the CARD memorandum. Reginald Freeson said that in his constituency (Willesden) there was plenty of evidence of discrimination and racial violence to justify the Bill. Mrs Shirley Williams also spoke forcefully in favour of legislation and pointed out that six Western European countries had laws against racial incitement. At the close the Government had a majority of nine on the closest of the two divisions (258–249), the Liberals voting for the Bill.

In the three weeks between the Second Reading and the opening of the Committee Stage the Home Secretary drafted amendments to his own Bill. From all sides had come support for the principle of conciliation and this was the major change. On the first part of the Bill, dealing with discrimination in places of public resort, the original remedy under criminal law was removed and a civil remedy was substituted. A national Race Relations Board is to be set up which will appoint and supervise the work of local conciliation committees. The local committees will investigate complaints of discrimination and where appropriate bring about the settlement of differences and induce compliance with the law. In the event of conciliation having no effect the local committee can report to the Board which, if it agrees that a pattern of discrimination exists, reports to the Attorney-General. If he agrees with the Board's judgment he can bring an action for injunction against the person discriminating; the ultimate penalty for defiance of such an injunction being imprisonment for contempt of court.

At first sight it seemed that CARD, Lester and company had got most of what they asked. Conciliation had been substituted for the criminal law but not in the areas where in fact they thought it was really important, namely, housing and employment. In fact, like Soskice himself, some of them felt there were very strong arguments in favour of retaining the criminal law to deal with discrimination in places of public resort — for instance, it was quick acting and an unambiguous statement of the public conscience. Consequently they felt that the advantages of the criminal law method had been lost without getting the full benefits of a properly constituted conciliation method. The Race Relations Board is not to be a Statutory Commission with full powers of investigation, subpoena and initiation of civil proceedings. The critics were also dismayed at the shape and powers of the Board in the event of Parliament wishing to extend its jurisdiction at a later stage to the more important fields of housing and employment. They saw such extension as inevitable in time and they were anxious lest it be poured into an ill-constructed mould just because that mould, namely, the Race Relations Board, was already in existence.

Politically, Soskice's changes to his Bill were astute. He made the Bill much less harsh and therefore acceptable to the vast majority of MPs in all three parties. Moreover, by taking up the one coherent point in the Opposition's Second Reading amendment, Soskice tied the Conservative Party as firmly as the Labour Party to supporting the Bill in principle. Those Labour critics of the Bill who said that it did not go far enough were really the only ones left with anything much to say and they determined to press their case in committee. As Soskice's amendments really introduced a new principle (conciliation) and a new instrument of government (the Board) the Committee Stage of the Bill should have been important. In fact the Labour critics of the revised Soskice Bill were not able to press home their points as hard as they would have liked because of the political situation. The economic situation was bad, the Opposition was winning minor skirmishes during the mammoth Finance Bill and parliamentary time was extremely short. In the end these helped to preserve Soskice's Bill as he had redrafted it.

## *The Committee Stage*

Before the Committee had its first meeting there was a good deal of manoeuvring behind the scenes in both parties to fix the membership. When the list for Standing Committee B was first published, Peter Griffiths got the Whips to change the Conservative membership so that two members with immigrant problems (himself and Harold Gurden, Birmingham, Selly Oak) were put on. To accommodate these two and Captain Orr (Down, South) who also came on at the last moment, two left of centre Conservatives were removed and even the Whip, Geoffrey Johnson Smith, stood down. This reshuffle of the Conservative membership shifted the balance of opinion among the Conservative members well to right. Only three of the Conservatives took a liberal view of race relations — John Hunt, Norman St John-Stevas and Sir George Sinclair — none of whom had immigrant problems in his constituency.

On the Labour side the critics who wanted to widen the Bill also ensured that they were well represented on the Committee. As a result, seven of the thirteen Labour members thought the redrafted Bill to be inadequate and Soskice found himself in a minority among his own party of four to seven with two other members absent more often than not. His support was limited to the three tied Government men, Edward Milne, his P.P.S., William Whitlock, a Whip, and George Willis, Minister of State for Scotland.

Of course, the theory behind choosing Committee members is to get as representative a range of party opinion as one can, mainly drawn from those who showed an interest on the Second Reading. But as neither the right-wing Conservatives nor the left-wing Labour members were so naïve as to let the membership of the Committee be nominated entirely at the whim of the Whips, it does seem curious that the Home Secretary allowed himself to be outvoted in his own party. The result was that on four important occasions he must have been embarrassed to find more support in front of him than behind. But for the change in the composition of the Conservative membership the Bill might even have come out of Committee considerably different from Soskice's second draft. Having changed the method for dealing with discrimination Soskice would not accept amendments to strengthen or widen the Bill in any way. Naturally the right-wing Conservatives supported him against the amendments put forward by his own side.

When the Bill reached Standing Committee B on 27 May the Opposition protested that Soskice really ought to have brought in a new Bill to be read twice before the whole House before being committed to a Standing Committee. It was a fair point. Soskice's excuse was that he was not extending the coverage but that he was only changing the method by which the House's original and approved aims were to be achieved.

Apart from this opening shot the Opposition welcomed Soskice's amendments and later agreed to the Third Reading. They only tried to change minor details in the Bill and pressed none of them to a division. Peter Griffiths and Harold Gurden were the most aggressive Conservative critics. In the third sitting they sought to remove the criminal penalties for racial incitement and to replace them with the same conciliation procedure as for discrimination.[20] Gurden

20 House of Commons, *Official Report, Standing Committee B* (1 June 1965) cols 104–17.

attacked Soskice for designing the Bill to protect only the Labour Party's friends. Indeed some of Soskice's friends had used the words 'leper' and 'vermin' about other people but that was not made illegal by this Bill. Gurden was not supported by his front bench and Sinclair and Stevas pointedly dissociated themselves from his views. But he would not withdraw his motion and it had to be negatived.

The seven Labour critics of the redrafted Bill were not an organised rebel group but acted roughly in concert with the aid of whispered consultations on the Committee Floor.[21] They pushed their amendments to a division four times. The closest they got to winning was a vote of seven to eleven but on three divisions there were more Labour members voting against Soskice than for him; each time the Bill remained as he wanted it only because of Conservative votes.

The Labour critics moved four substantial amendments to the discrimination section:

1. To make the definition of places of public resort *inclusive* and so allow the courts to widen it to include places unlisted if they thought necessary. Lost 2–10

2. To include shops as places of public resort where discrimination would be prohibited. Lost 6–10

3. To give the Race Relations Board authority to use the local Conciliation Committees for work on problems not actually outlined in the Bill. Lost 7–11

4. In the event of the Attorney-General not taking proceedings after a report from the Board, to allow the complainant to bring a civil action. Lost 6–11

The first and most important amendment was moved by Donald Chapman.[22] Soskice rejected it on the grounds that the law must be clear and list all the places which were included. Stevas spoke in its favour on the grounds that the principle of the Bill was that 'any discrimination in a place of public resort was contrary to public policy. . . . Nearly all arguments for the narrow definition of public places have gone with the disappearance of the criminal procedure.' Ivor Richard pointed out an inconsistency in the Bill in that all places maintained by a public authority were covered but only those privately owned places which were specifically mentioned. Thus a hairdresser operating on public premises would be included but one operating on private premises would not.

Chapman wound up by saying that he was extremely disap-

[21] Donald Chapman, David Ennals, Reginald Freeson, Dr M. S. Miller, Ivor Richard, Paul Rose, Mrs Shirley Williams.

[22] *Official Report* (15 June 1965) cols 201–24.

pointed; an elaborate machinery of conciliation had been set up to apply only to a limited number of places, in some of which there was no discrimination anyway. All places unlisted in the Bill would now have a licence to discriminate. Soskice replied by saying that it was not a narrow definition at all because it covered all the thousands of public-houses, hotels, restaurants and theatres in the country. On the division Stevas and Hunt voted for the amendment and six Conservatives and four Labour members voted against it; seven Labour members abstained. One of these Labour members confessed afterwards that it was really seeing the two Conservatives vote for this amendment that shamed the Labour critics into voting for the three later amendments against their own Minister.

Chapman introduced the amendment about shops on the grounds that it was illogical to exclude them because they were surely places of public resort. Soskice insisted that the Committee reject this on the grounds that a limit must be placed on the definition somewhere and that he thought of a place of public resort as a place where someone goes to stay for a time to enjoy the amenities: 'In these, discrimination is particularly injurious to one's feelings whereas in a shop it wouldn't be so much.' Chapman replied by saying that he and others would 'simply take this Bill and Clause as an instalment on civil rights legislation and go on for the rest if a deteriorating race relations situation arises'.

Mrs Shirley Williams moved the fourth main amendment because she was convinced by her own first-hand knowledge of American practice. Soskice rejected it because he said the whole object of his new discrimination section was to conciliate not to make matters worse by having court actions. 'The whole concept of the Bill is that of the public wrong.' Therefore it was a good thing to give the Attorney-General the last word. Reginald Freeson sharply countered by saying the rights of the individual were not enshrined in the Attorney-General. He argued that common law rights should be extended when the field of unlawful actions was extended as in this Bill. Soskice had said that the right to civil action would interfere with the process of conciliation, but, said Freeson, such would not be the case because a civil action could only be instituted after the conciliation process had run its full course and failed.

After this last division on 29 June the Act was virtually complete. The Labour critics were far from satisfied but they refrained from pressing further amendments at the Report Stage. The Chief Whip warned them that the Government could not afford to give the Bill any more time and that if the Bill was not finished in one day on Report then it would have to be dropped. The subsequent consideration of the Bill in the House of Lords made some minute changes which were of little consequence.

## *Conclusion*

The Race Relations Act will be the work of many hands. Prohibition of discrimination in places serving food, drink and entertainment was first put forward in a Bill by Sorensen; the inclusion of public transport and public premises comes from the Martin Committee. The Race Relations Board is the child of Soskice but the principle of conciliation was mooted by Little and refined by the Lester group. The prohibition against discrimination in the disposal of tenancies was simultaneously recommended to the Labour Party by Little and Ungoed-Thomas. Brockway should have the credit for proposing that racial incitement should be illegal and the Martin and Soskice Committees were together responsible for suggesting the actual legal means used. The maximum penalties for incitement started at £100 (Brockway), rose to three years and £10,000 (Soskice Committee), but were enacted at two years and £1,000. The penalty for discrimination started at £25 and later disappeared altogether.

Looking at it in retrospect it seems a haphazard, secret and inefficient process. The Labour Party kept its election pledge but one wonders if it feels happy that this is really the best way to begin in an entirely new field of legislation. The Home Secretary and his department eventually produced a Bill which was approved by Parliament but might not more extensive research and fuller consultation with the main interests have enabled them to be right first time? The gestation of this Act certainly adds more support to the case for revising our whole system of legislative drafting.

# AGRICULTURAL SUBSIDIES IN BRITAIN AND AMERICA[1]

*By* J. ROLAND PENNOCK

POLITICAL problems involving persisting and important negotiations between affected interests reflect continuing structural characteristics of government. Agriculture is one example of a persisting problem facing British government. Since agricultural problems exist in almost all countries, the subject is particularly suited to comparative analysis. J. Roland Pennock's study of agricultural policy in Britain and America shows how certain bargaining outcomes that seem natural in Britain depend upon specific features of party politics and cabinet government. It is noteworthy that since this article was published the growing importance of Common Market membership to both British parties has led the claims of British farmers for special subsidies to be downgraded with bipartisan agreement.

THE major objective of this essay is to study the politics of agricultural subsidies and price supports in Britain and America during the postwar period.[2] The general method followed is to combine empirical data from the case study with *a priori* arguments in such a way as to contribute both to the appreciation of the arguments and to their evaluation. The case material has two aspects, each of which has importance in itself and also gains support from the other. First, there are the substantive results. Political scientists, for understandable reasons, are inclined to focus largely upon governmental processes; yet surely the results — in terms of public policy, however formulated, adopted and executed — are normally of primary importance. It is true that effectuated policies tend to elude

[1] The basic research from which the materials for this article were drawn was made possible by the John Simon Guggenheim Memorial Foundation, for whose award the writer is deeply grateful. He is also indebted to Professor Charles E. Gilbert for helpful criticism and suggestions.

[2] For the most part the study was confined to the first decade following the Second World War, although in a few instances materials have been drawn from later years.

Reprinted in a slightly abridged form from 'Responsible Government', Separated Powers and Special Interests: Agricultural Subsidies in Britain and America', *American Political Science Review*, LVI iii (1962) 621–33.

objective evaluation. In this case, however, the policy results — in pounds and dollars — are objective enough, though hard to isolate for measurement. To be sure, there are other difficulties, with which, as we proceed, we shall have to cope as best we may. Are the situations truly comparable? — a problem with almost any comparative study. Are variations in results properly attributable to specifiable aspects of the political process? At this point the second aspect of the study — its procedural side — becomes significant. Analysis of process, of the steps leading up to the results, may be useful not only for its own sake but also by adding to or subtracting from the plausibility of the conclusions suggested by the substantive comparisons. In other words, if we identify a difference in results not clearly growing out of differences in the situations, and if we also identify phenomena on the procedural side that might lead to such a difference in results and in a given instance provide every evidence of having done so, we are better off in our search for understanding than we would be if we confined ourselves to investigation of either results or processes alone.

In point of fact, the substantive comparison gives no support to the view that parliamentary government, British style, has any special immunity to group pressure.[3] If anything, it appears that the balance is tilted in the opposite direction. From 1954 to 1961, Britain subsidised her farmers, by most tests, much more heavily than did the United States. For the benefit of a relatively much smaller percentage of the population, British farm subsidies during that period were absorbing nearly three times as large a share of the gross national product as the American. (The detailed figures, using various bases of comparison, together with a discussion of technical and other difficulties in making the comparison, are in the Appendix, pp. 217–20.) Moreover, the economic position of British farmers, as compared to the rest of the population, has improved tremendously over the prewar situation — far more than in the United States, where the relative standings are apparently about the same.[4] And more to the point, this relative gain on the part of British farmers

[3] Note that in selecting British government for this study, we are taking the example and type of parliamentary government that should, according to orthodox theory, present the sharpest contrast to the presidential system.

[4] Between 1938 and 1957 national income in the United Kingdom increased by 266 per cent, while farming net income increased by 461 per cent. On a *per capita* basis, national income increased approximately 237 per cent, while farming net income went up by 457 per cent (for persons engaged in agriculture). In the United States, contrasting 1957 with the 1935–9 average, the total net income of the farm population from farming sources increased by 141 per cent (150 per cent from *all* sources), and their *per capita* income from farm sources rose by 215 per cent (from *all* sources 285 per cent),

appears to be entirely attributable to the subsidy, which in fact constituted roughly two-thirds of their net income.

But, it might be argued, there may be good reasons, quite apart from group pressure, why the British should support agriculture more heavily than we do. There is no simple, conclusive answer to this. Nevertheless the writer has carefully examined the justifications advanced in each country for subsidisation, to try to gain some sense of whether they are more powerful in Britain than here. Most of the arguments, like the claimed sociological advantages of the small, family farm, are equally valid or invalid for the two countries. Two arguments, however, the validity of which is debated by the experts, apply uniquely to Britain. They are the strategic argument — that British agriculture must be kept in good fettle so that production can be quickly expanded in the event of war and blockade — and the balance of payments argument — that an expanded agriculture minimises the drain on foreign exchange for the purchase of feedstuffs. The first of these is not seriously regarded by most of the experts[5] but it undoubtedly possesses a considerable (though probably declining) appeal to the populace at large, inclining the electorate more favourably to agricultural subsidies than they otherwise would be. To what degree the relatively high subsidies are attributable to this factor it is impossible to ascertain. The second uniquely British argument, that of the balance of trade, being more technical, has more appeal in Government circles than with the citizenry. Yet it seems unlikely that the Government has been greatly moved by this argument, although on one occasion they used it as an excuse for setting supports at a higher level than could otherwise be justified.[6]

---

while the personal income of all persons was increasing by 285 per cent, on a *per capita* basis. In other words, in the United States, the average income from farming failed to keep pace with that of the rest of the population, while in the United Kingdom the farm population advanced at about double the rate of the country as a whole. (Calculations are based on figures from the *Annual Abstract of Statistics* (1958) and the 'Annual Review and Determination of Guarantees, 1958' (Cmnd. 390), for the United Kingdom; and, for the United States, from *The Farm Income Situation*, no. 169 (July 1958), United States Department of Agriculture, and the *Economic Report of the President*, Jan 1962.)

[5] They reason (1) that stockpiling can probably meet the challenge of a blockade, especially in view of the probability that a major war in the future will not be extended over many years, and (2) that in any case continuing dependence on foreign sources for food supplies is the best means of assuring the maintenance of a large merchant marine, which in the past has proved invaluable in the event of attempted blockade.

[6] My justification for this statement is partly that government economists themselves, in private conversation, lay little stress on this argument and

One other general difference in the agricultural situations of the two countries may be relevant. In the United States, farming is considerably more diversified and a far larger proportion of total farm output consists of feedstuffs — grain, etc., fed to hogs, cattle and poultry — and of agricultural products not destined for consumption as food — cotton, tobacco, soybeans for industrial uses, etc. — than in Britain. In the one case, one farmer's price is another farmer's cost, and in both cases the purchasers are not consumers, nor even wholesalers distributing to consumer markets but rather industrial processors, large commercial organisations and the like. So it may be that conflicts of interests among farmers reduce their political and bargaining strength. And if it is thought that the large buyers to whom these products are sold are better able to assert their interest in lower prices than are unorganised consumers or the suppliers who cater directly to consumer markets, then it might be supposed that the combination of forces working to limit farm subsidies would be relatively stronger in the United States than in Britain. But this is an oversimplified picture, blurring the market effects of farm co-ops, chain store processors, etc., and the political effects of federalism, a bicameral Congress and rural over-representation. There are too many factors to disentangle here, and their net effect in combination is not clear.

It might plausibly be argued that the difference in support levels is to be accounted for neither by governmental systems nor by different felt needs, but by the effectiveness of farm organisations. Most British farmers are members of the National Farmers Union of England and Wales, or the N.F.U. of Scotland. For purposes of representing farmers at Price Reviews (negotiations with the Government for subsidies) and similar occasions, the Unions act as one. There are also commodity groups and regional differences within the national unions that occasionally give the N.F.U. national headquarters a hard time. Nonetheless the degree of bargaining and pressure group unity they maintain is remarkable. American farmers

---

freely admit that subsidies should be lowered; and partly it is that economists generally, even agricultural economists, are divided on the validity of the argument, with the weight of opinion perhaps on the side of doubting it. Austin Robinson has argued the case for subsidies to save foreign exchange; see 'The Problem of Living Within Our Foreign Exchange', *The Three Banks Review* (Mar 1954) pp. 3–19. Other economists have disputed his interpretation and contend that, if anything, the balance of payments argument calls for limitation of agricultural subsidies; see Derek T. Healey, 'Increased Agriculture or Increased Exports?', *Westminster Bank Review* (May 1955) pp. 10–12, and Colin Clark, 'Britain's Dependence Upon Agricultural Imports', loc. cit. (Nov 1956) pp. 9–11.

have no such monolithic organisation. Many are unorganised. The others are members, often duplicating members, of numerous commodity groups and of certain general purpose farm organisations, of which the American Farm Bureau Federation — with a claimed membership of 1,591,777 farm families out of a total of 5,382,162 farms in 1953 — is the largest. Farm Bureau membership is drawn most heavily from the corn-hog area of Indiana, Illinois and Iowa, and from the South. Its political orientation is conservative. The National Grange, with under a million members, is the second largest general farm organisation, while the National Farmers Union, with perhaps 200,000 members during the period in question, heavily concentrated in Colorado, Minnesota and the Dakotas, represents a more militant and politically liberal group.

To what extent this difference in the pressure group organisation in the two countries qualifies any conclusions that might be drawn from the comparison it is difficult to say. The tendency towards monolithic social, economic and political structures that pervades English life manifests itself in two mutually contradictory ways, however, as far as it is relevant to our present concern. It tends to produce strong, centralised political parties and it also facilitates the formation of strong pressure groups, each representing virtually the whole of the interests affected. Here, it might be argued, we have a stand-off. The homogeneity of the country produces strong pressure groups and it also produces strong parties, the better to withstand the pressure groups. The homogeneity of the pressure groups may itself owe something to the concentration of power in British government.

Although we might leave the matter here, it is perhaps desirable to comment on the sharp policy division between the Farm Bureau and the Farmers Union.[7] It is by no means clear that this division of forces weakened the pressures for subsidy. A single, all-inclusive organisation is not necessarily more aggressive because of its unity;

[7] The difference can easily be exaggerated if we are thinking about the general level of subsidy. Both organisations favoured expenditure of government funds for disposal of farm surpluses in a variety of ways. Both favoured price supports. The Farmers Union favoured continuation of rigid supports at 90 per cent of parity for 'basic' commodities. The Farm Bureau favoured supports on a sliding scale, depending upon the supply situation. The Farm Bureau programme, a modification of which was enacted in 1954, almost certainly involved a somewhat lower subsidy rate than would have been entailed by the Farmers Union programme. On the other hand, in view of falling commodity prices, the Farm Bureau shortly after this date supported the 'Soil Bank' programme, which was enacted and which involved a much greater subsidy than any possible saving that might have been brought about by the lower support rates.

it must find a programme that can win the support of most of its members. A smaller, regional organisation, heavily representative of one or two commodities, can be more radical. Was even the Farm Bureau less aggressive in support of agriculture than the N.F.U. in Britain? Both organisations in practice recognised the necessity for some retreat from the wartime levels of subsidies or price supports, yet both wished to preserve the bulk of their wartime relative gains. In the United States, however, the Farmers Union was unwilling to make this concession. Inasmuch as this country, unlike Britain, had at least one organisation fighting for a more radical and expensive programme than featured the wartime experience, it might as plausibly be argued that any difference between the two countries with respect to pressure groups would lead one to anticipate a higher rather than a lower rate of government support for farming in the United States.

So much for the substantive comparisons. The end result of agricultural politics in the two countries has been to produce heavier subsidisation (in one form or another) in Britain than in the United States, instead of the reverse, which orthodox theory would lead us to anticipate. We have briefly canvassed two out of three possible sets of factors that might lead to this result: the needs or justifications and the organisation of interests most directly affected. On balance, it appears doubtful that there is enough here to account for the difference in results, although one can certainly not be dogmatic on the point. At the very least, the substantive comparison suggests the need for examining the matter procedurally — that is, for looking at the processes by which key decisions were made in the two countries and asking whether or not they give support to the standard propositions about the two forms of government.

If the electoral alternatives are kept simple, the man in the voting booth can understand them and wield his power effectively, and anything that strengthens the political effectiveness of the voter-at-large tends to weaken the special interests — so runs the argument. How do the two forms of government stack up in this regard? In one sense there can be no doubt whatever that the British form wins hands down by this test, for at election time there is but one question for the voter to answer — is he for the Government or against it? — with the further possibility that he may have one additional choice if he is against it. There is no question of splitting his ticket. But if we are considering a particular subject, such as agricultural subsidies, the realistic question is whether there is any alternative at all. Since the Second World War there have been five general elections in England. Throughout this period agriculture was the beneficiary of heavy subsidies.[8] At none of these elections was the extent of agricultural subsidy a point at issue between the parties. Yet the policy being pursued did not lack for critics. Such journals as the London *Economist* kept up a continuous drum-fire of criticism of agricultural policy under both Labour and Conservative Governments, alleging that subsidies were too high. An occasional Member of Parliament, like Stanley Evans, lashed out against 'featherbedding' the farmers.[9] And the weight of opinion of economists, including agricultural economists, favoured the view that the subsidies were at a higher rate than was justifiable. On the other hand, the farmers frequently complained that their profits were not keeping pace with the rising standards of living of other occupational groups. Nonetheless, at no election did the level of subsidies become an issue between the parties. Agricultural policy was greatly debated, but the debates consisted in such matters as rival claims for credit for the benefits the farmers had received, charges that the programme was being badly administered, that farmers lacked confidence in the Government (or in the Opposition, as the case might be), and so on. Labour, by promising the reinstitution of bulk purchasing and other devices, tried to hold out the prospect of greater price stability, but was careful not to suggest that average prices would be higher (or lower).

The sensitivity of the parties to the farm vote is nowhere better demonstrated than by the difficulties generally experienced by the Liberal Party in squaring its free-trade, anti-subsidy principles with electoral expediency in the matter of agricultural policy. In 1953 the Party Assembly adopted a resolution calling for the gradual abandonment of guaranteed prices and assured markets for agriculture. Not only did this action call forth heated debate but, after

[8] Until about 1953–4 the Government bought all farm products at fixed prices. Although these prices were much above the level charged for the food (the Government paying the difference), it is possible that no subsidy would have been needed during this period of food shortage had prices been allowed to find their own level. In other words, it might be argued that the subsidies during this period were really consumer subsidies, redistributing the available food among consumers rather than income among producers. For our purposes, then, the elections of 1955 and 1959 are of greatest significance, for by that time free market conditions prevailed and farmers depended heavily upon direct subsidy.

[9] Evans, a Labour MP, was forced to resign as Parliamentary Secretary for the Ministry of Food for persisting in this kind of criticism, including such charges as that the taxpayers had had to pay £12 million during the last year for the production of surplus potatoes (*Hansard*, vol. 475, col. 1042). The promptness with which the Government called for Evans' resignation and publicly disavowed his views made it clear that they had no intention of being tagged as favouring any diminution of agricultural support.

the adoption of the resolution, a prospective Liberal candidate for Parliament announced that 'speaking for at least twelve prospective Parliamentary candidates, we do not feel we can fight an election on the present policy, and give notice that we can not do so'.[10] Presumably as a consequence of this pressure, the resolution adopted in 1954 was much more qualified.[11]

A nice test case is supplied by a by-election held in the Division of South Norfolk in January, 1955. The election was of particular interest because the constituency is marginal as between the major parties and highly agricultural, being in the heart of one of the major farm areas of England. The writer followed the campaign closely, attending several campaign meetings. The constituency was actively cultivated by the candidates and by their supporters ranging all the way up to the Minister of Agriculture himself, Mr Heathcote Amory, on the Conservative side, and to Messrs Hugh Gaitskell and Aneurin Bevan on the Labour side. Both sides insisted that they would maintain subsidies, with no 'whittling away', while hinting that their rivals were not altogether reliable in this regard. Neither made any suggestion of increasing the subsidies.

The pattern revealed for this campain was substantially duplicated in the general elections of 1955 and 1959. In the latter year, for instance, the Conservative election manifesto pledged continuance of the long-term assurances to agriculture, continued support to horticulture by means of tariffs and also by means of new improvement grants to the extent of £7½ million. Labour promised to improve farm security, which, it claimed, had been 'whittled away' since 1951, and to give the farmer 'protection against unfair foreign competition'.[12]

In the United States the picture was quite different. The Agricultural Adjustment Act of 1938, permanent legislation, provided for price supports for 'basic' commodities by means of loan and purchase arrangements at rates varying in accordance with a formula relating the percentage of 'parity' at which they would be supported to the supply situation. By agreement of both parties the operation of this Act had been suspended during the war and afterwards in favour of provision for a rigid support of basic prices at 90 per cent of parity. This temporary legislation was scheduled to expire on 31 December 1948. By a series of extensions, however,

[10] *Farmer and Stock-Breeder*, LXVII (14–15 Apr 1953) 57. And see *The Times* (4 Apr 1953) p. 3, col. a.

[11] *Farmer's Weekly* (30 Apr 1954) p. 42.

[12] D. E. Butler and Richard Rose, *The British General Election of 1959* (London: Macmillan 1960) pp. 260 and 275.

the fixed supports at 90 per cent of parity were not allowed to die until six years later. By stages during this period the Democratic Party became identified with maintenance of the 'rigid' support system while the Republicans championed a 'flexible' arrangement. An Administration-sponsored bill providing for flexible supports was enacted in 1954 with overwhelming Republican support in both Houses, while the Democrats opposed the flexible principle (with its inevitable lowering of the extent of price support) by more than three-to-one. These positions have been adhered to subsequently and were reflected in the party platforms for presidential elections. In short, the American voter, unlike his British opposite number, had a significant electoral choice and accompanying possibility of control with regard to agricultural price supports during the 1950s.[13]

Closely connected to the question of choice and control is the matter of energising public opinion, also a feature included among the reputed attributes of the British system. It is not really a separate point so much as a presumed consequence of clear issues and simple methods of popular control. There can be no doubt that where the parties in Britain are divided on an issue, both the system of parliamentary debates and the election system tend to focus attention upon, and arouse interest in it. But where party competition produces identical positions on a given point, as it tends to do, and as has been the case with the level of agricultural subsidies in Britain, no occasion for public discussion arises. In this country, on the other hand, substantially this issue has played a significant role at each of the last three presidential elections. This is not to argue that there is anything inherent in the American system that accounts for this difference, or that a similar situation would be found if we examined other policy areas. It is merely to point out that the alleged advantage of the British system does not always materialise and that in certain cases the advantage may lie in precisely the opposite direction.

Having said this much, the supposed merit of clear and centralised responsibility in British government has already been dealt with, by implication. The responsibility for the level of agricultural subsidies in Britain is clear; it is pin-pointed. There is only one catch: to oust the Government would not alter the situation, although there is an abundance of opinion in the country at large and among experts to the effect that a change is in order.

[13] This does not mean he would necessarily elect to use it. To vote his convictions on price supports might mean going contrary to his beliefs on other matters which he deemed more important.

Among the *a priori* arguments advanced for the theory that British government is exceptionally well fitted to resist the demands of special interest pressures, perhaps the most frequently cited is the strength of party discipline. Members of Parliament, unlike members of Congress, are not generally susceptible to pressure from constituents to vote this or that benefit for them.[14] With rare exceptions, they will vote as the Whips instruct. Closely related to party discipline is the position of the Government. A single committee, the cabinet, thanks to the combination of the two-party system and strong party discipline, has the power, within limits, not only to formulate the Government's programme but also to implement it. Its party members in the House are in the majority and they may be counted upon to support the Government's programme. Since the Government will stand or fall, at the next election, on its record as a whole and before the electorate as a whole, so the theory goes, it will be to its interest to resist the pressures of special interests in so far as they appear to distort or run counter to the general interest.

How sound is this reasoning? Of course it is true that MPs seldom defy the Whips. But the Whips, as is well known, are two-way lines of communication. Through them the party leaders are kept informed of what the rank-and-file want and what they hear from their constituents and, even more pertinently, of how MPs, especially those from marginal districts, assess the impact of particular policies on their chances for re-election. Such information is of interest to party leaders in any democratic country. Even in the United States it is highly relevant to the party's welfare and to the outlook for its general policies. But in the United States a party may lose one House and hold the other or it may lose one or both Houses and hold the Presidency. And under such circumstances it may still see many of its policies effectuated — as was clearly demonstrated under the Eisenhower regime. In Britain, on the other hand, the winner takes all. Under such circumstances it is hardly to be supposed that the news that, say, a score of Members of Parliament might lose their seats at the next election unless something is done for the aged, e.g., or for the farmers, will be without influence on the Government.

In this connection, we may well remind ourselves of Hatschek's

[14] However, the writer was present in Westminster one day when a delegation of lobbyists for higher old age pensions called a large number of MPs, one by one, from the floor of the House, asked their position on the question and, if the reply was not fully satisfactory, informed them that canvassers would cover their constituencies informing the voters of their weakness on this matter. There is evidence to suggest that this kind of pressure was not without effect.

law,[15] according to which British political parties start out with well-defined sets of principles but progressively lose them and become concerned primarily with obtaining and keeping power. We need only consider the most recent general election campaign to see Hatschek's conclusions substantiated. Each of the major parties seemed to be engaged in trying to prove that, at least in certain important respects, it was not so different from the other as had been thought. The Conservatives proclaimed themselves as the great supporters of the 'welfare state', while Labour made light of its attenuated programme of nationalisation. Such a development undermines the theory that the Government — or for that matter either of the major parties — must have a consistent programme. The parties tend to become as free as American parties to bid for the marginal voter, to try to build a majority by seeking the support of various special interest groups — especially those that are particularly aware of their interests and whose votes are believed to be shiftable.[16] Of course, in so far as a bid to one group must obviously be at the expense of other groups or of the whole, some limit is placed to this process. But it is well known that this protective mechanism is very sluggish. Producers tend to be more aware of their interests than consumers or even taxpayers. Moreover, the existence of a large number of traditional or ideological voters strengthens the hand of the special interests by enabling party managers to manoeuvre without fear of losses from their hard-core supporters. The British situation with respect to special interests may be put in a nutshell. The parties discipline their members, but no one disciplines the parties; and the parties are subject to the same electoral logic that operates in this country: they must bid for the support of interest groups. Another way to put the matter, using Robert Dahl's expressive phrase, is to say that in Britain, too, what passes for 'majority rule' might be more aptly described as 'minorities rule'.

An examination of British agricultural politics during the post-war period provides numerous examples of the operation of this electoral logic. The case of Stanley Evans, above, is a clear instance of party discipline being used to prevent giving offence to a well-placed pressure group. Although Evans was somewhat of an extremist

[15] Julius Hatschek, *Englisches Staatsrecht*, II (1905) 8 ff. Hatschek's law is described and discussed in Carl J. Friedrich, *Constitutional Government and Democracy*, revised edition (Boston, 1950) p. 417.

[16] In an editorial entitled 'The Electoral Auction', the London *Economist* bemoaned the fact that 'election manifestoes have been corrupted into expensive shrimping nets for farmers', pensioners', tenants', cotton workers', shipbuilders', shipworkers', and cinema interests' votes....' (*The Economist*, 26 Sept 1959, p. 998.)

on this matter, the traditional orientation and class interest of the Labour Party is towards the interests of urban labour. Cheap food, rather than prosperous farmers, would seem to be their natural concern. Moreover, this is the definite and outspoken view of the Co-operative movement, which is affiliated with the Labour Party and sits regularly in its councils. Yet in recent times it has been the prospect of winning a few farm votes from their normal Conservative alignment that has consistently set the course of Labour policy.

How party discipline operates in this kind of situation is well illustrated by a revealing incident that occurred in late 1953 in connection with an Order, laid before Parliament for ratification, increasing the import duties on certain fruits and vegetables. This was an issue calculated to arouse Labour to an anti-farmer stand if anything would, because the cost of the proposed action would be borne directly by consumers. As a matter of fact Labour, then in Opposition, was sharply divided as to what position it should take. Many of its Members, especially those representing the Co-operative movement, were strongly opposed to the tariff increase. Indeed, it appears virtually certain that the Parliamentary Labour Party would have voted to contest the Order had it not been for a strong personal appeal by Tom Williams, Minister of Agriculture in the preceding Labour Government. Although the decision was close, and a number of Labour Members did express themselves vigorously against the order in the House of Commons, the significant fact is that the Party leadership threw its weight behind the farming interest, and prevailed.[17] Here was party discipline in operation — being used to force a reluctant majority to pursue a policy thought by the leaders to be essential for winning certain marginal districts. (Williams and other Labour leaders had often publicly expressed the view that Labour could not hope to return to power without winning back some of the country areas they had won in 1945 and lost in 1950.)

Compared to this situation, party discipline in the United States is notoriously weak. Orthodox theory holds that weak discipline favours the special interest; but it is not necessarily so. Big city Democrats may refuse to go along with their party's policy of favouring high price supports — and they frequently do; and Republicans from agricultural districts may vote against their party's adherence to 'flexible' price supports. Under such circumstances, special interests that are powerful in a minority of legislative districts may find it more difficult to obtain legislative support than under a regime

[17] *Farmer's Weekly* (18 Dec 1953) p. 26; *Hansard*, vol. 521, cols 2235–7 and 2251.

of strong party discipline, operating as described above. On at least two occasions during the Eisenhower administration major price support legislation opposed to the official policy of the Democratic Party (which had a majority in both houses of Congress) and opposed by the House Committee on Agriculture, was yet enacted into law.[18]

The British system is also often thought to be less easily influenced by special interests than the American system because of the subordinated role of committees. Congressional committees have great power and are notoriously likely to be controlled by Congressmen favourably disposed towards the interests whose affairs come under their jurisdiction. It is frequently overlooked, however, that the British system, structurally very different, may lead to functionally similar results. Parliament regularly delegates many important decisions to the Government or to particular Ministries. When legislation takes this form, the Ministries, in certain respects, are cast in the role of Congressional committees: they have great power; their decisions are likely to receive less publicity than those of Parliament, and in any case the process by which they reach their decisions is not one of public debate and ordinarily involves no public scrutiny; they have a tendency — so at least it is alleged in England — to become favourably inclined towards the interests under their wing; and they are readily accessible to those interests.

The case of agriculture illustrates all of these points. The controlling legislation leaves the rate at which agricultural products will be subsidised or supported entirely to Ministerial discretion, operating within the broadest of statutory policy directives.[19] It is true

[18] For an analysis of the voting on the first of these occasions, the Agricultural Act of 1954, see J. Roland Pennock, 'Party and Constituency in Postwar Agricultural Price-Support Legislation', *Journal of Politics*, XVIII (1956) 167–210, esp. pp. 184–210. The situation was decidedly complicated by the fact that the largest of the farm organisations, the American Farm Bureau Federation, was opposing the 'pro-farmer' policy of the Democratic Party. Consequently it is not a clear instance of a 'general interest' prevailing over the organised special interest. Of the 47 Democrats who went contrary to their party policy at this time, however, over half were from metropolitan areas. Their defection can hardly be charged to the position of the Farm Bureau. Similarly the 23 Republicans who voted against the position of their Party and of the Farm Bureau were clearly voting for what they considered to be the special interest of their constituencies in high price supports.

[19] Agriculture Act, 1947; 10 and 11 Geo. 6, ch. 48. The relevant provision reads, in a passage reminiscent of an American party platform, that powers under the Act shall be used, through the devices of guaranteed prices and assured markets, to promote and maintain 'a stable and efficient agricultural industry capable of producing such part of the nation's food and other agricultural produce as in the national interest it is desirable to produce in the

that the Treasury stands always in the immediate background, breathing down the neck of the Ministry, but it must depend largely upon the Ministry's estimate of the needs of the industry. Moreover, all orders made under this provision of law must be made after consultation with representatives of the interests concerned. In practice this means that each year, at what is known as a Price Review, representatives of the Minister of Agriculture sit down with representatives of the National Farmers Union and, in an often prolonged series of meetings, negotiate the guaranteed prices for the following year. Each side is provided with an abundance of data. Certain agreed but rather vague standards guide them. But there is much room for judgment, and hence for haggling; for what are sometimes embittered arguments; and for plain horse-trading. It has been said on good authority that the final decisions are frequently made on the basis of considering the effect in certain marginal constituencies.[20]

The experience of the 1955 Price Review is hardly atypical. It had been the expressed hope of those charged with administering the subsidy policy that Exchequer liability could be progressively decreased at a rate approximating, or at least approaching, the increase in farming efficiency, then estimated at about £25 million *per annum* for products covered by the Review. Applying the principles that had been enunciated to the data as to changed costs and the like, and deducting the presumed efficiency increment, the result would have been no net change in guarantees and subsidies. In fact, however, the Ministry granted a net increase of about £40 million. The reasons advanced for this action were two: (1) that during the previous year crops had been seriously damaged by bad weather; and (2) that the balance of trade situation made it desirable to produce more homegrown feedingstuffs. However, the first of these reasons was not supposed to be relevant, since all figures are based

United Kingdom, and of producing it at minimum prices consistently with proper remuneration and living conditions for farmers and workers in agriculture and an adequate return on capital invested in the industry'. [Part I, 1, (1).] Full power to carry out the purposes of this Act are vested in the Ministry of Agriculture and Fisheries (now the Ministry of Agriculture, Food and Fisheries), subject only to being laid before Parliament as an Order, which, theoretically, either House could veto.

20 One of the top Government economists dealing with these matters has been quoted as saying that the annual determinations of agricultural subsidy levels are 'primarily political' and hardly susceptible of being explained or justified in terms of 'statistical measurements'. Private correspondence from J. H. Kirk, quoted in J. Anthony Mollett's 'Britain's Postwar Agricultural Expansion: Some Economic Problems and Relationships Involved', *Journal of Farm Economics*, XLI (1959) 3–15, at p. 9, n. 15.

on 'normal' weather; and it was not even contended that the second argument was sufficient to justify the increases.[21]

To understand the Price Review of 1955 one must know that a General Election was imminent and that the farmers were known to be disgruntled. The mood of the annual meeting of the National Farmers Union in January was described in the pages of *The Economist* as one of 'gloomy resentment'.[22] A direct vote of no confidence in the Government's farm policy was narrowly averted; and, as it was, the Union condemned the Government for 'gradually undermining' the provisions of the 1947 Act.[23] Off the record, Government officials in a position to know were quite ready to concede (and decry) the effects of the political winds. In Parliament, Labour members, not surprisingly, testified to the same effect. George Brown, Parliamentary Secretary for Agriculture under the Labour Government, declared:

> The price this year was very nearly not an agreed one. It became an agreed price only because someone politically a little higher than the Minister came along and said, 'There will be an election soon, and we must have an agreed price.' The Council of the N.F.U. know that. My friends in the industry tell me what is happening.[24]

And Tom Williams, Labour Minister of Agriculture, asserted that the N.F.U. was on the point of voting its lack of confidence in the Government when the Chancellor of the Exchequer made his peace with them in a speech at the N.F.U.'s annual dinner.[25] Note that it was the Chancellor of the Exchequer who was chosen for this task. Possibly he was chosen (or invited by the N.F.U.) because he was a farmer. But if George Brown was right it appears that this was a clear case of political intervention, perhaps by cabinet action, to urge the Minister of Agriculture to go further on behalf of the farmers than even he was prepared to do on his own initiative.

This incident will also serve as a comment on the frequently heard claim that the British Treasury is a powerful roadblock in the way of special interest demands upon public expenditures. Undoubtedly it is, in many situations; but it may also be acutely vulnerable to electoral pressures.

In appraising the argument for, and evidence of, British vulnerability to the demands of a special interest group, it should be

[21] See 'Annual Review and Determination of Guarantees, 1955', Cmd. 9406; and The National Farmers Union of England and Wales, 'Information Service', x i (Jan/Feb 1955).

[22] 'Resentment on the Farm', *The Economist*, CLXXIV (29 Jan 1955) 345.

[23] Ibid.

[24] *Hansard*, vol. 540 (3 May 1955) col. 1622.

[25] Ibid. col. 1532.

remembered, too, that British farmers constitute a small part of the population. As a percentage of total production, agricultural production in Britain is less than two-thirds as large as in the United States. In terms of the percentage of the labour force involved, the discrepancy is even greater. Nor is the distribution of farm voters such as to increase their political effectiveness; but rather the contrary.

Touching another of the weaknesses often attributed to the separation of powers, the division of responsibility, we must be careful to examine both sides of the ledger. Divided responsibility does muddy the waters and so complicate the task of a displeased majority wishing to enforce accountability for the act of commission or omission that occasioned its displeasure. This much is true. But how often, on a particular issue, is there a majority? When pressure groups secure special consideration, it is generally the work of an active minority translating its demands into law thanks to the passivity of a large number of legislators. In the American system there are many checkpoints to the exercise of power; this is the very meaning of the system of checks and balances. If the farm lobby wins at one point its opponents may effectively defend a roadblock at another. This is precisely what often happens. Critics of the system who emphasise vulnerability to pressure groups all too frequently point to examples of success at a particular point in the process without following through to the ultimate result. Moreover, when that ultimate result is to prevent action, it follows from what has just been said that it is by no means necessarily true that a majority will is being frustrated. On the contrary, the necessity of mobilising more power, or making it effective at another point, tends to mean that there will be more debate, more public discussion, more general education with respect to the matter in question, with the result that other groups than those immediately affected, consumer groups, for instance, are aroused to support their own interests, with the further consequence that when action is taken it will have a wider representative base — and perhaps a very different one — from what would otherwise have been the case. There is every evidence that this is precisely what happened during the long debate over flexible *versus* rigid price supports. Farm leaders were outraged at moves by Secretary Benson that they interpreted as appeals for consumer support.

Finally, a special word should be said about the presidential veto power, even though it is one of the checks to which reference has just been made. Representing a national constituency, the President is generally in a better position than anyone else to resist the demands of particular interests. The same argument was cited in support of the view that it is to the interest of the Government in England to support a consistent policy, and one that does not give undue concessions to special interest. Applied to the presidency, this argument tends also to be subject to the same weaknesses. But here an important qualification is to be noted. A British Government desiring to remain in office is wholly dependent upon having its party continue to hold a majority of the seats in Parliament; hence it must consider the electoral situation in all of the constituencies. The President also has a large stake in having his party control the Congress. But it is not *so* large a stake. It is not all or nothing. He may remain in office even though his party is in the minority in both Houses of Congress and he may even continue to exercise very considerable power under such circumstances. To this extent the 'general interest' base provided by the veto power is stronger than its equivalent under the cabinet system.[26]

For examples from agriculture, we may go back to the spring of 1946. Wool production had been heavily subsidised during the war and was in excess supply. In spite of recommendations by the Secretary of Agriculture and a special committee established for the purpose, Congress failed to act. The Secretary of Agriculture then discontinued all support of wool prices, which had been provided under general war powers. Congress responded by passing a bill which included among its provisions a special fee on imported wool. This provision ran directly contrary to our postwar foreign trade policy and its enactment threatened to wreck the Geneva Trade Conference, then in session. In spite of the strong opposition of the Department of State, the bill passed both houses of Congress. The President vetoed the bill and Congress sustained his action. A new bill, omitting the import fee provision, was thereupon speedily enacted. A special interest that was threatening our foreign economic policy was successful in Congress, but was checked by action of the President.

Eight years later another President was able to take advantage of the special interest in wool to prevent the success of a move in behalf of high price supports for basic crops which he believed to be counter to the general interest. The President had recommended a system of production payments for wool, substituting this for commodity loans. He had also recommended reversion to a flexible price

[26] In referring to the 'general interest' base of the veto power I do not mean to obscure the fact that the veto may be used in support of special interests. It should be pointed out, too, that the peculiarities of our electoral college system are generally thought to operate in such a way as to favour certain special groups. It is arguable, however, that in a crude fashion, this inequality is offset by the rural orientation of the legislative branch.

support system for basic crops, as already mentioned. The House Committee on Agriculture, apparently in a move to outwit the President, combined his wool bill with an extension of the then-existing price supports for basics at a fixed 90 per cent of parity. However, they had miscalculated. On the eve of the crucial vote, Secretary Benson himself is said to have carried the word to Congressmen from wool states that the President would veto a 90 per cent bill even though it carried the wool payments plan with it. Thus in the end Congressmen from wool states had to vote for flexible supports for basics in order to get their wool subsidy. Five out of a possible 32 did so. This is not a particularly strong case, but it at least suggests the possibility of a situation in which the threat of a veto might bring some pressure on one interest group to help check another.

Many cases can be cited when the bicameral system has tended to work in the same way — to obstruct the demands of special interest groups. In both 1948 and 1949 the House of Representatives first voted to prolong the operation of high price supports, ultimately acceding to the Senate's insistence on a downward modification. Only the Korean war prevented this action from being allowed to take effect. One may find other instances in which either one House of Congress or the other or both or the Administration has manifested a great — perhaps too great — sensitivity to agricultural interests and demands. Frequently, however, the requisite concurrence of all three is lacking.

In spite of what has just been said, it is often true that the inertia of government tends to favour the special interest. Where an emergency situation develops, Congress may act fairly quickly — especially if a well-organised interest is prodding it; but, where legislation favouring a special interest is already on the books, it is difficult to get it removed even in the face of conditions that seem to call for such action. But for many situations there is a technique to counter this tendency, and Congress often sees fit to use it. This is simply the device of granting a demand for a limited period, requiring renewal if it is to be extended beyond the original grant. In this way the weight of governmental inertia is shifted. In the battles over flexible *versus* rigid price supports, the proponents of flexible (which in effect meant lower) supports always enjoyed the great advantage that inertia, and therefore the check and balance system, was on their side; for no action at all meant a return to an even lower level of price guarantees than they were proposing.

To summarise briefly what has been said: the purpose of this case study was to examine the commonly held belief that 'responsible government', British style, is markedly superior to the system of separated powers in its ability to resist the demands of special interests — to examine this belief in the light of the evidence of postwar agricultural subsidies and price supports. From that evidence it appears that in Britain, the all-or-none nature of party competition may make leaders extremely sensitive to the demands of pressure groups, and party discipline may be used to suppress elements in the party that would like to resist the demands of those groups. The American system, it is true, may be less responsive to a clear popular majority, when such a majority exists. But, in the more common event that only minorities have clear positions, these minorities have more hurdles to cross, more roadblocks at points where their demands may be checked, than similar groups face in Britain. No single case establishes a general rule. But viewing the case of agricultural subsidies and price supports in combination with more general analysis, the writer concludes there are strong grounds, at least, for doubting that the American form of democracy is any more susceptible than the British to the pressures of minorities.

## Appendix. British and American Agricultural Subsidies: Facts and Arguments

A comparison of rates of subsidy for British and American agriculture can only rest on approximations based on more or less arbitrary assumptions and allocations. The difficulties are several. In Britain, price controls were retained until 1953 and 1954. Before that, during the period of wartime and postwar shortages, the food and agriculture industry was heavily subsidised but (see note 10 above) it is arguable that the subsidies were consumer subsidies. In the United States, war-induced scarcities led to a similar ambiguity. Accordingly, the comparison is confined to the post-price control period.

For the United Kingdom, then, I shall use the years since the free market has been re-established, 1954–5 through 1960–1. The average annual cost of agricultural support in the United Kingdom for that period amounts to $716 million.[27]

For the United States, no such accurate measure of costs to the Treasury is possible. Here, in large measure, instead of paying a direct subsidy we (in effect) buy farm products and store them. Some of these stored commodities are eventually sold on the market, some

[27] Computed from official data. See *Hansard*, fifth series, vol. 618 (22 Feb 1960) cols 21–2; ibid. vol. 617 (9 Feb 1960) cols 35–6; and ibid. vol. 634 (8 Feb 1961) col. 71.

are given away, and some are diverted to secondary (and less remunerative) uses. What our price support programme for any given year will cost cannot be ascertained until long after the event, if at all — not, at least, until the commodities have been disposed of and the proceeds realised; these may be in blocked foreign currencies.[28]

TABLE 1

*Farm subsidy cost comparisons on a* per capita *basis*

| | *United Kingdom* | | *United States* | |
|---|---|---|---|---|
| | *Number* (*in millions*) | *Subsidy* per capita | *Number* (*in millions*) | *Subsidy* per capita |
| Population[a] | 51·0 | $ 13 | 164·3 | $ 13·44 |
| Population engaged in agriculture[b] | 1·1 | $ 651 | 9·0 | $246 |
| Farm operators[c] | ·29 | $2,469 | 5·4 | $409 |

[a] Population figures are for the year 1955.

[b] These figures are for the year 1951. I am informed by the Ministry of Agriculture, Fisheries, and Food that their estimate of the present farm labour in the United Kingdom, reduced by a complex calculation to full-time male adult equivalents, is ·9 million.

[c] The United Kingdom figure is from the 1951 census and is for 'farmers and farm foremen'. The Ministry of Agriculture, using different definitions, estimates that farm operators at present number about 350,000. (Information supplied by Mr J. H. Kirk, Ministry of Agriculture, letter of February 10, 1959, to the author.)

The costs actually realised each year can, of course, be calculated. These figures are made available by the Department of Agriculture and we rely on them here.[29] The comparisons set out in Tables 1 and 2 use the average of the realised cost for the six years ending 30 June, 1960, the latest for which figures are currently available. The figure so derived is $2,209·6 million.[30]

[28] During World War II, it may be recalled, the entire accumulation of price-supported farm surpluses from the depression years was disposed of at an over-all profit to the Government.

[29] It must be emphasised that we are considering the *cost of agricultural subsidies to the taxpayer*. Much of this sum is expended for storage and other costs that do not go to the farmer. Whether the farmers profit more or less than the cost of the programme is, fortunately, not a question that need be answered for the purpose of this article. Incidentally, it would be a difficult question to answer for Britain as well, although there most of the costs of the programme go directly into the farmers' pockets.

[30] This calculation includes all farm programmes classified by the Department of Agriculture as 'primarily for stabilisation of farm prices and income'

At this point a possible objection must be noted: the cost to the public treasury is only part of the social cost of price supports. How much has been added to the consumers' bill for farm products by the existence of price supports? This question takes us into a far more speculative field than the calculation of costs to the government. What would prices be if they were not supported? The answer

TABLE 2

*Farm subsidy cost comparisons in relation to various national income and expenditure figures**

| | United Kingdom | | United States | |
|---|---|---|---|---|
| | *Amount (in millions) Col. 1* | *Subsidy as a percentage of amount in Col. 1 Col. 2* | *Amount (in millions) Col. 3* | *Subsidy as a percentage of amount in Col. 3 Col. 4* |
| Gross farm income | $ 3,699·9 | 19·3 | $ 33,788 | 6·5 |
| Net agricultural income | $ 843·1[a] | 84·9 | $ 11,473 | 19·2 |
| Gross national product | $49,311·0 | 1·4 | $400,300 | 0·5 |
| Governmental expenditures (national govt.) | $13,821·6 | 5·1 | $ 68,122 | 3·2 |

* All figures are averages for the six fiscal years 1954–55 through 1959–60.

[a] After allowance for excess of replacement cost over original cost of certain assets used during the period. (Cmnd. 390, pp. 11 and 12.)

Sources for both tables: United Kingdom: *Annual Abstract of Statistics*; 1951 Census, *Occupation Tables*; Cmnd. 390; and private communications from the National Farmers Union and the Ministry of Agriculture, Fisheries, and Food; United States: 1950 Census; Census of Agriculture (1950); *The Farm Income Situation*, No. 169, July, 1958; *Agricultural Statistics, 1956*.

would depend in large measure upon how much would be produced in the absence of acreage controls. Even more difficult to calculate, and perhaps even more significant, is the effect of price guarantees in encouraging farmers to use more fertiliser, buy more labour-saving machinery, and in other ways improve their efficiency. It may

and also the item for Agricultural Conservation Payments. The latter is included to make the total comparable to the figures used for the United Kingdom where so-called 'production grants' (e.g., for lime and fertiliser) are used more or less interchangeably with 'deficiency payments' and other forms of direct subsidy. Costs of the soil bank 'acreage reserve programme' are included but, following the practice of the Department of Agriculture, the soil bank 'conservation reserve programme' is excluded. If the latter were included, the average annual cost figure would be increased by $112·5 million, or about five per cent.

be questioned, however, whether the average voter is much influenced by this factor. He hears about the cost of the farm programme to the government, but it is doubtful whether he gives much thought to that part (very small at most) of the cost of a shirt or a loaf of bread that can be charged to price supports.[31]

Using the crude cost figures that have just been developed, then, the next step is to make them more comparable, as between the two countries, by reducing them to ratios or percentages of such factors as population, farm operators, farm income, national income, and governmental expenditures for all purposes. This is shown on the previous page. It will be observed that, by all but one of these measures, during the period in question, British agriculture was subsidised at a much higher rate than America. For the one exception (subsidy *per capita* of total population), subsidy rates were substantially equal.[32] According to the other bases of comparison, the difference ranges (very roughly) from a factor of a little over one and one-half, using total governmental expenditures as the standard, to one of six in another instance (farm operators). Using a sort of rough average of these indices, it would not be grossly misleading to say that the rate of British agricultural subsidies was running, proportionally, at from two to three times the rate of their American counterparts.

[31] It may be that, under exceptional circumstances, some public opinion can be stirred up against a particular programme on the basis of its presumed effect in raising prices. The case of butter before Secretary Benson's cut in the support level of dairy products in the spring of 1954 may be a case in point.

[32] This basis of comparison, of course, leaves out of account the fact that *per capita* income in the United States is far in excess of that in Great Britain; hence the subsidy bears less heavily on the American taxpayer.

# PLANNING: THE NATIONAL HEALTH SERVICE

*By* HARRY ECKSTEIN

WHEN a political problem is a continuing or recurring one, there are substantial political and administrative arguments in favour of attempting to plan policies on some sort of regular basis. In recent years, publicity has been given to the application of planning techniques to economic problems; however, the influence of international economic fluctuations upon Britain makes this area poorly suited for planning. The National Health Service, the focus of Harry Eckstein's study, would seem to be more amenable to planning techniques, for the problems of health tend to persist in patterns relatively predictable in the short run. It is therefore of special significance that the author concludes that here too planners face important and potentially ineradicable obstacles in pursuit of a well planned and fully effective health service.

## I

IT is unfortunate that so much of the theoretical work on planning has been done by economists and others who expound theories about the mechanics of spontaneous individual economic activity and generally believe that the mechanics of market activity are, on the whole, beneficent mechanics. Such writers obviously approach planning with a bias; and they seem to think that they can explode the myths of planners simply by demonstrating that a planned system could not *duplicate* the supposedly benevolent mechanics of a 'market' system. Nor is this all: their approach to planning is, more often than not, exceedingly abstract, almost geometric, in character, and rarely seems to be rooted in, or even relevant to, any actual planning experience.

A good example of what I have in mind comes in the first two paragraphs of chapter eight in Professor Michael Polanyi's *Logic of Liberty*.[1] Polanyi here tells us that he is only labouring the

[1] M. Polanyi, *The Logic of Liberty* (1951) esp. p. 111. See also the enthusiastic review by J. W. M. Watkins, 'Organisation in Science and Society', *Ethics* (Apr 1952) pp. 201–4.

Reprinted in full from *Political Studies*, IV i (1956) 46–60, where it was originally published as 'Planning: a Case Study'.

obvious: central planning is 'strictly impossible', because 'the number of relations requiring adjustment per unit of time for the functioning of an economic system of $n$ productive units is $n$-times greater than can be adjusted by subordinating the units to a central authority'; not only would the rate of adjustments under planning be $1/n$th its value under perfect market conditions but *the rate of performance (production) would be reduced to the same fraction*! Note the implications and hidden premisses of this argument. Polanyi assumes that an absolutely rational and effective central planning authority could at best duplicate the complex of individual decisions in a 'polycentric' system. He also assumes that one decision-making 'unit' can adjust to only one series of relations over a given unit of time. One could argue, on the same ambivalent assumptions and in equally seductive pseudo-mathematics, that since every unit in a polycentric system of activity must adjust to all the other units in the system, that is, since every unit must, strictly speaking, make calculations qualitatively similar to those demanded of a central planning authority, the number of foolish decisions in an unplanned system is bound to be, mathematically, $n$-times greater than in a monocentric system, and the whole system $n$-times as absurd. Both of these arguments are, of course, ludicrous: they are merely mathematical arguments which pretend to say something about society when in fact they only say something about the writer's private assumptions. I do not object to mathematical models of the planning process, but they should be offered only as tentative hypotheses, or as symbolic representations of theories to be otherwise established. My purpose here is to present such a differently established theory.

Before the Viennese economists launched their classical critique of socialist planning there was already in existence another school of anti-socialist thought which, in my view, propounded a much more sophisticated critique. This school, despite the current popularity of its chief exponent (Max Weber) seems to have made no impression on current thought about socialism and the welfare state. I propose here to revive certain aspects of this school's critique, but in a version of my own designed to make it particularly relevant to the British Health Service, from which I wish to draw examples.

The Weberians were not committed to the market system, but they did consider that it made possible an extraordinarily high degree of 'rational action' by individuals. At the same time, they were not biased against planning, although they saw in it a tendency towards the diminution, perhaps the disappearance, of rational behaviour as a dominant mode of social conduct. But we can grasp the significance of this only when we understand the sense in which Weber uses the term 'rational'.[2]

Weber considered an action to be rational *in form* (formally rational) if it was the result of *ends-means calculation.* This conception is described as 'formal' because it does not imply *correct* calculation. Now, one can show a close relationship between liberal society (or *laissez-faire* society, whichever is preferred) and a high degree of individual formal rationality. First, and most obviously, liberalism was immensely destructive of conformitive behaviour by its attacks on tradition and its attachment to free rational calculation as a basis of action. Secondly, and more important, liberal ideology and society eminently satisfied the most important of the conditions on which rational activity (as here used) depends,[3] the condition that, to be fully conducive to rational action, the ends of the action must be *quantifiable* (since ends-means calculation is most easily performed in purely quantifiable terms),[4] must be *unambiguous* (since it is manifestly difficult to calculate the achievement of objectives which are only vaguely understood), and (if more than a single end is involved) be *internally consistent* (in the sense that the achievement of one valued end will not rule out the achievement of another equally valued objective). Economic liberalism supplied an over-riding objective which satisfied these criteria about as perfectly as any system of objectives could — profit, which it made into an ultimate end by equating self-interest with collective interest. It therefore made for a high degree of formally rational behaviour, not because it created a polycentric society (which it did) but because of its specific values and the specific institutional conditions — legal, political, fiscal, etc. — that it created.

But Weber was always careful to distinguish *formal* and *substantive* rationality. The first he used merely to refer to ends-means calculation, correct or erroneous; the second referred to *effectiveness*, that is, to the extent to which formally rational action is correctly adapted to its end. Now it does not follow that if an individual bases his actions on calculation he will achieve his objectives; he may make bad calculations. Nor will a society, a large number of whose

[2] The material from Weber comes from *The Theory of Social and Economic Organisation*, *passim.*

[3] For some others in a particular case — capital accounting in economic enterprises — see Weber, op. cit. pt. ii, sect. 30.

[4] Weber, indeed, uses the term 'formally rational calculation' as if it were synonymous with quantitative calculation. Note also his insistence that money is the most rational means of orienting economic activities and that the use of budgets maximises economic rationality. (Ibid. p. 186.)

members act in a formally rational way, or even one whose members are individually substantively rational, necessarily be a 'rational' society — if by this we mean a society which successfully achieves its shared values. Just the opposite may be the case. Hence, even if we grant that there is a relationship between liberalism and formally rational conduct we need not grant one jot of the *laissez-faire* economists' case. Weber saw this clearly enough, and was in fact no defender of the 'polycentric' order. Indeed, he looked upon socialism and planning as essentially attempts to achieve a *fully rationalised* society in place of the partially rationalised society created by liberalism. The purpose of planning was to introduce pattern and deliberate calculation into what was left of the 'swarm-life' of society (as Tolstoy would put it) by rationalising not only individual conduct but also the whole complex of market relationships.

But at this point there arises a crucial question. Is it really possible to create a 'fully rationalised' society — to have a high degree of formally rational conduct by individuals and yet a society which successfully achieves its ends? If a society values ends conducive to rational conduct and if it attaches intrinsic value to the institutional conditions required for rational behaviour, then the problem disappears. But if it aims at other ends and insists on inappropriate institutional conditions, then the attempt fully to rationalise society may have a very unexpected result: the diminution, perhaps disappearance, of rational conduct itself; although — and this must immediately be added as a qualification — the society need not therefore be less 'efficient' in terms of its shared values. Hence the chief problem Weber raised about planning was not whether it would improve or deteriorate society — that after all depends on one's values — but simply whether a high degree of rational conduct would be likely to survive a high degree of planning. The answer, of course, cannot be found abstractly and mathematically. It depends on the specific conditions under which planners have to function; because rational conduct itself depends on specific conditions. Hence I present here, not a general critique of planning, but a specific critique in the concrete case of the British Health Service.

## II

Undoubtedly the people who plan and control the National Health Service have to function under conditions which make a high degree of rational decision-making on their part difficult if not impossible. Their difficulties arise from three main sources: the sheer '*logical*' *difficulty* of the decisions they have to make, the *psychological pres-*

*sures* to which they are subjected, and their *lack of control over a multitude of factors crucial to adequate calculation.*

1. Their '*logical*' *difficulties* (i.e. difficulties in making calculations) arise from two factors: the inappropriateness to rational calculation of the objectives at which the process aims, and the very wide range of factors which they must take into account.

The Service aims at a large number of objectives, some of which are related, but not, because of that, consistent with one another. (i) Its most fundamental objective is to remove all barriers between patient and treatment. This implies not only, or even primarily, the removal of economic barriers. The most important steps required have been a geographical redistribution of doctors and facilities, a functional redistribution of manpower (e.g. among medical specialities), a general increase in trained personnel (especially nurses and technicians), a sizeable increase in the number of hospital beds and the amount of practically every sort of hospital equipment; in gist, more men and equipment, more rationally distributed. (ii) A second objective, closely related to the first, is to 'rationalise' medical services. This implies organisation that is economical, effectively adapted to the requirements of modern medical practice, and highly responsive to planning. This set of objectives is perhaps even more important than the first, since the pre-Health Service system was inadequate more because of its lack of organisation than because of shortages and maldistribution. (iii) Both of the above sets of objectives are to be pursued in a way which will not upset the extremely sensitive (and extremely ill-understood) 'doctor–patient relationship'. Medical practice has to remain independent, at least to the extent of protecting doctors against non-medical interference in medical matters; patients have to be guaranteed a workable system of free choice among doctors; and doctors have to be subjected to a minimum of purely administrative demands so that they will have time enough for practice and leisure enough for keeping up with their extremely dynamic field. (iv) The administrative structure devised for all of these purposes is to be significantly 'democratic', because the operative ideology of the British is significantly democratic. (v) Not least, the whole system has to be managed at a cost which the national budget can support, and this, in a period of constant inflationary pressure and given the existing prejudices about public spending, means at a financial minimum.

Clearly, these various sets of objectives do not begin to satisfy the conditions which make a series of ends fully conducive to rational action. They involve manifest inconsistencies: for example, between 'rational' and 'democratic' organisation, or, even more clearly, between minimising costs and removing all barriers to treatment. Moreover, some of the objectives involve unquantifiable considerations and considerable ambiguities. What, for example, is an appropriate doctor–patient relationship, and what sort of administrative demands might tend to deteriorate it? Take the simple problem of redistributing general practitioners from over-doctored to under-doctored areas. The most effective method would be direction. But would this method be consistent with 'democratic' values? If not, perhaps some system of incentives would be more tolerable; but would it be effective in anything short of the fatal long run? And if the incentives to be offered are financial, could the Exchequer stand the cost? This is one of the easier problems which have arisen under the Service, and it has been dealt with rather successfully; but it may convey some of the quandaries which arise simply from the objectives of the Service.

It is the task of the Health Service planners somehow to translate the 'values' of the Service, with all their ambiguities and inconsistencies, into a consistent, rationally calculated and — not least — politically defensible programme. The difficulties this involves can be summarised thus: (*a*) Where 'quantitative' decisions can be made fairly easily they generally impinge upon equally important 'qualitative' matters. For example, it is not too difficult to determine what should be the national cost of prescribed drugs and medicine. But any system designed to limit prescribing to the appropriate minimum will rub against the nebulous demands of the doctor–patient relationship. What sort of system could be devised which would sufficiently preserve the doctor's professional discretion and at the same time not be a blank cheque on the Exchequer? (*b*) Where it is possible to make decisions on clear and unambiguous grounds they generally impinge on entirely ambiguous matters. Take the problem of rationally distributing 'capital resources' (building materials, expensive equipment, etc). Given a limited quantity of such resources, especially a severe scarcity, it would certainly be necessary to lodge control of their distribution in some very high-powered authority dealing with a very wide area — perhaps, as has actually been the case during most of the existence of the National Health Service, in the Ministry itself. But is this 'democratic', if being democratic is taken to mean a high degree of local administrative independence?

These problems, in general outline, and with variations to fit the particular case, probably occur in planning of any sort. The deliberate political definition of social objectives is never likely to yield single-term, unambiguously quantifiable criteria of action —

except by accident. Liberal ideology was able to focus conduct to such an extent on such a criterion precisely because it left the realisation of its ultimate values to the implanted mechanics of society rather than to the constructive intelligence of the engineering individual. The planned society cannot similarly absolve the calculating reason from responsibility for shared social purposes. Whatever other conclusions might be drawn from this point, it should at least be clear that the demands which the planning process makes on the calculating intelligence are far greater than those implicit in the egocentric adjustments of the 'market'.

But planners must also make immensely difficult decisions even when the objectives do not clash and even when they are not ambiguously defined or unquantifiable. In particular, they must always make rationally related, consistent *series of decisions* where the 'market' demanded only single, supposedly 'self-relating' decisions.[5] To cite a simple example: the Health Service planners have to dole out a limited supply of capital goods in such a way that the most will be got from the outlay; how are they to do this in a 'rational' way? Obviously, they must weigh against one another all the needs of all the parts of the Service and then dole out the goods available where they are most needed. Hence the decision to install a maternity wing in hospital *A* located in region *X* demands a concomitant decision not to install one in hospital *B* in region *Y*. And since the Exchequer allocates funds, not maternity wings, to the Ministry of Health, the decision to install a maternity wing in hospital *A* may imply a decision not to improve the kitchen in hospital *C* or to build a new X-ray room in hospital *D*, and so on. Each individual decision logically implies a series of further decisions, stretching out almost *ad infinitum*, each one of which should also be made on rational grounds. It is clear that to make such decisions must require a far wider range of calculation — and concomitantly, a far greater range of information — than those demanded by the liberal market.[6]

The logical difficulties of the planning process are, of course, much more severe in bad times than in good. Almost all the most oppressive problems which have arisen in the Health Service so far are traceable to the fact that severe economic shortages have prevented

[5] This is the point that Polanyi should have made in the argument cited above.

[6] Here my analysis comes close to that of the economists who argue that no economy can function rationally without a spontaneous price system. But the question remains whether a price system really has the beneficent powers ascribed to it; whether spontaneously achieved values need coincide with actually desired values and whether there can be any price system at all (in the classical sense) in such areas as medicine.

the satisfaction of certain urgent wants which would certainly have been satisfied if circumstances had been more favourable. 'Abundance' cannot alter the essential difficulty of planning, but it can obviate a certain amount of practical decision-making, for instance, it may make it unnecessary at a given moment to decide between the extension of tuberculosis and mental hospitals where both are considered to need extension for different reasons. In other words, the very circumstances which create the greatest needs for planning (great scarcity) also account for its most vexing problems.

2. The second main aspect of the conditions in which Health Service planning must be carried on is the *psychological* situation of the planners.

Having assumed control, the decision-makers are held — and feel — fully responsible. Hence, the logical difficulties of planning inevitably lead to psychological tensions which may become quite unbearable in a period of serious scarcity. To decide between the relative weight of an improvement of the mental health *versus* the tuberculosis services, or between the demands of the Newcastle *versus* the Manchester Region, and to be aware of the human issues involved, may try emotional stability as much as the calculating intelligence. Moreover, the tensions arising from the planners' sense of social responsibility are heightened by the pressure exerted by parties affected by the decisions, by general criticism, and by institutionalised political accountability.[7]

[7] For example, in a single day, parliamentary questions were asked about the adequacy of mass radiography units in a particular locality; the remuneration of Junior House Officers acting as *locums*; the distribution of merit awards to specialists; the alleged abuse of sick-pay by part-time domestic staff in certain hospitals; expenditure on day nurseries in certain localities; the state of hospital waiting-lists; the supply of malt to T.B. patients; hold-ups in the supply of bone-conduction hearing-aids; the possible construction of a new out-patient department; political discrimination in appointments to a certain Hospital Management Committee; the distribution of nurses; the steps being taken to recruit mental deficiency nurses; the use of beds in mental deficiency institutions; the cost of maintaining greenhouses, gardens, and other such installations at a particular hospital; the number of empty rooms in the offices of the Leeds Regional Board; and the increases in the staff of the Pricing Bureaux (see *Hansard*, 7 May 1953). On the whole, about one day a week is devoted to parliamentary questions about the Service; some twenty to thirty questions are asked each time, about half of which concern the affairs of a single Health Service agency. Bevan realised well enough that this would happen before the Health Service came into existence. In an address before the Royal College of Nursing, he compared himself to St Sebastian, who was pierced by a thousand 'javelins'. He maintained that his own role in the Service would be to act as the 'central registrar of defects . . . for every mistake you make I shall have to bleed' (*British Medical Journal* (1948) vol. i, Supplement, p. 185).

3. The effect of the psychological pressures is further heightened by the fact that *many factors bearing on the decisions which the planners have to make are effectively beyond their control.* The amount of money they can use is fixed by broad national budgeting considerations. The amount of physical resources available is limited by national wealth and national planning decisions. The manpower available is determined by the birthrate, the educational system, and the general level of employment, among other factors.

The best example here is the subjection of Health Service budgeting to Treasury requirements. Not only the level of funds but the very process of budgeting is fixed by the Treasury; and in a sense the Health Service has been harmed more by this imposed budgeting process than by the actual severe limitation of funds.[8] It has been harmed by the need to prepare annual budgets which has prevented long-run planning in a Service where almost all large-scale planning is long-run. It has been harmed by the need to prepare budgets long in advance of events; in a chronically inflationary situation this has led to chronic over-budgeting. It has been harmed further by the denial of powers of *virement* to local administrative bodies and the demand that all savings in any year to be returned to the Exchequer; both of these requirements have led to very considerable waste: not only the whole budget but every part of it is inflated and distorted, and no real effort is made to achieve savings: there are frequently wild spending sprees at the end of the financial year to get rid of unspent funds.

Almost nothing can be done about this, because the Service is financed out of taxation. It has been widely suggested that the Service should be run on the University Grants system of long-period (e.g. five-year) appropriations. But as long as the Treasury is responsible for annual planning, and as long as the Health Service is the largest item in the Civil budget, it is impossible to exempt that Service from the normal budgeting process. And as long as there are violent fluctuations in price-levels, budgeting every five years in advance, in so large a service, would at the least be extremely difficult. If national budgets are to be prepared accurately, their constituent parts must be prepared long enough in advance to allow the Treasury to integrate them.[9] In gist, as long as the Treasury does national financial planning, and as long as the general economic welfare of the nation is given priority over the welfare of the Health

[8] *Hansard*, vol. 472, col. 937.

[9] Recent changes in the budgeting time-table (see Ministry of Health Memorandum R.H.B. 1951, no. 84) do not affect this argument, for reasons too complex to be set out here.

Service, annual budgets and long-range forecasts are inescapable. The restrictions on *virement* and on the spending of savings may be inescapable for another reason — because they are too deeply ingrained in Treasury usage. But the essence of the problem remains — that there is a point beyond which Treasury procedure cannot be adjusted to Health Service needs. Efficient public financial administration in general need not be efficient financial administration in every public service. What suits the hospitals need not suit the nation, and the nation clearly has first claim.

## III

The tendencies of the planning process are all attributable to the demands it makes on planners and the attempts of the planners to make these demands as bearable as possible. The principal adjustment they make involves the reduction of the area of rational decision-making, and, in some cases, the manifest abdication of rational decision-making.

This dynamic is evident, first of all, in the substitution of 'routine' rules for rational calculation wherever the logically most difficult and psychologically most oppressive decisions are required.

The clearest instance is the distribution of funds to the hospital system. It has, of course, been necessary to distribute funds to the hospitals in terms of what the nation could spare in relation to other requirements. How has the Ministry adjusted the hospitals' estimates of their individual needs to the funds available for hospital purposes? Although local budgeting is known to be distorted and local spending to a large extent irrational, it has either cut all estimates uniformly or determined future in terms of past expenditure.[10]

Exactly the same thing happened in the case of the so-called 'staff surveys'.[11] The purpose of these was 'rational' enough. Most of the Health Service budget goes to the hospitals; most of the hospitals' budgets goes into wages and salaries; and hospital staffs had greatly increased since the inception of the Service.[12] Hence, the Ministry decided on a series of surveys to detect unnecessary staffing. But the decisions which emerged from the surveys were certainly other than rational, simply because it was extremely difficult

[10] These methods were first used in 1949, i.e. well before the imposition of the ceiling on expenditure. See *Seventh Report from the Select Committee on Estimates*, 1948–9, qu. 947. See also J. S. Ross, *The National Health Service in Great Britain* (London: Oxford University Press, 1952) p. 162.

[11] See *Hospital*, vol. 46, p. 432.

[12] See, e.g., *Eleventh Report from the Select Committee on Estimates*, 1950–1, qu. 232, paras. 24–5.

(if not, again, impossible) to devise rational standards for measuring objective staffing needs and to apply them without stirring up hornets' nests of pressure. The Health Service planners again avoided the problem by using routine formulae. First, they froze the levels of hospital staffs at those prevailing by making all future appointments depend on Ministry approval and demanding that a reduction in staff cancel every addition; then they asked all hospitals to cut staffs by 5 per cent.[13] It is difficult to believe that these were anything more than decisions of convenience which could have been reached without a single local survey being made.[14]

Stereotyped rules have again been applied in almost every instance in which the objective appraisal of individual cases would entail great difficulties and pressures. For example, to distinguish genuine from bogus medical partnerships,[15] the Ministry has ruled that any partnership of less than a year's duration is not 'genuine' for Health Service purposes. Stereotyped rules have been applied perhaps most ludicrously to surgical operations, which are now divided into major, intermediate, and minor, the surgeons being paid prescribed maximum fees by their 'pay-bed' patients in accordance with this classification. (The same distinctions were used under the old system for the purpose of charging patients, but they then referred to the objective difficulty, not to 'types' of operations, and the surgeon was the final arbiter as regards the degree of difficulty involved. A similar procedure in the Health Service would have run the risk of abuse or of intolerable clinical arrangements, such as the appointment of assessors to attend the operating theatre or to sit on some distant surgical estimates board. The only workable procedure was not to judge individual cases on their objective merits at all, but to lump all operations together in a prearranged typological scheme. The result, of course, is that surgeons may now receive more money for an easy operation than for a really difficult one.)[16]

This tendency to elaborate standardised or routine procedures as alternatives to objective decision-making on the individual merits of concrete cases has two principal functions: to reduce the logical difficulty of decision-making by providing clear and simple rules

13 Ministry of Health Memorandum R.H.B. no. 133, and *Hansard*, 7 May 1953.

14 There is some evidence, indeed, that the survey teams did not do their job at all thoroughly. See *Hospital*, vol. 48, p. 3. The secretary of one hospital told me that the jobs of its hundred employees were 'evaluated' by two people in two days. What could they have learned?

15 This is a matter of some importance since general practitioners in partnership are given certain advantages over single-handed practitioners in the Service.

16 See e.g. *Eleventh Report from the Estimates Committee*, qu. 414.

into which concrete cases may be compressed, and to reduce psychological pressure by similarly providing clear and simple standards of justification.[17]

A second tendency is closely related to the first. It consists of the elaboration of procedure which can make a kind of rational calculation possible but not one efficiently suited to the substantive goals of calculation, and sometimes, indeed, one tending to obstruct the achievement of these goals. Such are procedures involving standard formulae — simple yardsticks which obviate a multitude of decisions on their own merits. The clearest example furnished by the Health Service is the frenzied quest for costing procedures, simple and universally applicable to formulae by which to assess individual hospital needs and to pass judgements on individual hospital demands. Costing procedures, however useful for other purposes (e.g. as an indication, but an indication only, of uneconomic management in individual cases) cannot, for a host of reasons, be used as an absolute means for determining budgets unless they are so meticulously detailed that their application would involve treating almost every individual case on its particular merits; in which event, of course, little would be gained by using them. Despite this, the Ministry still seems to be searching for them, and many hints have been dropped that the ultimate goal is to use them as universally applicable standards for determining the 'objective' requirements of every part of the hospital service.

All this illustrates one of the fundamental dilemmas of the planning process: the need to operate either without standards of calculation or with over-standarised procedures. In a situation which practically precludes fully rational behaviour, planners try to create a set of conditions in which a high degree of calculated decision-making becomes possible, even if these conditions are irrelevant to, or impede, the achievement of their goals. They try, indeed, to maximise the conditions of formally rational at the expense of substantially rational behaviour, in short, to re-create in the planned system the very faults of the spontaneous system.

A third tendency is that towards what Sir Oliver Franks has

[17] The same tendencies may, of course, be observed in the operation of judicial systems.

More examples of 'routine' in the Health Service could be cited: e.g. certain of the procedures used by the Dental Estimates Board, and the methods used to check on the prescribing habits of general practitioners and opticians. In most of these cases, however, a real effort is made to come to grips with the objective merits of individual cases, the routine procedures being used only to detect cases on which objective individual judgements should be made. This is perhaps the most 'rational' use to which routine can be put.

called 'rigidity and inertia'. This tendency manifests itself in three ways.

*First*, originally makeshift arrangements tend to become permanent. 'The word "temporary" ', said a witness before the Committee on Estimates, 'is a term of art in the Civil Service.'[18] There are good reasons why it should be. The re-examination of any decision reimposes a need for making difficult calculations. Moreover, almost any arrangement will adjust itself at least to some extent to the demands made on it, and can therefore be defended by the claim that 'it works', even if it does not work too well. Finally, almost every arrangement leads to the formation of vested interests and therefore to resistance to change. The clearest example in the Health Service may be found in the remarkable tenacity of the supposedly temporary Supplementary Ophthalmic Service and especially in the considerable consolidation of parties interested in its persistence. A further example may come to be provided by the current hospital grouping arrangements: these are obviously meant to be makeshift, they obviously 'work' in some sense, and they are obviously creating considerable interests, both administrative and political, in their preservation. As yet, they have scarcely been altered at all.

The *second* manifestation of the tendency is an extension of the first: in general it is difficult to get any decision changed once it has been acted upon. There is an extremely important reason for this: decision-makers who are fully and publicly accountable acquire political and psychological stakes in their own decisions and develop a justificatory rather than a critical attitude towards them. The best example in the Health Service may be found in the Ministry's defensive attitude towards changing the areas of the South-West Metropolitan and South-Western Regions. But in general major changes in the Service have been made much more as the result of outside pressures than as a result of internal initiative, for instance, certain changes in the budgeting time-table, and the suddenly concerted attack on tuberculosis in 1951.

The *third* manifestation of the tendency appears in the indefinite postponement of action for the sake of more and more inquiry, however superfluous this may be. It is accounted for by reasons already cited and one other — the frequent feeling of the decision-makers that they do not possess the technical competence required for rational action. Its obvious forms are the abdication of decision-making to specially competent outside bodies, the accumulation of report upon report, and the parliamentary reply that 'the matter is under consideration'. The best example in the Health Service may

18 *Seventh Report from the Estimates Committee*, qu. 23.

be found in the Ministry's enlightened procrastination towards the construction of Health Centres and towards the employment of dental nurses and dental hygienists.

A fourth tendency is seen in the substitution of political for rational decision-making. (By political decision-making I mean decision-making which either aims more at being acceptable than at being efficient, or which is more a product of influence and persuasion than of rational calculation.) A disposition to choose actions for their defensibility follows almost logically from the disposition towards justification already discussed, and is most likely to be a factor where rational calculation and defence of a decision are most difficult. In the Health Service the best examples may again be found in hospital finance. The Ministry realises that its budgetary formulae do injustice in individual cases; it is also obsessed with making defensible decisions. Hence it permits local representations after making its general decisions, and frequently, if the pressure is strong enough, gives in. The result is not rational budgeting, but arbitrary budgeting, revised to keep local criticisms to a minimum. In this process, a great deal obviously depends on the influence a local administrative body has at Ministry level, e.g. the personal relationships of its chairman with important people in the Ministry. Other examples are also likely to be found where decisions call for technical competence. In the Health Service the operative criterion has often been acceptability to the profession. Indeed, deference to professional viewpoints rather than subservience to parliamentary opinion has been the tendency, although the latter obviously also plays a role. Since the Service was instituted the medical profession has hardly ever failed to get its way on issues involving any sort of technical considerations, and it has been successful on a great many non-technical matters as well.

The first, third, and fourth tendencies all imply either the suspension or the breakdown of rational action. The fifth, like the second, serves the purpose of making rational action possible regardless of substantive consequences. It involves the centralisation of administrative powers.

It would take much too long to list all the instances in which there has been a flow of administrative powers from the periphery to the centre in the case of the Health Service; but, not surprisingly, the chief instance is once again in financial administration. No doubt the scarcities of the post-war years made necessary some centralisation of financial administration. But the tendency towards centralisation can be attributed also to the normal situation of the planners. Centralisation serves above all the purpose of reducing the area of factors over which the decision-makers have no control. In this sense it is clearly designed to facilitate both calculation and control. But in so far as it increases both the number of factors which must be taken into account by a single authority and the range of that authority's direct responsibility for the consequences of decisions, it increases precisely those tensions which lead to the breakdown of rational action. Once more, the best example is hospital finance. The greater the need has been for a really rational distribution of funds among the hospitals, the more have financial procedures been centralised; the more these procedures have been centralised, the more they have been dominated by routine and arbitrary formulae, by snap decisions in place of rational calculations. This constitutes another fundamental dilemma of the planning process. In the first place, the process seems impelled, for logical reasons, to enlarge the area of factors which are subject to the control of a single authority as much as possible; in the second, it is impelled, for psychological as well as logical reasons, to reduce the scope of rational decision-making as much as possible, and the more the range of calculation is enlarged the more it is necessary to reduce it. In so far as this is the case, the two major tendencies of the process — towards maximising the conditions of formally rational action and towards the breakdown of rational action — are intimately related.

## IV

I must repeat that these arguments and hypotheses, although some of them have been stated in general terms, are specifically relevant only to the British Health Service. But suppose that on further inquiry they are found to have general applicability, what larger implications do they contain?

In the first place, they do not imply, by any stretching of logic, that an unplanned system will always, or even sometimes, be more 'effective' than a planned system. If my arguments have general validity, and if we at the same time give up *laissez-faire* theory, then we seem impelled to assert a final melancholy generalisation which the *laissez-faire* economists are trying to avoid. Let me state it in Weberian language:

*The chief condition for the existence of a high degree of formally rational conduct is, generally speaking, a high degree of substantive irrationality in society; and the most probable result of the deliberate attempt to make society substantively rational is the breakdown of rational conduct altogether.*

On this basis the fully rational organisation of society is impossible, and we seem to have no choice but either to renew our belief in *laissez-faire* or to live with a sense of utter futility. But is there really no other possibility?

The answer is emphatically that there is one. The arguments I have outlined do not deny the engineering reason; they merely circumscribe its effectiveness and indicate its extreme instability when it is taxed too much. However much the experience of planning in the Health Service may reflect adversely on the absolute efficiency of the process, any fair appraisal of the work of that Service to date would have to be more favourable than unfavourable.[19] What the tensions we have discovered imply is that a society can be rationally organised only if it does not insist on too much of either formal or substantive rationality. Liberalism, by taking itself too seriously, was corroded by the Marxist and nihilist reactions against its inconsistencies in practice. The corrosion of the planned society, if the argument here is correct, may take the form of its utter routinisation or 'politicalisation'. The villain of the piece, in other words, is neither *laissez-faire* nor planning: it is perfectionism — the desire for an absolutely rational and benevolent social mechanism, or the desire for a set of absolutely rational and benevolent social engineers. Perfectionism is deeply ingrained in Western culture, beginning with the Christian belief in a single, omnicompetent, entirely benevolent God, and developing through the social application of the Newtonian notion that the universe is a divinely engineered self-regulating mechanism, held together in perfect 'equilibrium' by the magnetism of the planets. Once one has become a perfectionist, it is difficult to be anything else. The appeal of inevitable progress, immutable harmony, absolute freedom or absolute well-being, is too seducing to be resisted. *Per contra*, anti-perfectionism becomes equated with absolute pessimism. But in fact it is the perfectionists who are themselves the worst pessimists and who inculcate pessimism. Proceeding from the absolute benevolence of the market mechanism, they argue the impossibility of effective planning; or, proceeding from the benevolence of the planning process, they argue the utter evil of the spontaneous society.

[19] It would take a separate article to document this assertion properly. But it must be granted that the Health Service is at least an improvement over the old system. Great strides forward have been made in the redistribution of general practitioners; the hospital grouping arrangements have made possible great improvements in administrative co-ordination and the allocation of medical work; the greatest defects of the old system, especially the lack of proper dental and ophthalmic care, have been remedied. Compare, for example, the findings of the ten *Hospital Surveys* (1945) with the Ministry's annual reports on the condition of the hospital service; or the first annual report of the Medical Practices Committee with the latest.

Asking us to believe in one or other version of the millennium they invite cynicism or, worse, frustration, the chief curse of modern society. But we are not constrained to regard planning with either cynicism or frustration: it is not only possible, but sensible, to regard it with what one might call pragmatic, optimistic *im*perfectionism.

# SOME REFLECTIONS ON THE REPORT OF THE ROYAL COMMISSION ON THE POLICE

*By* Jenifer Hart

For more than a century, British governments have made use of Royal Commissions to deliberate upon major policy issues that do not require immediate decision. The use of Royal Commissions is well known, but the practice of these bodies has been little studied. Jenifer Hart's analysis of the Royal Commission on the Police is of value not only as a study of an important method of government, but also as a study of the operations of a Royal Commission. It raises questions about the general suitability of Royal Commissions as an instrument of policy-making, as well as questions about the conduct of a branch of British government that in modern times is often treated as beyond examination or reproach.

In 1958 one of the worst scandals in the history of the British police came to light. After a trial lasting nineteen days, two C.I.D. officers of the Brighton police force were sentenced to five years' imprisonment for having conspired to obstruct the course of public justice during the previous nine years. The Chief Constable, Mr Ridge, after trial on the same charges, was found not guilty, but was subsequently dismissed from the force as negligent and unfit for his duties. He had been in the Brighton C.I.D. for twenty-one years before he became Chief Constable in 1956. The Home Secretary, the Queen's Bench and the Court of Appeal all upheld his dismissal, but the House of Lords on appeal held that the decision of the Watch Committee to dismiss him was null and void as contrary to the principles of natural justice, Mr Ridge not having been given a proper opportunity to defend himself. The case for the Crown was that all the accused had refrained from making proper inquiries and instituting criminal charges when they ought to have been made, that they had tipped off law breakers, including a receiver of stolen goods, and given them warning when police action was afoot. One of the cases in which obstruction had taken place involved a £15,000 theft of cigarettes. In the course of sentencing the C.I.D. officers, the trial judge made a statement which included grave reflections on

Reprinted in excerpt form from *Public Law* (Autumn 1963) pp. 283–98, 303–4 (Stevens & Sons).

the Chief Constable's conduct. He also drew attention to the fact that one of the convicted policemen had been on holiday with a local man with a serious criminal record. It was widely suggested that several other members of the force must at least have known a good deal about what was going on. Throughout these nine years, during which other police forces not unnaturally lost faith in the Brighton force, it was certified as efficient by H.M. Inspector of Constabulary; and the Inspectors in their joint Report for England and Wales in 1957 said there was 'ample evidence that the guardianship of the Queen's Peace was secure'. Mr Ridge's appointment as Chief Constable in 1956 was approved by the Home Secretary presumably on the advice of H.M. Inspector. The Watch Committee, ignorant it seems of what was going on, took no action. The MP for Brighton alone appears to have been uneasy, but had no success when he tried to raise the matter with the Home Secretary in Parliament.

The same year the Chief Constable of Worcester, Mr Davies, was found guilty of fraudulent conversion of over £1,000 of certain police club funds and was sentenced to eighteen months' imprisonment. During the trial it was alleged that the conduct of the Chief Constable's predecessor, Mr Tinkler, who had retired in 1955, had been grossly irregular for many years. He had run up large debts at the police club for drinks and borrowed money from police funds to settle this account and for various other private purposes. The money borrowed by Mr Tinkler from police funds was eventually repaid, but the trial revealed a shocking state of affairs. For instance, the secretary of the club, a police inspector, signed blank cheques at Mr Davies' request for several years. Mr Davies was treasurer of the club from 1946 and connived at Mr Tinkler's activities. Moreover, when Chief Constable, he intercepted a letter of complaint sent by the Police Federation (the policemen's organisation) to the Mayor, and also instructed the chief clerk to delete passages from a report which the Federation was trying to send to H.M. Inspector. He considered that the Federation had 'let him down' by asking for an inquiry into the management of the club. (Loyalty is a virtue much stressed in police circles.) Mr Davies' appointment as Chief Constable of Worcester in 1955 was approved by the Home Secretary, presumably on the advice of H.M. Inspector, and the force was throughout this period certified as efficient.

Meanwhile strange things were happening in Cardiganshire. These were skilfully unravelled (no mean feat) by Mr H. J. Phillimore Q.C. who was appointed by the Home Secretary in 1957 at the request of the Police Authority to inquire into the administration of the Cardiganshire Constabulary and the state of discipline of the force. Anyone with an appetite for intrigues and sharp practices will enjoy this report about the behaviour of public persons in a small Welsh county.[1] Mr Phillimore found that there was a serious and justifiable lack of confidence among the public in the efficiency and administration of the police force, and he apportioned the blame fairly widely. The Chief Constable, whose appointment beyond the age of sixty-five had been prolonged in 1954 for five years, had been slack in some matters of discipline and administration. The influence of two Aldermen had been harmful to the force. One, who was in Holy Orders, had intervened successfully with the Chief Constable to get a charge for speeding against a friend of his, also in Holy Orders, reduced to a caution. The Clerk to the Police Authority also came in for criticism for the way in which he tried to get rid of the Chief Constable. He succeeded at one time, but the Chief Constable was reinstated on appeal to the Home Secretary. Mr Phillimore pointed out that in a little over ten years two Chief Constables had been involved in disciplinary proceedings. He considered that the force was too small, that it gave little scope to an officer of real ability and that favouritism or the suspicion of it inevitably affected morale. The Police Authority took strong exception to the report, but the Home Secretary accepted its findings and considered that the events of the previous eighteen months called for urgent and drastic remedy. At one time, the payment of Exchequer grant was nearly withheld. In the end the solution adopted was the amalgamation of the force with a neighbouring one.

These disturbing cases were soon followed by the protracted dispute at Nottingham between the Chief Constable and the Watch Committee. In 1959 the Watch Committee asked the Chief Constable to report on police inquiries which concerned a member of the Nottingham City Council; the Chief Constable refused and was suspended from duty by the Watch Committee. The Home Secretary intervened and the Chief Constable was reinstated. This controversy, which was the culmination of a long history of antagonisms between the local labour party and the Chief Constable, aroused a great deal of passionate feeling locally and appeared to the public at large as an undignified pantomime.

## I

These were some of the incidents which gave rise to the appointment of a Royal Commission on the Police in 1960.[2] The Commis-

[1] Cmnd. 251, Aug 1957.

[2] Final Report, Cmnd. 1728 (1962).

sion was not asked explicitly to investigate bribery and corruption or other misconduct by the police, but it was told to review *inter alia* 'the arrangements for their control and administration', and to consider their 'accountability'. One would have thought that these tasks could not be fulfilled without first attempting to define the precise character of the problem and to estimate its magnitude. For how can one advise on controlling the police until one knows their weak spots, what there is to guard against, and how often things go wrong? But the Commission apparently thought otherwise. Thus it did not, for example, collect figures about the number and nature of disciplinary charges against policemen, the number of police convicted of criminal offences, the number of Chief Constables who have had rows with their police authorities or who have left under a cloud, etc. Facts such as these covering, say, the last twenty or thirty years, with the ranks of the offenders, would have made a solid basis from which to start discussing control. Some witnesses gave some figures, but they are not complete, and in any case they were not collated by the Commission but remain scattered about in the evidence.[3] Indeed, the Commission seems to have made no real attempt to give a down-to-earth, particularised picture of the police service today. Instead, we are given an unrealistic, glamourised and too general acount of it; we are treated to lengthy disquisitions about the formal legal framework, and about the purpose of the police, on which we are all surely agreed; we are constantly taken back into the past for which the Commission has great respect; and, unless careful, we are mesmerised by verbiage and hollow phrases.

Admittedly the Commission was not assisted by much of the evidence given to it, at least by the evidence from official bodies and organisations, which tends to be unrealistic, complacent and too general. For instance, the Home Office memorandum declares that in practice friction between the Home Secretary, police authorities and chief officers does not occur.[4] (What about Cardiganshire and Nottingham?) The Association of Chief Police Officers (England and Wales) says that H.M. Inspectors 'get to know a great deal about the state of efficiency of the various forces in their area and of the personal qualities and characteristics of the Chief Constables themselves'.[5] (Then why, we may ask, do they not act on their knowledge?) The Association reaffirmed 'their confidence in the general standards of integrity and conduct among all ranks of the

[3] Association of Municipal Corporations, Minutes of Evidence 11–12, p. 637; Commissioner of Police of the Metropolis, M. of E. 20, p. 1172; Bow Group, M. of E. 24, p. 1299, and Questions 4652 to 4656.

[4] Appendix II to M. of E., p. 9, para. 17. [5] M. of E. 15, p. 860, para. 99.

police' and their 'faith . . . in the general administration and operation of the component forces and the Service as a whole'.[6] One police authority which gave evidence considered that 'the rules governing the appointment [of Chief Constables] are such that only men of the highest integrity are likely to fill these positions'.[7] The MP for Carlisle, with the apt name of Dr Johnson, was, however, more realistic when he declared that if Chief Constables are 'speaking broadly, rogues, you get them in the end, but they can put up a pretty good smokescreen in the meantime'.[8]

The Commission itself is, however, partly to blame for the inadequacy of much of the material put before it. Thus it often failed to ask sufficiently clear and detailed questions, or the questions which would have been the most revealing. Moreover members of the Commission, and especially the Chairman, spoke at far too great length, instead of eliciting information from witnesses. Further, almost every time a witness referred to a particular happening, the Commission was reluctant to hear about it. But how else can a picture of what in fact happens in bad cases be built up? It would obviously be an error to generalise from these, but it is important to know the worst that does ocur. Of course, these impressions are necessarily based only on the published evidence; things may have been different in the private sessions, but if so the report is reticent about what emerged at them.

As examples illustrating these criticisms of the work of the Commission, the following may be cited: the report speaks of Chief Constables as 'able and intelligent men, growing in professional stature and public esteem' (para. 82), and of 'the able men who command our police forces' (para. 301); it says that the system has 'stood the test of time and emerged successfully after severe strains' (para. 141); 'it has not failed' (para. 148); our police system is sound partly because 'reasonable people operate it successfully' and 'because it follows a tradition of local policing which is traceable back for many centuries' (para. 142); 'there are black sheep in most families. Moreover, news that a policeman has been prosecuted before a criminal court ought to be regarded as evidence of a Chief Constable's determination to deal properly with his men, rather than as an indication of widespread criminal conduct among policemen' (para. 399); as the system 'commends itself strongly to the Home Departments, the local authorities and the chief constables, [it] must obviously have strong claims to public confidence. . . . The recent events which led to public criticism of the police . . . did not

[6] M. of E. 15, p. 864, para. 126.
[7] M. of E. 20, p. 1130, para. 2.
[8] M. of E. 22, Q. 4442.

reveal major defects in the system, so much as occasional failures in human relationships and a lack of clear definition of fields of responsibility' (para. 141). In fact, only one, or at the most two (Nottingham and perhaps Cardigan), of the six events which led up to the appointment of the Commission fell into this category. The Commission had previously pointed out that in assessing the value of evidence some allowance must be made for the influence of vested interest (para. 140), but it then proceeds to give far more weight to the opinion of those with a vested interest in the system as it is than to the views of outside critics. The Commission's statement that it does not propose to give a detailed history of the police (para. 25) raises one's hopes, but these are soon dashed, for at once we are back in the Middle Ages and plunged into Courts Leet and the Statute of Winchester of 1285 (paras. 26 and 27). It is significant that we are referred to a very old (1895) and greatly overworked article by a member of the Home Office on 'The Office of Constable' and not to more recent and relevant writings. Far too much time is taken up with explaining why things are as they are: why, for instance, we have so many small forces, and why the legal position is uncertain and confusing. This is a largely pointless activity for a Royal Commission, except in so far as it helps them to decide whether there are now good reasons for leaving things as they are. The Willink Commission does not seem to have worked on this criterion. The old familiar catchwords and phrases are trotted out without any attempt to analyse them. We are, for instance, told by the Commission that 'The police and the community are one. The police act for the community in the enforcement of the law and it is on the law and its enforcement that the liberties of the community rest' (para. 326). One does not have to have read Bentham to know that this is misleading: one merely has to have tried to sell the *Daily Worker* or *Peace News* in the street or to have demonstrated in some minority cause. And does the law against public indecency as enforced by the police really protect our liberties? Further, what does it add to our knowledge to say that 'The police are recruited from the public, and remain members of the general body of citizens' (para. 362)? In another place the Commission says that our police system 'provides for the central pooling of knowledge and experience gathered from the whole country' (para. 142). This is hardly true whilst H.M. Inspectors do not inspect the Metropolitan Police and whilst the Inspector for Scotland works very much on his own. Nor will the vague and ambiguous recommendation made by the Commission that the Metropolitan Police should 'receive the advantages of the reorganised inspectorate' (para. 252) go far towards realising J. S. Mill's ideal that knowledge should be centralised.

II

The Commission says that it has tried to 'define the complementary roles of the police authority and the central authority in the administration of the police service, and to remove any uncertainty due to overlapping responsibilities' (para. 324). How far is this claim justified? The Secretary of State is to be made 'statutorily responsible for the efficiency of the police' (para. 230), and this will involve *inter alia* being responsible for ensuring 'the effective execution by police authorities of the authorities' duties' (para. 231). If we turn back to see what duties the report has assigned to police authorities (para. 154), we find among their four main duties these two:

(1) 'to constitute a body of citizens concerned with the local standing and well-being of the police, interested in the maintenance of law and order, and able to give advice and guidance to a chief constable about local problems'; and

(2) 'to play an active role in fostering good relations between the police and the public'.

Apart from difficulties due to the vagueness and generality of these duties, there are certain further ambiguities and unresolved problems. For instance, the report does not say how a Secretary of State is to know whether these duties are being performed by the police authority. Surely he must know this if he is to be 'responsible for ensuring the effective execution by police authorities of their duties'. It is not apparently the job of H.M. Inspectors to report on these matters (see list of their duties in para. 250). Indeed, when reviewing the Inspectors' relations with police authorities, the report says that the Inspector should on the occasion of his official inspection discuss with the police authority matters for which they are legally responsible (para. 160), and it would seem only such matters, and the duties described at (1) and (2) above are not part of their legal responsibilities (see list of legal responsibilities proposed by the Commission in para. 233). Further, even assuming that the Secretary of State thinks he knows that a police authority is not fulfilling these duties (*e.g.*, that they are not fostering good relations between police and public, or are not able to give advice to their Chief Constable), what can he do about it? He would apparently not be entitled to withhold grant, since he can only do this if they do not satisfactorily discharge their legal responsibilities (para. 233).

Or let us consider what being statutorily responsible for the police does not involve according to the recommendations of the Commission. The Secretary of State is not given 'complete responsibility for the police service': he is not to be responsible 'for the acts of individual policemen or for the day-to-day enforcement of the law'. He is only to have 'a general duty to ensure that the police operate efficiently'; and he is to have 'no powers of direction' (para. 230). The Commission does not define precisely what it means by 'a general duty to ensure that the police operate efficiently' except by appearing to equate this general duty with 'central responsibility for an efficient organisation, both central and local' (para. 230). But how can a Secretary of State be sure that the organisation of a local police force is efficient unless he can find out what individual policemen do and how the law is actually enforced? The concept of day-to-day enforcement is also very obscure. With what is it being contrasted? One may ask how this clarificatory allocation of functions would have worked at Brighton. The organisation of the force (whatever that means) may well have been efficient: at least the Brighton police were no doubt paid, equipped and housed properly. But if someone had suspected that certain 'individual' police officers were not doing their work properly, that they were corrupt or lax in the enforcement of the law, what could that person have done about it? If the Secretary of State is not to be 'responsible for the acts of individual policemen or for the day-to-day enforcement of the law', he will presumably not be willing to listen to and investigate complaints that this or that policeman was corrupt or lax, and the person who suspected irregularities would have to wait until several or perhaps even many police officers behaved badly before the Secretary of State would look into the allegations. This view is supported by the passage in the report which says that the responsibility of the police for the enforcement of the law is 'neither central nor local' (para. 230). It seems to follow from this that if a police officer is slack in enforcing a particular law against a particular person or institution (*e.g.*, a club as at Brighton), no member of the public could get the matter investigated by the Secretary of State, the police authority or indeed by the Chief Constable if he were not willing to do so. Thus it appears improbable that the Commission's proposals would have helped to bring the Brighton scandals to light any sooner. If the Commission considered that in order to put teeth into the Secretary of State's statutory responsibility for the efficiency of the police, he should investigate allegations of this kind, whilst not being responsible for the acts of individual policemen, it should have said so.

Just as the Commission assigns a 'general duty' to the Secretary of State to see the police operate efficiently, so it recommends that the general policies of a Chief Constable in regard to certain matters should be more effectively supervised than they are at present (para. 92). These matters are such things as law enforcement, the disposition of the force, the concentration of police resources on a particular type of crime or area, the manner in which the Chief Constable handles political demonstrations or processions, allocates and instructs his men for handling industrial disputes, the methods he employs in dealing with an outbreak of violence or of passive resistance to authority, and his policy in enforcing traffic laws and in dealing with parked vehicles (para. 89). Who under the Commission's scheme is intended to provide the increased supervision which is recommended? Mainly it would seem the local police authority, though this is by no means clear. At any rate they do not seem to be included in the matters for which the Secretary of State has a 'general responsibility' as listed in para. 231. Perhaps they are the kind of thing on which he could call for reports from Chief Constables; these are not specified in the passages in the Commission's report where this power is recommended (paras. 134 (f) and 322). So we must conclude that it is for the police authority to provide the 'more effective supervision'. But this supervision seems to have no bite in it until things have gone so far that the police authority has lost confidence in the Chief Constable and makes him retire. For the Commission says that in the field of law enforcement in relation to particular cases, a Chief Constable should be 'free from the conventional processes of democratic control and influence' (para. 87). All a policy authority seems able to do until things have got really bad is (a) to ask for reports from the Chief Constable on his general policies as to the disposition of the force, etc., and even then they may not be able to get them (para. 163), and (b) to give him advice and guidance which he is not bound to take (para. 162). They will also normally acquire rather more information than they have at present from the annual report which the Chief Constable will be required to submit to them (para. 164). For instance, information about complaints against the police (their number, nature and disposal) will, if the Commission's recommendation is followed, be included in these annual reports (para. 468), but the police authority is not to have the power to intervene in a particular case. It will only be able 'to scrutinise the manner in which the Chief Constable discharges this part of his duties' (para. 469). Here again they can do nothing it seems unless they resort to the drastic step of forcing him to retire. The Commission also recommends that a member of a Council should have a right to ask questions of the Chairman of the police authority, though he would not be obliged to reply if, in his judgment it seems, this would be contrary to law or to the public interest (para. 165).

III

One of the matters which had caused much public concern in recent years was the inability of MPs to raise in the House of Commons questions about the police outside London except in very general terms. It seemed to many people anomalous and indeed indefensible that a service to which the Exchequer contributed about £40 million a year, and over which the Secretary of State had in fact a considerable degree of control, should be immune from effective parliamentary oversight, especially as the activities of the police affect the liberty of the subject in so many ways. Nor could it be said that this did not matter because at least the ratepayers or their elected representatives had control over the organisation and actions of their local police force, for they clearly did not. Although there are as many as one hundred and eleven conclusions and recommendations at the end of the Commission's report, these contain no reference to Parliament. The body of the report, however, seems to intend that the Secretary of State should be more accountable to Parliament on police matters than he is at present. It is, one imagines, in order to secure this that he is to be made statutorily responsible for the efficiency of the police. At any rate, the chapter on 'The Central Authority' ends up with these words: 'The Secretaries of State will be accountable to Parliament for the efficient policing of the whole country' (para. 325). And a little earlier, after recommending that the Secretary of State should determine whether a Chief Constable was justified in refusing to give a report to his police authority, the Commission comments: 'An advantage we see in this arrangement is that it will serve to regulate and guide relations between a police authority and a Chief Constable in a manner open to Parliamentary criticism' (para. 323). This presumably meant that Parliament could criticise a decision of the Secretary of State about the refusal of a Chief Constable to give a report to his police authority. The section on 'Complaints against the Police' also seems to contemplate some role for Parliament; at least we are told that if an aggrieved citizen fails to secure redress locally, it will be 'open to him to complain to his MP, or to any other person whom he regards as influential' (para. 470). But a little later the Commission seems to go back on this, for it says, 'Those who favoured making the Secretary of State responsible to Parliament for the police contemplated that complaints might, if necessary, be dealt with by means of Parliamentary Question and Answer.... We ourselves are unanimously of the opinion that the present procedure, amended as we have proposed, will almost always provide for the proper and impartial investigation of complaints' (paras. 467–77). The amendments proposed by the Commission for dealing with complaints do not include any mention of Parliament. If an MP cannot ask a question about the handling of a complaint against the police, it is difficult to see what the aggrieved citizen will gain by taking the matter up with him as is suggested earlier by the Commission. The lack of any clear recommendation on this very important and difficult matter is greatly to be regretted. It may be that the Commission felt it would be exceeding its proper sphere if it expressed a view on what could be regarded as a matter of parliamentary procedure to be determined by the officers of the House of Commons, though one can think of no good grounds for such a self-denying ordinance. But in any case the Commission does not stick firmly to this line, for it touches on the subject.

## IV

One of the most crucial questions in connection with the British police is how many separate forces we should have — one? fifty? a hundred? or over 150 as now? The Commission starts boldly, saying that 'there is no excuse for shirking some fundamental re-thinking' about the structure of our police system (para. 18). Then we are told that the organisation of the police should be such that they will achieve maximum efficiency and that our present system does not (paras. 19 and 20). (No objection can be raised so far except that the concept of 'maximum efficiency' is not defined.) Next we are told that the Commission had received no evidence that the system of local forces was in some measure to blame for the inability of the police in the post-war years to halt the rise in crime (para. 22). This suggests that no witnesses considered that the fight against crime would be helped if there was a national police force, or fewer police forces. This is simply not true. For example, the Chief Constable of Lancashire in his memorandum (which is a breath of fresh air in the generally turgid atmosphere) states that detective staff are handicapped in their work by being for the most part organised on local authority boundaries,[9] and the Inns of Court Conservative and Unionist Society argues that, for various reasons which they give, a small number of regional forces would improve police efficiency.[10] However, the Commission admits that there is much to be said for having a unified or national police force, for (in para. 147) it says:

[9] M. of E. 15, p. 927, para. 40. [10] M. of E. 11–12, p. 690, para. 36.

'That there is a strong case for bringing the police of this country under complete central control is undeniable. Such a step might well enable the service more effectively to fulfil its purposes.' As the Commission had decided, albeit after much heart-searching, that a national force would not be constitutionally objectionable or politically dangerous (para. 139), one would expect them to come down in its favour. But the fundamental re-thinking we had been promised is abandoned, and we are told that in turning down direct control of the police by the government, the Commission had borne in mind that 'it is in the tradition of this country to allow institutions to evolve and change gradually, encouraged, guided and supported by public opinion' (para. 150). This is not a very convincing ground for rejecting the policy which the Commission itself considered might well enable the police to be more effective. The only member of the Commission who spotted the weakness of this reasoning was Dr Goodhart, who took a less inbred view of the British police system (see his *Memorandum of Dissent*).

However, when it comes to abolishing the smaller forces, the Commission is distinctly bolder, in spite of not being given much lead on this matter by the official witnesses. The Home Office Memorandum virtually ignores the question altogether; the nearest it gets to the point is to say (hopefully) that 'it ought to be possible to resolve' the disadvantages and problems due to the existing system, by consultation between the Home Office, police authorities and chief constables.[11] The Association of English and Welsh Chief Constables, on the other hand, knows there is danger in the air and emphasises the co-operation and co-ordination which they allege exist between forces, and the advantages of local connections. One might almost infer from their memorandum that every force was always rushing to the aid of its neighbours and that the laws of the country were enforced on uniform lines in all areas. The Association of Municipal Corporations also emphasised that co-operation was extensive and argued for a large number of independent police authorities.[12] In support of this, one of their representatives said that if an area was not efficiently policed the Watch Committee would soon hear of it and in those circumstances the electors would be very much concerned.[13] (How does one work Brighton into this picture?) Nevertheless, the Commission recommends the elimination of the smaller forces. It does not get down to the final details, but it talks of 500 as 'the optimum size' (para. 280), meaning presumably 'minimum', since it does not propose that no force should have *more* than

[11] Appendix II to M. of E., p. 9, para. 19.
[12] M. of E. 11–12, pp. 626–7, paras. 4–7. [13] M. of E. 11–12, Q. 2307.

500 men (forty-four now have). The procedure recommended by the Commission would, however, be slow and cumbrous: a working party issuing a series of reports and then local inquiries into schemes proposed by the central departments (para. 286). Are H.M. Inspectors really not in a position to advise departments at once on suitable new police areas? Even the Commission regards the matter as urgent and important.

## V

One of the matters which the Commission was asked to investigate was 'the relationship of the police with the public'. It found an acute conflict of evidence on the question whether the present relationship is better or worse than in the past. Among those who held there was no significant deterioration in recent years were the central departments, police authorities and chief officers of police. Another group thought relations were possibly slightly worse than they used to be; these included the Superintendents of Great Britain, and the Police Federation of England and Wales. A third group thought there had been a significant decline; these included the Scottish Police Federation, the Magistrates Association of England and Wales, the Law Society, the Inns of Court Conservative and Unionist Society, the Society of Labour Lawyers, the Bow Group, the Institute of Journalists, the Institute of Public Relations and the National Council of Civil Liberties. This conflict of evidence puzzled the Commission. All they could suggest by way of explanation was that:

> 'Perhaps there is a tendency for any judgment on such an intangible subject as the popularity or otherwise of a class of public servants to be too subjective to be wholly reliable if it is based on personal experience alone. It was because we recognised this difficulty', the report continues, 'that early in our inquiry we asked the Government Social Survey, a division of the Central Office of Information, to undertake a survey in an attempt to establish authoritatively both what the British public think of the police, and what the police think about the public' (para. 332).

These passages imply that the Commission thought there were objective criteria which could be applied to the question of deterioration, and that these tests must not be based on personal experience, or at any rate not on personal experience alone. But, we may ask, are there such criteria or tests? and, if so, did the Government Social Survey use them? It would no doubt be reasonable to take the number of assaults on the police by the public and the number of complaints received by the police as tests of relationships. But otherwise it is difficult to think of objective tests independent of personal experience which would help to produce an answer to the question:

have relations between police and public deteriorated? In any case, the Social Survey did not try to find such tests. It recognised (and rightly) that the answer to this question, as to many others about these relations, must be based either on what people think has happened or think is happening, or on their actual experience. We find, therefore, that all the questions asked by the Survey are either of the form 'Do you think x?' or 'Have you experienced y?' Indeed it is in the nature of a social survey of this sort to ask questions of these types.

Maybe what the report was trying to say in the passage quoted above is that perhaps the witnesses before the Commission were not a representative cross-section of the whole community. This is no doubt true, and if one wants to know what the 'man in the street' thinks about something, one must go and ask him. (Whether this was a useful activity on this issue is another question.) Or maybe what the Commission was getting at was that the witnesses were generalising unwarrantably from their own experiences. This seems to be what it had in mind when, writing of the malpractices of the police, particularly perjury, it said that, 'The preoccupation of the legal witnesses with the behaviour of the police in the courts may well have led them to exaggerate the significance of occasional allegations of this kind' (para. 335). Whether these witnesses were generalising unwarrantably or not, the Survey and the Commission itself use concepts which are so general as to be virtually useless. Thus many of the questions asked of the public use the collective term 'the police' as if policemen were all identical units: or, in other words, many of the questions do not enable the person answering to say 'I think this of some policemen, but not of others', or 'I have great respect for 95 per cent of the police but not for 5 per cent of them.' This in turn leads the Commission off into generalisations about 'the police' which obscure the fact that, though, no doubt, relations between most policemen and most members of the public are usually good, relations between some policemen and some members of the public are sometimes bad.

At first the Commission says that relations are 'on the whole very good' (para. 338), but later this becomes 'We have already refuted any suggestion that relations between the police and the public are bad' (para. 414), and further on 'the relationship between the police and the public is good' (para. 478). This tendency to deal in generalities colours the approach of the Commission throughout its work: the chairman in his questioning of witnesses professed himself more interested in 'the general public' than in particular sections of it.

However, if the Survey does not get us into the realm of objective criteria and impersonal experiences (as, indeed, it could not), does it fulfil some useful purpose? There is, in fact, quite a lot of interesting information to be found in its report.[14] But some of the conclusions drawn by the author of the Survey and accepted uncritically by the Commission seem entirely unwarranted. Take, for example, the information elicited about changes in relations between the police and the public during the last ten years, which, expressed as percentages of the samples, was as follows:

| | *Public's view of their own feelings towards police* | *Police view of public's opinion of police* |
|---|---|---|
| No change or don't know | 89·2 | 27·6 |
| Change for better | 6·6 | 3·6 |
| Change for worse | 3·7 | 68·8 |
| Change, but not clearly for better or worse | 0·5 | — |
| | 100 | 100 |

On the basis of these figures the author of the Survey concludes that 'the majority of the police thought that the public's opinion of them had changed for the worse whereas, in fact, it had changed for the better rather than the worse' (para. 41 of Survey.) He also speaks of 'the police having a distorted impression of their standing in the eyes of the public'. The Commission interprets the results of the Survey in the same way. It speaks of 'the inaccuracy of police opinion as to their standing in the eyes of the public' (para. 350), and it summarises the position by saying that 'public opinion of the police has changed for the better rather than the worse' (conclusion 71). All this cheerfulness, however, does not seem to be warranted by the evidence; for the fact is that, as shown above, the great majority of the public (89·2 per cent) reported *no* change in their feelings towards the police during the last ten years. The proportion reporting a change (10·8 per cent) is so small that it is not of much significance that two-thirds of these reported a change for the better.

Further, where the views of the two groups surveyed differ, why should the verdict of the public be accepted as against that of the police, as is done by the author of the Survey and by the Commis-

[14] The Relations between the Police and the Public, by R. Morton Williams. Appendix IV to M. of E.

sion? Neither of them gives any reasons for taking the views of the public as correct and those of the police as false, though, having made this assumption, they explain why in their view the police get a distorted impression of what the public feel about them. On the contrary, on questions on which significant comparisons can be made, there would seem to be good reasons for attaching more rather than less weight to the views of the police group than to the views of the general public group. For the police could with justification be considered to have more knowledge and experience of many of the matters dealt with in the questionnaires than had the general public, and they are trained to observe carefully and accurately. It seems strange to prefer the less well considered views of a random section of the public.

In the case of some other matters, *e.g.*, the actual behaviour of the public apart from changes in behaviour, the police were asked very few questions. This is a pity, because if the police had been asked about actual behaviour, one could have considered how the public translated into practice the great respect the vast majority of it (82·7 per cent) said it felt towards the police. The nearest we can get to seeing from the Survey if they act respectfully as well as feeling respect, is to take the fact that 88·7 per cent of the police said they thought something should be done to improve relations between the police and the public and that 97 per cent of the police suggest the public could do more to help them prevent crime and enforce the law. Respect by itself is clearly not enough.

Moreover, some of the things found by the Survey are prima facie improbable, or at any rate in need of further analysis which is not provided. For instance, the survey of the public (not that of the police) was used in order to try to estimate the actual amount of serious misconduct by the police. This was no doubt a good idea, but the results were astonishing and the conclusions drawn from them by the author of the Survey and by the Commission were absurd. For about 2 per cent of the sample of the public said they had personal knowledge of serious misconduct by the police during the past ten years — that is knowledge of the police taking bribes, using unfair methods to get information, twisting evidence and using too much force. 'Personal knowledge' excluded knowledge gained from friends or relatives, newspapers, radio or television. The compiler of the Survey does not consider the alleged incidence serious; nor does the Commission feel any concern at this finding (para. 373). But if the figure of 2 per cent were correct, about 65,000 instances of serious misconduct by the police would have taken place every year, which is nearly one per police officer per year. It seems unlikely from the way the sample was selected that many of the persons interviewed were referring to the same case, and it was surely irresponsible of the author of the Survey and of the Commission neither to have assessed the veracity of these answers nor to have explored the implications of the figures, before deciding that the position was satisfactory. The Commission might have sensed that something needed further exploration if it had compared the incidence of serious misconduct as alleged by the public with the numbers of offences proved against policemen under the Police Discipline Regulations and of convictions against the police. Such a comparison would have suggested either that the public was wildly wrong in its estimates of police misconduct or that chief constables were very lax in taking action against policemen who had done wrong.

The conclusion drawn by the Commission from the Survey is as follows: 'The findings of the survey constitute an overwhelming vote of confidence in the police, and a striking indication of the good sense and discrimination of the bulk of the population in their assessment of the tasks that policemen have to carry out. It is clear that such change as there has been in public opinion in recent years has been mainly in favour of the police. We, therefore, assert confidently, on the basis of this survey, that relations between the police and the public are on the whole very good, and we have no reason to suppose that they have ever, in recent times, been otherwise. This is a finding which we believe will give great satisfaction to Your Majesty, to the police, and to the public' (para. 338). In another place the Commission refers to: 'This valuable report [which] reveals an attitude of mind on both sides that augurs well for the continuance of good relations between the police and the public in years to come' (para. 350). But for the reasons suggested above, it would seem that the Commission was not justified in rating so highly the value of the Survey, and that their conclusions do not follow from the evidence it provided.

## VI

There is some grain among the chaff, but by and large the report is a disappointing document both on its descriptive and on its prescriptive sides. Reflection on its deficiencies makes one wonder whether Royal Commissions as we know them to-day are the best method, or even a good method, of tackling problems of this kind. For they are normally composed of representatives of different outlooks. No doubt outlooks are sometimes altered in the light of the evidence submitted, but on the whole this is probably a rare occurrence. Therefore if the fifteen or so members of a Royal Commission are to produce an agreed report, one of two things must happen, or both. Either (*a*) the report must be in the nature of a compromise between the views of the members, or (*b*) it must be vague, general, ambiguous, or perhaps even express conflicting views in different corners. Neither solution is satisfactory. Perhaps we should consider replacing Royal Commissions of the modern type with much smaller investigatory groups of say three people who would be charged with the duty of hearing evidence from all the conflicting interests. The members of a small group can usually be made to think more closely and thoroughly than those of a larger group, and their report would not be liable to suffer from the defects noted above.

# THE MARKET FOR STRATEGIC IDEAS IN BRITAIN: THE SANDYS ERA

*By* LAURENCE W. MARTIN

IN many policy areas, the congeries of people who influence policy communicate through an informal network of contacts. Laurence Martin's metaphor of a 'market' is apt, for it calls attention to the ease of communication between individuals concentrating their political activities in London. The market described here differs from the forum of classical models of democracy, for it is far more specialised in the character of activities and far more exclusive in the numbers of its participants.

EVEN after the tentative movement toward a policy of nuclear deterrence in White Papers since 1953, the *Outline of Future Policy*[1] issued in April 1957 by Duncan Sandys, Minister of Defence in Harold Macmillan's new Cabinet, created the impression of being a new departure. In this respect it was accorded a general welcome, for the Suez affair had induced wide agreement among military commentators at least upon the need for a close scrutiny of existing programmes.

The contents of Sandys' paper have become well known. Doctrinally it was characterised chiefly by frank recognition that active and passive protection of Britain against nuclear attack was impossible and that defence must therefore be by deterrence, with active defence limited to safeguarding retaliatory forces. The process by which the decision was taken displays an interesting interaction of personal, political and organisational influences.

Although the White Paper was discussed in a series of highly acrimonious meetings between the Minister and the Chiefs of Staff, it was very much the personal achievement of the Minister, who, on good account, paid scant regard to protests and on occasion refused even to consider dissenting papers. Such advice as the Minister did employ in his remarkable *tour de force*, which entailed some dozen

[1] Cmnd. 124, accompanied by *Defence Statistics*, Cmnd. 130.

Selected and abridged from the *American Political Science Review*, LVI i (1962) 23–41.

drafts, came largely from senior civil officials of his Ministry, particularly the Chief Scientist, and—allegedly—from one Colonel Post, a personal confidant. Inspiration for the line taken came also from the Prime Minister, who had himself served a brief and unprofitable period as Minister of Defence and who had endowed his deputy with the more generously defined authority he would himself have liked. In an announcement to the House of Commons on 24 January 1957, the Prime Minister authorised the Minister of Defence to decide matters of general defence policy affecting the 'size, shape, organisation and disposal of the armed forces and their equipment and supply including defence research and development', and to interfere in matters of particular importance within each Service, all with a view to 'a substantial reduction in expenditure and manpower'. At the same time the Chairman of the C.S.C. was given the parallel office of Chief of Staff to the Minister.

Each of the Service chiefs was unhappy with Sandys' policy. None questioned the principle of a British deterrent, but each, including the Chief of Air Staff, in whose hands the deterrent was primarily placed, deplored the effect of economy on his own Service.

The disposition of the Army's case serves to illustrate the extent to which economic and political guidelines took precedence over military opinion in 1957. The new, all-regular, 'streamlined' Army was to be 165,000 strong.[2] Under Antony Head, who became Minister of Defence in October, 1956, and had previously been Secretary of State for War, various studies and ministerial urgings had reconciled the Army to a strength of 200,000, the ultimate figure embodied in Eden's plans. This acceptance was based on use of Gurkhas in Asia, reductions of garrisons, severe weakness east of Suez and, in general, upon a number of optimistic assumptions as to capabilities and commitments. It also rested on promises of the very best equipment, tactical nuclear weapons and provision for air mobility. Even so, when actuaries of the Central Statistical Office were called upon to estimate the highest possible voluntary recruitment for the Army, their answer of 165,000 left a gap which, if small enough to make all-regular forces enticing, was large enough to be of critical military consequence. As a result, after Suez made economy urgent, a sharp dispute developed between Head and the Chancellor of the Exchequer, Harold Macmillan. Neither a Cabinet meeting nor a conference between the two Ministers could resolve the difference, and, before further debate was possible, Macmillan became Prime Minister.

[2] The exact figures for individual services were not in Cmnd. 127. See George Wigg's analysis of the arithmetic, *Hansard* (29 Feb 1960) col. 909.

Head's refusal to retain office under Macmillan thus represented his unwillingness to be the Prime Minister's agent in reducing the Army against military advice. The new force level, based on the estimate of recruitment, was naturally declared to be militarily adequate by the Government. Of course the C.S.C. strongly disagreed but no appeals were successful in the face of the determination of the Prime Minister and Minister of Defence. The C.S.C. had also been persuaded, unwisely as some thought, to prepare a plan for the deployment of a hypothetical army of 165,000 and presentation of this as a workable professional proposal, it has been said, enabled the Minister to conceal the full extent of service anxiety even from some members of the Cabinet.[3]

It seems reasonable to say that this represented a distinct departure from precedent in method as well as doctrine. There was a marked change in the tone of policy-making and in the character of political direction. Fears voiced in the press that the economy would come across-the-board, in the old percentage style, proved wrong. On the contrary, the Minister came down heavily for a particular doctrine and imposed a number of very far reaching consequent changes upon the military posture of the nation. The question remained, however, as to whether this decisiveness had been wisely exercised. It is not surprising that these formative months proved to be but the beginning of a prolonged public and private debate.

The dispute between the Services and Mr Sandys as to both the content of his policy and his method of making decisions continued during the months when the bare bones of his outline were being fleshed in detail. In this running dispute the two elements of content and method were inextricably entwined. Anxiety about Sandys' plans for reshaping the formal machinery of making defense policy was given point by dislike for the use he could be expected to make of it. Protests against the detailed applications of his policy and the manner in which these were made, implicitly criticised the way the machinery was working.[4]

The nature of British defence machinery being what it is particulars of the heated, high-level controversy which continued after publication of Sandys' White Paper are hard to acquire. This

[3] This must rest in part on private information, but Head's later speech of 28 July 1958 (*Hansard*, col. 988 ff.) goes a long way.

[4] The difficulties raised by economies already envisaged in the White Paper were sharpened for some months by the anxiety of the Chancellor of the Exchequer to secure still further reduction of expenditure. This ultimately terminated in the resignation of the Chancellor, Peter Thorneycroft, in Jan 1958.

observation, indeed, touches directly on a main service grievance. For the C.S.C. were now made painfully aware that the traditional reticence which preserved them from close public scrutiny of their achievements could cut two ways. They now felt that the pattern of closed debate and service reticence was being exploited to impose unsound policies while concealing from the public and Parliament and even from the full view of the Cabinet, risks which were being taken and the extent to which professional military opinion was united in misgiving if in little else. The Minister, they felt, was refusing his military advisers the justice of a fair hearing and was reaching firm agreement with the Prime Minister before going through the semblance of debate in the Defence Committee. It was also suggested that Sandys encouraged service rivalries so as to prevent formation of a solid front against him. Admittedly it would be difficult to distinguish precisely between making use of divisions amongst advisers to railroad home a plan condemned by all, and being compelled to devise and insist upon a scheme because the advisers could not themselves hit upon an agreed policy. Yet many apparently felt they could distinguish the difference, which in itself indicated a grave absence of mutual trust in military affairs. Perhaps the *Economist* best expressed what was felt to be at stake when it declared that there must be authority, and that the authority must be the Minister's, but that authority should be used to extract agreement from the military leaders, not merely to squash them and ride roughshod over their views.[5] The danger of authoritarianism was also well put during a later parliamentary debate by Sandys' immediate predecessor: 'My right honourable Friend has great qualities of strength of character and determination. He is known for it inside and outside the House. They are fine qualities in a Minister provided he is right. If, however, he introduces a policy which may lead the country into danger, such qualities can be calamitous.'[6] Thus while there was no question of the Government's right to lay down the law, considerable uneasiness arose from the feeling that this was being done without a full and free flow of ideas within the official machine. A further question also existed as to whether a wider public had no right to learn the broad lines upon which professional debate was proceeding on a matter of such moment.

As to formal organisation of defence policy, the amplified powers of the Minister of Defence, defined by Macmillan in January 1957, were confirmed in a major restatement of *Central Organisation for Defence* in a White Paper of July, 1958.[7] This paper apparently represented a compromise between the Minister's inclination to carry

[5] 7 Dec 1957. [6] 28 July 1958 (*Hansard*, col. 994). [7] Cmnd. 476.

the centralisation of authority further and the desire of the services and the service ministers to maintain their autonomy. The arrangement was worked out in a hotly contested debate of many months, some rumours of which reached the press.[8] Once more the overall authority of the Minister was asserted, though with the omission of his right to interfere with matters internal to the services which he considered important.[9] He secured a right of review over senior appointments and the power to transfer functions to his own Ministry. Moreover the Minister was made the fount of operational orders, for which purpose he was given a Chief of Defence Staff (C.D.S.) to replace the jointly held offices of Chairman of the C.S.C. and the Chief of Staff to the Minister. This perpetuated the *ad hoc* arrangement whereby the Suez operation had been directly controlled by Eden by way of the Chairman of the C.S.C. Appointment of the C.D.S. was also intended to provide a head for the C.S.C. equipped to give independent advice to the Minister. For this purpose the new Chief was authorised to call on the Joint Staff for assistance.[10] The collective responsibility of the C.S.C. to the Government for professional advice and the individual right of each Chief to have access to the Minister and Prime Minister were, however, reaffirmed.

The second major change made in the White Paper was the announcement that the membership of the Defence Committee would be regarded as a floating one, with attendance at particular meetings being decided *ad hoc* by the Prime Minister.[11] At the same time a lower level Defence Board was created to contain, under the Minister of Defence, both the service ministers and the C.S.C. together with the Permanent Secretary and Chief Scientists of the Ministry. This Board was to deal with all purely military affairs while the Defence Committee would normally confine itself to problems related to financial, foreign, colonial and commonwealth affairs.[12] According to well informed sources, Sandys' original plan had been to confine the service ministers to the Board, excluding them from the cabinet committee. This the Cabinet overruled, leaving their attendance subject to discretion, and it was made clear that minutes of the Defence Committee would always be circulated

[8] Cf. *Daily Telegraph*, 28 Feb, 25 Apr, 10 July 1958; *The Times*, 26 June 1958; *Observer*, 29 June, 6 July 1958.

[9] In Apr 1957, Sandys had announced a Defence Administration Committee to consider service unification but little more was heard of it.

[10] For explanation of all this see Sandys' contribution to the debate on the White Paper, 28 July 1958 (*Hansard*, cols 954 ff.).

[11] The Chiefs of Staff would apparently attend as of right. See Para. 4 of Cmnd. 476.

[12] In this respect it partly replaced an informal Service Ministers Committee in which the Minister of Defence had periodically met the service heads.

to all the nominal members.[13] The service ministers also retained their right to 'make submissions to the Cabinet'. The actual effect of this reorganisation on the relationship between the Minister of Defence and the services thus remained to be seen. In general the increase in power received by the Minister in 1957 seemed to be confirmed, and the service ministers further reduced in status. The exact effect of the changes in staff organisation was also uncertain. Would the C.D.S. be the ally or the rival of the Minister? Some believed the whole reform to be an unsatisfactory hybrid, as a result of the deadlock between the ambitions of the Minister and the services, and that such features as increasing the responsibility of the C.S.C. to the Minister while at the same time affirming the right of the services to appeal over his head, might confuse rather than clarify matters.

### *The Service Appeal Against Sandys*

While the services thus continued to put their case through formal channels they did not confine themselves to these when they felt the results to be unsatisfactory. In Britain, the ultimate objective of an attempt to revise a matter of broad policy must be to change the mind of the cabinet. This has increasingly come to mean the mind of the Prime Minister and his closest advisers, who may be senior civil servants as well as ministers. For this the obvious recourse of the services is to the formal processes of the governmental machinery. But they are not without further resources if these processes fail to serve their ends. There are devious methods to change the government's mind: by efforts to bypass unreceptive superiors to ensure that they have not left ministerial colleagues in ignorance of the service case, for example, or by representations to influential unofficial circles within the ruling party. Failing success in this way there is the possible expedient of attempting to change the climate of opinion within which the inevitable adjustments of policy will be made, by appeals to the attentive public.

For all the legendary service abhorrence of such unorthodox methods in Britain there are numerous well known historical instances of such campaigns.[14] And, in fact during the Sandys' era when the services felt they were not receiving a fair hearing, there

[13] i.e. Prime Minister, Home Secretary, Foreign Secretary, Chancellor, Commonwealth Secretary, Minister of Defence, Minister of Labour, the Service Ministers, and the Minister of Supply.

[14] It is perhaps worth recalling that as a Territorial Army officer before the war Duncan Sandys caused a furore by denouncing deficiencies in anti-aircraft preparations.

was a marked increase in behaviour so frequently thought of as peculiar to Americans.

There is a wide impression among British politicians particularly concerned with defence that during the Sandys' era there was an appreciable increase in the number of 'leaks' of information both as to planned developments and as to interservice disputes.[15] Not all of this came from the military; indeed some suggest that civil servants were an especially prolific source.[16] Nor can all leaks be regarded as intended to obstruct the Minister's policy. Some are doubtless accidental, some made for personal reasons, and others may be intentional trial balloons and manoeuvres by the Government. Nor, of course, were leaks intended to influence interservice disputes unprecedented. Nevertheless, with all these reservations, there appears to have been a marked increase in the willingness of serving officers to talk in confidence with the press, with backbenchers and even with individual leaders of the Opposition.[17]

It is not necessary, however, to confine oneself to this elusive phenomenon, for there was also a remarkable number of more overt and dramatic 'demonstrations' in the years following 1957. Each of the services was associated with one or other of these. The most noted and sensational were Conference and Exercise Prospect, mounted by the R.A.F. in the spring of 1958 and organised by the Director of Plans. This was a three-day briefing session for a selected group of R.A.F. officers and Air Ministry civil servants, later followed by a one-day performance held in the Royal Empire Society Hall on 6 May 1958 for selected correspondents and others.[18] At these affairs the emphasis upon deterrence, wielded by the R.A.F., was upheld as the only practicable policy. The press directed its

[15] For one public reference to this see George Brown's — Labour's chief spokesman on defence — observation, 'We . . . have had almost every member of the Services' team . . . making quite sure that their particular angle on what was happening was well known and well publicised.' (*Hansard* (28 July 1958) col. 971.)

[16] A one time minister has suggested to me that leaks are particularly prevalent in areas where private contractors have an interest in boosting or detracting from a particular weapon, e.g. in the missile and aircraft field, as compared to programmes handled by national arsenals, etc.

[17] Again note George Brown's allegation: 'The Service Chiefs spoke in public, against all traditions, taking that risk in order to get round the Ministers whom they could not persuade in private. There was virtually nobody in the Service Departments at that time who was not taking the trouble to tell anybody about it who would listen. I have minuted notes of receptions and of conversations in which leading Service men made only the reservation, "Do not quote me" . . . other Service advisers had articles written in leading journals with only the thinnest of pseudonyms hiding the authority behind them. . . .' (*Hansard* (27 Apr 1960) col. 221.)

[18] See *Air Power* (Summer 1958) pp. 283 ff.

attention, however, chiefly to the degree to which the R.A.F. of the future was depicted in a fashion which differed in several prominent respects from that implied in the White Papers, especially in the matter of manned aircraft. A second generation of strategic bombers, of tactical bombers and of fighters were all held essential. A call was also issued for an airborne missile,[19] reflecting reluctance to depend entirely on fixed bases. 'Prospect' aroused a public sensation, though the results were apparently mixed. The discussions then going on as to procurement of a new medium-range nuclear strike aircraft, the TSR2,[20] and a fighter, the Lightning, were shortly settled in favour of the R.A.F. But the press sharply criticised such demonstrations and it is said that the incident strengthened the Minister of Defence in the strenuous Cabinet discussions then proceeding on his plans for reorganisation.[21]

Naval efforts were more discreet, as by repute they have always been. Throughout these years senior naval officers continued to maintain particularly close liaison with certain newspapers, such as the *Observer*. Early efforts to enhance the Navy's role under the Sandys regime were directed towards anti-submarine warfare.[22] To the extent naval opinion contemplated a part in deterrence, it was in terms of the carrier, for which were being developed ship-to-air missiles and a low-level strike aircraft, which was regarded as a rival to the R.A.F.'s TSR2. The carrier was under heavy criticism on grounds of vulnerability, but the Navy was slow to develop an alternative interest in the Polaris. A number of considerations reportedly still underlay this caution; doubt as to the availability of nuclear propulsion, a 'cavalry' traditionalism in which submarines were not a suitable backbone for a fleet; and, perhaps most of all, fear of being compelled to undertake development within existing limits of the naval budget. Nevertheless, during 1958, especially after amendment of the MacMahon Act, interest in a naval deterrent grew and senior naval officers provided information for certain newspaper articles extolling the merits of seaborne deterrence and casting doubt upon the efficacy of the R.A.F.'s striking force.[23]

[19] As far as I can discover, this was not, as is now sometimes said, an anticipation of the Skybolt airborne ballistic missile later made the mainstay of British policy, but a cruise missile for low-level radar penetration.

[20] For the history of this aircraft, see the *Observer*, 4 Jan 1959.

[21] The *Economist* once more provided the most incisive comment, 'Whose Hand on the Tiller?', 10 May 1958.

[22] See Admiral Sir John Eccles' outburst, 'repudiating' the White Paper and reverting to the concept of 'broken-backed' war. (*Economist*, 5 Oct 1957.)

[23] A telling broadside under the *nom de plume* of Nucleus, in the *Observer*, was said, by those in a position to know, to be the direct contribution of a just retired, very senior naval staff officer; see *Observer*, 7 and 28 Dec 1958.

The most dramatic instance of the Army speaking up was the lecture that Lieutenant General Sir John Cowley delivered to the Royal United Service Institution on 4 November 1959. In this highly publicised pronouncement the General, while admitting the danger of service parochialism, criticised reliance on deterrence on both moral and practical grounds, and outspokenly deplored neglect of the conventional forces, drawing a critical comparison between the proportion of expenditure devoted to the deterrent and that to the Army. Cowley wrote a little verse on this theme:

> I also have a plan to spend a thousand million pounds
> To buy some guided missiles and to hide them in the ground,
> And then to clearly paint on each 'these things must not be used',
> No wonder that our citizens are getting confused.

This was one man, but a man who spoke as Controller of Munitions in the Ministry of Supply, who drew attention to the fact that he was on active service, and whose remarks had been cleared by the Secretary of State for War. Press comment and correspondence in the *Journal* of the R.U.S.I. were noticeably more favourable than in the Prospect case; perhaps a reflection of the headway made by Sandys' critics. The Prime Minister himself was reportedly much annoyed by this incident and it was announced that henceforth such utterances would require clearance not merely by the services but also by the Minister of Defence.[24]

Public complaints of this kind might be expected to attract more attention in a period of doctrinal change but such a number of incidents in so short a period tends to confirm the belief that unaccustomed contraints on the interplay of views within the official machine encouraged dissent to seek other channels. Certainly the demonstrations were successful in communicating professional misgivings to a wider circle of attentive opinion, and thereby placed the Government under the necessity of justifying its policy before a critical audience.

### *The Wider Market for Strategic Ideas*

Service leaders were, of course, only one of many sources of attempts to manipulate the wider market and through it, the Government. This market ranges in a complex fashion from the narrower influential circles, a twilight zone between direct influence and the creation of generally favourable opinion, to the broadest forms of public

[24] A text of the Cowley lecture is in the *RUSI Journal*, Feb 1960. An exchange in the House of Commons, in which the new rules on clearance were stated, is in *Hansard* (11 Nov 1959) cols 378 ff.

advocacy. In Parliament the various kinds of influence are inextricably entwined, and the service leaders are the targets as well as sources of attempts at influence.

The nature of the market for strategic ideas in Britain and its relation to official processes is ill understood, but the higher temperature of military affairs under Sandys made it somewhat easier than usual to discern the cruder patterns.[25] By their very character the points at issue were conducive to public debate. The basic question of nuclear deterrence, and the shortage of manpower, had a deceptive simplicity which encouraged lay discussion; and the simplicity of doctrine which permitted Sandys to seize the reins also gave scope to his critics. Quite apart from service grievances, the White Papers of 1957 and 1958 and particularly the latter's willingness to contemplate the initial use of strategic nuclear weapons, aroused considerable public misgiving.

Service demonstrations of dissent reinforced unofficial anxiety by providing evidence of specific grievances and, perhaps even more, simply by revealing the existence of general professional unrest, of which these partial glimpses may even have given an exaggerated notion. *The Times* commented eloquently on the dangers of this at the time of General Cowley's outburst. Admitting the undesirability of every senior officer repeatedly holding forth in public, *The Times* continued:

> It would be equally dangerous on the other hand, if none of them was ever allowed to express an honest criticism publicly. But we have come perilously close to this in recent years. There has been no way for the public to know whether or not crucial defence decisions were being taken against the advice of the Government's professional military advisers. Strategy has had to be accepted in a vacuum. Public opinion has been denied its proper part because there has been no access to the views of the senior officers of the three services.[26]

Press comment on defence matters in general was frequent and lively, though spasmodic during these years. The so-called quality press paid particular attention to defence. Certain individuals, the defence correspondent of *The Times*, Alastair Buchan[27] of the *Observer* and the defence writers of the *Guardian* and *Economist*, became especially prominent in maintaining a drumfire of sceptical comments on official doctrine and in drawing attention to

[25] It should be observed that the unusual intensity of feeling may have distorted as well as intensified the normal pattern.

[26] *The Times*, 12 Nov 1959. On the effect of secrecy on trust in the Government, see the exchange between Sandys and Brown (*Hansard* (11 Feb 1957) cols 1155 ff.).

[27] Since 1958 Director of the Institute for Strategic Studies.

military unrest. Certain of the more popular papers were perhaps the most fertile in publication of the various leaks. Press comment was not, of course, uniformly opposed to the Government. The *Daily Telegraph* and *Sunday Times* fairly staunchly defended official policy, *The Times* chiefly criticised overemphasis on deterrence, while the *Observer* and *Guardian* went much further and appeared ready to abandon the deterrent should that be the only way to refurbish conventional forces. By late 1958 the press comment was overwhelmingly critical in one way or another. The prestige papers, above all *The Times*, were also the vehicles for correspondence on military affairs, which a number of well qualified students of British affairs believe to have perhaps even greater influence in sowing doubt in official minds than editorial comment.[28]

The press embodies a considerable number of that small group of professional and semi-professional students of defence who are perhaps best described as commentators. There has in point of fact been a small discussion group called the Commentator's Circle, with Liddell Hart as head, which is credited with no little influence in developing informed opinion and colouring the tone of the mass media. The notion of commentator embraces the leading defence correspondents, such eminent military historians as Liddell Hart, and articulate retired officers such as Sir John Slessor and Sir Anthony Buzzard, together with such politicians as Richard Crossman, George Wigg and John Strachey who write and engage in journalistic debate. These would also rank high among the contributors to such specialised journals as that of *RUSI*, *International Affairs* and *Air Power*, or to general periodicals like *Encounter*, in which an extended series on the theme of 'Their Bomb and Ours' attracted much attention in 1958.

In some respects a broader extension of the concept of a commentator's circle is the Institute for Strategic Studies set up in 1958, and intended both to further study of military affairs and to bring together people concerned with military affairs from varying points of view. The Council of the I.S.S. contains several of the most influential commentators. The I.S.S. has apparently won greater countenance from those officially engaged in military and foreign affairs than is common for private bodies in England; it includes a number of senior officials among its members and enjoys the favour of the present Chief of the Defence Staff. From time to time the I.S.S. is used for briefing sessions in which official infor-

[28] Captain Liddell Hart, for example, firmly maintains that a well-written critical letter to *The Times* does more to influence leading civil servants than a wealth of books or articles.

mation is confidentially conveyed. This is thought to serve the dual purpose of broadening support for policies which are based on information not suitable for general dissemination — the 'scrambling' performance of the V-bomber force being an example. In return the audience receives more substance for its unofficial assessments and may presumably hope that its own views may not be without influence on the officials.

This kind of activity is a particularly clear illustration of the way in which the roles of publicist and confidential adviser may blend. Even the press may have its direct influence on the important officials as well as its general effect on the tone of public opinion. Thus there may be combined in a single person or organisation types of influence ranging all the way from the undoubted achievement of the Campaign for Nuclear Disarmament in raising the level of public attention to military questions by the most overt possible activities to the contribution that confidential representations by the Society of British Aircraft Constructors are said to make to resisting the elimination of aircraft.[29] Parliament itself, the single most important sounding board for opinion on military affairs, is at the same time the scene of much confidential interchange.

Because the formal legislative and financial powers of Parliament are under the effective control of the government these days, Parliament's influence on defence policy depends chiefly on the quality of the arguments it can generate and the attention it can secure for them. The difference between Parliament and Congress in this respect is perhaps not as large as one might think, for we have recently become aware of how rarely Congress directly enforces a change in American military policy. It is rather in Parliament's lack of Congressional resources for securing information that its chief disadvantage lies. George Brown, then defence spokesman for the

[29] The effect of the arms industry is still an obscure issue much beclouded by old emotions. Equally hard to evaluate is the coincidence between strategic views advocated by certain leading, articulate, retired officers, and the kinds of equipment manufactured by firms of which they are directors. The fact that many of the retired officers most respected as commentators are connected with armaments firms is sometimes said to be due to their advantage in keeping up with technical developments, but it seems at least equally probable that it is their articulateness or reputation as publicists which secures them the favour of manufacturers. Most of these pundits, one notices are drawn from the R.A.F. or the Navy, the 'weapons services'. For a reference to this at the highest level see Sir Frederick Brundrett's speech to the R.U.S.I., 16 Mar 1961. Sir Frederick was Chief Scientist to the Ministry of Defence until Dec 1959 and closely associated with the Blue Streak. Quite apart from vested interests there are of course powerful arguments for the preservation of an aircraft industry on grounds of employment and the export trade.

Labour Party, has gone so far as to declare that 'in this area, we are given so little information in the House, less I rather think, than anywhere in any democratic country in the world....'[30] This difficulty has repeatedly drawn comment and has led to proposals for a specialised committee on the American pattern, or at least for examination of the service Estimates before a select committee.[31] Such a device would not only provide information but also enable Members to make use of what they know without fear of damaging the national security.

The expedient of secret briefings for leaders of the opposition, tried under the Labour Government, was soon abandoned by Churchill on the ground that it unduly hampered criticism, and an offer of similar consultations made during the reorganisations of 1958 was immediately rejected by Gaitskell for the same reason. The prejudice on all sides against private communication of official information seems reinforced by distaste for characteristics of the American system associated with Congressional independence, as well as by the desire of all parties to enjoy the fruits of executive privacy in power.[32] Such information as is received other than openly from government pronouncements therefore comes from the public media and from the leaks and private channels mentioned earlier. Occasionally Ministers informally give a courtesy briefing to their opposite numbers in the shadow cabinet, but this, by all accounts, is usually advance notice of an imminent public announcement and never in the nature of prior consultation. The White Papers on defence, particularly the routine annual issues, are frequently envied in the United States but though they do offer the advantage of a single focus for debate, informed British observers believe they are as much a vehicle for deception as for enlightenment, and at best a partisan brief. Scepticism has gone to the length of a proposal for issuing White Papers only quinquennially or at important departures, for some critics feel that the need to produce an annual report encourages over-dramatisation and a search for illusory achievements.[33]

[30] *Hansard* (13 Dec 1960) col. 226.

[31] See F. J. Bellenger's suggestion (*Hansard* (26 Feb 1958) col. 427), that of W. Wyatt on 27 Apr 1960 (*Hansard*, col. 288) and Gaitskell's complaint (*Hansard* (1 Mar 1960) col. 1140). Wyatt was concerned that 'We are handicapped at present in this country because we have not adequate machinery for going into these highly important but complex and technical matters in any satisfactory way'.

[32] In contrast to which the C.I.D. had a certain amount of bipartisan representation in early days.

[33] The Paper of 1959 was dubbed by *The Economist* 'Blank White Paper'; cf. *Daily Telegraph*, 7 Feb 1958, and *Hansard* (26 Feb 1958) cols 561–4; (29 Feb 1960) col. 903.

The unofficial contacts of politicians outside the government with officers and civil servants are reportedly more numerous and intimate with Conservatives than Labour, and, consequently, a Conservative opposition may be better informed than a Labour one. The chief alternative sources of the opposition are the press, certain recently retired officials, authors, private commentators and a small number of Members especially interested in and informed about Defence. George Wigg, a veritable mine of information, is a pre-eminent Labour example of the last. A considerable number of references in debate to expert writings are to American commentators, reflecting the paucity of English equivalents,[34] while the flow of information about United States policy provides facts about matters of allied concern and technological information which can be applied to British circumstances.

Lack of information is undoubtedly a handicap to the opposition, though it probably does not undermine their arguments to the extent that governments not unnaturally suggest. Some would say that a more serious limitation on the effectiveness of Parliament as a forum is the surprisingly small number of Members who show much really sustained interest in military affairs.[35] Despite the common idea that the House of Lords is a superior senate of experience, very few indeed of the myriad ex-service peers use their right to debate, to an extent which has drawn direct reproachful comment in the Lords itself.[36] Moreover, parliamentary attention to defence is heavily concentrated in the first half of the year under influence of the schedule for the White Paper and budget, and many feel that Government frequently escapes sustained attack as a result of this, of adjournments, and of the pressure of other issues on parliamentary time. It is revealing to note that when forming his governments, Sir Anthony Eden regarded the parliamentary duties of the Minister of Defence as exceptionally light.[37]

In the workings of the present Labour Opposition the formal committees of the Parliamentary Party, though much used to register differences, are apparently not the forums for a great deal of debate, still less for the formulation of the leader's policy or sifting of information. There is a committee of members of the Shadow

[34] The debate in the Lords on 5 Mar 1958 is full of examples of this (*Hansard*, cols 1095 ff.).

[35] The Bow Group, a collection of young Conservative thinkers, is said to have found it difficult to recruit a working party to prepare a study on defence to match their publications on other topics.

[36] *Hansard* (5 Mar 1958) col. 1248.

[37] *Full Circle*, p. 354. The intensification of interest in defence matters in the last few years, however, might lead him to modify that assessment.

Cabinet holding the ghostly defence and foreign affairs portfolios, and at Transport House a defence adviser, serves the whole Party. But far and away the most influential body would seem to be a confidential committee gathered by the shadow defence minister, comprising two or three congenial Members of Parliament, with a small entourage of commentators and informants, supplemented from time to time by special working parties. This device is useful not only to inform and advise the leaders but also to avoid the pressures of internal party differences.

This recalls that there are centres of dissentient opinion in Parliament other than the Opposition front bench. In the Labour Party the nuclear disarmers have been an obvious influence on the climate of debate. George Wigg and Richard Crossman have formed the nucleus of another line of criticism both of Government and official Opposition policy, standing out for greater emphasis on conventional forces and maintaining the impracticability of both the strategic and tactical nuclear elements of existing policies.[38] Critics of this kind are inclined to say that the official Labour leaders have tried to maintain a monolithic allegiance to front bench views akin to that sought by Sandys himself. Certainly Gaitskell made several efforts to suppress Wigg's criticism of official Opposition policy, especially as enunciated by John Strachey, and Crossman was ousted from the Shadow Cabinet, partly for his failure to support an Opposition amendment in the defence debate of 1960. The damage such dissidence may do to the effectiveness of an opposition is hard to assess, but there seems little doubt that the present Conservative Government has been greatly relieved of need to re-examine and justify its policy by the conflict of views among its critics, which prevents the emergence of an image of a clear-cut alternative policy.[39]

As it happened, the leaders of the Labour Party did not seem to want to advance a policy much different from the Conservatives. While they joined in criticism that the Government placed excessive faith in deterrence and opposed the prospect of initiating the use of nuclear weapons, the Labour front bench was unwilling to accept the onus of continued conscription or higher expenditure.

The degree of agreement which existed between the two front benches was paralleled by a similarly cross-bench alliance of critics who particularly deplored the neglect of conventional forces. This

[38] See especially their joint articles in the *New Statesman*, 14 May, 11 June 1960.

[39] Unfortunately for the Labour Party, of course, its constitution and its ideological bent tend to compel it to try to draw up a coherent policy despite frequent pleas that an opposition is only obliged to criticise.

alliance produced harmonious mutual support in debate between such otherwise dissimilar individuals as George Wigg and Antony Head, Sandys' predecessor. Indeed, disgruntled Conservative back-benchers have as good a claim as the Opposition to have resisted the Government in recent years. Supposedly, dissent within the governing party often does more to give British government pause than the attacks of the official opposition, for such criticism comes from relatively trusted sources and raises a threat to the effectiveness and enthusiasm of the party. When such dissent becomes public, it weakens the impression of confident official policy based on inside information that is so discouraging to the opposition. A number of Conservative back-benchers have enjoyed a special reputation for wisdom on defence matters during the Sandys era, among them Fitzroy Maclean, Viscount Lambton, Nigel Birch and Antony Head. These offered a natural focus for criticism among those, probably more numerous among Conservatives than Labour, who normally took an interest in military affairs and maintained an association with one or other of the services.[40] Head's disagreement with official policy was well known as a result of his resignation, but, in the Tory tradition, he behaved with great discretion and for some time limited himself to private remonstrances and to remarks in party committees. In 1958, however, something of an open Conservative revolt began against the trend of official policy and, in the debate on reorganisation, Head partially unfolded the story of his resignation. While the facts had long been suspected, this explicit and undeniably well informed account came with all the more telling effect against the normal fog of secrecy penetrated only by hearsay. By 1961 unrest had gone far enough for a Young Conservative convention deliberately to avoid giving a vote of confidence in Government policy.[41]

The tendency of British military planners and civil servants is to deny that public criticism has much effect on their recommendations. By the time events have stimulated such comment, it is said,

[40] Retired officers, particularly from the Army, are numerous in the Commons and were especially alarmed by reductions in manpower. On the subject of retired officers, mention should be made of such service-related interest groups as the Navy and Army Leagues. With the exception of such special efforts as the Army League's occasional study reports — and the unique but elusive influence of the service clubs — these organisations would not seem to be sufficiently up to date in their thinking to contribute much to the supply of ideas, though they may have some restraining influence on the desire to eliminate established formations. See Armstrong, op. cit. pp. 101–2.

[41] *Sunday Times*, 26 Feb 1961; and see Viscount Lambton's privately printed pamphlet, *Inadequacy*, 1961.

the same stimulus has set on foot official studies which are more prompt and better informed. But even the proudest claimants for professional imperviousness agree that public sources and debate influence their political chiefs. Certainly it seems beyond question that press and Parliamentary criticism reinforced the case for reassessment at this time. The course of debate in Parliament supports this judgment by the frequency of references to well known commentators and the energy devoted to arguing as to whose side of the question particular pundits supported. One can often trace a notion from a commentator in one year, to the lips of a Parliamentary critic in the next, and to the White Paper or ministerial speech in the third. One of the clearest, though perhaps unintentional, tributes to the role of public debate was paid by Watkinson when, in defending the time taken to decide on abandonment of Blue Streak, he explained that, 'Of course the decision was a narrowly balanced one. All big decisions are. Among the surrounding experts, the advisers, the newspaper correspondents, and so on, there are conflicting views.'[42]

[42] *Hansard* (27 Apr 1960) col. 237.

# THE PLOWDEN REPORT: A TRANSLATION

*By* W. J. M. MACKENZIE

INFORMATION is at a premium in policy-making, for people who do not know what is happening can hardly exert intentional influence upon government. The conventions of British government involve contrary assumptions. On the one hand, the government of the day is expected to explain and justify its actions publicly in Parliament and in official statements. On the other, the norms of policy-makers — both ministers and civil servants — place a high value upon maintaining a dignified silence about much that is done in Westminster. In order to satisfy these conflicting expectations, many policy-makers have devised a form of communication in 'code', that is, statements have specific meaning only to those who possess sufficient inside knowledge to penetrate beyond the superficial and cryptic character of public and published discussions. As a former classical philologist and wartime civil servant, W. J. M. Mackenzie is doubly qualified to attempt the difficult feat of decoding the language of the Plowden Report, a major Treasury study of the control of public expenditure.

Translator's note. *The report reached me when I was busy with other things, and a reading of the summaries, a quick perusal, conveyed nothing to me at all. My interest was reawakened by a note in Mr Anthony Sampson's book* The Anatomy of Britain *at page 284 that this was a 'revolutionary and critical document' written in an unknown tongue. I used to be a philologist, sometimes I wish I still was; here is a shot at a translation. Much is of necessity conjectural, but this version has a certain internal coherence which gives it plausibility, like the stuff about clerical officers doing imprest accounts which the late Michael Ventris got out of Minoan Linear B. So I hope some editor will take a chance with it.*

*W.J.M.M.*

Reprinted from *The Guardian*, 25 May 1963. The Plowden Report's text, approximately five times the length of the translation, was published as *Control of Public Expenditure*, Cmnd. 1432, (London: H.M.S.O., 1961). For a more customary discussion of the Report, see e.g. D. N. Chester, 'The Plowden Report: Nature and Significance', *Public Administration*, XLI i (Spring 1963) 3–15.

1. For various political reasons we were asked to attempt the impossible; to accept criticisms without accepting them, to have a public inquiry which is not public.

2. At first I was expected to carry the can alone. Then I got them to add three pretty safe people:

Sir Sam Brown, war-time Under-Secretary at MAP, now a City solicitor of distinction (born 1903).

Sir Jeremy Raisman, a most distinguished member of the I.C.S. now Vice-chairman of Lloyds Bank (born 1892).

Mr J. E. Wall, a war-time temporary, who stuck in the Civil Service till 1952, and is now a director of E.M.I. (born 1913).

3. Naturally, there was a great wrangle about what should be published, and this was ended by a nonsensical compromise embodied in this document. The Civil Service members of the inquiry (who are officially nameless, but you can easily find who they were) do not agree to this paper, but they do not disagree in any respect whatever.

Plowden
Chairman

## Report

1. We proceeded on two principles: no dirty linen in public; outside critics are bores.

2. We did however chat to a great many civil servants, and two years of that is more than enough.

3. Unluckily, it turns out that the real problem is about the nature of government in general, and of British government in particular. This is what we are discussing, but of course we have to wrap it up in Mandarin prose.

4. Our general impression is that the Civil Service is extremely old-fashioned and riven by jealousies: but there is public spirit there, and some of them do try quite hard.

5. This report is just 'key-note' stuff: detailed proposals have been handed in separately.

## Part I. The Need for a Revolution

6. Public expenditure is not a separate problem. It involves all government action and all participants in government.

7. To be rational in government involves ranking objectives in order of priority, quantifying their rank order, and giving effect to it in action till such time as it is specifically changed.

There has been much debate as to whether this is possible in theory.

*The Traditional System*

8. As a matter of practice, it has not even been attempted in Britain hitherto, except to a limited extent in regard to public investment.

9. The only rational principle followed has been to resist all pressure equally, until it proved too strong or skilful.

10. This was well enough while public expenditure was relatively small but to follow that principle now is to abandon the whole economy to pressure politics.

11. There is no going back now.

*Principles of Reconstruction*

12.

A. Forward look.
B. Settled decisions.
C. Measurement.
D. Reform of Cabinet and Commons.

*A. Forward Look*

13. This is being tried, but no one really knows how to do it. Some of our members feel it would do more harm than good to make a 'thing' of it at this stage.

14. It is at least notionally possible to run the exercise for all direct expenditure by public authorities, and they ought to be made to try it.

15. But the result could easily be misleading. Some central government expenditure is not subject to control from year to year; e.g. doles to unemployed and to farmers. In any case, the line between 'public' and non-public expenditure now has little economic meaning.

16. Similarly, on the revenue side of the account, this really amounts to making guesses about the national income.

17. However, it would be feeble not to try; and (as we explain later, paras. 26, 58, 75, 106) the result might be very valuable in educating public opinion. Unfortunately we can't believe that politicians would have the nerve to publish it, nor could we, in our capacity as political secretaries, advise them to take the risk.

*B. Settled decisions*

18. One can easily trace the psychological damage and actual waste of resources caused by chopping and changing in the 1950s.

19. There is not much excuse for this where investment is a matter

of straight building programmes and the need is uncontroversial. For instance, educational building and motorways have been tidied up fairly well: but there is a lot to do yet in other fields. By studied omission we note particularly the field of housing and urban renewal.

20. In some fields the results are fairly obvious, and new procedure would not make much difference. In others, like defence, the whole situation is crazy, and there is really nothing we can do about it. But let us at least have a general pro forma for expenditure over five years, the first year clear, the four later years shading off into impenetrable fog. This will make us all feel better about it.

21. But of course it may have no practical meaning for a Government caught between pressures at home which want scaling up, pressures abroad which want scaling down.

22. Let us, however, put it on record that the Keynesian idea of using public expenditure to keep the economy in balance has been completely abandoned. It makes no sense at all for current expenditure; (23) at most, there are a few small things that could be done in relation to capital programmes, if we were ready for it in time, as we never are.

24. As we said above, the worst result of the present situation is psychological. Departments think that the 'forward look' is phoney, therefore they take little trouble about forward planning. Unfortunately they are right, but this is partly because of their own actions.

*C. Measurement*

25. Nobody knows how different bits of public expenditure affect the economy.

26. The public accounts are unintelligible.

27. *Estimates.* One thing we *have* done is to get through a revision of the form of the Estimates, which will be reflected in the form of the Accounts.

28. The next step is to train politicians, civil servants, the City, the press, to 'read' these cash accounts alongside the economic accounts about national income and expenditure.

29. *Accounts.* This is just as bad a mess, but less urgent as no one uses the accounts anyhow. Progress is likely to be very slow.

30. *Statisticians and Accountants* (see also para. 53). The whole thing is very amateurish in method: but it is hard to see where we can find properly trained professionals in the face of present competition.

*D. The Cabinet*

31. The thing is, of course, now regarded as a game, Treasury versus the Rest, at Cabinet level as well as in Whitehall.

32. We have some thoughts about this, but are not very well agreed among ourselves, and are afraid of getting dragged into public controversy. So much depends on political power, since this is a question of increasing the power of central control in government, decreasing the weight of departmental interests. You can do this up to a point by increasing the weight of the Treasury in the Cabinet (as the Prime Minister has now done): but (as some of us have pointed out) this is as likely to increase the hostility of Departments and their pressure groups as to make for closer integration.

## Part II. The Treasury as Holding Company

33. There is much friction between Departments and the Treasury: this is to some extent routine fuss over trivialities, but it reflects an obsolete frame of mind.

34. It should be made perfectly clear in future that this is not to be regarded as a game between equal players.

35. The Departments are in effect operating companies, and the job of their managers is to manage; not to try to act as directors of the holding company.

36. The functions of policy-making are now concentrated in the Treasury, and it has been given ample power to keep lower management in its place. It is in the hands of the Treasury alone to measure the efficiency of management, and to apply rewards and sanctions by posting and promotion.

37. *Supply.* The old 'Estimates Cycle' is obsolete as a procedure for making policy.

38. Our alternative is:

(*a*) Treat Estimates procedure as Executive Class routine.

(*b*) Have occasional 'big dos' over the 'forward look'.

(*c*) Let the Treasury participate fully in each big departmental decision when it is being taken. This will slow things up, but how else can you get away from the present situation, in which the Treasury never really understands departmental policy at all, and Departments are ranked according to their strength and skill in 'bouncing' the Treasury?

39. This does not mean that we think the Treasury should keep out of small departmental decisions. It cannot train its young men except by giving them small game to chase; but it really must emphasise to them that these are only tests of speed and agility, not the real thing.

40. *Establishments.* The Treasury and the Staff Associations are in complete agreement that strict centralisation is essential, and the Departments realise that they are helpless in this pincer grip.

41. It is however a matter of common courtesy that there should be a show of consultation, and this can do no harm if it is confined to trivial matters.

42. *Changes.* Things do happen, but too slowly: we can only think of five changes in the last five years — forward look, hospital revenue (we have referred to these), general grants to local authorities, changes in agricultural price review procedure, and some minor changes in Civil Service pay negotiation.

43. The great thing is not to let these timid initiatives die out.

44. *Management.* One of our members got in Mr E. F. L. Brech, and he worked up the old idea that the Civil Service could learn a good deal from business practice.

45. We have all realised that 'management' is an OK word ever since Fleck got at the Coal Board in 1953. But some of us note that there are important Departments (the Foreign Office, for instance) where present doctrines about 'management' are quite irrelevant.

46. In this terminology a Department is the equivalent of an operating company within a group.

47. Within a Department the Principal Establishment Officer is supposed to be expert on managerial efficiency: but few P.E.O.s are up to this. The job therefore falls back on the P.U.S., who has no time for it, and even on the Minister.

48. Hence the whole thing has to begin from the Treasury. There will be no improvement unless it assumes the normal responsibilities of top management in relation to 'management succession' throughout its group of companies.

49. What is more, it must control effective services for 'management assessment.' It is not staffed or organised at present to discharge either of these functions; and it will not be able to do so without unrelenting and bitter opposition, unless our analogy of 'holding company' and 'operating companies' is understood and accepted throughout the Civil Service.

50, 51. *Management Services.* A few big departments are fairly well briefed on these; to the others they mean nothing at all.

52. The Treasury does lay on courses, but the general practice is to send to these only Assistant Secretaries who have just about reached their ceiling.

53. Real progress has been made in O. and M. costing, and the use of computers: but the bottleneck is in expert staff and it is not

realistic to think that these can be bought from outside at present rates. They must be home grown.

54. More could be done about common services.

55. For the hospitals, for instance; 56, 57. And perhaps for local authorities, but really we know nothing about these.

58. In fact it all needs more public discussion.

59. *The Treasury.* We have seemed to criticise the Departments, as independent satrapies, pressing their own ideas of public policy, ill-managed, ill-informed, and inbred. We have suggested a new model, based on that of progressive private enterprise. We realise that in doing so we have cast the Treasury for a part which it is at present ill-fitted to discharge. If it cannot adapt itself, the thing is hopeless.

## Part III. The Reform of Parliament

60. It is obvious that in our 'model' the role of the Commons is quite subsidiary: but it could be a help to the Government in minor ways if it were prepared to sacrifice some of its old mumbo-jumbo.

61. *Annual finance procedure.* The present legislative procedure is absolute gibberish: but we have not the nerve to recommend a frontal attack on it.

62. A two-year cycle has been suggested: but inflation goes too fast for that. Even private business finds it necessary to strike a fresh balance each year.

63. *Penny Exercise Book Accounting.* This is silly, but it has advantages as a system of policing fraud, and those who have looked at it carefully have all looked away again in horror at the work and dislocation involved in introducing a more logical system.

64, 65. There would be no real advantage in having sophisticated accounts except for trading services, and most of these have now been hived off to public corporations and so on. The others have trading accounts already.

66, 67. Trading accounts won't help at all in settling priorities where the determinants are political and social, and that is most of the story, as we explained earlier.

68. *Claw-back.* It is always said that this causes a rush to get rid of money somehow, before the financial year ends. In fact, the sums involved are not very big; it is more a question of attitudes than of accounts.

69. In an organisation as big as this, large autonomous units cannot be denied the power to 'fiddle' at the margin; this is a built-in tendency, but controlled by mutual understandings. No tightening up can control it without ridiculous repercussions.

70. The Departments themselves know how to work with the present system:

71. And its worst defect is that subordinate authorities like H.M.C.s don't understand it, in fact they think it is mad. It will be easier to make some concessions than to explain it to them.

72, 73. *The Commons and Commitments.* The Commons have at present no organisation for discussing departmental decisions at the time when they are taken.

74. A reorganisation would be useless unless the Government were prepared to give the House access to the information it possesses itself. This no Government would do.

75. Up to this point we are agreed; but some of us feel that the rest of our recommendations will fall to the ground unless something is done to secure better informed debate in public.

76, 77. *P.A.C., E.C., S.C.N.I.* The present effect of these committees on administration is bad. They are old-fashioned in approach, are interested primarily in trivialities, and waste the time of very busy men who have more important things to do.

78. The position is nearly, but not quite, intolerable; yet there is no hope of relief unless these committees begin to understand what they are doing.

79. *Change.* The theory of the old system, set up in the 1860s, is that the Commons control finance and the Treasury acts as its intermediary in dealing with Departments.

80. This gave paramountcy to the Commons and limited the Treasury to strict terms of reference. We recommend the paramountcy of the Treasury, and complete flexibility in its powers. There is likely to be a battle about this; fortunately or otherwise, the Commons do not realise what is at stake.

81, 82. *Losses.* For instance, the Public Accounts Committee have always been interested in specific cases of defalcation. But these are in total insignificant, and it is nonsense that the Treasury should be forced by the P.A.C. to concern itself with each case individually. Its job is to see that the system is right.

83, 84. '*Regularity.*' Similarly, the old business of 'policing' the appropriations is quite out of date; the risk of that sort of 'fiddle' is now negligible. The old procedure can be somewhat simplified (see para. 27); the main thing however is to interest the P.A.C. in the things about efficiency which now interest the Treasury.

85. *Nationalised Industry.* The ideas of the White Paper (Command 1337 of April, 1961) are relevant.

86, 87. The industries cost public money; the Commons therefore seek detailed control; this is likely to cost more money and to decrease efficiency further.

88. The Government's policy is to assimilate nationalised industry to other forms of big business; and this means that the Commons must be prepared to accept the limited role of shareholders.

89. They should be treated to a certain amount of blarney, stuffed with unusable figures, and allowed to take part in set-piece debates. But they really must not try to join in policy decisions when they are being made. We hope that if Dr Beeching and others can establish this rule for public enterprise the precedent will have good effects in other fields of Government expenditure.

## Part IV. Summing Up

90. Our main themes have been the Forward Look: the Management Model; effective Treasury control over the Commons.

91. Do not think we are very confident about success in any of these. The problem is vast and complex; (92) much of the departmental organisation is obsolete and resistant to change.

93. *Right strategy.* There must be a group of top people sharing a picture of the situation and its difficulties.

94. They have two main instruments of control: (a) to study men and organisations at work in individual cases; (b) to set up adequate systems of comparative analysis.

95, 96. Skill consists in using these two instruments judiciously in combination. (a) is quite well used now, (b) is still very poorly developed.

97. *Wrong strategy.* The thing not to do is to concentrate only on the total of public expenditure. This is nearly (though not completely) meaningless; and it is apt to have awkward political consequences in the shape of a demand for percentage cuts all round. This is exactly the wrong way to proceed.

99. *Danger points.* We analyse these as follows: (1) The routine cost of administration must of course be screwed down: but that is a regular management job, already quite well done.

100. (2) There is always a risk of uncontrollable extravagance as a result of electoral politics. (3) But the really big waste of the 1950s has come in three ways:

101. (*a*) The maintenance of obsolete firms, industries, and areas, which have no hope of running except at a loss. Economic liabilities should be shed.

102. (*b*) Obsolete subsidies; those who are given Government money come to regard this as their right, unconditionally and for ever.

103. (*c*) Sudden reactions to temporary situations, military or technological.

104. In the nature of things the Treasury is bound to be 'bounced' from time to time. Its best safeguard against this is to take decisions slowly, secure Cabinet backing, and fight attempts at sudden change.

105. *The Public.* We are agreed that this is a hopeless task unless the Treasury has the backing of an 'informed' public opinion. We disagree about the steps to be taken. Most of us think that public relations might easily make things worse. People can never be got to understand this kind of problem, and anything you say gives a handle to opposition.

106. A minority of us think that the risks entailed by excessive discretion are even greater. There is a national emergency, and we shall not get through unless we can somehow tap the stock of common sense used by citizens in their personal affairs.

107. Acknowledgments.

## CHAPTER IV

# THE POLICY PROCESS

ANY attempt to generalise about the process of policy-making in Britain must be treated cautiously, for statements based upon case studies should implicitly carry prefatory statements such as: 'In the case of race relations...', or 'In the case of the national health service...'. Alternatively, statements meant to apply to underlying attributes found diffusely through British politics might require the *caveat*: 'While exceptions may be found to the following statement, on balance...'. Because the constant repetition of such qualifications would be obvious as well as tedious, they are rarely found in writings about British government. It is worth calling attention to the point from time to time, especially at the beginning of a concluding chapter.

Conventionally, models of policy-making in Britain assume that the process of government is the same, whatever the problem at hand. If government is said to be 'the Crown in Parliament', then the vagueness of this abstraction may make it equally relevant or irrelevant whatever the circumstances. If the model posits government by a Prime Minister — rightly or wrongly compared with an American President[1] — then there is usually a saving clause indicating that this model only fits 'important' policies. Important policies are, by a convenient tautology, only those policies dealt with by the Prime Minister.

The idea of government by Act of Parliament is precise, as far as it goes, but leaves undefined the origins of Acts of Parliament and the range of policies that can effectively be made by legislation. Dividing policy-making into 'political' and 'administrative' areas, with the former the exclusive province of elected politicians and the latter the province of civil servants, imposes a dichotomy upon a continuum. At the extremes, one can recognise a distinction between a policy such as the declaration of war and one concerning post

[1] When the Anglo-American comparison is invoked, no explicit reference is made to the particular President after whom British Prime Ministers are supposed to model their actions — Herbert Hoover, Franklin D. Roosevelt, Dwight D. Eisenhower, or John F. Kennedy. Some parallels with each of these can be found among recent occupants of 10 Downing Street.

office sub-stations. Most political issues, however, mix administrative problems and conflicts of principle and interest. Even so seemingly clear-cut an issue as the Suez War of 1956 involved questions about the administrative competence of those planning the attack upon Egypt as well as debates about the principle of the use of force there.

The selections in this chapter gradually expand the field for generalisation about British government. The selection about parliamentary legislation from *The Times* shows how restricted is the field within which MPs can exert influence by legislation. The selection by Richard Neustadt indicates the problems small groups of elected politicians face when they seek to influence policy. George Jones's contribution on the power of the Prime Minister shows that he too is restricted in his impact on policy. The articles by Samuel Brittan and D. N. Chester extend the analysis to include senior civil servants, men whose work is not only crucial in policy-making, but also suffers from many constraints felt by their political superiors. The concluding article by F. M. G. Willson draws together the two main themes of the reader — the importance of institutional and structural limitations upon policy-makers, and the significance, within this context, of small groups of very disparate men.

## Bibliographical Note

The conventional view of post-war British government is most clearly stated in Lord Morrison's *Government and Parliament* (London: Oxford University Press, 3rd ed., 1964). In the 1960s, attention has increasingly been given to the idea of British government as a kind of Prime Ministerial government. This view tends to be supported by J. P. Mackintosh, *The British Cabinet* (London: Stevens, 1962), and is present, *à outrance*, in R. H. S. Crossman's Introduction to the Fontana Library edition of Bagehot's *The English Constitution* (London, 1963). For alternative revisionist views, see e.g. Bernard Crick, *The Reform of Parliament* (London: Weidenfeld & Nicolson, 1964) and A. H. Birch, *Representative and Responsible Government* (London: Allen & Unwin, 1964). The institutions of policy-making are most ferociously (if not thoroughly) criticised in Brian Chapman's *British Government Observed: Some European Reflections* (London: Allen & Unwin, 1963). A more careful critique is contained in Kenneth Waltz's *Foreign Policy and Democratic Politics: the American and British Experience* (Boston: Little, Brown, 1967). Bagehot's nineteenth-century classic, *The English Constitution*, remains worth reading in the lifetime of Mr

Wilson's Labour Government, if the reader will set aside the institutional trappings and concentrate upon the author's main theme of the dissociation between the dignified appearance of British government and the workings of its more-or-less efficient parts.

# MANY BILLS COMPETE FOR PRIORITY IN A PARLIAMENTARY SESSION

By *The Times* POLITICAL STAFF

IN so far as a government makes policy by legislation, all its measures must be discussed and approved by both Houses of Parliament. In a situation defined by the Government as an emergency, such as the German breakthrough in France in May 1940, or the alleged influx of coloured British citizens from Kenya in February 1968, a government may push legislation through in a few days. In the ordinary course of events, the promoters of non-emergency legislation must compete with each other for a favourable position in the timetable for a parliamentary session. As the following survey by *The Times* illustrates, major government departments and pressure groups compete against each other for allotments of limited parliamentary time. Since the timetable of a parliamentary year is relatively inelastic by comparison with the possible subjects for legislation, the leaders of the Cabinet use the technicalities of parliamentary timetabling as a means of manipulating political priorities and playing off pressure groups. In instances not chronicled in the following article, the government of the day may itself be the victim of a shortage of parliamentary time. Alternatively, leading ministers may seek broad discretionary powers, allowing them to take decisions without reference to legislation.

THIS is the season of the year when Mr Macmillan and the principal managers of Government business have to make up their minds about the scope of the Queen's Speech.

As is clear from the review below of Bills that are strong candidates for a place in the Parliamentary programme for next session, the difficulty does not lie in scraping together enough legislation to keep the two houses occupied but in making choices between Bills competing hotly for priority.

All the Bills mentioned here have been promised by Ministers,

---

Reprinted from *The Times*, 19 Sep 1963. For similar but shorter articles concerning other sessions, see e.g. *The Times*, 25 Sep 1961; 8 Oct 1962; 17 Oct 1966; and 13 Oct 1967.

sometimes firmly for the coming session, sometimes simply with the hope that parliamentary time will permit. But it will be wise to bear in mind that Mr Macmillan and Mr Macleod, particularly, this time have to frame a Queen's Speech that will fit into their plans for a general election.

In other words, in the fifth and final session of the present Parliament they now have their last chance to put first things first and to fulfil all the firm promises that have been given, without crowding the programme to the point where a general election after next year's Budget would catch them with important work only half done.

The following Bills are among the main candidates for a place in the Queen's Speech:

1. *Defence Reorganisation.* — Legislation to create a unified Ministry of Defence absorbing the Admiralty, the War Office and the Air Ministry (whose Ministers will become Ministers of State) has a high priority. All statutory defence powers vested in the Service Ministries will be transferred to the new Secretary of State for Defence. Under him the Defence Council will exercise the powers of command and administrative control previously exercised by the Board of Admiralty and the Army and Air Councils.

Mr Thorneycroft, Minister of Defence, told the Commons on 31 July that the aim was legislation in the autumn and a vesting day next April.

2. *Ports.* — Accepting the major recommendation of the Rochdale committee, the Government have set up a National Ports Council under Lord Rochdale to formulate a plan and supervise its execution. Legislation is needed to put it on a statutory basis; to give it the powers necessary to exercise its functions of advice and regulation effectively; and to give the Minister of Transport powers to ensure that the national port development plan is carried out. This will be done by Government control of capital investment.

3. *Credit for Shipbuilding.* — A Bill to be introduced early in the session will authorise loans of up to £60m. for financing orders from British owners for new ships built in British shipyards. Loans will be made available to cover up to four-fifths of a ship's cost, the terms of each loan being decided on merit after advice from a committee under Lord Piercy, chairman of the Ship Mortgage Finance Company.

The original £30m. offer, made at the end of May, was doubled in July. The Cunard Steam-Ship Company have since applied for a loan to replace the *Queen Mary* with a smaller ship.

4. *Provision for Redundancy.* — Both Mr Hare, Minister of Labour,

and Mr Maudling, Chancellor of the Exchequer, have said that proper financial provision for workers made redundant is of vital importance for economic growth. In the Commons in April Mr Maudling said that the Government intended to tackle this complicated problem vigorously with a view, if necessary, to introduce legislation this autumn.

Mr Hare has said: 'Should a national redundancy scheme prove to be the answer, there is one thing of which I am quite certain: the Government should not simply take over from the industry the responsibilities and obligations which are an essential part of the relations between employers and their workpeople.' If managements knew change would be resisted because of redundancy fears they would hesitate to modernise.

5. *Industrial Training.* — The Government have prepared legislation on the basis of recommendations made in the White Paper on Industrial Training (Cmnd. 1892). In July, Mr Hare said that consultations with the British Employers' Confederation and the Trades Union Congress had enabled good progress to be made in the drafting. He promised to legislate when parliamentary time permitted.

6. *Police.* — Accepting the majority view of the royal commission which rejected the idea of a national police force, the Government recognised that much legislation administering the police in England and Wales is vague and out of date. Mr Brooke, Home Secretary, said in May that the aim was to make a fresh start and to define as precisely as possible the powers and duties of the police authorities and of the Home Secretary and the relations between them.

The Bill would seek to give the Home Secretary new functions, including power to require a police authority to retire its chief constable, and to call for reports from chief constables. A proposed new power would enable the Home Secretary to secure the proper co-ordination of the work of local police forces. Questions of the Home Secretary's answerability to Parliament on police matters outside the Metropolitan police area may also be settled.

7. *Underground Storage of Gas.* — The Gas Council's projects for storing gas in porous rock below ground are being held up for want of legislation. The Council's private Bill to authorise a store near Winchester was withdrawn because of local objections and the Government said that national legislation was necessary 'to provide a framework of control'. Consultations began in July 1962. Although a Bill was ready no time could be found for it last session.

8. *Public Library Service.* — Based on the recommendations of the Roberts committee, this Bill would give the Minister of Education the general responsibility for the oversight of the public library

service in England and Wales, and require public library authorities to provide an efficient service. A national scheme for co-operation between libraries is likely to be provided for in the measure.

9. *Public Works Loan Board.* — In October 1962, Mr Maudling expressed concern about the steep increase in the temporary debt of local authorities and said that before Easter 1963 a Bill would be needed to extend the powers of the Public Works Loan Board. In August this year Mr Lubbock, Liberal member for Orpington, suggested that since the interest on P.W.L.B. loans was ½ per cent above the open market charge urgent action was needed.

Mr du Cann, Economic Secretary to the Treasury, replied that discussions had taken place with the local authority associations and a White Paper would be published this autumn. Legislation would be necessary, he said, because only £50m. was now available to the P.W.L.B.

10. *Scottish Law of Succession.* — This Bill has already been published and a promise has been given that it will be included in next session's programme.

11. *Airports Authority.* — A 1961 White Paper promised a Bill to establish an authority to own and manage Britain's four main international airports: London, Gatwick, Stansted, and Prestwick. Conservative MPs have since complained of Government inaction. When Mr Amery, Minister of Aviation, was asked in July this year about legislation to create a separate authority for London Airport, he replied: 'Most of the preparatory work has been done; further progress depends on when parliamentary time can be found.'

12. *Fire Protection.* — The Home Secretary, the Minister of Housing and Local Government and the Scottish Secretary have decided that the law on residential establishments and clubs needs to be strengthened and rationalised. Amending legislation has been discussed with interests concerned.

13. *Drugs.* — Mr Powell, Minister of Health, is preparing 'a comprehensive modernisation of the whole of the law on drugs and poisons' to ensure that dangerous drugs are not placed on the market. He has hinted that it was being treated as urgent. Legislation could be ready for the coming session.

14. *Common Land.* — In May it was stated that it remained the Government's 'firm intention' to introduce a scheme of commons registration broadly on the lines recommended by the royal commission in July 1958.

15. *Nigeria.* — Mr Sandys, Commonwealth and Colonial Secretary, said in August that Nigeria was to become a republic on or about 1 October 1963, but, pending information on the precise form of the

republican constitution, legislation would be deferred until the next session and then introduced retroactively.

16. *Legal Aid.* — A Bill to provide for the payment out of the legal aid fund of costs incurred by successful opponents of legally aided litigants was withdrawn last session because of procedural difficulties in the Lords. It will begin its passage in the Commons next time.

17. *Kenya Independence.* — Legislation is needed to enable Kenya to become independent on 12 December.

18. *Malta Independence.* — The Government have decided that Malta should become independent not later than 31 May 1964, but the form of the constitution has yet to be settled.

Legislation has also been promised on a number of other subjects, without a clear commitment on timing. They include:

19. *Consumer Protection.* — In the debate on consumer protection in May a Government speaker said that, after the Molony committee report, new or amending legislation relating to the Hire Purchase, Merchandise Marks, Sale of Goods and Trade Marks Acts was being considered.

20. *Transactions in Seeds.* — Legislation based on the recommendations of the Committee on Transactions in Seeds has been promised. The committee recommended that plant breeders should be given the opportunity to acquire rights in their new varieties for a period of 15 to 25 years during which they would obtain royalties from persons licensed to grow or sell them, and that an independent Plant Variety Rights Office, analogous to the Patent Office, should be set up.

21. *Undersea Resources (Oil and Gas Reserves).* — The Minister of Power said in May that legislation to ratify the international convention concerning oil and natural gas reserves under the North Sea would be introduced as soon as there was time.

22. *Classified Roads.* — Evidence was given to the Estimates Committee in 1962 that a complete revision of the system of making grants for work on classified roads was being prepared. Discussions with the local authority associations may not be completed in time for a Bill to be introduced this time.

# WHITE HOUSE AND WHITEHALL

*By* RICHARD NEUSTADT

THE growth in popular references to a 'Presidential-style' government in Britain has not been matched by a growing interest in the systematic comparison of the processes of government in the two countries. Richard Neustadt's article is unusual in the author's explicit concern with comparative analysis of cabinet government and the American style of executive government. It is also unusual in that the author writes from first-hand experience as a White House staff official, as well as considerable first-hand knowledge of government in Whitehall.

CABINET government, so-called, as practised currently in the United Kingdom, differs in innumerable ways — some obvious, some subtle — from 'presidential government' in the United States. To ask what one can learn about our own system by viewing theirs, may seem far-fetched, considering those differences. But actually the question is a good one. For comparison should help us to discriminate between shadow and substance in both regimes. A look down Whitehall's corridors of power might suggest a lot of things worth noticing in Washington.

For a President-watcher, who tries to understand the inner workings of our bureaucratic system by climbing inside now and then, and learning on the job, it is no easy matter to attempt comparison with the internal life of Whitehall. How is one to get a comparable look? Those who govern Britain mostly keep their secrets to themselves. They rarely have incentive to do otherwise, which is among the differences between us. Least of all are they inclined to satisfy the curiosities of academics. Even we colonials, persistent though we are and mattering as little as we do, find ourselves all too frequently treated like Englishmen and kept at bay by those three magic words: 'Official Secrets Act'. Why not? Nothing in the British Constitution says that anyone outside of Whitehall needs an inside view.

---

Reprinted from *The Public Interest*, II (1966) 55–69 

Quite the reverse. If academics know, then journalists might learn, and even the back-benchers might find out. God forbid!

In Britain governing is *meant* to be a mystery. And so it is. Only in the memoirs of participants does one get glimpses, now and then, of operational reality. And even the most 'indiscreet' of recent memoirs veil the essence of the modern system: the relations between ministers and civil servants in the making of a government decision.

For four years I have made a hobby of attempting to poke holes in Whitehall's defences, and to take a closer look than either interviews or books afford. Partly this has been a 'busman's holiday': having roamed one set of corridors, I find the temptation irresistible to look around another. Partly, though, I have been tempted by the thought that a comparison of set likenesses and differences would add a new dimension to President-watching.

To test that proposition, let me raise two simple points of difference between their system and ours.

First, we have counterparts for their top civil servants — but not in our own civil service.

Second, we have counterparts for their cabinet ministers — but not exclusively, or even mainly, in our cabinet.

If I state these two correctly, and I think I do, it follows that in our conventional comparisons we all too often have been victims of semantics. Accordingly, in our proposals for reform-by-analogy we all too often have confused function with form. I find no functions in the British system for which ours lacks at least nascent counterparts. But it is rare when institutions with the same names in both systems do the same work for precisely the same purpose. Thus, the most important things that I bring back from my excursioning in Whitehall are a question and caution. The question: what is our functional equivalent? The caution: never base analysis on nomenclature. These seem to be embarrassingly obvious. But it is astonishing how frequently they are ignored.

## I

'Why are your officials so passionate?' I once was asked in England by a bright, young Treasury official just back from Washington. I inquired with whom he had been working there. His answer: 'Your chaps at the Budget Bureau.'

To an American, those 'chaps' appear to be among the most *dis*passionate of Washingtonians. Indeed, the Budget staff traditionally prides itself on being cool, collected, and above the struggle, distant from emotions churning in the breasts of importunate agency officials. Yet to my English friend, 'They took themselves so seriously ... seemed to be crusaders for the policy positions they thought made sense ... seemed to feel that it was up to them to save the day....' If this is how the Budget Bureau struck him, imagine how he would have felt about some circles in our Air Force, or the European Bureau of the State Department, or the Office of Economic Opportunity, or the Forest Service for that matter, or the Bureau of Reclamation, or the National Institutes of Health!

His inquiry suggests two further queries. First, out of what frame of reference was he asking? And second, is it sensible of him (and most of us) to talk of our own budgeteers as though they were his counterparts? These questions are pertinent because I think we are very far from candid with ourselves about the way we get *his* work done in *our* system.

This young man was a Principal-with-prospects at the Treasury. By definition, then, he was a man of the Administrative class, the elite corps of the British civil service. More important, he was also an apprentice-member of the favoured few, the elite-of-the-elite, who climb the ladder *in* the Treasury. With skill and luck and approbation from his seniors he might someday rise to be a Mandarin. And meanwhile he would probably serve soon as personal assistant to a Cabinet minister. In short, he had the frame of reference which befits a man whose career ladder rises up the central pillar of the whole Whitehall establishment towards the heights where dwell the seniors of all seniors, moulders of ministers, heads of the civil service, knights in office, lords thereafter: the Permanent Secretaries of the Cabinet and the Treasury.

English civil servants of this sort, together with their foreign office counterparts, make up the inner core of 'officials', civilian career men, whose senior members govern the United Kingdom in collaboration with their ministerial superiors, the front-bench politicians, leaders of the parliamentary party which commands a House majority for the time being. Theirs is an intimate collaboration, grounded in the interests and traditions of both sides. Indeed it binds them into a Society for Mutual Benefit: what they succeed in sharing with each other they need share with almost no one else, and governing in England is a virtual duopoly.

This is the product of a tacit treaty, an implicit bargain, expressed in self-restraints which are observed on either side. The senior civil servants neither stall nor buck decisions of the Government, once these have been taken in due form. 'Due Form' means consultation with these senior civil servants, among other things; but having been consulted, these officials act without public complaint or private evasion, even though they may have fought what they are doing up to the last moment of decision. They also try to assure comparable discipline in lower official ranks, and to squeeze out the juniors who do not take kindly to it.

The senior politicians, for their part — with rare and transient exceptions — return this loyalty in full measure. The politicians rarely meddle with official recruitment or promotion: by and large, officialdom administers itself. The politicians preserve the anonymity of civil servants both in Parliament and in the press. Officials never testify on anything except 'accounts' (an audit of expenditures), and nobody reveals their roles in shaping public policy. Ministers take all kudos for themselves — likewise the heat. They also take upon themselves protection for the status of officialdom in the society: honours fall like gentle rain at stated intervals. They even let career civil servants run their private offices, and treat their personal assistants of the moment (detailed from civil-service ranks) as confidentially as our department heads treat trusted aides imported from outside. More important, the politicians *lean* on their officials. They *expect* to be advised. Most important, they very often follow the advice that they receive.

This is an advantageous bargain for both sides. It relieves the politicians of a difficult and chancy search for 'loyal' advisers and administrators. These are in place, ready to hand. And it relieves civil servants of concern for their security in terms both of profession and of person. No wonder our career men appear 'passionate' to one of theirs; theirs have nothing at stake except policy!

So a Treasury-type has everything to gain by a dispassionate stance, and nothing to lose except arguments. To be sure, since he feels himself with reason to be one of an elite, ranking intellectually and morally with the best in Britain, this is no trifling loss. If parliamentary parties were less disciplined than they now are, or if he had back-benchers who identified with him, he could afford to carry arguments outside official channels, as his predecessors sometimes did a century ago — and as *military* officers still do, on occasion. But party discipline calls forth its counterpart in his own ranks. And party politicians on back benches have no natural affinities with civil servants—quite the contrary. The civil servant really has no recourse but to lose his arguments with grace and wait in patience for another day, another set of ministers. After all, he stays, they go. And while he stays, he shares the fascinating game of power, stretching his own mind and talents in the service of a reasonably grateful country.

The Treasury-type is a disciplined man; but a man fulfilled, not frustrated. His discipline is the price he pays for power. Not every temperament can take it; if he rises in the Treasury, he probably can. But there is more to this than a cold compromise for power's sake. Those who rise and find fulfilment in their work do so in part because they are deliberately exposed at mid-career to the constraints, the miseries, the hazards which afflict the human beings who wield power on the political side. They know the lot of ministers from observation at first hand. Exposure makes for empathy and for perspective. It also makes for comfort with the civil servant's lot. Whitehall's elites gain all three while relatively young. It leaves them a bit weary with the weight of human folly, but it rids them of self-righteousness, the bane of *our* career men — particularly endemic, of course, among budgeteers.

A Treasury-type gains this exposure through that interesting device, the tour of duty in a minister's private office as his personal 'dogsbody'. The private secretary, so called, serves his master-of-the-moment as a confidential aide, minding his business, doing his chores, sharing his woes, offering a crying towel, bracing him for bad days in the House, briefing him for bad days in the office. Etcetera. Remarkably, by our standards, the civil service has pre-empted such assignments for its own. (Do not confuse a minister's private secretary with mere *parliamentary* private secretaries who are drawn from the back benches of the House.) Still more remarkably, the politicians feel themselves well served and rarely dream of looking elsewhere for the service. I know an instance where a minister confided in his private secretary a secret he told no one else save the Prime Minister, not even his Permanent Secretary, the career head-of-department, 'lest it embarrass him to know'. The Permanent Secretary was the private secretary's boss; yet the secret was kept as a matter of course. This, I am assured, is not untypical: 'ministerial secrets' are all in the day's work for dogsbodies.

Accordingly, the one-time private secretary who has risen in due course to be permanent secretary of a department knows far more of what it feels like to perform as a politician than his opposite number, the department's minister, can ever hope to fathom in reverse. A William Armstrong, for example, now joint-head of Treasury, whose opposite number is the Chancellor of the Exchequer, spent years as private secretary to a previous Chancellor who was among the ablest men in the cabinets of his time. Draw the contrast with our own career civil servants.

Our budgeteers imagine that they are the nearest thing to Treasury civil servants. For this, no one can blame them. Much of our literature suggests that if they are not quite the same as yet, a little gimmickery could make them so. Many American political scientists have bemused themselves for years with plans to borrow nomenclature and procedures from the British side, on the unstated premise that function follows form. But it does not.

Functionally, our counterparts for British Treasury-types are *non*-career men holding jobs infused with presidential interest or concern. They are 'in-and-outers' from the law firms, banking, business, academia, foundations, or occasionally journalism, or the entourages of successful Governors and Senators — along with up-and-outers (sometimes up-and-downers) who relinquish, or at least risk, civil service status in the process. Here is the elite-of-the-elite, the upper-crust of our 'Administrative class'. These are the men who serve alongside our equivalents for ministers, and who share in governing. One finds them in the White House and in the *appointive* jobs across the street at the Executive Office Building. One finds them also on the seventh floor of State, and on the third and fourth floors of the Pentagon; these places among others.

Let me take some names at random to suggest the types. First, the prototype of all: Averil Harriman. Second, a handful of the currently employed: David Bell, William Bundy, Wilbur Cohen, Harry McPherson, Paul Nitze. Third, a few recent 'outers' almost certain to be back, somehow, sometime: McGeorge Bundy, Kermit Gordon, Theodore Sorensen. Fourth, a long-time 'outer' who is never back but always in: Clark Clifford. Three of these men got their start as government career men, two as academics, two in banking, two in law, and one on Capitol Hill. The numbers are but accidents of random choice; the spread is meaningful.

The jobs done by such men as these have no precise equivalents in England; our machinery is too different. For example, McGeorge Bundy as the President's Assistant for National Security Affairs was something more than Principal Private Secretary to the Prime Minister (reserved for rising Treasury-types), a dogsbody-writ-large, and also something different from the Secretary of the Cabinet (top of the tree for them), a post 'tradition' turns into an almost Constitutional position, certainly what we would call an 'institutional' one. Yet the men in those positions see a Bundy as their sort of public servant. They are higher on the ladder than my young friend with the question; they do not take budgeteers to be their counterparts; they know a Senior Civil Servant when they see one.

Every detail of our practice is un-English, but the general outline fits. One of our men appears on television; another testifies against a bill; a third and fourth engage in semi-public argument; a fifth man feeds a press campaign to change the President's mind; a sixth disputes a cabinet member's views in open meeting; a seventh overturns an inter-agency agreement. So it goes, to the perpetual surprise (and sometimes envy?) of the disciplined duopolists in Britain. Yet by *our* lights, according to *our* standards, under our conditions, such activities may be as 'disciplined' as theirs, and as responsive to political leadership. The ablest of our in-and-outers frequently display equivalent restraint and equal comprehension in the face of the dilemmas which confront our presidential counterparts of their Cabinet politicians.

The elite of our officialdom are not careerist men in the British sense (although, of course, our in-and-outers have careers); why should it be? Neither is it the President with his department heads. They, too, are in-and-outers. We forget that the duopoly which governs Britain is composed of *two* career systems, official and political. Most ministers who will take office through the next decade are on the scene and well identified in Westminster. The permanent secretaries who will serve with them are on the Whitehall ladders now; a mere outsider can spot some of them. Contrast our situation — even the directorships of old-line bureaus remain problematical. Who is to succeed J. Edgar Hoover?

We have only two sets of true career men in our system. One consists of Senators and Congressmen in relatively safe seats, waiting their turn for chairmanships. The other consists of military officers and civil employees who are essentially technicians manning every sort of speciality (including 'management') in the Executive establishment. Between these two we leave a lot of room for in-and-outers. We are fortunate to do so. Nothing else could serve as well to keep the two apart. And *their* duopoly would be productive, not of governance, but of its feudal substitute, piecemeal administration. We can only hope to govern in our system by, and through, the Presidency. In-and-outers are a saving grace for Presidents.

## II

Since 1959, English commentators frequently have wondered to each other if their government was being 'presidentialised'. In part, this stemmed from electoral considerations following the 'personality contest' between Harold Macmillan and Hugh Gaitskell in that year's general election. In part, too, it stemmed from the impression left by Macmillan's active premiership — re-inforced this past year by the sight of still another activist in office, Harold Wilson.

Despite their differences of style, personality, and party, both Macmillan and Wilson patently conceived the Cabinet Room in Downing Street to be the P.M.'s office, not a mere board-room. Both evidently acted on the premise that the P.M.'s personal judgment ought, if possible, to be decisive. Both reached out for the power of personal decision on the issues of the day. Macmillan did so through offstage manoeuvre, while avowing his fidelity to cabinet consensus. With perhaps a bit more candour, Wilson does the same. Hence discussion about trends towards 'presidential' government.

Yet between these two Prime Ministers there was another for a year, Sir Alec Douglas-Home. And by no stretch of the imagination could his conduct in office have been characterised as presidential. On the contrary, by all accounts he was a classic 'chairman of the board', who resolutely pushed impending issues *out* of Number 10, for initiative elsewhere, by others. He managed, it is said, to get a lot of gardening done while he resided there. I once asked a close observer what became of the initiatives, the steering, the manoeuvring, which Home refused to take upon himself. He replied:

> When ministers discovered that he really wouldn't do it, they began to huddle with each other, little groups of major figures. You would get from them enough agreement or accommodation to produce the main lines of a government position, something they could try to steer through Cabinet. Or if you didn't get it, there was nothing to be done. That's how it began to work, outside of Number 10, around it.

That is how it would be working now, had there been but a slight shift in the popular vote of 1964.

The British system, then, has *not* been presidentialised, or not at least in operational terms. For, as we learned with Eisenhower, the initiatives a President must take to form 'the main lines of a government position' cannot survive outside the White House precincts. Toss them out and either they bounce back or they wither away. A president may delegate to White House aides ('ok, S.A.'), or to a Foster Dulles, but only as he demonstrates consistently, day-in-and-out, that they command his ear and hold his confidence. Let him take to his bed behind an oxygen tent and they can only go through motions. Eisenhower's White House was a far cry from 10 Downing Street in the regime of Douglas-Home. That remains the distance Britain's system has to travel towards a presidential status for prime ministers.

But even though the system did not make an activist of Douglas-Home, his predecessor and successor obviously relished the part. The system may not have required them to play it, but they did so, and the system bore the weight of their activity. In externals, Number 10 looks no more like the White House under Wilson than it did a year ago. But, in essence, Wilson comes as close to being 'President' as the conventions of *his* system allow. He evidently knows it and likes it. So, I take it, did Macmillan.

How close can such men come? How nearly can they assert 'presidential' leadership inside a cabinet system? Without endeavouring to answer in the abstract, let me record some impressions of concrete performances.

First, consider Britain's bid for Common Market membership four years ago, which presaged an enormous (if abortive) shift in public policy, to say nothing of Tory Party policy. By all accounts this 'turn to Europe' was Macmillan's own. The timing and the impetus were his, and I am told that his intention was to go whole-hog, both economically and politically. As such, this was among the great strategic choices in the peacetime politics of Britain. But it never was a 'Government decision'. For those, by British definition, come in Cabinet. Macmillan never put the issue there in candid terms. Instead he tried to sneak past opposition there — and on back-benches and in constituencies — by disguising his strategic choice as a commercial deal. The Cabinet dealt with issues of negotiation, *en principe* and later in detail, for making Britain part of Europe's economic union without giving up its Commonwealth connections (or farm subsidies). One minister explained to me:

> Timing is everything. First we have to get into the Common Market as a matter of business, good for our economy. Then we can begin to look at the political side.... Appetites grow with eating. We couldn't hold the Cabinet, much less our back-benchers, if we put this forward now in broader terms....

Accordingly, the move towards Europe had to be played out in its ostensible terms, as a detailed negotiation of a commercial character. This took two years; and while the tactic served its purpose within Tory ranks, these were the years when France escaped from the Algerian war. By the time negotiations neared their end, Charles de Gaulle was riding high at home. Macmillan tiptoed past his own internal obstacles, but took so long about it that his path was blocked by an external one, the veto of de Gaulle.

Second, take the Nassau Pact of 1962, which calmed the Skybolt crisis between Washington and London even as it gave de Gaulle excuses for that veto. Macmillan was his own negotiator at the Nassau Conference. He decided on the spot to drop his claim for Skybolt missiles and to press the substitution of Polaris weaponry. He wrung what seemed to him an advantageous compromise along those lines from President Kennedy. Then and only then did he 'submit' its terms to the full Cabinet for decision (by return cable), noting the concurrence of three potent ministers who had accompanied him: the Foreign, Commonwealth, and Defence Secretaries. With the President waiting, the Cabinet 'decided' (unenthusiastically, by all accounts) to bless this *fait accompli.* What else was there to do? The answer, nothing — and no doubt Macmillan knew it.

Third, consider how the present Labour Government reversed its pre-election stand on Nassau's terms. Within six weeks of taking office, Wilson and his colleagues became champions of the Polaris programme they had scorned in opposition. Their back-benchers wheeled around behind them almost to a man. It is no secret that the Prime Minister was the source of this reversal, also its tactician. So far as I can find, it was his own choice, his initiative, his management, from first to last. He got it done in quick-time, yet he did it by manoeuvring on tiptoe like Macmillan in the case of the Common Market (with just a touch of the shot-gun, like Macmillan in the Nassau case). When Wilson let Polaris reach the Cabinet for 'decision', leading ministers, both 'right' and 'left', already were committed individually. By that time also, Wilson had pre-tested back-bench sentiment; he had 'prematurely' voiced to an acquiescent House what would become the rationale for Cabinet action: keeping on with weapons whose production had already passed a 'point of no return'.

Superficially, such instances as these seem strikingly unpresidential. In our accustomed vision, Presidents do not tiptoe around their Cabinets, they instruct, inform or ignore them. They do not engineer *faits accomplis* to force decisions from them, for the Cabinet does not make decisions; Presidents decide. A Kennedy after Birmingham, a Johnson after Selma, deciding on their civil rights bills, or a Johnson after Pleiku, ordering the bombers north, or Johnson last December, taking off our pressure for the multilateral force, or Kennedy confronting Moscow over Cuba with advisers all around him but decisions in his hands — what contrasts these suggest with the manoeuvres of a Wilson or Macmillan!

The contrasts are but heightened by a glance at their work-forces: Presidents with twenty-odd high-powered personal assistants, and a thousand civil servants in their Executive Office — Prime Ministers with but four such assistants in their Private Office (three of them on detail from departments) and a handful more in Cabinet Office, which by definition is not 'theirs' alone. Differences of work-place heighten the effect still more: 10 Downing Street is literally a house, comparing rather poorly with the White House before T.R.'s time. The modern White House is a palace, as Denis Brogan keeps reminding us, a physically-cramped version of the Hofburg, or the Tuileries.

Yet beneath these contrasts, despite them, belying them, Americans are bound to glimpse a long-familiar pattern in the conduct of an activist Prime Minister. It is the pattern of a President manoeuvring around or through the power-men in his Administration *and* in Congress. Once this is seen, all contrasts become superficial. Underneath our images of Presidents-in-boots, astride decisions, are the half-observed realities of Presidents-in-sneakers, stirrups in hand, trying to induce particular department heads, or Congressmen or Senators, to climb aboard.

Anyone who has an independent power-base is likelier than not to get 'ministerial' treatment from a President. Even his own appointees are to be wooed, not spurred, in the degree that they have their own attributes of power: expertise, or prestige, or a statute under foot. As Theodore Sorensen reported while he still was at the White House:

> In choosing between conflicting advice, the President is also choosing between conflicting advisers.... He will be slow to overrule a cabinet officer whose pride or prestige has been committed, not only to save the officer's personal prestige but to maintain his utility.... Whenever any President overrules any Secretary he runs the risk of that Secretary grumbling, privately if not publicly, to the Congress, or to the press (or to his diary), or dragging his feet on implementation, or, at the very worst, resigning with a blast at the President.

But it is men of Congress more than departmental men who regularly get from Pennsylvania Avenue the treatment given Cabinet ministers from Downing Street. Power in the Senate is particularly courted. A Lyndon Johnson (when he served there), or a Vandenberg in Truman's time, or nowadays an Anderson, a Russell, even a Mansfield — to say nothing of a Dirksen — are accorded many of the same attentions which a Wilson has to offer a George Brown.

The conventions of 'bipartisanship' in foreign relations, established under Truman and sustained by Eisenhower, have been extended under Kennedy and Johnson to broad sectors of the home-front, civil rights especially. These never were so much a matter of engaging oppositionists in White House undertakings as of linking to the White House men from either party who had influence to spare. Mutuality of deference between Presidents and leaders of congressional opinion, rather than between the formal party leaderships, always has been the essence of 'bipartisanship' in practice. And men who really lead opinion on the Hill gain privileged access to executive decisions as their customary share of 'mutual deference'. 'Congress' may not participate in such decisions, but these men often do: witness Dirksen in the framing of our recent Civil Rights Acts, or a spectrum of Senators from Russell to Mansfield in the framing of particular approaches on Viet Nam. Eleven years ago, Eisenhower seems to have kept our armed forces out of Indo-China when a projected intervention at the time of Dien Bien Phu won no support from Senate influentials. Johnson now manoeuvres to maintain support from 'right' to 'left' within their ranks.

If one seeks our counterparts for Wilson or Macmillan as Cabinet tacticians, one need look no further than Kennedy or Johnson manoeuvring among the influentials both downtown *and* on the Hill (and in state capitals, or among steel companies and trade unions, for that matter). Macmillan's caution on the Common Market will suggest the tortuous, slow course of J.F.K. towards fundamental changes in our fiscal policy, which brought him to the point of trying for a tax cut only by the end of his third year. Macmillan's *fait accompli* on Polaris brings to mind the Southeast Asia Resolution Johnson got from Congress after there had been some shooting in the Tonkin Gulf — and all its predecessors back to 1955, when Eisenhower pioneered this technique for extracting a 'blank cheque'. Wilson's quiet, quick arrangement for the Labour Party to adopt Polaris has a lot in common with the Johnson *coup* a year ago on Federal aid to education, where a shift in rationale took all sorts of opponents off the hook.

British government may not be presidential, but our government is more prime-ministerial than we are inclined to think. Unhappily for clarity of thought, we too have something called a Cabinet. But that pallid institution is in no sense the equivalent of theirs. Our equivalent is rather an informal, shifting aggregation of key individuals — the influentials at both ends of Pennsylvania Avenue. Some of them may sit in what we call the Cabinet as department heads; others sit in back rows there, as senior White House aides; still others have no place there. Collectively these men share no responsibility nor any meeting ground. Individually, however, each is linked to all the others through the person of the President (supported by his telephone). And all to some degree are serviced — also monitored — by one group or another on the White House staff. The former 'Bundy Office', or the 'Sorensen Shop' which one might best describe now as the Moyers 'sphere of influence', together with the staff of legislative liaisoners captained until lately by Lawrence O'Brien — these groups, although not tightly interlocked, provide a common reference-point for influentials everywhere: 'This is the White House calling....' While we lack an institutionalised Cabinet along British lines, we are evolving an equivalent of the Cabinet Office. The O'Brien operation was its newest element, with no precursors worthy of the name in any regime earlier than Eisenhower's. Whether it survives, and how and why, without O'Brien become questions of the day for Presidency-watchers.

The functional equivalence between a British Cabinet and our set of influentials — whether Secretaries, Senators, White House staffers, Congressmen, or others — is rendered plain by noting that, for most intents and purposes, their Cabinet members do the work of our congressional committees, our floor leaderships, and our front-offices downtown, all combined. The combination makes for superficial smoothness; Whitehall seems a quiet place. But once again, appearances deceive. Beneath the surface, this combine called 'Cabinet' wrestles with divergencies of interest, of perspective, of procedure, of personality, much like those we are used to witnessing above ground in the dealings of our separated institutions. Not only is the hidden struggle reminiscent of our open one, but also the results are often similar: 'bold, new ventures' actually undertaken are often few and far between. Whitehall dispenses with the grunts and groans of Washington, but both can labour mightily to bring forth mice.

It is unfashionable just now to speak of 'stalemate' or of 'deadlock' in our government, although these terms were all the rage two years ago and will be so again, no doubt, whenever Johnson's coat-tails shrink. But British government is no less prone to deadlock than our own. Indeed I am inclined to think their tendencies in that direction more pronounced than ours. A keen observer of their system, veteran of some seven years at Cabinet meetings, put it to me in these terms:

> The obverse of our show of monolithic unity behind a Government position, when we have one, is slowness, ponderousness, deviousness, in approaching a position, getting it taken, getting a 'sense of the meeting'. Nothing in our system is harder to do, especially if press leaks are at risk. You Americans don't seem to understand that....

In the Common Market case, to cite but one example, the three months from October to December, 1962 were taken up at Brussels, where negotiations centred, by a virtual filibuster from the British delegation. This drove some of the Europeans wild and had them muttering about 'perfidious Albion'. But London's delegates were not engaged in tactical manoeuvring at Brussels. All they were doing there was to buy time for tactical manoeuvring back home, around the cabinet table. The three months were required to induce two senior ministers to swallow agricultural concessions every student of the subject knew their government would have to make. But Britain could not move until those influential 'Members of the Government' had choked them down. The time-lag seemed enormous from the vantage point of Brussels. Significantly, it seemed short indeed to Londoners. By Whitehall standards this was rapid motion.

One of the checks-and-balances in Britain's system lies between the P.M. and his colleagues as a group. This is the check that operated here. A sensible Prime Minister is scrupulous about the forms of collective action: overreaching risks rejection; a show of arbitrariness risks collegial reaction; if they should band together his associates could pull him down. Accordingly, the man who lives at Number 10 does well to avoid policy departures like the plague, unless, until, and if, he sees a reasonable prospect for obtaining that 'sense of the meeting'. He is not without resources to induce the prospect, and he is at liberty to ride events which suit his causes. But these things take time — and timing. A power-wise Prime Minister adjusts his pace accordingly. So Macmillan did in 1962.

Ministerial prerogatives are not the only source of stalemate or slow motion in this system. If members of a Cabinet were not also heads of great departments, then the leader of their party in the Commons and the country might be less inclined to honour their pretensions in the Government. A second, re-enforcing check-and-balance of the system lies between him and the senior civil servants. To quote again, from the same source:

> The P.M. has it easier with ministers than with the civil servants. The ranks of civil servants do not work for *him*. They have to be brought along. They are loyal to a 'Government Decision' but that takes the form of action in Cabinet, where the great machines are represented by their ministers.

The civil servants can be his allies, of course, if their perceptions of the public interest square with his; then all he needs to do is to bring ministers along. Something of this sort seems to have been a factor in the Labour Government's acceptance of Polaris: Foreign Office and Defence officials urged their masters on; Treasury officials remained neutral. The P.M. who first manages to tie the civil servants tighter to his office than to their own ministries will presidentialise the British system beyond anything our system knows. But that day is not yet. It may never come.

So a British Premier facing Cabinet is in somewhat the position of our President confronting the Executive Departments and Congress combined. Our man, compared to theirs, is freer to take initiatives and to announce them *in advance* of acquiescence from all sides. With us, indeed, initiatives in public are a step towards obtaining acquiescence, or at least towards wearing down the opposition. It is different in Downing Street. With us, also, the diplomatic and defence spheres yield our man authority for binding judgments on behalf of the whole government. Although he rarely gets unquestioning obedience and often pays a price, his personal choices are authoritative, for he himself is heir to royal prerogatives. In Britain these adhere to Cabinet members as a group, not to the Prime Minister alone. True, he can take over diplomacy, as Neville Chamberlain did so disastrously, and others since, or he can even run a war like Winston Churchill. But Chamberlain had to change Foreign Secretaries in the process, and Churchill took precautions, making himself Minister of Defence.

Still, despite all differences, a President, like a Prime Minister, lives daily under the constraint that he must bring along *his* 'colleagues' and get action from *their* liege-men at both ends of the Avenue. A sensible Prime Minister is always counting noses in Cabinet. A sensible President is always checking off his list of 'influentials'. The P.M. is not yet a President. The President, however, is a sort of super-Prime Minister. This is what comes of comparative inquiry.

## III

For over half a century, a great number of studious Americans have sought to fasten on our system, frankly imitating Britain, both a senior civil service drawn from career ranks and a Cabinet drawn from Congress. Meanwhile, without paying much attention to such formulations, our governmental practice has been building *ad hoc* counterparts. I have given two examples and could offer many more, but I hope these suffice to make the point.

The in-and-outers on whom we depend to do at presidential level what the Treasury-types of Whitehall do at Cabinet level deserve much more notice than they have so far received. They are a political phenomenon to study. They also are a political resource to nurture. Their care-and-feeding should concern our schools of public service not less but rather more than that of civil servants who remain in career ranks. (At least this is a proposition we shall test at Harvard with the new resources we are to obtain in memory of that notable recruiter, John F. Kennedy.)

As for our Cabinet-substitute, the shifting set of influentials, few things are more interesting in our system than the still inconclusive signs that we *may* now be on the verge of a new institutional breakthrough, a pragmatic innovation in our Constitution which might match those of the Roosevelt–Truman years. For White House staffing in the years of Kennedy and Johnson, combined with Johnson's tendency to use some senior Senators as though they were Executive advisers — these together, if sustained, could lay the basis for new patterns of relationship we someday would discover had become an institution. It is, of course, too soon to tell. Truman, in his early years, also leaned a lot on certain Senators. Eisenhower's staffing innovations mostly were a flash-in-the-pan. Influentials on the Hill are not yet tied into the presidential circle with anything like the firmness or the mutual satisfaction (relatively speaking) of the ties which bind their counterparts downtown. Perhaps they never will be. But if they ever are to be, the Johnson years appear a likely time.

These among others are the thoughts a look at Whitehall can suggest to a watcher of Washington — provided one is careful to distinguish form from function.

# THE PRIME MINISTER'S POWER

*By* George W. Jones

Personality bears the burden of much contemporary writing about the office of the Prime Minister. Yet this position has only recently been held by men as different in character as Sir Winston Churchill, Clement Attlee, Sir Alec Douglas-Home and Harold Wilson. Such men come and go in Downing Street; the institutional features of the office persist. George Jones's review of these characteristics provides an unemotional and detailed account of the constraints that operate upon the Prime Minister of the day, whatever his personal characteristics.

It has become part of the conventional wisdom expressed by some academics and journalists that the position of the Prime Minister in the British system of government has altered significantly in recent years. No longer, they assert, is he merely *primus inter pares* or just the leading member of the Cabinet, but he has been transformed into something quite new, perhaps a quasi-President, or an elected monarch or even an autocrat. The Prime Minister's predominance, attained by Churchill during the Second World War, is said to have persisted in peace-time during the administrations of Attlee, Churchill again, Eden, Macmillan, Douglas-Home and now Wilson. If this view is correct then Cabinet Government is a dignified façade behind which lurks the efficient secret of Prime Ministerial power.[1]

[1] R. W. K. Hinton, 'The Prime Minister as an Elected Monarch', *Parliamentary Affairs* (Summer 1960) pp. 297–303.

D. J. Heasman, 'The Prime Minister and the Cabinet', *Parliamentary Affairs* (Autumn 1962) pp. 461–84.

R. H. S. Crossman's Introduction to Walter Bagehot's *The English Constitution* (London: Fontana, 1964) pp. 51–7.

B. Crick, *The Reform of Parliament* (London: Weidenfeld & Nicolson, 1964) pp. 34–9.

J. P. Mackintosh, *The British Cabinet* (London: Stevens, 1962) is often quoted as supporting this argument, but the book contains serious inconsistencies, noted in D. N. Chester, 'Who Governs Britain?' *Parliamentary Affairs* (Autumn 1962) pp. 519–27. However, Mr Mackintosh clearly supports this argument in an I.T.V. broadcast on 10 Jan 1965 — 'Power in Britain'.

Reprinted in full from *Parliamentary Affairs*, xviii ii (1965) 167–85, by permission of A. D. Peters & Co.

It may not be possible to test the validity of these suppositions until the Cabinet papers are made available, fifty years after the events they refer to have taken place, and until the politicians and civil servants involved in the process have published their memoirs. But even with the scanty evidence at present before us, there are grounds to argue that the Prime Minister's power has been exaggerated and that the restraints on his ascendancy are as strong as ever, and in some ways even stronger. The aim of this paper is to consider the argument that the Prime Minister has become more powerful and to suggest some countervailing factors which seriously inhibit his freedom to initiate and manoeuvre.

The elevation of the Prime Minister is attributed to many trends. The extensions of the franchise, the growth of nation-wide mass parties and the development of the mass media of communications[2] are said to have changed the nature of a General Election. From a number of separate constituency contests it has become almost a plebiscite, a gladiatorial contest between the party leaders. On them are concentrated the efforts of the party propagandists and the attentions of the press, radio and television. Their words and nuances of expression are carefully analysed to expose their parties' policies, which they are supposed to embody. This personalisation of political issues and allegiances is said to be essential if most of the electors, who are not very politically conscious, are to be reached, interested and won over. They may not understand or follow debates about policies, but they appreciate a clash of personalities. The leaders appear to be the only significant contestants during the campaign; neither the calibre nor the personal views of the other candidates count for much more than 1,000 votes, since the electoral swing over the whole country or at least regionally at a General Election is fairly uniform. Candidates seem to attract or repel voters solely on the basis of which leaders they will support in the House of Commons.

Thus the only mandate given by the electorate to an MP is to

---

A. Sampson, *Anatomy of Britain* (London: Hodder & Stoughton, 1962) pp. 330–3.

P. Johnson, *New Statesman*, 14 Feb 1964.

P. Worsthorne in the *Sunday Telegraph* quoted by J. P. Mackintosh, op. cit. p. 437, and Professor M. Beloff (in the *Daily Telegraph*, 2 Aug 1960) quoted by Sampson, op. cit. p. 330.

[2] 'Radio and television bring him more frequently than any other politician into the homes of the people, who therefore see in his personality the embodiment of the party and, in times of emergency, the trustee of the national cause.' J. Harvey and A. Bather, *The British Constitution* (London: Macmillan, 1964) p. 224.

support his leader.[3] The Prime Minister therefore can be sure that his party in the Commons will back him. Obedience to the Prime Minister, however, rests not just on the commands of the electors. Some commentators claim that the Prime Minister's power to obtain a dissolution of Parliament from the Crown deters his supporters from rebellion, since they wish to avoid a costly and arduous election campaign which may jeopardise their seats.[4] Others stress that if MPs voted against their party in the House, their constituency parties would be likely not to readopt them as official candidates, and without party endorsement the former MPs would be defeated ignominiously, like Dr Donald Johnson at Carlisle in October 1964. Party loyalty, feelings of personal attachment to a group of colleagues and fear of letting the other party either damage the standing of his own party or even gain office, are additional pressures on an MP to follow his party's line.

The party policy which the MP has to follow is most likely the Prime Minister's policy, rather than a collective party policy which all members have helped to form. A Prime Minister, whether Conservative or Labour, effectively controls his party and is not restrained by it, despite the differences in the formal constitutions of the parties. The limitations which the Labour Party's constitution places upon its leader fall away when he becomes Prime Minister, and are superseded by the conventions of the British Constitution, which put into his hands the power to choose his colleagues and decide policy. The powers of a Conservative and a Labour Prime Minister are identical:[5] they have the freedom to choose whom they will to be members of their Governments. One appointment in particular is of special importance in sustaining the Prime Minister's sway over his Parliamentary colleagues, and that is the Chief Whip. As a Lord of the Treasury he is directly responsible to the Prime Minister for the performance of his duties. He lives at 12 Downing Street, close to the Prime Minister, with whom he can communicate unobtrusively whenever required. They have daily sessions together, called 'morning prayers', when they discuss the state of the Parliamentary party. The Chief Whip has to maintain discipline amongst its ranks, and he does this not just by bullying, but also by explaining and clarifying the Prime Minister's views to those who are anxious.

[3] W. G. Andrews in 'Three Electoral Colleges', *Parliamentary Affairs* (Spring 1961) describes a General Election as conferring imperative mandates for the designation of the Prime Minister (p. 182) and as 'an indirect way of voting for prime ministerial candidates' (pp. 184–5).

[4] Harvey and Bather, op. cit. p. 224.

[5] R. T. Mackenzie, *British Political Parties* (London: Heinemann, 2nd ed., 1963).

He also assists the Prime Minister to dispense a host of honours, awards, decorations, knighthoods and peerages, and of particular significance for the MPs, Government offices.[6] MPs are said now to have less scope to make reputations as mere backbenchers.[7] They want Government office, and the easiest way for them to earn this reward is to give loyal service to the Prime Minister and not to appear to him or the Chief Whip as nuisances. Criticism of the Prime Minister will bring his disfavour which will block future prospects of advancement. The importance of the power of patronage has increased as the number of Government offices has grown. Conservatives have recently attacked Harold Wilson for enabling more MPs to hold Government offices, on the grounds that he is reducing the independence of the legislature, by packing it with placemen dependent on the executive and his will.[8] Alarm has also been expressed that even Parliamentary Private Secretaries are being regarded as junior members of the Government, liable to lose their unpaid offices, if they oppose a Government decision.[9] Promotion seems to depend on knuckling under to the Prime Minister's decisions. Thus the loyalty of the MPs is cemented to the Prime Minister because the Chief Whip, who maintains discipline and helps to bestow patronage, is a personal agent of the Prime Minister, and because the amount of patronage at the Prime Minister's disposal has increased.

Through his control of his party the Prime Minister can be certain that the Commons will support his Government and accept his measures. His will becomes an Act of Parliament, for the House of Lords is no obstruction to Commons' decisions and the Queen's assent is automatic. The Courts, too, will not resist a statute. Parliamentary Sovereignty means Prime Ministerial Sovereignty. It does not mean Cabinet Sovereignty, because the Prime Minister is said to dominate his Cabinet through his power to appoint and dismiss its members, to control its operations and even to bypass it altogether by the use of Cabinet Committees and informal conversations with individual Ministers.

The Prime Minister's power of patronage is said to enable him to master his Cabinet. Able to hire and fire, to demote and promote and to allocate particular offices to whomever he pleases, he holds the political future of his colleagues in his hands. He can advance the

[6] P. G. Richards, *Patronage in British Government* (London: Allen & Unwin, 1963).

[7] Because of the declining public interest in Parliament and politics. Mackintosh, op. cit. p. 389.

[8] *Hansard*, vol. 702 (19 Nov 1964) cols 671–2 and vol. 703 (10 Dec 1964) cols 1839–42.

[9] *The Economist*, 27 May 1961.

careers of those he favours and check those he dislikes according to the positions he gives them, for some offer the chance to make a good reputation, while others can bring the holder little esteem. Thus a Minister who wants to climb is dependent on the Prime Minister, and the easiest way to earn his gratitude is to serve him loyally. Ministers are not usually keen to retire. Since the Cabinet consists of a fairly formal hierarchy of Ministers, resignation would take a man out of the queue for higher office. Few want to lose their places, so they stay, often consoling themselves and others with the thought that they can be more influential on future policy inside rather than outside the Cabinet. If they do resign, they will be asked to explain why, and if the reason is a disagreement over policy, then the Opposition is given an opportunity to damage the party, which injures even more the reputations of those who resigned. The Prime Minister is strengthened because of his Ministers' reluctance to resign. Even when some important Ministers do resign, the Prime Minister can remain secure and laugh the episode off as a little local difficulty. He can dismiss a large part of his Cabinet and still stay secure. The famous purge of 12 July 1962, when Harold Macmillan sacked one third of his Cabinet, made twenty-four Governmental changes in all and brought eleven back-benchers into the Government, is said to indicate the great power of the Prime Minister and the dependence of his colleagues on his whims. He creates and destroys his Cabinet at his pleasure. When he retires, so do all his colleagues; his successor has a free hand in forming his own administration.[10]

Once the Cabinet is chosen the Prime Minister is said to have a free hand in managing its operations. It meets in his house; its members wait outside the door of the Cabinet room until he is ready to start. He controls the agenda; his Ministers send their papers to the Cabinet office, whose Secretariat prepares the agenda, which the Prime Minister has to approve. He can therefore keep off the agenda anything he wishes, include what he wants and stop the circulation of any memoranda he objects to. No Minister, it is claimed, can get anything discussed at Cabinet which is not on the agenda. If he tries to raise such an item, the Prime Minister as Chairman can rule him out of order and even walk out, thus closing the meeting. During the proceedings he guides the discussion,

10 'The Prime Minister expresses his changes of mind and emphasis by changing his colleagues, they themselves being given scant opportunity to modify their own positions.' (Heasman, op. cit. p. 479.)

'The uncertainty among ministers resulting from frequent changes and dismissals consolidated his power.' (H. Daalder, *Cabinet Reform in Britain, 1914–1963* (Oxford: University Press, 1964) p. 125.

naturally along the lines he wants, and when he is ready, he can end the discussion with his summary and assessment of the sense of the meeting. He may have listened to the Cabinet's advice, but the last word is his. Since no votes are normally taken, it is hard for opposition to his views to crystallise, and it is rare for his decision to be challenged.

It is often claimed that the Prime Minister has scant concern for his Cabinet, whose approval of his decisions is a mere formality, or which he can side-step completely. Through informal talks with individual Ministers, who are more amenable alone than in Cabinet, he can infiltrate his views, influence and even reshape the Minister's proposals.[11] At his house, at Chequers, over meals, or through the network of private secretaries,[12] he can arrange with Ministers the main outlines of what they will present to the Cabinet. Policy will have been settled before the Cabinet stage. The Prime Minister can set up Cabinet Committees, chaired by himself or a trusted colleague, to watch over certain topics or certain Ministers. Here issues can be thrashed out in a thorough discussion and policy proposals agreed. Members of the Cabinet not in on these discussions find it very difficult to raise objections in Cabinet when these matters arise.[13] They lack knowledge about the problems involved; they would be unlikely to prevail and fear to make fools of themselves through their ill-informed contributions. The crucial policy decisions, it is said, are taken not in the Cabinet, but in inter-departmental Committees after consultation with the interests concerned, in Cabinet Committees, or in conversations between the Prime Minister and an individual Minister. This downgrading of the Cabinet is said to have been encouraged recently by some new methods introduced by Harold Wilson; working weekends at Chequers for the Ministers and officials concerned to discuss defence and economic policies, working dinners at 10 Downing Street for Vice-Chancellors and exporters, and the meetings between the Prime Minister and the heads of the aircraft industry. These developments show once again

[11] e.g. see Lord Hill of Luton, *Both Sides of the Hill* (London: Heinemann, 1964) pp. 236–7. Junior Ministers are said to have to give the Prime Minister reports on progress in their departments. (*New Statesman*, 23 Jan 1965.)

[12] Sampson describes this network as 'the bush-telegraph of Whitehall', op. cit. p. 334.

[13] When discussing Harold Macmillan's chairmanship of the Cabinet, Lord Hill of Luton said, 'If I have a criticism it is that, now and again, the Cabinet was consulted at too late a stage in the evolution of some important line of policy: he seemed to forget that many of us had not been present at the Cabinet committee concerned with the topic' (Lord Hill of Luton, op. cit. p. 235).

that the Prime Minister and not the Cabinet is the crucial element in the decision-making process.

Some commentators have said that an inner Cabinet has emerged, the efficient part, which really directs the formal Cabinet's activities. It is said to comprise the Prime Minister and a clique of his personal cronies. They take the important decisions and get them through the Cabinet or else avoid it. Churchill is said to have ruled in this manner; Attlee began the large-scale production of atomic weapons and Eden carried out his Suez policy by means of these techniques of government. The Cabinet as a whole and individual Ministers are kept very largely in ignorance; a Minister may find that a decision is taken concerning his own department without his being consulted. Thus the traditional concept of collective Cabinet responsibility applies no longer, or else applies in a new way. Ministers have the choice now if they disagree with the Prime Minister's decisions either of resigning or of accepting them. The concept of collective responsibility is used to muzzle the opponents of the Prime Minister in the Cabinet. The Cabinet has been transformed into a network of Committees and individuals, all subordinated to the Prime Minister who controls them. His personal policy is endorsed automatically as Cabinet policy.

The concept of individual Ministerial responsibility has also been transformed, since a Minister is said now to be the public relations man for his department and the errand boy for the Prime Minister. This change is supposed to have been revealed in 1962 by the Foreign Secretary (Lord Home) when he said in an interview. 'Every Cabinet Minister is in a sense the Prime Minister's agent — his assistant. There's no question about that. It is the Prime Minister's Cabinet, and he is the one person who is directly responsible to the Queen for what the Cabinet does.

'If the Cabinet discusses anything it is the Prime Minister who decides what the collective view of the Cabinet is. A Minister's job is to save the Prime Minister all the work he can. But no Minister could make a really important move without consulting the Prime Minister, and if the Prime Minister wanted to take a certain step the Cabinet Minister concerned would either have to agree, argue it out in Cabinet, or resign.'[14]

The Civil Service is also said to be dominated by the Prime Minister.[15] As Government has expanded its activities, there has

[14] *The Observer*, 16 Sept 1962.

[15] Crossman, op. cit. pp. 49–51, says that the Prime Minister is the 'apex not only of a highly centralised political machine, but also of an equally centralised and vastly more powerful administrative machine', and that in both 'loyalty has become the supreme virtue'.

been a growing need to centralise and co-ordinate the administration to ensure coherence of policy. Free of departmental entanglements the Prime Minister is able to survey the whole range of Government and to intervene where he likes. He is aided by the Cabinet office and his own private office, both of which act as his intelligence agencies. Through their work 10 Downing Street is said to be much better informed about the full spread of Government business than any other department, and this factor tends to set the Prime Minister apart from his colleagues. 'In the nervous system of Whitehall, the Prime Minister's office must be the ganglion.'[16] His control over the Civil Service is achieved also by his close links with the Treasury. The personnel of the Civil Service are managed by the Establishment Division of the Treasury, whose Joint Permanent Secretary, the Head of the Home Civil Service, is directly responsible to the Prime Minister in his capacity as First Lord of the Treasury. He is, therefore, able to decide which Civil Servants will hold the most important positions in the departments. This patronage is said to enable his will to prevail in Whitehall.

Thus the Prime Minister controls his party, Parliament, the Cabinet, and the Civil Service. But he can also control to a great extent the succession to his position. If he retires in mid-term, he is strongly placed to pass on his office to the man of his choice. This is somewhat easier for a Conservative than a Labour Prime Minister to do, since the Labour Party's constitution lays down that the MPs shall elect a new leader, while the Conservative Party uses certain processes of consultation, which allow the outgoing Prime Minister great scope to gain support for his favourite. It seems that Harold Macmillan's activities helped Sir Alec Douglas-Home to succeed him.[17] A Labour Prime Minister, however, can smooth the path of his choice and obstruct the course of another through his power to allocate Governmental offices. His candidate can be given a position from which to earn a good reputation, while the other can be landed with a difficult assignment unlikely to advance his career.

When the Prime Minister has finally to face the people at a General Election, he does not undergo a severe ordeal. He can decide when to appeal to the country within the statutory limit, and since opinion polls furnish him with a fairly accurate assessment of the likely result, he can pick a favourable time. For the actual campaign he has many advantages over the Leader of the Opposition.

[16] Sampson, op. cit. p. 331.

[17] Iain Macleod, 'The Tory Leadership', *The Spectator*, 17 Jan 1964. R. S. Churchill, *The Fight for the Tory Leadership* (London: Heinemann, 1964) pp. 94–139.

Publicity is showered on him as Prime Minister, wrestling with the nation's problems and speaking for the whole country. He can be depicted as more constructive and less partisan than his apparently party-minded and carping opponent. He can turn his whole term of office into a permanent election campaign, using the manipulative techniques of the advertisers and public relations men to create for him a favourable image in the eyes of the gullible public. Prime Ministers have rarely lost elections in the twentieth century. Sir Alec almost won, and might have succeeded if he had been able to stay on longer.

The Prime Minister, therefore, is in a position of unrivalled predominance, and one ex-Prime Minister has been prepared to admit this himself. Lord Avon has said, 'A Prime Minister is still nominally *primus inter pares*, but in fact his authority is stronger than that. The right to choose his colleagues, to ask for a dissolution of Parliament and, if he is a Conservative, to appoint the Chairman of the party organisation, add up to a formidable total of power.'[18] So powerful has he become that one journalist has advocated that he should give regular press conferences to let 'a window into the Prime Minister's mind'.[19] Apparently he is the only individual who counts. His supremacy was shown in 1963 when the opening of the Commons session was delayed until Lord Home was made a commoner and an MP.

The arguments which have been outlined so far neglect many factors which restrain the Prime Minister in the exercise of his power. His actual position is not as predominant as has been presented.

Election studies and opinion poll data present no firm evidence for a categorical statement that people vote for or against party leaders.[20] What can be said is that voters are greatly influenced by the images they have in their minds of the parties, and the image is not composed just of the leader but it is a compound, whose main component is the record and achievement of the party when it was in Government. The overall performance of the Government and not the activity of the Leader shapes the image of the party. Other less significant elements of the image consist of the main figures of the party, their views and attitudes, the ways they behave to each other, the history of the party, its traditional and present

[18] Lord Avon, *The Memoirs of Sir Anthony Eden, Full Circle* (London: Cassell, 1960) p. 269.

[19] P. Worsthorne, *Sunday Telegraph*, 5 May 1963.

[20] J. Blondel, *Voters, Parties and Leaders* (Harmondsworth: Pelican, 1963) pp. 81–4.

associations, its past and present policies and its broad ideals. These, however, are not as decisive as the conduct of the party when in office. This creates the impression of the party in the minds of most electors. Elections then are won or lost by Governments not by Oppositions, and not just by the leaders. If the role of the leaders were as important as some suggest, then it might be expected that the electoral swings in the constituencies where they stand would show significant variations from the regional and national swings. In fact no such divergencies can be shown. The leader is as much the prisoner of the image of his party as the other candidates. Although much of the propaganda of the parties concentrates on the leaders, there is no evidence that it is effective. Studies of the effects of television show that most people display a sturdy resistance to the blandishments of the manipulators. They seem to absorb from a programme only what fits in with their preconceived notions. Their previous attitudes are reinforced not overturned. The claims that advertisers and public relations men make for their techniques are exaggerated in the face of the dogged obstinacy of the public.[21]

If the leader is not the individual whom the electors vote for or against, then there is no mandate on the MPs to support their leaders.[22] Their obedience to their leader is not based on the wishes of the electorate, nor does it arise because of his ability to call for a dissolution when he likes. The cost of an election campaign is no burden to an MP, since his expenses are paid by his party. The campaign is not very arduous; for most MPs, a three weeks irritation at worst, while it is more arduous for the leader who is the leading campaigner, having to travel over the whole country. Since the bulk of Parliamentary seats, over two-thirds, are safe, few MPs worry that they will lose.[23] Thus dissolution is not a very realistic threat against potential or actual rebels. Indeed, the individual who has most to lose from a dissolution is the Prime Minister himself, who may lose his Government office, his prestige, power and high salary. Further, since he wants to win, he is hardly likely to enter an election campaign wielding the weapon of dissolution against his own party, for the Opposition will make much capital out of the splits within his party. If dissolution is the potent device some suggest, then there should be a tendency for rebels to sit for safe seats, immune from the changes of electoral fortune. But there is no cor-

[21] J. Trenaman and D. McQuail, *Television and the Political Image* (London: Methuen, 1961). A. H. Birch, *Representative and Responsible Government* (London: Allen & Unwin, 1964) pp. 171–88.

[22] On the 'mandate' see Birch, op. cit. pp. 114–30.

[23] C. O. Jones, 'Inter-Party Competition in Britain — 1950–1959', *Parliamentary Affairs* (Winter 1963–4) pp. 50–64.

relation between the tendency to rebel against the party leadership and the size of the MP's majority. Thus neither the actual use of nor the threat to use the power of dissolution are the means of enforcing discipline on MPs.[24] They are kept in line by their constituency parties who may not readopt them. But local parties do not penalise their members for all acts of rebellion. MPs can expect trouble from their local parties if they go against their Parliamentary party over a period of time by taking up a position close to that of the Opposition party. A revolt to the centre will arouse the anger of the local parties far more than a revolt to the extreme wing, farthest from the position of the Opposition.[25] A revolt therefore is not completely out of the question.

Parties are not the monoliths as depicted by some commentators. Neither inside nor outside Parliament are the parties tamely subservient to the will of the Prime Minister. They are riven with factions, divided over both short and long term policy objectives, the claims of various interests and local and regional issues.[26] More commonly in the Labour than in the Conservative Party the alignment over one topic persists for a whole range of others, so that more permanent cleavages exist in the Labour Party than in the Conservative.[27] The most important factions in both parties are those which coalesce around the main figures in the party. Each of the chief colleagues of the Prime Minister has a personal following which would prefer to see their man leader rather than the actual leader. There is no loyalty at the top because the Prime Minister's colleagues are his rivals, eager to replace him, and he is engaged in a constant battle to fend them off. Many attempts were made to displace Mr Attlee, but they collapsed because his prima donna rivals failed to unite around a successor.[28] Churchill, it seems, had to retire earlier than he wanted in order to please Sir Anthony Eden and his following.[29] Even before the Suez venture there were serious

[24] On the power of dissolution see W. G. Andrews, 'Some Thoughts on the Power of Dissolution', *Parliamentary Affairs* (1960) pp. 286–96.

[25] L. D. Epstein, 'British MPs and their Local Parties: The Suez Cases', *American Political Science Review* (June 1960) pp. 374–90.

[26] R. Rose, 'Parties, Factions and Tendencies in Britain', *Political Studies* (Feb 1964) pp. 33–46.

[27] S. E. Finer, H. B. Berrington and D. J. Bartholomew, *Backbench Opinion in the House of Commons, 1955–59* (Oxford: Pergamon, 1961).

[28] L. Hunter, *The Road to Brighton Pier* (London: Arthur Barker, 1959) and H. Dalton, *High Tide and After* (London: Frederick Muller, 1962).

[29] McKenzie, op. cit. p. 581, especially n. 2. R. S. Churchill, *The Rise and Fall of Sir Anthony Eden* (London: MacGibbon & Kee, 1959) p. 192. Lord Dalton in an obituary of Sir Winston Churchill said that ' his younger colleagues pushed him overboard' (*New Statesman*, 29 Jan 1965).

rumblings against Eden, and if he had not retired through ill-health after the Suez affair, it is most likely that he would have been forced out.[30] Mr Macmillan had to fight hard to remain leader, and but for his operation he too might have been forced out. Sir Alec Douglas-Home became Prime Minister not because Mr Macmillan or the Queen chose him but because his chief rivals tolerated him and led no revolt against him. It is significant that the Queen asked him at first only to try to form an administration. He kissed hands as Prime Minister twenty-four hours later. These were the crucial hours when he sought to win over Butler, Maudling and Hogg; it was during those hours that he was chosen as Prime Minister, by his colleagues. Today Harold Wilson is not secure; George Brown's reputation has risen considerably. Some commentators detect opposition to Wilson from within his own party. He has been described as tending 'to look more and more like a Labour Foreign Secretary, with Mr Brown as Prime Minister'.[31] The Prime Minister is only as strong as his colleagues let him be. Without their support he falls. To become and remain Prime Minister a man must work hard to retain the support of his main colleagues and not present them with an opportunity to remove him.

Television has enhanced the stature of the Prime Minister's rivals far more than his own standing. Gladstone and Disraeli, Asquith and Balfour, MacDonald and Baldwin were at the centre of the stage because of the office they held; their colleagues did not have the opportunities to display themselves to their party members and public which the colleagues of a post-war Prime Minister have. Today television brings into almost every home not just the Prime Minister, who cannot be on the screen all the time, but also the major Ministers, his chief colleagues. They have the chance to win, consolidate and encourage a personal following, which their pre-war counterparts never had. They have been strengthened in their relations *vis-à-vis* the Prime Minister. Thus the significance of the development of television is not that it has elevated the Prime Minister but that it has contributed to undermining his position. Maudling, Heath, Macleod, Brown and Callaghan are the men who have been helped by television. Even if the Prime Minister does receive considerable attention from television, it is not necessarily a one-sided blessing. Much depends on his telegenic qualities. Sir Alec

[30] McKenzie, op. cit. pp. 582–6. R. S. Churchill, *Rise and Fall*, p. 309. Lord Hill said that Eden was made a scapegoat for Suez (op. cit. p. 179).

[31] *The Spectator*, 8 Jan 1965. A *Times* leader noted that 'the word is going round that he [Mr Wilson] has not got a good backbone' (19 Jan 1965).

Douglas-Home seemed to think that exposure together with Mr Wilson would not help his cause in the 1964 election campaign. The standing of a Prime Minister can be damaged, if he gives a poor performance, and a skilful interviewer may make him seem very foolish. Thus the case that the Prime Minister has been strengthened by television is not proven.

The Prime Minister if he is to remain in office must carry his leading rivals with him. He might withstand a backbench revolt with their support, but if a backbench revolt found a spokesman of leadership calibre, who could win the backing of his other colleagues, then the Prime Minister would be in a very insecure position. To avoid this fate he must woo and coax his colleagues and party to support him and his policies. He is engaged in a continual dialogue with his party both inside and outside Parliament. The Whips act as his eyes and ears, conveying to him through the Chief Whip the feelings of the Parliamentary party. The Chief Whip's job is to tell the Prime Minister what the MPs will not stand; he restrains the Prime Minister as much as the MPs; he mediates between the two, explaining each to the other. The Whips are responsible for knowing thoroughly the views of certain groups of MPs divided into the geographical areas of their constituencies and they also attend the specialist party Committees in the House. Whenever any policy or tendency of the leadership is found to be creating displeasure then the Whips inform the Prime Minister and try to effect a reconciliation. The Whips should not be regarded as the bullying agents of the Prime Minister.[32] By other means also he keeps in close touch with the feelings of his party, through individual trusted MPs, his private secretaries, his own personal contacts in the House, in its tea room, dining room, bar and corridors and through more formal meetings with back bench committees. It would be fatal for a Prime Minister to set himself apart from his Parliamentary party. It requires management. So too does the extra-Parliamentary party, especially the Labour Party which has less of a tradition of loyalty to the leadership than the Conservative Party. To keep the outside party conversant with the policy of the Parliamentarians, Ministers, since the Leyton by-election, are to explain their positions to area conferences of party members all over the country and a liaison Committee has been established to mediate between the Parlia-

[32] On the role of the Whips see 'The Commons in Action', and interview with M. Redmayne (*The Listener*, 19 Dec and 26 Dec 1963). Lord Hill said that 'A Chief Whip's job is to listen and to learn, to gather up the scraps of gossip, to assess other people's opinions. He is the Prime Minister's ears and eyes in the smoking room and the lobby' (op. cit. p. 242). See also *The Economist*, 15 July 1961.

mentary Labour Party and the National Executive Committee.[33] The leaders in Parliament recognise that the basis of their power would vanish if they alienated their party activists. Thus the Prime Minister is not the master of his party. Leaders can lose their parties' support and be toppled. They lead only with the sufferance and by the courtesy of their followers. A Prime Minister is only as strong as his party, and particularly his chief colleagues, lets him be.

The Prime Minister's power of patronage has been exaggerated as a means of keeping his supporters loyal. Careerists can argue with great force that the way to achieve top office is not to give loyal and silent service, but to build up a following, to gain a reputation of having expertise in a certain sphere and to make a nuisance of oneself. The Prime Minister will then be forced to give the man office to quieten down his attacks, to restrain his following and generally to keep the party contented. But once in Government office the man is not necessarily neutralised and muzzled. He will still maintain his following and keep open his informal contacts with them: indeed his stature amongst his faction may be enhanced by his performance in office. Thus he will be able to bring forceful pressure to bear on the Prime Minister whenever a policy is contemplated that he thinks undesirable. And if the opponent is a leading figure in the party with a significant following, the Prime Minister will be most reluctant to force the matter so far that he will be faced with a rebellion and resignation which will injure the reputation of his Government. The Prime Minister's power to offer office and promotion to backbenchers and Ministers is not a sure-proof device for obtaining their obedience to his wishes. He is seriously checked by his major colleagues who can rally other Ministerial and formidable backbench support against him. The MPs then are not mere 'lobby fodder' for the Prime Minister, nor is the House of Commons just a 'rubber stamp' or 'talking shop'. MPs can bring their views to the notice of the Prime Minister, individually or collectively, through discussion with the Whips, in the specialist Committees, and by approaching him themselves directly. Since he depends on their allegiance, he will try to accommodate his policies to their wishes.

The Prime Minister's influence over policy has been exaggerated. Government business has so increased and involves many technical and complex factors that no one man is able to survey the whole field. Policy initiatives come from many sources, not just from the Prime Minister, but from party policy, from the recommendations of Civil Servants who have worked out schemes with various interests often before the Prime Minister knows about them, from administra-

[33] *The Times*, 28 Jan 1965.

tive necessity, from the sheer pressure of events at home and abroad and from the demands of public opinion channelled upwards in various ways. The House of Commons itself is no negligible factor and even the Opposition is influential. On some issues the arguments of the Opposition may gain favour with the electorate and then the Government party, especially if an election is imminent, will take over some of the Opposition's suggestions as its own, so as to blunt the force of its attack. Before the last election the Labour Party frequently claimed that its policies had been filched by the Government. Debates in the House of Commons, therefore, are not a meaningless charade; they can help shape the Government's policy. The Prime Minister has also to take into account the views of his own party both in and outside the House. Through their specialist Committees MPs have opportunities for gaining expertise in the work of particular departments and can therefore keep significant checks on the policy of the Government. The coming of Independent Television indicates that a specialist Committee can even impose its policy eventually on a reluctant Cabinet.[34] Thus the Prime Minister is not necessarily able to initiate the policy he wants, nor shape policy as he desires. There are too many political pressures which he has to take account of.

A Prime Minister has a free hand constitutionally to form his own Cabinet, but politically he is limited. He has to include the leading figures in the Parliamentary party, and they may be so influential within the party and in the country that they may even dictate which office they will have. His Cabinet must represent a cross-section of opinion in the party and contain the main faction leaders. Harold Wilson before the election said that Sir Alec Douglas-Home's Cabinet was too large. It revealed, he said, the Prime Minister's weakness, because he had had to strike a large number of bargains. He promised to form a smaller Cabinet.[35] In fact it was exactly the same size, again evidence of the number of powerful figures and interests the Prime Minister had to conciliate. Moreover, the actual offices to which he allocated the individuals showed very few surprises and suggested that he had not had much freedom to manoeuvre. Most went to offices to which they had already staked a claim, as members of the Shadow Cabinet, as front-bench spokesmen, and because they had some expertise or interest in the subject.[36]

34 H. H. Wilson, *Pressure Group; the Campaign for Commercial Television* (London: Secker, 1961).

35 *Whitehall and Beyond* (London: B.B.C., 1964) p. 26.

36 R. M. Punnett, 'The Labour Shadow Cabinet, 1955–64', *Parliamentary Affairs* (Winter 1964/65) especially on p. 70 where he says, 'On the whole

Thus the Prime Minister has not a free hand in the choice of his colleagues or the allocation of their offices.

Nor has he a free hand in dismissing them. None of the Ministers who were dismissed or retired after disagreement with the Cabinet in the post-war years were men of sufficient standing in their parties to present a significant challenge to the Prime Ministers, with the exception perhaps of Aneurin Bevan. No Prime Minister threw out or forced the resignation of a man who had support enough to displace him.[37] Even in the July purge of 1962 no serious contender for the leadership was removed. The Prime Minister took good care to keep in the Cabinet his main rivals. His display of butchery illustrated further the limitations on his freedom of action. It did not enhance his position, rather it damaged an already fading reputation. He appeared to be making scapegoats of Ministers who had served him loyally and carried out policies he had agreed with. He seemed to be sacrificing them to save his own skin. His actions did not increase confidence in his powers of judgment or timing. He made enemies inside the Parliamentary Party and inside the Conservative Party outside Parliament. He did not increase the popularity of the Government. He undermined his own position by his purge.[38] The incident also illustrated the point that loyal service is not enough to bring a Minister promotion and to prevent dismissal. None of those axed had a reputation for being awkward or nuisances or opponents of the Prime Minister. They were removed because they were easy targets and appeared to have no significant following among the remaining leading Cabinet Ministers or the MPs generally. Thus the importance of the Prime Minister's powers of appointment and dismissal has been grossly overestimated, perhaps most of all by Harold Macmillan.

Although the proceedings of the Cabinet follow a formal protocol, the predominance of the Prime Minister suggested by the customs

---

there was very little change in the allocation of senior responsibilities in the transition from opposition to power, and the Ministerial duties are very largely based on the allocation of responsibilities that applied in the 1963–64 session.'

[37] Attlee never threw out Bevin, Cripps or Morrison.

[38] Even Crick points out (op. cit. p. 39) that by-election reverses continued; opposition in his own party was brought out into the lobbies when 70 backbenchers held a protest meeting against the dismissal of Selwyn Lloyd, and it led to the revolt of Oct 1963.

See also Lord Hill, op. cit. pp. 246–8, and Lord Kilmuir, *Political Adventure* (London: Weidenfeld & Nicolson, 1964) pp. 322–4; Reginald Bevins said that 'In July 1962 Harold Macmillan committed political suicide more certainly than if he had himself resigned' (*Sunday Express*, 17 Jan 1965).

of Cabinet etiquette has been exaggerated. His control over the agenda is not as absolute as has been presented. He may temporarily be able to keep off the agenda an item he dislikes, but he would be unable to prevent permanently a group or even one of his major colleagues from bringing up a matter they wished to discuss. If he did try to obstruct them, he would be acting senselessly, stirring up their opposition and encouraging them to rally support amongst the rest of the Cabinet and the MPs against him. It would be very foolish for a Prime Minister to storm out of a Cabinet meeting when one of his leading colleagues brought up an issue which the bulk of the Cabinet wished to discuss. To walk out on such an occasion would seriously damage his reputation in their eyes.[39] The actual drawing up of the agenda is not solely dictated by Prime Ministerial whim. Outside pressures are significant, from his colleagues, departments, the party in and out of Parliament, public opinion and events both domestic and external. Nor is he in command of the final verdict of the meeting. His summary and decision cannot go against the sense of the meeting. He cannot impose his own views on a reluctant session, especially if the chief figures in the Cabinet oppose him. He may see his ideas modified and even rejected in the give and take of discussion.[40] To carry on as leader, the Prime Minister must retain the confidence of his Cabinet, which means that he cannot dictate to it. Just because there is little evidence of revolts against the Prime Minister within the Cabinet, does not indicate that its members are tamely subservient to him. Most likely it shows that the final decisions are agreed ones, reached after discussion and compromise. Harmony implies not so much obedience to the Prime Minister's will as general agreement amongst the Cabinet members, including the Prime Minister.

The charge that the Prime Minister bypasses the Cabinet through conversations with individual Ministers, cronies, Cabinet Committees, and experts outside Government, loses sight of the important fact that any major decisions, which such meetings come to, have to pass through the Cabinet before they can be implemented. Any participant in such sessions with the Prime Minister, who objects to any decision, can get it discussed and decided at Cabinet level, and any member of the Cabinet can query any decision of such sessions,

[39] Enoch Powell said, 'A Minister clearly has a right to bring a matter to his colleagues if he wants to. The very nature of collective responsibility implies that if a man wants his colleagues' assent or advice he can have it' (*Whitehall and Beyond*, p. 59).

[40] Lord Hill said of Macmillan that 'if he found himself in a minority he accepted the fact with grace and humour' (Hill, op. cit. p. 235).

get a discussion started and a Cabinet decision taken.[41] The doctrine of collective responsibility is still meaningful. By it, Ministers are encouraged to take an interest in the work of other departments than their own. It is a myth that a Minister is so completely absorbed in the work of his own department that he neglects the other aspects of Government policy.[42] Ministers are still members of the House of Commons and members of their Party. They have to defend the whole range of Government policy and not just that of their department. Moreover, they are usually keen on promotion, and thus do not immerse themselves in a single subject to the exclusion of other topics.

It is only sensible for the Prime Minister to keep on specially close terms with his chief colleagues and major rivals. These are the men with most weight in the Cabinet; to square them would be the first stage in getting a policy through the Cabinet. This inner Cabinet has no formal structure, nor is it a collection of the Prime Minister's personal friends. He consults them not because he likes their company but because they are the most powerful men in his Government. This kind of grouping is quite different from those meetings which Churchill used to hold late at night with some cronies. These were his personal friends with whom he enjoyed discussing matters, using their ideas to stimulate and sharpen his own.[43] The chief men in his Cabinet were a different set. The former had not the real influence in Government which the latter had, who could block some of Churchill's own objectives.[44]

Harold Wilson's meetings with Ministers and officials to discuss particular topics are not innovations. Other Prime Ministers have had such meetings, and dinners with experts;[45] what is new is the publicity given to them. This is part of the technique of government, creating the impression that the Government is active.

The two instances always quoted to show the great scope of Prime Ministerial power, the decisions to produce atomic weapons and to

[41] Mr Wilson in the I.T.V. broadcast on 'Power in Britain' said that it was open to any member of the Cabinet to question any of the assumptions of the Cabinet Committees, and Ministerial meetings at Chequers which he said were like Cabinet Committees (10 Jan 1965). Also see *The Times*, 11 Jan 1965.

[42] See Enoch Powell's view on this point in *Whitehall and Beyond*, p. 58.

[43] Lord Kilmuir noted that Macmillan refused to have an inner Cabinet (op. cit. p. 309). Mackintosh, op. cit. p. 434. Lord Woolton points out in *The Memoirs of the Earl of Woolton* (London: Cassell, 1960) that this was not Government by cronies (pp. 377–8).

[44] Mackintosh, op. cit. p. 435, especially n. 2.

[45] Harold Wilson claimed to be returning to the practices of Attlee and Churchill. (*Whitehall and Beyond*, p. 26.)

carry out the Suez venture, have been presented in a very biased way. The decision to produce atomic weapons was taken after thorough discussion in the Defence Committee of the Cabinet; it was circulated in the Cabinet agenda, but not discussed in Cabinet because the decision was accepted by the Cabinet Ministers; the decision was also announced to Parliament, and again no discussion took place because at that time in 1948 there was no significant opposition to the manufacture by Britain of such weapons.[46] The Suez affair was not the personal policy of the Prime Minister. The policy was discussed and initiated in a Committee of the Cabinet, comprising the chief men in the Cabinet; the full Cabinet was kept informed about the Committee's decisions, and objections seem to have been raised by a few members; but clearly the majority of the Cabinet was behind the policy of the Committee.[47] Thus in neither case were these decisions taken solely by the Prime Minister. He had to carry with him his chief Colleagues and the majority of the Cabinet.

The standing of the individual Minister has not been so depressed as some have suggested. The quotation from Lord Home, as he then was, has been overrated. It may tell us something about his relations with the Prime Minister, but nothing about Harold Macmillan's relations with other Ministers. Some said that Lord Home was appointed Foreign Secretary because Macmillan wanted a man who would agree with him, performing much the same role as Selwyn Lloyd. In any case it has long been the custom for the Prime Minister to be virtually his own Foreign Minister. Only Austen Chamberlain and Ernest Bevin since 1919 were allowed a significant measure of independence by their Prime Ministers. The Foreign Office has often succumbed to Prime Ministerial intervention. Thus, since the relations between the Prime Minister and the Foreign Secretary are of a special character, any statement about their relations is not a general statement about the Prime Minister's relations with other Ministers. A more apt quotation by a Minister about Harold Macmillan's practices comes from Iain Macleod, 'Mr Macmillan set a new standard of competence in the business of forming, controlling and guiding a Cabinet. He knew how to delegate to individual Ministers and to leave them alone. It was because the whole Cabinet worked so well and so smoothly that people formed the impression of an absolute personal ascendancy, and the notion

[46] See the correspondence between R. H. S. Crossman and G. R. Strauss in *New Statesman*, 10, 17, 24, 31 May 1963, 7 June 1963, and in *Encounter*, June 1963 and Aug 1963.

[47] Mackintosh, op. cit. pp. 435–6. Lord Avon, op. cit. p. 432.

grew up that we were changing from a Cabinet to a Presidential system of Government. In fact the reverse was happening. Mr Macmillan by his skill, restored a great deal of vitality to the Cabinet as a body.'[48] And Sir Alec Douglas-Home in a later interview in the *Observer*, when he was Prime Minister, said, 'A good Prime Minister, once he had selected his Ministers and made it plain to them he was always accessible "for comment or advice", should interfere with their departmental business as little as possible.'[49] Harold Wilson has described the task of a Prime Minister as 'conducting an orchestra and not playing the instruments oneself'.[50] The only post-war Prime Minister who claimed that he was more than *primus inter pares* and acted as such by for example interfering and fussing with Ministers and their Departments was Sir Anthony Eden.[51] His activities did not gain him the support of his colleagues, and he can hardly be called one of the more successful Prime Ministers of Britain.

The Prime Minister is at a serious disadvantage with his colleagues. Unlike most of them he has no department to keep him informed and to brief him. He is not able to check the information flowing to him from the departments and their Ministers. Without alternative sources of information he cannot easily evaluate their advice.[52] He is especially weak in that he cannot involve himself in the 'germinating stage' of a policy,[53] when the Civil Servants and Ministers are mulling over some proposals. He is most likely brought

[48] *The Spectator*, 14 Feb 1964. Lord Kilmuir noted that 'Macmillan's approach to Cabinet business was businesslike and firm; all important issue [sic] would be dealt with by the Cabinet, to remove the very real possibility that some unconsidered independent action by a junior Minister might damage the Government as a whole' (Kilmuir, op. cit. p. 308).

[49] *The Observer*, 13 Sept 1964.

[50] In the I.T.V. broadcast 'Power in Britain', 10 Jan 1965 and in *The Times*, 25 Jan 1965. The Political Correspondent of the *New Statesman* said 'The Labour leadership is composed of a full (if at times discordant) orchestra, rather than a one-man band' (29 Jan 1965). Earlier he had claimed that Harold Wilson showed a readiness to delegate responsibility (*New Statesman*, 22 Jan 1965).

[51] Mackintosh, op. cit. p. 435. Dalton, op. cit. p. 20. Kilmuir points out that Eden annoyed Macmillan by interfering in his department (Kilmuir, op. cit. pp. 243–4), and that Macmillan interfered far less than Eden 'unless he judged that they [departmental matters] merited Cabinet consideration' (op. cit. p. 308).

[52] Because he is so weak in this respect there have been suggestions that he should have a department of his own, a Prime Minister's office. *The Economist*, 8 June 1963, or Lord Shawcross in *The Times*, 11 Oct 1963. *The Guardian*, 26 Feb 1964.

[53] Lord Bridges and Harold Wilson have noted the restraints on the Prime Minister's power because he was absent at the 'germinating stage'. (*Whitehall and Beyond*, pp. 68–9.)

in when discussions are completed, and opinions have solidified. His private office and Cabinet office are not comparable to the departments behind his Ministers, nor do they approach the large number and expertise of the advisers of the American President.[54] Harold Wilson, before becoming Prime Minister, expressed the view that the Prime Minister needed to be served by a briefing agency to ensure that he was as fully informed as a departmental Minister, and that the Prime Minister should come in on policy discussions at an early stage.[55] Harold Wilson's sessions at Chequers, which he claims are a return to the methods of Churchill and Attlee, are attempts to bring the Prime Minister into this early stage, and his attaching to the Cabinet office of certain academics and civil servants, economists, scientists and technologists in particular, is an attempt to provide himself with new sources of information and advice. He has not added them to his private office, which has remained very much the same as before, but to the Cabinet office. It is, however, not just the servant of the Prime Minister; it has a collective loyalty to the Cabinet and its prime function is to serve that body not a single man. Indeed Wilson's refusal to turn his private office into a strong central intelligence service for himself indicates some limits on his power. If he had done so he would have irritated his Ministers and civil servants.[56] To avoid their displeasure he had to strengthen the Cabinet office. But far from enhancing the position of the Prime Minister above his colleagues the Cabinet office has served to sustain the doctrine of collective responsibility, since it has been loyal to its function of serving the Cabinet as a whole.

Even if he had established a stronger private office, it is unlikely that it would have prevailed against older and larger departments. They have usually triumphed over small *ad hoc* teams of civil servants attached to new fangled Ministries with lofty aims and no traditional establishment. Non-departmental Ministers and Prime Ministers have had little success when fighting the entrenched departments, who remain impervious to take-over bids.[57] The civil service consists of a number of departments, each possessing a strong *esprit de corps*. It is not as centralised and monolithic as some have suggested and therefore not so easily amenable to Prime Ministerial control. His power over appointments is not such that he can put exactly whom he wants in any position he likes. He has to defer to

[54] R. Rose, *Politics in England* (London: Faber, 1965) p. 195. Sampson, op. cit. pp. 334–5. G. Smith, 'The political prisoner', *Sunday Times Colour Magazine*, 18 Sept 1963. Interview with Sir Alec Douglas-Home, *The Observer*, 13 Sept 1964. Interview with R. Neustadt, *Sunday Times*, 8 Nov 1964.

[55] *Whitehall and Beyond*, p. 26.

[56] Interview with R. Neustadt, op. cit.

[57] *The Economist*, 13 Aug 1960.

the advice of the Joint Permanent Secretary to the Treasury and the consensus amongst the top echelons of the civil service about who should fill the major posts. Even if a personal choice is put in charge, there is no guarantee that he will remain a loyal servant of the Prime Minister. He will most likely become the spokesman of his department's view, defending its interests against all comers.

It is hard for an individual Minister to know all that is going on in his own department, and therefore even harder for a Prime Minister to know all that is going on in the whole machine of Government. If on one item he does exert himself to influence the course of a decision, he will have to expend much energy and effort, and in so doing will naturally neglect other aspects of policy. If he does prevail in one area, he fails in others, because he cannot influence everything at once.[58]

The Prime Minister has no executive powers vested in him. To achieve anything he must work with and through his Ministers who have executive power vested in them.[59] These men have powerful and independent departments to brief them and possess significant followings in their party who hope to see their man one day leader. To become and remain Prime Minister a man must carry these major colleagues, who are his rivals, with him. He cannot dictate to them, but must co-operate, consult and negotiate with them and even at times defer to them. Cabinet Government and collective responsibility are not defunct notions. Shared responsibility is still meaningful, for a Prime Minister has to gain the support of the bulk of his Cabinet to carry out his policies. He has to persuade it and convince it that he is right. Its meetings do not merely follow his direction. Debate and conflict are frequent. It cannot be bypassed and he cannot be an autocrat. To attempt to become one presages his political suicide.

The Prime Minister is the leading figure in the Cabinet whose voice carries most weight. But he is not the all powerful individual which many have recently claimed him to be. His office has great potentialities, but the use made of them depends on many variables, the personality, temperament, and ability of the Prime Minister, what he wants to achieve and the methods he uses. It depends also on his colleagues, their personalities, temperaments and abilities, what they want to do and their methods. A Prime Minister who can carry his colleagues with him can be in a very powerful position, but he is only as strong as they let him be.

[58] Daalder, op. cit, p. 248.

[59] G. C. Moodie, *The Government of Great Britain* (London: Methuen, 1964) p. 85.

# THE IRREGULARS

*By* Samuel Brittan

Following the return of the Labour Government in 1964, efforts were made to introduce into the structure of British government the type of 'irregulars' or 'in-and-outers' whom Richard Neustadt regards as of special importance in the American executive. By customary standards, the number of new recruits to special posts around ministers was significant, although the absolute total could be counted in the dozens. The innovation in manning departments did not seem to produce a commensurate innovation in the form or content of policy-making. Samuel Brittan, himself an irregular recruit at this time, indicates that the failure lies partly in the role definitions of the irregulars, and partly in the institutionalised inertia of patterns of civil service–ministerial relationships.

It was often argued in the period before the 1964 election that ministers were too dependent on the regular civil service and that it would be beneficial to bring more outsiders into Whitehall. Like so many other innovations the introduction of 'irregulars' into the Government machine came under a cloud, as a result of the Labour Government's economic performance in its initial years of office. The case for introducing irregulars had largely been argued in terms of the economic mistakes of the previous Conservative governments. Yet judged, not merely by its own promises, but by any fair-minded criterion of efficient economic management, Labour's performance in 1964–7, makes that of its Conservative predecessors seem dazzling by comparison. After three years of office, it was clear that any belated change of course was more likely to be the result of external events, or of politicians or orthodox civil servants changing their minds, than of the activities of irregulars.

Those of us who believe that the injection of new men and ideas was, is, and always will be necessary to bring a breath of fresh air into Whitehall have therefore the obligation to shed any light we can on why the practical results in 1964–7 were so disappointing and draw a few lessons for the future. It would be a tragedy if the

---

This article was revised and expanded before the devaluation of November 1967 by the author from 'The Irregulars', *Crossbow*, x xxxvii (1966) 30–3.

economic-policy blunders after the 1964 and 1966 elections were to make people think that all was fine with the government machine as it had previously existed.

I must however warn at the outset that my own experience and knowledge are confined to the central economic departments — the Treasury, Department of Economic Affairs and some aspects of the work of the Bank of England, Board of Trade and Foreign Office. I have to omit from consideration extremely important departments such as Education, Defence, Health and even Technology. These spend much of the taxpayer's money and employ a large proportion of all civil servants; and their activities are highly relevant even to economic policy in its broadest sense, let alone other areas of Government.

Since a book of mine, *The Treasury Under The Tories*, has sometimes been cited as a source of the argument for bringing in 'irregulars', I may perhaps be forgiven for drawing attention to the subsidiary nature that this reform actually occupied in my own proposals. The final two pages stated:

> If we are to maintain a faster economic growth than in the past, we require not a reshuffle of desks and ministries, but a clear-cut economic decision. It needs to be accepted that the maximum expansion of real wealth (of which leisure is a part) is the main aim not of human life, nor necessarily of national policy as a whole, but certainly of *economic policy*.

The concluding paragraph of the book actually ran:

> If this new order of priorities is accepted, we shall somehow get the right institutions. But it is all too beguiling an error to suppose that some institutional trick can be an adequate substitute for the right policy decisions.

The suggested new order of priorities was not accepted, and in practice the sterling parity and 'orthodox' trade policies were put first — although for its two years of office the Government insisted that no choice was necessary. Given these two facts one would always have predicted a worse performance than in the past, however many irregulars were introduced.

My excuse for bringing in this personal aspect is that part of the reason why Labour did not fulfil its promise to get Britain moving again and instead introduced the biggest economic freeze that the country has ever seen is that the Party leaders spent too much time before the 1964 Election on questions, such as: 'Should we have a separate Economics Ministry?' 'Who will get which jobs?' and 'Who will report to whom?' and not nearly enough on questions of substance.

## *The Case for Irregulars*

The 'irregular' official or adviser, who has been a feature of the Whitehall scene under Labour is not the same thing as the traditional 'temporary'. Many years before 1964 there were temporary civil servants in the professional grades, recruited for specific purposes. The Economic Section of the Treasury, for example, was for long recruited on this basis. The basic difference between the temporaries and the 'irregulars' is that ministers are much more involved in the appointment of irregulars than of temporaries. The 'irregular' does not owe his appointment to the civil service machine, and his place in the hierarchy is less closely defined. He ought therefore to be in a better position both to challenge accepted departmental attitudes at the vital stage before policy alternatives are presented to ministers and also help to alert the latter to the full range of choice. In practice the distinction is blurred at the edges. There are many people of whom it is quite impossible to say whether they are temporaries or irregulars, and one can think of permanent civil servants who have proved more independent-minded than some irregulars.

Moreover as time goes on former irregulars become established (technically or in spirit); while ministers as they come to know their career civil servants better, and as lines of policy become established, feel less need for outside contacts. Indeed one can generalise that irregulars are a phenomenon of new governments, or very occasionally of new ministers. (There were a few irregulars in and around the newly elected Conservative Government of 1951). This timing is a misfortune. For irregulars come in when they and their ministers both are very 'green'. They would be more useful several years later when ministers have become part of the machine and their ideas have dried up, but that is when they least feel the need for outside influences.

In stating the case for irregulars one should not overestimate the extent to which permanent civil servants are influenced by conscious views on policy. Like most other human beings permanent officials want to get to the top in their jobs and dislike avoidable complications and unpleasantness. They know they are judged not by their policy views, but by their ability to do a series of practical tasks, such as drafting reports on which committee-members can agree, chairing difficult meetings, and above all else in getting documents cleared quickly with all the many interested parties.

A surprising amount of time is spent at a high level in organising future meetings, recording discussions or arguing about which committees should take which papers. Moreover, much of the civil servant's work is neither administration nor policy, but providing briefs, setting out for ministers and senior officials previously agreed positions in innumerable different forms for innumerable different occasions.

Much of this work is far more high-grade than the description would suggest, and calls for considerable finesse. Nevertheless, it is hardly surprising that a flair for policy questions is only one of the qualities — and in itself neither sufficient nor necessary — required in a good civil servant. The sheer process of getting something out and agreed (or clearly disagreed) exerts a great pressure for orthodoxy and following precedent. The most valued man of all — as in other walks of life — is the one who can cope with a sudden flap.

The proliferation of new ministeries under Labour, so far from being an improvement, has in fact made committeemanship, appeasement and face-saving even more important than they were before. A limited degree of informality and frank conversation on a personal basis is possible within departments before papers and positions are formalised, which is much more difficult when the same men are separated by a departmental wall.

In principle, there are many opportunities for dissenting views to reach the top. But it is other-wordly to suppose that a civil servant of any ambition or common sense would want to acquire a reputation for being troublesome or unhelpful, as he would if he were deliberately insensitive to the way in which the powers-that-be wanted an issue to be handled. One must never forget that the same superior officials to whom younger men are supposed to be free to offer radical policy suggestions make regular reports on which their future careers depend. This is all human and inevitable, and only mentioned because it is sometimes denied.

One trouble is that officials at the top are too busy to think imaginatively about issues and are in fact dependent on policy papers originating in the middle or lower reaches of their departments. Yet all these lower officials are in practice bound by the over-all policy framework laid down from above. The net result is that major policies change very infrequently and slowly, and usually in response to, rather than in anticipation of, external disturbances.

One aspect of the Treasury, not often stressed, is the influence it has had on the careers of officials through its control of establishments, a fact which few civil servants forget. But even when the management of the civil service is hived off into a separate department, there will still be a central group of senior officials centring around the Treasury and the Cabinet Office, whom ambitious junior officials would be extremely unwise to alienate. At the very highest levels, ministers, too, have a say on promotion and appointments; and the same considerations of tact and caution apply. There is a limit to which one will want to rub a minister's face in an awkward truth unless one has a desire to end up in the Yemen — or its many equivalents in the Home Civil Service.

It is sometimes argued that these inevitable bureaucratic phenomena do not matter in practice. Conservative ministers, it is argued, frequently saw outsiders and were influenced by critical published comment. But this is neither here nor there. Even my own brief experience has confirmed how little chance such outside influences have of influencing policy in a *specific way.* It is really unthinkable that officials who have spent a long time hammering out a position, and have with the greatest difficulty agreed a line, first within and then between departments should suddenly start all over again because of an article in a Sunday paper, or a letter from an academic that has caught the attention of a minister. Outsiders, who have not seen the confidential minutes of all the meetings and do not know the stage which departmental thinking has reached, have not the slightest chance of winning any battle of memoranda against a minister's official advisers. They can only hope to make an impact if they are taken into a department as antibodies and participate in the real discussions where policy is made. (I believe that a number of established civil servants who were originally most opposed to the new recruits would now regard them as a stimulating influence). Those few occasions in which ministers have been influenced by a general climate of outside opinion which has not been argued out and accepted inside the official machine have not been fortunate precedents. One has only to think of the Macmillan Government's conversion to a 4 per cent rate of growth.

## *Reasons for Disappointment*

Why, in view of the theoretical strength of the case, have the practical results of recruiting irregulars been so disappointing? The main reason lies in the style of policy-making adopted by the incoming Labour Government in 1964. It very quickly acquired a reputation for rushed decisions, inadequate long-term strategy and an approach to policy resembling (and this is rather more than an analogy) the preparation of tomorrow's newspapers. It is unnecessary to look around for a Hungarian scapegoat, still less to blame the system of outside recruitment, when a Prime minister can say, as Mr Wilson did to the New York Economic Club in April, 1965: 'If an incoming government were at any time likely to consider devaluing the nation's currency, political considerations would have dictated doing it on that first day, when the fault would clearly and unequivocally lie with those who had charge of the nation's affairs for 13 years. So that decision once taken, was a decision for good.' This is an indefensible approach to a major decision of policy — as if it were possible to give a once-for-all answer to the question of whether the currency is overvalued in a few hours on the first day of a government. Equally alarming is the assumption, regarded as too elementary to require justification, that the timing of one of the most important decisions in a nation's economic history is to be decided exclusively by considerations of party tactics.

The above is not simply a criticism of the Government for refusing to devalue in 1964 or 1966. If the Prime Minister's mind was closed to argument on the exchange rate, and he was unwilling to risk effective trade controls, he should then have deflated right from the beginning instead of waiting until July 1966 and hitting the economy when it was already on the point of turning down, and after several confidence-sapping crises. Nor can this delay be cynically attributed to electoral motives. The shock of the July 1966 crisis well after the second election was genuine enough. Although practically all outside experts stressed the need for choice, the government could not rid itself of the belief that there was a 'third way' between devaluation and deflation. Even as late as the 1967 recession, the government still persisted in believing that a series of *ad hoc* industrial gestures could provide a substitute for economic policy.

In this kind of situation an enormous responsibility rests on the senior irregulars, as the one group that can speak out. For that reason it would be better if they did not have too strong a political commitment to the Government of the day — as distinct from a commitment to certain views, or a personal loyalty to a particular minister. Ideally too, they should be the sort of people who can live happily outside the governmental web, and are prepared to quit at the drop of a hat. It is unrealistic to ask for moral supermen; but it is not a good thing if irregular advisers attach more importance to keeping a particular government in power than to seeing their own professional policy views prevail. The doctrine that civil servants should not resign on policy may be applicable to permanent officials, although even here it becomes utterly immoral if carried to extremes. It has no place at all among irregulars; and it was sad that no one more senior followed the example of Mr Richard Pryke who resigned from a junior post in the Cabinet Office in July 1966, although there were several others who quietly went away.

Where many reformers, including the present writer, may have gone wrong in the past was in taking for granted that it would be desirable to strengthen the influence of politicians against officials. The day-to-day horizons and public relations obsessions of most ministers in any administration are no more worthy of reinforcement than the intellectual conservatism of most senior officials. Indeed in some ways the greatest criticism of conventional civil servants is that they let ministers get away with too much nonsense, and do not sufficiently push forward unpalatable points of view. Yet at the same time ministers are terribly in the hands of the civil servants for the analysis of problems, and the enumeration of practical policy alternatives. Such is the inwardness of the system that both these statements can be simultaneously true. Perhaps, at the root of it all is the view of the civil servant as a Court eunuch who has his own special kind of influence but must not presume to argue with his ministerial overlord on equal terms.

Two gold medals — one for patriotism and one for public administration — should be given to anyone who can devise a method for forcing on ministers' attention as forcefully and frankly as possible the real thought of civil servants and professional advisers at working level, irrespective of whether they are 'regulars' or 'irregulars'. Of course, differences of opinion, between departments, or between different sections of differentiated departments, may go up to ministers, but never dissension from below. The fact that the departmental or inter-departmental line put forward is itself influenced by ministers' known views or prejudices makes matters worse. For senior politicians are thereby often insulated from franker comments on their policy attitudes, whether by regular or irregular civil servants.

The insulating mechanism is strengthened by the fact that a large number of the briefs put up to ministers are not advice on matters of policy at all, but defensive briefs for use in speeches, meetings, negotiations, or even social occasions where ministers may expect to be questioned. The job of any civil servant, regular or irregular, in writing such briefs is, like that of a barrister, to put up the best case he can for his client, whether he believes it himself or not; with imagination it is possible to put up a good brief for almost any policy under the sun. The constant exposure of ministers to briefs of this kind encourages self-delusion, both on the strength of their case and the degree of expert support it commands. Perhaps all such briefs ought in future to have a one sentence postscript stating what the author really believes.

I sometimes think that if the Prime Minister and his senior colleagues could hear the lunchtime conversation in the execrable canteen on the fifth floor of the New Public Offices in Great George Street this would do far more good than any further administrative shake-up. Indeed, I often wonder whether it would not be a good idea to take a secret ballot on unmentionable subjects, such as devaluation was in 1964–7, among all government economists for the Prime Minister's benefit. Without some such device, there is no way of finding out what knowlegeable people really think and forcing it on ministers' attention.

### *The Difficulties of the Irregular*

Apart from the political style adopted by ministers in the years under discussion, there are secondary factors arising from the very nature of much civil service work which puts the irregular at a disadvantage.

The scarcest commodity in the civil service is information, and like all scarce commodities it is not freely exchanged. It is quite wrong to think that someone in another department (or even always in one's own) will give freely of his knowledge. Therefore those with the knack of finding out what is really going on are off to a head start; and these are usually the established professionals.

Despite their title, the administrative civil servants in the central policy-making departments such as the Treasury or the D.E.A. are not administrators and are not on the whole responsible for the detailed formulation or execution of policy. For this they are dependent on the men-on-the-ground in departments such as the Inland Revenue, Customs and Excise, Board of Trade or Ministry of National Insurance (or, in a different category, the Bank of England). The really successful policy-making civil servant is the one with the knack of getting these less glamorous departments to produce ideas of their own, or to envisage in outline schemes which fit the long-established administrative habits of these departments.

Such qualities may be regarded as aspects of the more obvious, but all-important, knack of knowing what buttons to press to make things happen in Whitehall. Clearly these qualities are by their nature more likely to be found among regular civil servants, and it is not surprising that the lists of new appointments suggested that the regulars were rapidly regaining the ground they lost in October 1964. The most effective of the original irregulars, Mr Robert Neild, left the Treasury in 1967 for a post in Sweden. Dr Thomas Balogh's deputy at the Cabinet Office, Mr Michael Stewart, took up in the same year a post in Kenya. Inside the Department of Economic Affairs, the Chief Industrial Adviser, Mr Fred Catherwood, who went to N.E.D.C., was not replaced at his old level, and in the course of 1966–7 there was a marked strengthening of the regular element, with few net additions to the economists or industrialists. The departure of Mr George Brown in 1966 marked one stage in the reduction of the D.E.A.'s influence on economic management. The one exception is the Board of Trade, where Mr Anthony Crosland appointed a personal economic advisor in 1967.

The assumption by Mr Harold Wilson of the overlordship of the D.E.A. in the late summer of 1967 might seem to mark a revival in its fortunes. Historians will search the official records in vain for any announcement of this take-over. Its only existence was in off-the-record guidance for lobby correspondents. A responsibility of so shadowy a kind can be gradually and quietly shed at any time. Most important was the loss of co-ordinating powers in external economic policy to the Board of Trade, and the appointment to the D.E.A. of a minister newly promoted to the Cabinet, whose seniority could not be compared with that of either Mr George Brown or Mr Michael Stewart.

As a result of the factors discussed above, irregulars inevitably run with leaden boots in any race against professionals. The Labour Government unnecessarily increased their handicap in the crucial months after 1964 by putting the vast majority of them in newly created departments outside the traditional centres of power. Most of the industrial advisers seconded from management positions went to the Department of Economic Affairs. Not a single one was taken into the Treasury. The same applies incidentally to the Foreign Office, which, even after Mr George Brown took over in 1966 was quite untainted with irregulars.

In *The Treasury under the Tories* I advocated a real Economics Ministry based on, and including, the economic and financial divisions of the Treasury. Contrary to what is sometimes supposed, I came out strongly against any split of responsibility for managing the economy between the Treasury and a separate D.E.A. The split has had a predictably unfortunate effect on the Treasury itself. It has given it encouragement to concentrate on the short-term and to revert at times to some of the attitudes characteristic of an old-fashioned Finance Ministry.

### *Untouched Defects*

For those who are interested in institutional reform, there is one further defect of the existing machinery of government which is never mentioned and had hardly been touched by the changes of 1964. It is remarkable how few are the departments primarily concerned to put forward the interests of *this* country, rather than those of our allies and trading partners.

Starting off as I do with a strong anti-nationalist bias, this is a complaint I am surprised to find myself making. But one is led to it by reflection on the great number of departments which approach economic problems primarily from the point of view of international negotiations. The Foreign Office has special responsibility for EFTA; the C.R.O. and Colonial Office for the Commonwealth; the Board of Trade for our general relations with our trading partners and for organisations such as GATT; the Treasury is concerned with international financial negotiations and institutions; and the D.E.A. had in its heyday a strong section concerned with overseas relations. This is all very necessary, worthy and proper, but there is a danger that the interests of the British economy suffer by default.

Finally, one of the main reasons why officials and advisers down the line can have so little effect on policy decision is the ridiculously exaggerated stress on secrecy that governs so much of British public life. To enforce this, the smallest possible number of civil servants, whether regular or irregular, are brought in on many of the really key decisions; and a large number of officials, whose own work might have had a useful contribution to make to the discussion, are presented with a *fait accompli* arrived at during high-level huddles.

The result of the obsession with security is to create an inquisition atmosphere throughout the civil service. Each spy story adds to the influence of the little men who search waste-paper baskets or the big men who ask 'When did you last speak to a journalist?' Peter Jenkins has alleged in *The Guardian* that whenever an outside writer happens to hit the mark — usually by putting two and two together — a leaks procedure is set in motion in which all officials with access to the information are interrogated directly or through their superiors.

In this situation it is much more important to keep one's advice confidential than to get it right. The secrecy aspect is perhaps more than anything else responsible for the monastic isolation often alleged of departments such as the Treasury. However many outsiders are brought in, it will not take long for them to acquire the same remoteness, if they are forbidden to discuss any of their ideas and plans with the outside world.

The ruling establishment, whether politicians or civil servants, will always have an interest in concealment, or rather in selective revelation, and the dice are loaded absurdly in their favour by the Official Secrets Act. The civil service may yield to prevailing fashion on the employment of irregulars, training methods or any other subject; but it will stand in the last ditch against any revelation of advice given to ministers.

This is all the more reason for waging battle in this direction. For no democrat can assume that either the analysis of officials or the ministerial reaction to it is so invariably inspired that it can never profit from informed and detailed outside scrutiny.

*Postscript*

The principle of having a few temporary ministerial advisers received the blessing of the Fulton Committee which reported on the Civil Service in 1968. Unfortunately, it will no longer be possible to use the expressive term 'irregulars', as the Committee suggested, with an irony which was probably conscious, that the practice should be put on a 'regular' basis. My feeling that any change of economic direction would be the result of external events, or of orthodox advisers changing their minds, was confirmed sooner than I expected by the circumstances leading up to the 1967 devaluation. One story going the rounds of Whitehall at the time was that when the Prime Minister eventually agreed to the Treasury's recommendation that the pound should be devalued he remarked, 'All right; but don't tell the economic advisers.' Perhaps the last word should be given to the anonymous Principal who told one of Fulton's researchers that 'without tackling such questions as the dogma of Ministerial Responsibility Parliamentary and Public Accountability', and 'the relationship between the Executive and Legislature', nothing very much would emerge from the Committee on the crucial issues. And so it proved.

*September 1968*

# THE WARTIME MACHINE

*by* D. N. Chester

In the course of two world wars. British governments have been drastically adapted to meet *ad hoc* challenges and to meet them successfully, judged by comparison with their enemies. The adaptability and success of government in wartime raises several questions: Is this a sign that normal peacetime arrangements are less adequate than wartime methods of governing the country? Are the unique problems of war amenable to solution more readily than peacetime problems, or in a different way? Does the tendency to agree upon war aims result in better co-ordination of activities and less dissipation of resources in internal conflict? British government in the period 1940–5 provides ideas useful in beginning to frame answers to such questions. D. N. Chester served during the Second World War as a member of the Secretariat of the War Cabinet; he draws upon this experience in formulating his account of British government in wartime.

The characteristics of the Whitehall machine which struck me most forcibly were: the great weight and vastness of the machine which on occasion almost amounted to an immovable object, if you were against it, but was an irresistible force if you were on its side; the tremendous power which lay in the hands of Ministers and in the hands of their nearest personal advisers; the heavy burden borne by a small number of people and their ability to act irrespective of the formal machinery through which they had to operate; and the remoteness of all the apparatus from most of everyday life and happenings except in so far as these could be translated into statistics or a general report. Let me say something of each in turn.

The Whitehall machine during the war consisted of some thirty departments, several of which had a staff of more than 30,000 and branches in many parts of the country. Some were conducting

---

Reprinted from *Lessons of the British War Economy*, ed. D. N. Chester (London: Cambridge University Press, 1951) pp. 19–33. For a long-term comparative analysis of British government in wartime, see Mancur Olson, Jr, *The Economics of the Wartime Shortage* (Durham, N. C.: Duke University Press, 1963).

operations in different parts of the world, others were dealing with many countries and keeping British policy in line with that agreed with those countries. The problem always was to get a policy decision which fitted into the total jig-saw puzzle. Few things affected only one department, most affected many departments and might even have to be cleared with other countries. At the top was a small War Cabinet which, however, confined itself to major issues of the war and foreign policy, and now and again some important issue on the home front, e.g. the introduction of a new rationing scheme. Under the War Cabinet there were at varying times a dozen or so ministerial and official committees and beyond these several hundred interdepartmental committees of varying degrees of importance mostly serviced by the departments concerned.

In so far as the decision required fitted readily into the current pattern and had no peculiar difficulties or newness the machine dealt with it efficiently and reasonably expeditiously. It dealt best with cases which could be decided in the light of general principles already laid down, especially if these were clear and well known. But great difficulties arose when a marked change in the situation or in attitude at the highest level required a revision and therefore a re-learning of the general principles. The machine would work best if it could be given one or two clear leads — such as everything must be done to economise refrigerated shipping space or drop-forgings or bricklayers. More usually the central criteria by which departments had to make their day-to-day decisions were much less exact, but vague rules — such as departments must get the most out of their available resources — would seldom have secured coherence in the action of different departments or facilitated the making of inter-departmental decisions.

It was never easy for such a vast machine to deal quickly and readily with small adjustments and slight shifts of emphasis. Some dramatic decision in clear quantitative terms — such as '1,000 additional heavy bombers are required by such and such a date' or 'The manufacture of tanks has been given the highest priority by a Prime Minister's directive' — could usually get a clear response from the machine. But the more one moved into the realms of a little more of this or of that or of securing a slightly freer attitude towards the use of a particular material, especially where such matters required an interdepartmental decision, the less perfectly the machine responded.

The general problem was really twofold — how to get clear, definite decisions out of the top committee machinery and how to keep everybody in touch with such decisions and any changes which took place in them. In certain fields the application of quantitative methods enabled quite precise decisions to be handed down, e.g. in respect of the allocation of manpower or of imports. But even here the difficulties were not altogether overcome, for within any departmental allocation there was often room for use of the allocation on several differing activities. Moreover, the situation might change dramatically or imperceptibly, and so make adherence to the existing allocation unwise, yet a fresh decision took time to make.

## *Communication*

Communication was the main problem here. By communication I mean not merely an awareness that such a decision had been taken, but also an understanding of the principles on which the department should act. There was also the need for an awareness of the current attitude of the key Ministers and of any tendencies towards a new attitude. The formal apparatus of communication was the minutes of committee meetings from the War Cabinet downwards; and in addition, when Mr Churchill was Prime Minister, a series of directives. But the most effective method was the close personal contact which existed between a comparatively small number of Ministers and civil servants — permanents and temporaries. From their daily attendance at this or that committee they took back to their departments the current attitude. By lunching, dining, even breakfasting together, during the long days worked during the war they not merely kept in touch with what was happening — and the situation was always changing — but also developed a corporate thought which was more effective than any series of minuted decisions. Indeed, I should imagine the war historians will have difficulty in tracing changes of policy merely from a study of Cabinet or Cabinet committee decisions: some such decisions were a dead letter very shortly after being made because the situation or atmosphere changed, yet no new decisions were formally put in their place. Indeed, formal committee decisions were perhaps among the least important of the devices of the central machine, save on purely statistical matters. Of primary importance was keeping all the top people in touch with the current situation — the facts of the military, economic and production situation and in particular with any important changes of emphasis — such as shipping is now tighter than dollars. In the phrase 'current situation' must be included any changes in the attitude of the Cabinet and of the few people who counted in the formulation of major decisions of policy — and the earlier such changes could be foreseen or forecast the better. Some of this was gossip or pure speculation, but from it all emerged important pointers to individual department policy. It might be only that X — a powerful Minister — was known to have expressed a view that a line of policy — say conscription of women — to which he had hitherto been opposed had become inevitable; or that at a meeting of Ministers held yesterday there was a clear view that something would have to be done quickly about a particular matter even though no formal decision was recorded; or that there was the likelihood of more steel or timber from this or that country. In the committee room, in corridors, over the phone, over a meal at the club, or in the many other ways of human contact, so the process of communication, of sifting, of formulation went on and from it emerged — sometimes clearly, sometimes rather muddled — the current attitude in Whitehall. It was this attitude which gave cohesion to the vast mass of daily departmental decisions.

Though this process worked reasonably well for the small number of top level and centrally placed people, it was obviously less effective as a device for keeping informed the lower levels of the administration in the many departments. Departments differed in their capacity to keep their large staffs in touch with changes in the situation or in policy. On matters which bore directly on the work of a particular Principal or Assistant Secretary in a department, the departmental machine usually worked all right; indeed, it was most likely that the official concerned would have been in the decision from the earliest stage. But in respect of general matters where the bearing on any particular job was indirect or less obvious it was not uncommon to find some officials completely unaware of the change, even some weeks later. Indeed, so vast was the machine that I suspect that in various comparatively minor fields of Government activity a policy continued to be followed long after it had been replaced by quite a different Government policy of general application. Sometimes the fault could have been avoided had the Permanent Secretary's office been able to circulate more widely the key documents; for example, some Cabinet committee minutes or papers. But even had they wished to do so they were unlikely to have sufficient copies to circulate widely and quickly, for it was the general policy on security and other grounds to restrict to a bare minimum the number of copies of Cabinet documents circulated to departments. Moreover, the reading of papers could take up a large part of one's day, however clever one became at picking out the essential bits, and though this may have been a worthwhile use of the time of a person whose main concern was with general policy its value was less apparent to the official dealing with a vast number of actual problems and indeed might be incompatible with his getting through his other work.

At various times the suggestion was made that some kind of official periodical should be circulated internally designed to keep a wide range of civil servants in touch with the economic situation,[1] the main lines of policy and the changes which might occur from time to time. The suggestion was not taken up, at least during the war years. It would have been an interesting and probably worthwhile experiment and might have gone a long way to speed up the process of communication and of securing a consistent policy at all levels. But it would not have been an easy undertaking and it certainly could not have removed the need for an efficient system of internal communication within departments or for those personal and informal explorations which I have described earlier.

One final point needs to be made on this important question of communication. The existence of a small group of economists who were closely in touch with the situation and with current lines of central policy and who had close contacts with the departments and with the main interdepartmental committees was undoubtedly an important element in securing the spread of information and ideas. Freed from the rigidities which come from rank and status and as yet untrammelled by the formalities of departmental procedure, they could act, sometimes most irregularly, in forging a closer link between central policy and departmental action. This rather roving commission was one of the most important continuous functions and one which again emphasised the importance of such a group being in close practical touch with the departments but not too formalised inside a department.

### *Positions of Power*

Notwithstanding the vastness of the machine and the many stages which might have to be gone through before a decision could be reached, it could be galvanized into sudden action or the course of policy dramatically changed by the actions of a comparatively small number of people. In the sphere of general economic policy there were probably twenty to fifty people in Whitehall who if their views coincided could do almost anything. In case this statement should give an exaggerated impression, perhaps I should add that most of these people were usually closely in touch with the views of other Ministers and officials, perhaps working more remotely from the

[1] The Economic Section prepared a survey of the economic situation from time to time which was circulated to Ministers and senior officials.

central machinery, and on occasion may have been the interpreters rather than the originators of policy. Nevertheless, in the final instance it was this very small group which really determined economic policy. Of primary importance in the group were the small number of Ministers who had to make final decisions on any matter of major or political importance. This was the last hurdle confronting all important matters, and whatever might be the power of officials or the cogency or otherwise of their advice, in the end the decision could be taken only by the Ministers (Ministers and officials do not, of course, ever mix so far as voting at a committee is concerned). Even the most powerful official committee could never give a decision which had the definiteness or finality of a committee of their Ministers.

It follows from this that among officials the most powerful, in the sense of influencing policy, were those who saw most of or had the confidence of a Minister. No Minister, however gifted, could examine and decide for himself the correct line to be taken on the hundreds of matters which come before him during the year. The most he could do would be to satisfy himself on a small number of major issues and for the rest see that he had the kind of advisers whom he could trust. Under this system, inevitable though it may be nowadays in view of the wide range and complexity of government functions, there is a tendency for all but the most able and energetic Ministers to become but mouthpieces of their advisers.

It might appear at first sight that the power of the officials concerned would be the greater the less capable their Minister. For he might rely on their advice for almost everything and so they would always get their own way. In actual practice, however, the reverse is usually the case. For the Minister who accepts readily and without question the advice of his officials is unlikely to be good at getting this advice through a hostile or critical committee. He may read his brief very well, but he is unlikely to be prepared for matters which come up unexpectedly and are not covered in the brief. Moreover, not having taken a personal part in the formation of the policy of his department he is less likely to fight tenaciously for it in committee. Whereas the powerful Minister who dominates the policy of his department raises the status of his immediate advisers, for he is likely to be the kind of Minister who gets his Ministerial colleagues to accept the views of his department, views to which he has made a major contribution. In the long run, and not very long either, no official however senior or however able can be in a stronger position in the interdepartmental struggle than would his Minister be if the struggle were taking place in a Ministerial committee.

When I entered the civil service I was inclined to believe the view sometimes expressed that power had now passed from Ministers to the permanent civil service. Experience showed this to be quite untrue — one had only to see the Ministry of Labour, for example, during Mr Bevin's period as Minister there and contrast it with the period before and after to appreciate the vast change a dynamic powerful Minister could make not merely in his department's policy, but in the power and prestige of his officials. The official with a strong Minister as his head goes to an official committee knowing that if the decision goes against him there he has every chance of winning it at the Ministerial level, whereas the official serving under a weak Minister knows that he is likely to lose the fight in the end. And officials know this of each other's position — the ups and downs caused by a change of Minister can be most striking.

Ventriloquist dummies never get very far or wield much power, nor do the officials who serve them. A strong Minister may, of course, be handicapped by a weak set of officials, for a major part of the interdepartmental discussion and agreement must necessarily be conducted at the official level. And, however able he may be, a Minister must rely a good deal on departmental advice. When you get a good Minister and a good Permanent Secretary working closely and enthusiastically together, as was the case at the Ministry of Agriculture during the war, then the department and the interests which it handles are very fortunate.

The position of those who were not part of the normal departmental machine but who were near one or more Ministers, as was, for example, the Economic Section, was powerful but sometimes delicate. The Economic Section normally worked to the Lord President of the Council, who from the beginning of 1941 onwards was in a strategic position so far as decisions affecting economic policy and the home front were concerned. Some departments, at least when they were in opposition to the advice they knew was being given by the Economic Section, felt that the position of the Section gave its members too much power. I think this criticism, which subsequently declined in volume, was partly due to the early inexperience of the members of the Section in handling interdepartmental matters. Usually issues come up to Ministers only at the end of a process of clearing at the official level. During this process misunderstandings are cleared out of the way, issues on which all are agreed are sorted out leaving for Ministerial consideration those matters on which agreement cannot be reached at the lower level. At least, that is how it works when done properly. If, however, there is introduced into this tidy system a small group who without taking part in the earlier processes can at the final stage brief a Minister to raise issues not considered earlier or, if considered, dealt with or rejected, in these circumstances departments may justifiably get angry or complain. This is really another aspect of the back-room/front-room boys issue. If the academic economists are shut away from departmental discussions, but nevertheless are asked to brief a particular non-departmental Minister on matters coming before him there will always be exasperation. For if their views are good, departments will be annoyed that they had not had a chance to consider them earlier, whilst if their views are unsound or impracticable departments will be annoyed at having to deal with matters which had already or should have been cleared at an earlier stage. Here again the solution must lie in bringing in such a group into the discussions at the earliest stage; this would not exclude their disagreeing with the decisions reached at the official level or in briefing their Minister accordingly (a right enjoyed by any departmental official), but it would ensure that the views they expressed to their Minister were made in the light of all the previous discussions and that departments had clear notice of these views. This was actually how the Economic Section operated as it rapidly acquired experience during 1940–1 and, towards the end of the war, my impression is that it was well integrated into the normal Whitehall process.

### *Significance of Committee Structure*

At the top it is personal ability and power rather than any arrangement of offices or of committees which really matters. During the war there were from time to time discussions in the House and the Press about the structure of the Cabinet committees, and now and again the Government felt it necessary to give a list of the main committees and their functions. Much of this public discussion appeared to proceed on the assumption that committees could be discussed without regard to the character of their membership, and in particular, of their chairman. Yet time and time again committees which appeared well on paper and to the public, which had clear terms of reference and well-balanced membership, would splutter out after a short, uneasy and unfruitful life, whilst other committees would go from strength to strength. It was almost uncanny on occasion to see the rise and fall of particular committees, almost as though they had a life of their own. Some would start out with apparently rosy prospects, with a flourish of announcements, perhaps even with a public statement; they would have several regular meetings, minutes and papers would be circulated, and then even though the work for which they were originally set up still continued they would become less active, they would cease to meet, to all intents and purposes they were dead even though not formally wound up. Decisions in this field would still be taken, but probably in another committee or in the Cabinet, or might even be largely working understandings without any formal committee decision. Broadly speaking if the Ministers (and their advisers) who really held the power were in agreement, the precise committee machinery was of little importance: if they were not in agreement, then the committee would not work anyhow. There is, of course, much more in the arrangement of Cabinet committees than this, but I have purposely oversimplified the issue because in its final form it is so simplified. The committee structure of 1940–1 in the sphere of economic and production policy failed partly because it was too complicated, but mainly because it did not coincide with political and personal realities. Yet the establishment of a Shipping Committee in 1942, with limited terms of reference, by providing a formal forum and point of focus undoubtedly added something to Government efficiency.

## *Burden of Responsibility*

It follows from what I have been saying earlier that this small group of Ministers and officials carried a heavy burden not only of responsibility but also of sheer hard work. During the years with which I am concerned there was never a period in which events and policy stood still and those concerned with policy formation could take a breather and mark time. Even when the major decisions as regards military preparations and production of armaments had been made, indeed even before that, there started the pressure of preparations for the peace. All through 1944, for example, winning the war and planning the peace went hand in hand, and it was largely the same group of officials which was concerned in each. The preparation of a policy of full employment was going on and taking the time of Ministers and senior officials even before the invasion of Europe had started. There can hardly have been such a strenuous time in the history of British government.

Few of the issues which came up in those years were clear or the answers obvious. A good deal of the work was pioneering and involved new techniques of government, new attitudes of mind. So far as I can see there was no method whereby most of these major decisions could be made other than by the small group of Ministers and their immediate advisers. Sometimes the attempt was made to give important tasks to, say, a committee of Parliamentary Secretaries or of middle layer officials chosen by their departments to specialize in a particular aspect of their work, e.g. reconstruction studies. But while such experiments did sometimes lead to useful preparatory work being done, the results achieved were often thin and tentative. Such committees carried little weight, and the mere fact that leading Ministers and their senior officials were prepared to delegate consideration of these issues to them usually showed that the issues were not at that time considered of real importance. As soon as they became important the earlier committees vanished almost overnight and much of the work was done over again. Sometimes, however, committees of this kind, though not of first-class quality, might find themselves taking a major hand in policy because events had moved too rapidly or because departments had failed to appreciate the urgency of the subject.

There are, of course, devices for reducing the load of work on the small number of key Ministers and officials. But the fact remains that during the war there were so many decisions to be made, of such importance and affecting such a wide range of interests — in Whitehall and overseas — and the number of people in the position to make or capable of making such decisions was so limited that no devices other than an outright rejection of responsibility could have relieved these persons of a very heavy load. Only people of a strong physique could stand for long the strain involved; indeed, it is doubtful whether any ordinary human being could stand the strain for more than a few years without his health being impaired and his losing efficiency through sheer loss of staying power. Any government machine which continued at such a pace year after year could only maintain its initial vigour and freshness by replacing this small key group at regular intervals.

Whilst on this point I would like to mention the contrast which is usually made between the position of a departmental and of a non-departmental Minister. It is popular to assume that the former is heavily burdened with day-to-day work which exhausts him, whereas the latter is free to deal with a succession of problems which in some way or other is considered an easier task than running a department. My general impression is that the burden of the non-departmental Minister who is acting as chairman of various Cabinet committees can be much heavier than that of a Minister in charge of a department. It is the constant succession of widely differing issues which have to be understood and their details mastered which makes the task of the non-departmental Minister more heavy. Some departments were, of course, so large and covered such a wide range of activities as to put their Ministers in the category I have just described. But a departmental Minister has a large and well-established staff under him, whereas the non-departmental Minister is usually given but meagre assistance. The departmental Minister can without appearing to be lazy or irresponsible confine his attention to matters of immediate concern to his department, whereas the non-departmental Minister must concern himself with matters covering a wide range of departments. If the Lord President had to deal with a problem during the war one could be certain that it was both important and difficult — when things were going well he was not brought in. Finally, the non-departmental Minister is always in danger of being in a lonely or delicate position in the committee. The departmental Minister speaks with the authority and experience of his department behind him; unless his views directly affect other departments the Ministers concerned may not be greatly interested or may confine themselves to their own departmental viewpoints. Or on occasion there may be a strong conflict of interests between Ministers. The non-departmental Minister acting as chairman is faced with the difficult problems of achieving results without estranging personal relations and of influencing departmental policy without taking responsibility out of the hands of the departmental Minister. And for all this hard and difficult work he gets little or no direct Parliamentary credit. It can be done, but only by a Minister whose authority and standing are not open to question, who has a great capacity for mastering a series of problems and who has the services of a small but qualified staff. Sir John Anderson during his period as Lord President of the Council raised the position of the non-departmental Minister and Cabinet committee chairman to a remarkably high level — but then he had a unique combination of qualities for the task.

### *Danger of Remoteness*

My final point concerns the remoteness of all this policy-making machinery from the everyday life of the people and therefore from the effects of many of its decisions. It is only necessary to recall the kind of life led by most of those concerned to appreciate this point. If one includes lunch-time, as lunch was usually consumed while talking shop, most of the senior Ministers and officials spent at least ten to twelve hours a day in Whitehall and would frequently take home a bag of papers to read in the evening or during the week-end. Many slept in or near their office for many of the war years. But even without these rather exceptional circumstances the life of Ministers and particularly of senior civil servants is hardly characteristic of the lives of the people their decisions affect. Seldom are they dealing with the persons actually affected, almost inevitably their decisions are based on memoranda and statistics, on impersonal rather than on personal factors. They read official minutes and memoranda, reports of committees, *Hansard* and *The Times* and probably *The Economist* and anything in the main national dailies which deals with Government policy. The people they deal with in other occupations are usually national leaders or the secretaries of national organisations having their headquarters in London, people equally in danger of being remote from what is actually happening in areas away from London.

In such surroundings there is always a danger of a lack of reality. What can come to be important, if one is not careful, is not how decisions affect people, but how they are thought to operate by people in the Whitehall circle. The leader or letter in *The Times* or *Economist* can become the reality by which one's actions are judged. Quite small snippets of technical or local knowledge can pass for expertness. The important thing is not to offend against the conception of events and action which is accepted as real by one's colleagues. This, of course, is an exaggeration, but there is sufficient truth in it to be disquieting.

Any occupation has its own little world and set of values. An Oxford college, a mining village, the City — all have accepted modes of thought, taboos and customs — sometimes harmless, sometimes dangerous, but all making it difficult to accept new ideas. If the wartime process were reversed and permanent civil servants found themselves temporary academics or stockbrokers, no doubt they would be aghast at many things they found and their fresh outlook would undoubtedly have a good influence on the institutions they entered. But it is doubtful whether in any of these institutions they would find any great gulf between their decisions and the immediate personal consequences. As college tutors, for example, they could not but be quickly aware of the effect of changes in teaching methods, curricula, and frequency of examinations, etc., on their own lives, or on the lives of their immediate colleagues and pupils.

A similar personal impact is, of course, experienced by those responsible for many government decisions. Ministers and civil servants cannot but be painfully aware of the effect of raising the rate of income tax. I well remember one Minister coming in on a Monday morning burning with his wife's indignation at the high price of lettuces and greengroceries generally and writing a most powerful

Cabinet paper in consequence. And once when discussing the question of a joint sweets-tobacco rationing scheme I remember watching the look of doubt grow on the face of a senior official when he was told what the weekly tobacco ration would be under the proposed scheme — to me, a non-smoker, it seemed a very satisfactory amount, but for him, a heavy smoker, it was well below normal consumption. But, mercifully so in many respects, most of the major decisions could be made in an impersonal, dispassionate manner and there was seldom any apparent clash between the decision taken and personal feelings or experience. Many decisions of Government are only possible if made in the most impersonal way: decisions to call up men in particular occupations, to curtail production in particular industries or to requisition certain properties are not taken lightheartedly, but they would be less easy to make, and infinitely more painful if the Ministers and officials concerned knew the personal circumstances of all the people who would be affected or were they themselves directly affected. Statistics are the great help here, statistics of manpower, of production, etc., which can be discussed and used as a basis for a decision in the most impersonal way. So impersonal, for example, that a decision to call up, say, an extra half-million men can appear as a change in a few figures in the manpower budget; as a transfer between columns on a piece of paper. Here again there is exaggeration, but again it is sufficiently near the truth to be rather frightening.

### *Some Implications*

This analysis has, I suggest, three implications for central government machinery. First, it stresses the importance of departments in the policy-making process as against the tendency in some theoretical discussions to treat departments as being mainly there to carry out decisions made by some super central body of Ministers and officials. Even in a department most decisions have to be impersonal, but at least the officials in the department do come into direct touch with many of the immediate results. To a department such as the Ministry of Labour, for example, with its exchanges spread over the whole country, its regional staffs, and its many headquarters links with employers and trade unionists, the manpower figures are not just statistics; they represent people with whom the staff are in daily contact, to whom they have to explain things, and whom they must satisfy and live with. The tendency in recent years has been to shift power away from those parts of the government machine in direct touch with affairs. The growth of central planning machinery, with its emphasis on statistics and overall decisions, has weakened the sovereignty of the individual departments and within the departments has probably opened up a gulf between those officials who spend their time dealing with the central allocations and plans and the officials who are actually administering the decisions in the field. This is an important problem in the machinery of economic planning. There are some who have stressed the merits of a central planning body situated in the Cabinet offices, or in the Treasury, a department almost equally remote from the public. Such people usually tend to regard the departments as being mere executives, carriers-out of a policy dictated by this centrally placed body. During the war the emphasis shifted from time to time. During the second half of 1940, for example, the arrangements were undoubtedly based on the idea of central policy direction, but Sir John Anderson as Lord President had a very sure sense of the importance of bringing departments fully into all policy decisions and yet at the same time he was able to make effective use of Cabinet committees. His emphasis on departments in the planning process was, I feel sure, due to his appreciation of the facts that economic policy decisions which did not make the fullest use of departmental experience would be unrealistic and, in any case, decisions taken without the clearly expressed support of the department which had to administer them might well be ineffective.

Second, there is the danger that the heavy burden carried by most Ministers is likely to reduce their value as interpreters of public opinion. Senior Ministers have to do a very large amount of reading of papers and memoranda and attend very many committees, and certainly during the war there was a danger that so far as their contact with politics and the man in the street was concerned they would be in very little different position from their official advisers. This is particularly the danger with the non-departmental Minister with a heavy load as chairman or member of Cabinet committees. The departmental Minister is brought into close contact with the day-to-day affairs of his department. He has a large correspondence with MPs and he meets numerous delegations. The non-departmental Minister, however, has none of these aids, and therefore unless he spends a deal of his time in the House of Commons, or makes a special effort to keep himself in touch with what is happening up and down the country he may well become but a super civil servant. This is the danger in the Prime Minister ceasing to be Leader of the House of Commons, however desirable such a development may be in allowing him to concentrate on guiding policy and major issues of political difficulty.

Third, it is now clear, looking back, that one of the great benefits which the academic and business temporaries brought to the Government service during the war was a fresh outlook. Had the Government, for example, started the war with a body of economic advisers who had been in their service for, say, ten or more years, it is doubtful whether such a body would have been anything like as useful. The temporary recruitment was due to the accident of war, yet can it be doubted that this new blood would have benefited the service even had there been no war? I think it is also true that by the end of 1945 the temporaries were beginning to lose their value in this respect; their earlier experiences had become heavily overladen with their civil service experience and they were in danger of losing their different outlook.

# POLICY-MAKING AND THE POLICY-MAKERS

*By* F. M. G. Willson

The character of policy-making in Britain can only be very crudely approximated by a simple, abstract model involving voters and elected office-holders, or by a multi-volume study of administrative history. One must have some general theoretical structure to give meaning to details, yet the abstractions cannot be so high-level that particularly important individuals or institutions are lost from sight. F. M. G. Willson's article is appropriate as a conclusion to this reader, for it places specific details within the context of a general framework of government which gives ample attention to the importance of the roles of individuals, as well as to the weight of the system that the individuals are trying to work.

In this paper an attempt is made to answer three questions:

(1) Who are the people concerned in the making of policy? This is broken down into two sections dealing with politicians and officials respectively.

(2) What are the organisation and procedures of the Government at the policy-making levels? The answer to this covers departments, the inter-departmental co-ordinating mechanism and the position of the Treasury, and the Cabinet and its committees.

(3) How are the policy-makers influenced, what is their place in a more general setting, and what is the relative importance of the politician and the official?

## I Personnel

### (*a*) *Politicians*

At any one time there are about 100 politicians holding offices of ministerial or quasi-ministerial character. They fall into several categories, and one group of about a dozen — the Government Whips in Parliament — can be excluded from the policy-making fraternity, though the advice of the Chief Whip, who holds the post of Parliamentary Secretary to the Treasury, might on occasion be

Reprinted from a previously unpublished paper, delivered to an Anglo-French study-group conference at Nuffield College, Oxford, 23–5 Oct 1959.

crucial to a policy decision. The remaining categories, in order of importance, are:

(i) *Full Ministers*, which includes

(*x*) Heads of the 20–5 major departments;

(*y*) The holders of certain non-departmental posts — including the Premiership — who may have 'roving commissions'; or may be entrusted with some special job involving the work of several departments (e.g. the Free Trade Area negotiations are the business of the Paymaster General; or may be party managers. There are never more than four or five such ministers.

The Cabinet is drawn from the 25–30 ministers in (*x*) and (*y*), and nowadays rarely exceeds 18 or 19. Those outside the Cabinet receive cabinet papers; they are members of cabinet committees relating to their particular departmental interests, and may be called in to cabinet meetings when those interests are being discussed.

(ii) *The Law Officers* — two for England and Wales and two for Scotland, whose part in policy-making is largely restricted to the role of expert legal consultant. (No Law Officer has been a member of the Cabinet since 1928.)

(iii) *Junior Ministers*, attached to particular departments. There are two groups, the first being of considerably higher status than the second, though the boundary line between them is a little hard to draw.

(*o*) Ministers of State (at four departments) and the Financial and Economic Secretaries to the Treasury;

(*p*) Parliamentary Secretaries at all departments (though some have other names, such as the Assistant Postmaster General and the Civil Lord of the Admiralty.

At present (September 1959) there are 7 in (*o*) and 28 in (*p*). Some departments have large establishments of junior ministers. The Foreign Office has two Ministers of State and two Parliamentary Secretaries: the Scottish Office has one Minister of State and three Parliamentary Secretaries. Each department has at least one Parliamentary Secretary.

No junior minister has any responsibility to Parliament for actions of the department he is attached to: constitutionally he is merely the mouthpiece of his minister, and sometimes — though not in the majority of cases — he is a Member of the House to which his minister does not belong. In practice the role of the junior varies widely. In some departments, like the Scottish Office, the work is divided functionally between the Parliamentary Secretaries, who are thus drawn into the regular administrative routine. In departments where there is no such distribution of work the junior's activity and influence depend largely on the minister, who may be willing to delegate substantially or, at the other extreme, may allow the junior almost no discretion. In very general terms, the junior normally stands outside the hierarchy of a department: senior officials do not approach the Minister through the junior unless the latter has been clearly charged with responsibility for a particular subject by the minister. Moreover the junior minister is not superior to the Permanent Secretary of the department.

(iv) *Parliamentary Private Secretaries.* These are not ministers but are MPs (or, very occasionally, Peers) of the governing party who are attached to and chosen by ministers (and in a few cases by junior ministers) with the tacit approval of the Prime Minister and the party whips. The P.P.S. does not receive any salary other than that as an MP. He acts as a general channel of liaison between the minister and Members of both Houses. There are about 30 P.P.S.'s.

It it is accepted that, while individuals in all the categories may have no little influence — even if only as planters of seed — all the P.P.S.'s and probably half to two-thirds of the junior ministers are essentially trainees, then the politicians whose words carry real weight in the making of policy number no more than approximately forty. And of those, less than half have the final say in Cabinet and perhaps only five or six will exercise a pervasive influence on all major questions.

It is rare for this team of politician policy-makers to remain completely unchanged for more than a few months at a time. There is a regular turnover of members, but even those who stay for several years tend to change their jobs — often quite radically — after two or three years at the most. They are, of course, people who have grown up together within the fold of one political party, and have lived their adult lives in the atmosphere of Parliament and Government. They suffer from no institutional incompatibilities, and are used to the essential compromises of existence in the internal politics of parties whose range of interests and attitudes is enormous. Once in office they find themselves living the inevitable hand-to-mouth routine of men in positions of real power whose attention is absorbed for 95 per cent of the time by the problems of the present and the immediate future. This is not unduly difficult or unwelcome to the professional politician, whose character and aptitudes tend to be mercurial. But it means that he can only find an opportunity to discipline himself to long-term thinking when he is in opposition. He may arrive in office with certain ideas: they will have to last his tenure — he is unlikely to have any opportunity to think out new ones until he is in no position to carry them into immediate effect.

(*b*) *Officials*

The official policy-making fraternity is much more numerous. The Home Civil Service is divided up into the well-known general or Treasury classes — Administrative, Executive, Clerical, etc. — and into a large number of special departmental and technical classes. Only a handful of the most senior Executive Class officials and a sprinkling of people from the special departmental and technical classes come within the policy-making field, whereas all the Administrative Class with the exception of most of the lowest grade — really a Cadet Grade — of Assistant Principals, must be included. The order of seniority in the Administrative Class is as follows, from the top downwards:

Permanent Secretary.[1] He is in full charge of a department subject only to the minister, and is the latter's main adviser on policy and administration. In addition he is the Accounting Officer with full personal responsibility to Parliament, through the Public Accounts Committee of the House of Commons, for the manner in which money voted for the use of the department is spent.

Deputy Secretary.[1]
Under Secretary.[1]
Assistant Secretary
Principal.
Assistant Principal.

There are about 2,200 men and women in the Administrative Class above the rank of Assistant Principal. To them must be added an indeterminate stratum from the tops of the Foreign and Overseas Civil Services, some of the Executives, etc., mentioned above, and a small group of high-level advisers such as military officers, scientists and economists. In all, this gives a total of about 3,000 officials, but if only those who are in regular personal contact with ministers are counted, then the figure is nearer 300.

Like their much less numerous political counterparts, the policy-making officials, in all save a very small handful of cases, are members of a closed community. It is less true now than in former years that senior civil servants are bound together by social ties — birth,

[1] In departments headed by Secretaries of State (which does not indicate any real difference in status from other full ministers) the three top civil service ranks are called Permanent Under Secretary of State, Deputy Under Secretary of State and Assistant Under Secretary of State.

schooling, university, clubs, etc. — though there are still some signs of weight being given to these phenomena in Whitehall. But if the service is less socially homogeneous it is professionally more closely integrated. Whatever his origins, by the time a civil servant has risen to the policy-making levels he has been conditioned into professional conformity — a conformity based on the inherited patterns of behaviour of the Administrative Class. He is a 'generalist' as opposed to a 'specialist'; a man with an intellectual grasp disciplined and limited by several years spent in absorbing the 'rules of the game'; a man shrewd in judgement of the latent power of a politician and of the full political implications of a situation; a man sceptical of the enthusiasms of his masters — not only because of his official experience, but basically because by nature he is, as it were, politically 'unsexed'. In contemporary Britain there is little chance that a civil servant by temperament would even try, in choosing a career, to become a politician, and *vice versa.* Even so, there are regulations and traditions which restrict all the official policy-makers in the context of political activity. They cannot stand for Parliament nor hold office in a political party: they cannot speak in public on matters of political controversy nor write letters to the Press setting out views on party political matters: and they are forbidden to engage in canvassing on behalf of candidates for Parliament. They can, if they observe a code of discretion, take a limited part in local government and politics, but while there are no statistics to quote, the chance that even a handful take advantage of this opportunity is remote.

Above all, the policy-making civil servant is in a sense independent of and indifferent to the politician because his career is influenced only very marginally by the politician. It is not impossible that places at the heads of departments may be filled by men who are known and preferred by ministers of the day rather than by other civil servants of equal capacity who suffer from not being known and trusted by such ministers; or that lower down the hierarchy of a particular department good service and/or a degree of favouritism when a minister happens to stay a long time in one position might improve somewhat the immediate promotion prospects of a junior Administrative Class man. But the rapid turnover of ministers, the influence of the top Treasury officials in matters of filling the highest posts, and the relative difficulty that ministers would have in moving particular civil servants with them from department to department, all make the intervention of the politician neither particularly likely nor particularly sought after in this context. For in a group so conscious of its separate existence, so used to the concept of being in charge of its own promotion race, the perils of ministerial favour are obvious.

The exceptions to normal civil service rules and backgrounds are confined to a fairly small number of specialists who do not belong wholeheartedly to the sort of official society described above. Nonetheless a considerable proportion of them have been organically linked with certain departments for so long that the mixed personnel of those departments has been recognised as a special species of normality. The military experts, concentrated in the Ministry of Defence, the three Service Departments and the Ministry of Supply constitute the largest group — senior officers with 'staff' training behind them (training with an increasingly 'civil' element about it) seconded for periods of service alongside the civil servants. Legal, medical and most scientific advisers are established civil servants, though one or two eminent scientists are brought in from time to time on short-term appointments. Economic advice is tending to become similarly 'established', though especially during and for a few years after the Second World War there were a number of economists appointed at policy-making levels from the academic world. The Prime Minister's Public Relations Officer has normally been a journalist generally sympathetic to the politics of the government of the day, but it is not beyond the bounds of possibility that even this position may be absorbed eventually into the civil service — it is notable that one of the most 'political' jobs in the government, Secretary to the Government's Chief Whip — is now held as a civil service post!

In short, jobs at policy-making level outside the normal civil service hierarchy are almost all technical or specialist in character, and their holders are either already in some sort of public service (e.g. the Army) or are recruited at mature ages in line with their professional qualifications, not on political grounds, and may stay for a limited period (thus some Oxford economists have been released by the University for a maximum of two years) or be absorbed into new established positions. The nearest approach to outside 'lay political' advisers have been such innovations as Lloyd George's 'Garden Suburb' — short lived (1917–22) and deeply resented by the professional administrators — or the appearance of some *eminence grise* like Lord Cherwell during the Second World War, who was soon translated into impeccable constitutional respectability by being made a minister.

The policy-making centre of British government thus consists of a group at the most 3,500 strong, of whom only 100 are politicians or in any sense at all 'party political' appointees. These figures can be reduced to a nucleus of some 350, of whom not more than 50 — and probably nearer 30 — are 'party political'.

## II Organisation and Procedure

The great bulk of the policy-makers are members of the staffs of individual departments with operating responsibilities. A small percentage are grouped in the Treasury (which will be dealt with separately); in the Ministry of Defence, whose major function is the co-ordination and leadership of the other defence departments; and in the Cabinet Secretariat. The last named is in no sense a policy-making unit but is perhaps the most vital communications and secretarial organisation, on which the smooth working of policy-making and execution depends. It is staffed by Administrative Grade officials seconded from departments for short periods and is headed by the Joint Permanent Secretary to the Treasury and Head of the Home Civil Service who, in effect, is the highest official adviser to the Prime Minister and might be regarded as the latter's top personal staff officer. One or two senior ministers, as we have seen, may from time to time hold 'roving commissions', and each has a very small personal staff. There are thus two worlds to describe — the operating departments, how they work internally; and the system of co-ordination.

### (*a*) *The Departments*

While each of the major central departments has its own peculiar organisational characteristics, in our context they fall into two groups: those which are headed by single political officers — ministers — and those whose supreme direction is carried on by boards. This is a distinction in administrative practice rather than in constitutional form and procedure, though the two aspects are mixed in a rather confusing way. Constitutionally there is always one man who is 'responsible' to Parliament for the conduct of his department, and in the majority of cases he is also the person in whom the powers exercised by the department are vested by statute or prerogative. But four of the Defence departments are each headed by a board — the Defence Board for the Ministry of Defence, the Board of Admiralty for the Admiralty, the Army Council for the War Office, and the Air Council for the Air Ministry. Each of these bodies is a group comprising the minister as Chairman, his junior ministers (never more than two), the most senior officers of the Service, the Permanent Secretary of the Department, and, in the case of the Defence Board, a Chief Scientific Adviser. The Defence Board is a recent innovation and has no legal powers — those being vested in the Minister of Defence himself. But the three Service departments exercise powers vested in their collegiate leaderships, and the ministers have few or no powers vested in themselves in law. In practice, however, it is well understood that the minister could exercise an absolute veto by means of his power (if backed by the Cabinet) to dissolve the Board or Council should he be outvoted and to appoint more amenable members. In one civil department — the Post Office — the system of collegiate headship is also used, but here the constitutional position is more akin to the Ministry of Defence. The Post Office Board has no legal basis, and the powers it exercises are in fact the powers of the Postmaster General.[2]

There is no record of any crises caused by disagreements within any of these boards leading to their dismissal and replacement, and in any event the exact legal and constitutional position is of less concern as regards policy-making than the difference between this sort of organisation of authority and that found in all the other departments. For in a single-headed department the hierarchy is a simple pyramid with the minister at the apex and ever wider layers of officials below him. In the board or council type of department the organization chart shows a series of pyramids each headed by a member of the board. Thus in a single-headed department the Minister receives his official advice through one supreme official head of the department — the Permanent Secretary — and from any subordinates whom he may wish to consult: in a council-headed department the Minister is advised by eight or nine people all of whom have a very similar status and most of whom are the presiding heads of functional divisions of the department.[3] Moreover, in all such departments the board members are predominantly technical experts, whereas in a single-headed department even the most senior technical adviser, like the Chief Medical Officer at the Ministry of Health, is not on quite the same level as the Permanent Secretary, though he is guaranteed direct access to the minister.

No authoritative studies comparing the two sorts of department have been made, but it would seem to the lay observer that the processes of policy-making could be substantially different in the two types of organisation because of the different structural pattern and the different positions of the main participants *vis-à-vis* one another.

[2] In the later years of the First World War the Ministry of Munitions was organised on conciliar lines, as were the Ministries of Supply and of Aircraft Production in the Second World War. The present Ministry of Supply does not appear to use the council system.

[3] Even in conciliar departments the Permanent Secretary is the only official in a position to have an over-all view of the organisation.

Nonetheless, at the crucial point — the minister himself — the internal organisation of all departments is very similar, and this may modify some of the contrasts which might be expected from the wider institutional variations.

Whatever the department the minister has immediately around him a similar group of people. He has a Private Secretary who is invariably an Administrative Grade Civil Servant — usually a Principal, though sometimes an Assistant Secretary, and in the case of the most senior ministers even an Under Secretary — chosen from among the department's staff after consultation between the minister and the Permanent Secretary. There may be an Assistant Private Secretary, also a career civil servant, and in a highly technical department the minister may have in addition a 'technical' secretary — e.g. the Military Secretary to the Secretary of State for War. On the political side there is the Parliamentary Private Secretary. The minister also has his own retinue of civil service typists. The whole group comprises the minister's Private Office. Each junior minister has a similar though less liberal secretarial establishment, and only rarely has a P.P.S. The Permanent Secretary and the other chief officials each have their own civil service secretaries, also usually juniors in the Administrative Grade.

The nerve centres of a British department are these Private Offices of the minister, his junior minister(s) and his senior officials, which collect, collate, negotiate, smooth over, record and see executed the information and the decisions which flood into and from them. They form a superstructure — or perhaps a labyrinth — above the operating divisions, usually headed by Assistant Secretaries. The divisions are primarily concerned to carry on the routine work and to recognise and forecast difficulties and pressures which will need to be made matters of 'policy' and discussed and decided in the Private Offices.

### (*b*) *Co-ordination*

Perhaps the basic tenet of co-ordination in British government is that nobody should do anything unless he is certain that everyone else who is likely to be concerned, even remotely, has been first 'put in the picture'. To express this and extend it in rather pretentious terms, the cross-fertilisation of ideas is a built-in feature of the whole central administration. Whitehall is not fairly represented as a collection of pyramids, even if it is stressed that there is close contact between their apices. It is better thought of as a honeycomb, in which there is as constant a movement between cells horizontally as vertically — though it is important to note that horizontal movement between departments is always at similar levels — thus Assistant Secretaries deal with Assistant Secretaries and Senior Executive Officers with their counterparts, but Principals in one department do not deal with Under Secretaries in another department. And the inevitable concomitant of this close horizontal contact is the existence of innumerable inter-departmental committees, many of them working at the levels of the operating divisions. It is from these committees and from the divisions themselves that problems are pushed upwards for solution in principle to the world of the Private Offices, cabinet committees and the cabinet itself, and to which outline decisions return for translation into daily routine practice. But before coming to those higher strata, it is necessary to put in a word about the position of the Treasury.

The Treasury's unique status is due to its responsibility (subject only to the ability of its minister, the Chancellor of the Exchequer, to carry his case through Cabinet) for controlling departmental expenditure — a control which extends to the size, structure, pay, etc., of the civil service, and influences considerably the organisational efficiency of departments, and the general arrangement of the work of the entire central administration. Its importance in policy-making can be illustrated by one example — no policy proposal will be accepted for discussion by the Cabinet or a cabinet committee unless it has first been discussed with the Treasury. A high proportion of interdepartmental consultation involves the Treasury, therefore, and takes the form of a set of continuous dialogues between departmental officials and their opposite numbers in the Treasury. The proportion of policy-making officials in the Treasury is much greater than in any other department, and the intellectual calibre of the senior staff is unquestionably high.

Above the level of the operating divisions in the departments, therefore, we find the major decisions on policy made in negotiations involving the Private Offices of the relevant departments, parts of the Treasury and, topping all, the structure of cabinet committees — i.e. committees composed of ministers who may or may not be members of the Cabinet, with a senior cabinet minister as chairman — and their equivalent official committees comprising some of the most senior officials from the departments concerned. (It is very rare for ministers and officials to sit together as members of a committee, though of course, all committees are serviced by civil servants.) At these levels procedure is intimate and negotiation subtle: the whole complex is often characterised as the 'Private Secretary network', or even more widely as the 'Old Boy network'. It may be recalled that there are only some 300 to 350 people concerned. They can be likened to a small sieve, finely meshed, the final filter through which only the most recalcitrant problems pass to the Cabinet, and through which on their downward journey major decisions begin their metamorphosis into administrative reality.

## III Wider Issues

How are the 350 top policy-makers, and the 2,500 or so less prominent policy-makers, influenced in their work? As in any other western democratic state, they are bombarded with suggestions and grievances from every organised sector of the community, and there is no need to do more than mention this 'interest group' aspect of policy-making. In Britain there is remarkably little direct pressure applied by Parliament *qua* Parliament. Because of the two-party system and the strong party discipline, no committee structure comparable to the French or American is allowed to flourish, and effective parliamentary inquisition is normally restricted to Question Time and to *ex post facto* examination by Select Committees of how policy was administered. The policy-makers, therefore, usually have little to fear in the way of parliamentary harassment, though the influence of individual MPs as representatives of particular interests may well be notable on occasion.

But while the party system reduces the scope of Parliament and, to no small extent, provides a bulwark against the most violent of interest group pressures, it also helps to ensure that there is an intermediate area of policy-making between the more obvious 'interests' on the one hand and the formal institutions of government on the other hand. In this intermediate area the most prominent actors are the major political parties themselves, each of which maintains a sizeable research organisation and publishes regularly material on which policy might be based and discussions of future policy. Other intermediate bodies are more or less politically aligned with parties, such as the Conservatives' Bow Group, and the Labour Party's intelectual ally, the Fabian Society, but there are also institutions with a less committed or at least more academic and disinterested approach, such as Political and Economic Planning, the Royal Institute of Public Administration, and the Acton Society Trust. In addition there are a handful of people in universities who make their contribution to party discussions.

It is impossible to make any precise calculation of the influence which this mixed cluster of policy middle-men has, and it might be argued that to differentiate it from other more obvious interest groups is mere pedantry. The existence and the output of such intellectually curious organisations may perhaps be viewed as more likely to influence the 'climate of opinion' than to sway directly the makers of policy decisions. But the writer feels that the role of such a layer of people and institutions has some significance: for this is the only segment of politically inclined British society which has the time to devote thought and action to policy-making of the relatively long term sort. Such organisations do attempt to reduce the facts and the powers of public affairs to some sort of rationality (albeit a biased rationality) and to put forward for the consideration of the busy worlds around them some alternative courses from which immediate policies can be developed. At the very most, these middlemen may bring forward some compelling new ideas; at the very least, they help to separate the wheat from the tares in matters appertaining to public policy. In either respect they relieve the pressure on the government itself. For within the maelstrom of day-to-day government, most students would endorse the empiricism of the *Oxford English Dictionary* that 'policy' is 'a course of action adopted and pursued . . . any course of action adopted as advantageous or expedient'. Not for those in office is the formulation of ideas about the place and proper functions of government in society, or the evolution of the great governmental philosophies of the age. For these practical men in charge of administrative organisations 'policy' really does mean courses of action to 'adopt and pursue'.

Nobody believes any more in a clear distinction between policy and execution, yet the democratic theory of government still presupposes its existence and acceptance. Politicians make policy decisions, civil servants advise and make executive decisions within the policy laid down. In fact what is now realised is that practically all decisions of any non-routine character are an amalgam of 'policy' and 'executive' considerations to which both the politician and the civil servant (not to speak of the outside world) contribute, though the constitutional proprieties are observed by the 'responsibility' being vested in the politician. The meaningful distinctions, therefore, are not between 'policy' and 'execution', but between the more and the less 'political' decisions in government, and the main point of interest is the degree of influence which the politician and civil servant respectively exerts on the making of the 'more political' of those decisions.

It has been a popular theory that ministers have no time to think and are only in office for short periods anyhow, while civil servants have permanent tenure, familiarity with the administrative machinery, all the facilities for fact finding and research, and must, therefore be in a favourable position for long term reflection and the production of long term policies. Whatever truth there was in this in the past, there are only a few backwaters between St James's Park and the Thames where this might still be true. Of course, the civil servant has all the facilities mentioned, but in truth the atmosphere could scarcely be described as being conducive to reflection. The higher one goes the less conducive it becomes, and it may be that the lower down the policy-making scale the better are the ideas being evolved. But where the final decisions are made and where the 'pace' and 'attitude' are set, life for the senior official is almost as full as that of the minister, though less varied and, because it may go on much longer, the narrower concentration may have a greater numbing effect on the imagination than the shorter if more spectacularly wearing ministerial tenure.

The policy-makers — and especially the top 350 — are, in fact, a focal point for the ideas and the pressures of organised groups in society, of Parliament, of the party machines, of that infra-structure of non-governmental policy middle-men described earlier, and of the administrative machine of the government itself. They are not — cannot be — reflective moulders of ideas: they are the recipients, the collaters, the compromisers, among a mass of persuasive influences and persistent people. They do not — and have not time — to 'think': they respond intuitively, instinctively, to produce decisions, often under considerable political pressure, which strike the mean most acceptable to the forces they are struggling to keep in equipoise. And this process does not entail their working as a 'solid' block of administrative automata. They are divided in two different ways, as we have seen. One division is that of personnel — the politicians and the civil servants, two closed circles which overlap only slightly: each knows the set-up of the other, each realises their interdependence, but each retains its own independent set of values: there is a mutual constitutional respect, largely based on self interest, for each other's limits, but perhaps marked by some trace of superiority and cynical impatience on the part of the civil servant, by some degree of suspicion and self-righteous impatience on the part of the minister. The other division, muted but not dissolved by the system of co-ordination, is that by departments, by loyalties to an organisation and to the social interests which that organisation represents.

Nonetheless, it is permissible to think of the top level of governmental policy-making as being, in the last resort, the function of a closely integrated group of 300-odd people, whose membership is subject to constant fluctuation but whose pattern of behaviour remains more or less constant. Within that group the relative importance of men and women is not really arguable in terms of political or official status alone. No one would support the suggestion that ministers are 'run' by officials, but at any one time there will be some officials who count more in policy-making — i.e. in the finding of practical courses of action within the greater philosophy of the ruling party — than some ministers. And just as within the Cabinet itself there is always a small inner ring of the most powerful, so in the larger mixed policy-making group there tend to be perhaps fifty people spread over Whitehall who together can carry any case through. The art of getting one's policy proposals accepted is the art of manoeuvring for the support — active or passive — of that crucial two and one-half score.

# A BIBLIOGRAPHY OF ARTICLES

SINCE influences of so many different sorts affect the making of public policy, no bibliography of this field can be comprehensive. This one concentrates exclusively upon studies published in periodicals, since books in the field are frequently mentioned in the text. A detailed bibliography of books in print can be found in John Palmer, *Government and Parliament in Britain* (London: Hansard Society, 2nd ed., 1964). This can be brought up to date by consulting reviews in subsequent issues of *Political Studies*.

Effectively, the definition of articles for inclusion arose from their relevance to the main chapter headings. Certain topics, such as local government, are therefore excluded by definition. Since material on such subjects as Parliament and the civil service is only intermittently related to policy-making *per se*, what follows is in no sense comprehensive in its treatment of the institutions of British government. A lengthy bibliography for institutions can be found in R. M. Punnett, *British Government and Politics* (London: Heinemann, 1968) pp. 423–65. A complementary bibliography in political sociology can be found at pp. 331–40 of Richard Rose, *Studies in British Politics*. The sections on pressure groups and parties are specially relevant.

Because the value of an article to a particular reader depends not only upon the insight of the author but also upon the interests of the person reading it, a range of citations have been included on topics rarely written about, without regard to the intellectual perspective from which they are written.

*Abbreviations*

*APSR* — *American Political Science Review*
*BJS* — *British Journal of Sociology*
*PS* — *Political Studies*

## I Political Recruitment

BERRINGTON, H. B., and FINER, S. E., 'The British House of Commons', *International Social Science Journal*, XIII iv (1961) 600–19.

BIRCH, A. H., 'Citizen Participation in Political Life: England and Wales', *International Social Science Journal*, XII i (1960) 15–26.

BOCHEL, J. M., 'The Recruitment of Local Councillors: a Case Study', *PS*, XIV iii (1966) 360–4.

BONNOR, J., 'The Fourth Labour Cabinet', *Sociological Review*, VI i (N.S., 1958) 37–48.

BUCK, P. W., 'Election Experience of Candidates for the House of Commons, 1918–1955', *Western Political Quarterly*, XII ii (1959) 485–91.

BUCK, P. W., 'By-Elections in Parliamentary Careers, 1918–1959', *Western Political Quarterly*, XIV ii (1961) 432–5.

BUCK, P. W., 'M.P.s in Ministerial Office, 1918–1955 and 1955–1959', *PS*, IX iii (1961) 300–6.

BUCK, P. W., 'The Early Start Toward Cabinet Office, 1918–55', *Western Political Quarterly*, XVI iii (1963) 624–32.

BUCK, P. W., 'First-Time Winners in the British House of Commons Since 1918', *APSR*, LVIII iii (1964) 662–7.

DODD, C. H., 'Recruitment to the Administrative Class, 1960–64', *Public Administration*, XLV i (1967) 58–80.

EPSTEIN, L., 'Candidate Selection in Britain: a Comparative Study', *PROD*, II iv (1959) 16–18.

EPSTEIN, L., 'British Class Consciousness and the Labour Party', *Journal of British Studies*, II ii (1962) 136–50.

EPSTEIN, L., 'New M.P.s and the Politics of the P.L.P.', *PS*, X ii (1962) 121–9.

FINER, S. E., see BERRINGTON, H. B.

GARCIA, T. V., see HARRIS, J. S.

GUTTSMAN, W. L., 'The Changing Social Structure of the British Political Elite, 1886–1935', *BJS*, II ii (1951) 122–34.

GUTTSMAN, W. L., 'Aristocracy and the Middle Class in the British Political Elite, 1886–1916', *BJS*, V i (1954) 12–32.

HARRIS, J. S., and GARCIA, T. V., 'The Permanent Secretaries: Britain's Top Administrators', *Public Administration Review*, XXVI i (1966) 31–44.

HEASMAN, D. J., 'The Prime Minister and the Cabinet', *Parliamentary Affairs*, XV iv (1962) 461–84.

HEASMAN, D. J., 'Parliamentary Paths to High Office', *Parliamentary Affairs*, XVI ii (1963) 315–30.

JENKINS, ROBIN, 'Who Are These Marchers?', *Journal of Peace Research*, IV i (1967) 46–60.

JONES, C. O., 'Inter-Party Competition in Britain, 1950–59', *Parliamentary Affairs*, XVII i (1964) 50–6.

KING, A. S., 'Britain's Ministerial Turnover', *New Society*, 18 August 1966, pp. 257–8.

LUPTON, T., and WILSON, C. S., 'The Social Background and Connections of Top Decision-Makers', *Manchester School of Economic and Social Studies*, xxvii i (1959) 30–52.

Mackenzie, W. J. M., 'Local Government in Parliament', *Public Administration*, xxxii iv (1954) 409–23.

McCorquodale, S., 'The Composition of Administrative Tribunals', *Public Law* (Autumn, 1962) pp. 298–326.

Miller, D. C., 'Industry and Community Power Structure', *American Sociological Review*, xxiii i (1958) 9–15.

Miller, D. C., 'Decision-Making Cliques in Community Power Structures', *American Journal of Sociology*, lxiv iii (1958) 299–310.

Pickering, J. F., 'Recruitment to the Administrative Class, 1960–1964', *Public Administration*, xlv ii (1967) 169–99.

Ranney, A., 'Inter-Constituency Movement of British Parliamentary Candidates, 1951–1959', *APSR*, lviii i (1964) 36–45.

Rasmussen, J., 'The Implication of Safe Seats for British Democracy', *Western Political Quarterly*, xix iii (1966) 516–29.

Richards, P. G., 'A Study in Political Apprenticeship', *Parliamentary Affairs*, ix iii (1956) 353–7.

Robinson, K., 'Selection and the Social Background of the Administrative Class', *Public Administration*, xxxiii iv (1955) 383–389.

Rose, R., 'The Emergence of Leaders', *New Society*, 17 October 1963, pp. 12–13.

Ross, J. F. S., 'Women and Parliamentary Elections', *BJS*, iv i (1953) 14–24.

Sainsbury, K., 'Patronage, Honours and Parliament', *Parliamentary Affairs*, xix iii (1966) 346–50.

Subramaniam, V., 'Representative Bureaucracy; a Reassessment', *APSR*, lxi iv (1967) 1010–19.

Turner, R. H., 'Sponsored and Contest Mobility and the School System', *American Sociological Review*, xxv vi (1960) 855–67.

Watkins, A., 'Portrait of a Labour Member', *New Statesman*, 12 April 1968, p. 470.

Willson, F. M. G., 'The Routes of Entry of New Members of the British Cabinet, 1868–1958', *PS*, vii iii (1959) 222–32.

Wilson, C. S., see Lupton, T.

## II Political Roles

Devons, E., '"Intelligent laymen" in Whitehall', *The Listener*, 21 May 1964, pp. 819–20.

Dowse, R. E., 'The M.P. and his Surgery', *PS*, xi iii (1963) 333–41.

KAVANAGH, D., see ROSE, R.

MILLETT, J. H., 'The Role of an Interest Group Leader in the House of Commons', *Western Political Quarterly*, IX iv (1956) 915–926.

MILNE, R. S., 'The Junior Minister', *Journal of Politics*, XII iii (1950) 437–50.

MOSSAWIR, H., see ROSE, R.

ROCHE, J. P., and SACHS, S., 'The Bureaucrat and the Enthusiast: an Exploration of the Leadership of Social Movements', *Western Political Quarterly*, VIII ii (1955) 248–61.

ROSE, R., 'Complexities of Party Leadership', *Parliamentary Affairs*, XVI iii (1963) 257–73.

ROSE, R., and KAVANAGH, D., 'Campaigning for Parliament', *New Society*, 28 July 1966, pp. 122–4.

ROSE, R., and MOSSAWIR, H., 'Voting and Elections: a Functional Analysis', *PS*, XV ii (1967) 174–201.

SACHS, S., see ROCHE, J. P.

STARBUCK, W. H., 'The Efficiency of British and American Retail Employees', *Administrative Science Quarterly*, XI iii (1966) 345–385.

WALKER, P. C. GORDON, 'On Being a Cabinet Minister', *Encounter*, XXI (1956) 17–24.

## III CASE-STUDIES IN PUBLIC POLICY

BRAND, J. A., 'Ministry Control and Local Autonomy in Education', *Political Quarterly*, XXXVI ii (1965) 154–63.

BRANDON, H., 'Skybolt', *Sunday Times*, 8 December 1963.

CHAPMAN, R. A., 'The Bank Rate Decision of the 19th September 1957', *Public Administration*, XLIII ii (1965) 199–213.

CHESTER, D. N., 'The Crichel Down Case', *Public Administration*, XXXII iv (1954) 389–401.

DAHL, R. A., 'Workers' Control of Industry and the British Labour Party', *APSR*, XLI iv (1947) 875–900.

DEAKIN, N., 'The Politics of the Commonwealth Immigrants Bill', *Political Quarterly*, XXXIX i (1968) 25–45.

DEVONS, E., 'An Economist's View of the Bank Rate Tribunal Evidence', *Manchester School of Economic and Social Studies*, XXVII i (1959) 1–16.

DOWSE, R. E., and PEEL, J., 'The Politics of Birth Control', *PS*, XIII ii (1965) 179–97.

ECKSTEIN, H., 'Planning: a Case Study', *PS*, IV i (1956) 46–50.

FINER, S. E., 'Les Silences de Sir Frank Newsam', *PS*, III i (1955) 17–27.

FLETCHER, R., 'Social Change in Britain', *Political Quarterly*, XXXIV iv (1963) 399–410.

GREGORY, R., 'The Minister's Line: or, the M4 Comes to Berkshire', *Public Administration*, XLV ii (1967) 113–28, and XLV iii (1967) 269–86.

GUNN, L. A., 'Organising for Science in Britain: Some Relevant Questions', *Minerva*, V ii (1967) 167–97.

HART, J., 'Some Reflections on the Report of the Royal Commission on the Police', *Public Law* (Autumn, 1963) pp. 283–304.

HEUBEL, E. J., 'Church and State in England: the Price of Establishment', *Western Political Quarterly*, XVIII iii (1965) 646–55.

HINDELL, K., 'The Genesis of the Race Relations Bill', *Political Quarterly*, XXXVI iv (1965) 390–405.

JOHNSON, F. A., 'The British Committee of Imperial Defence', *Journal of Politics*, XXIII ii (1961) 231–61.

LANE, R. E., 'Problems of a Regulated Economy: the British Experience', *Social Research*, IX iii (1952) 277–99.

LEE, J. M., 'The Overseas Development Institute and Its Publications', *Journal of Modern African Studies*, II iv (1964) 565–571.

MACKENZIE, W. J. M., 'The Plowden Report: a Translation', *The Guardian*, 25 May 1963.

MARTIN, L. W., 'The Market for Strategic Ideas in Britain: the Sandys Era', *APSR*, LVI i (1962) 23–42.

NETTL, J. P., 'Consensus or Elite Domination: the Case of Business', *PS*, XIII i (1965) 22–44.

PEEL, J., see DOWSE, R. E.

PENNOCK, J. R., 'Agricultural Subsidies in England and America', *APSR*, LVI iii (1962) 621–33.

RICHARDSON, J. J., 'The Making of the Restrictive Trade Practices Act 1956', *Parliamentary Affairs*, XX iv (1967) 350–74.

STARZINGER, V. E., 'The British Pattern of Apportionment', *Virginia Quarterly Review*, XLI iii (1965) 321–41.

TARKOWSKI, Z. M. T., and TURNBULL, A. V., 'Scientists versus Administrators', *Public Administration*, XXXVII iv (1959) 213–256.

TURNBULL, A. V., see TARKOWSKI, Z. M. T.

VIG, N. J. and WALKLAND, S. A., 'Science Policy, Science Administration and Parliamentary Reform', *Parliamentary Affairs*, XIX iii (1966) 281–94.

WALKLAND, S. A., see VIG, N. J.

WILLIAMS, B., 'Science and Technology as Development Factors: United Kingdom', *International Social Science Journal*, XVIII iii (1966) 408–26.

## IV THE POLICY PROCESS

BEER, S. H., 'Pressure Groups and Parties in Britain', *APSR*, L i (1956) 1–24.

BRAIBANTI, R., 'The Civil Service of Pakistan', *The South Atlantic Quarterly*, LVIII ii (1959).

BRANDON, H., see NEUSTADT, R.

BRITTAN, S., 'The Irregulars', *Crossbow*, x xxxvii (1966) 30–2.

BROWN, A., 'What Power Has a Prime Minister?' *New Society*, 1 June 1967, pp. 790–2.

CHASE, E. P., 'The War and the English Constitution', *APSR*, XXXVI i (1942) 86–98.

CHESTER, D. N., 'Research as an Aid in Public Administration', *Public Administration*, XL i (1962) 53–64.

CHRISTOPH, J. B., 'The Study of Voting Behavior in the British House of Commons', *Western Political Quarterly*, XI ii (1958) 301–318.

DAVIS, M., 'Some Neglected Aspects of British Pressure Groups', *Midwest Journal of Political Science*, VII i (1963) 42–53.

DEVONS, E., 'Governing on the Inner Circle', *The Listener*, 27 March 1958, pp. 523–5.

FINER, S. E., 'The Individual Responsibility of Ministers', *Public Administration*, XXXIV iv (1956) 377–97.

FRANKEL, J., 'Towards a Decision-Making Model in Foreign Policy', *PS*, VII i (1959) 1–11.

HOWARD, A., 'Washington and Whitehall', *The Listener*, 21 July 1966, pp. 75–6.

JONES, G. W., 'The Prime Minister's Power', *Parliamentary Affairs*, XVIII ii (1965) 167–85.

NEEDLER, M., 'On the Dangers of Copying from the British', *Political Science Quarterly*, LXXVII iii (1962) 379–96.

NEUSTADT, R., 'White House and Whitehall', *The Public Interest*, date?', *Sunday Times*, 8 November 1964.

NEUSTADT, R., 'White House and Whitehall', *The Public Interest*, II (1966) 55–69.

PLOWDEN, W., 'The Hidden Machine', *New Society*, 22 June 1967, pp. 912–13.

RASMUSSEN, J., 'Problems of Democratic Development in Britain: an American View', *Political Quarterly*, XXXV iv (1964) 386–96.

SCHAFFER, B. B., 'The Concept of Preparation: Some Questions about the Transfer of Systems of Government', *World Politics*, XVIII i (1965) 42–67.

TIVEY, L., 'The System of Democracy in Britain', *Sociological Review*, VI i (N.S., 1958) 109–24.